MARX AND EDUCATION IN RUSSIA AND CHINA

MARX AND EDUCATION IN RUSSIA AND CHINA

RONALD F. PRICE

CROOM HELM LONDON

ROWMAN AND LITTLEFIELD TOTOWA N.J.

© 1977 R.F. Price
Croom Helm Ltd, 2-10 St John's Road, London SW11

British Library Cataloguing in Publication Data

Price, Ronald Francis
    Marx and education in Russia and China.
    1. Communist education—Russia 2. Communist
    education—China
    I. Title
    370'.947   LA832.7

    ISBN 0-85664-507-9

First Published in the United States 1977 by
Rowman and Littlefield
81 Adams Drive, TOTOWA, New Jersey.

Library of Congress Cataloging in Publication Data

Price, R   F
    Marx and education in Russia and China.

    Bibliography: p. 349
    1. Communist education—Russia. 2. Communist educa-
tion—China. 3. Marx, Karl, 1818-1883. 4. Education—
Philosophy. I. Title.
LA832.P68 1977   370'.947   77-8590
ISBN 0-87471-873-2

Printed in Great Britain by offset lithography by
Billing & Sons Ltd, Guildford, London and Worcester

CONTENTS

Foreword   10

1. Marx and Education   11

2. The School System: Part One   76

3. The School System: Part Two   109

4. Education and the Economy   163

5. Labour and Education   184

6. Educating the New, Socialist Man   220

7. The Collective as Educator   269

8. Education and the Social-Political Reality   332

Abbreviations   347

Bibliography   349

Index   371

To the memory of Roger and Marjorie Manning
who once helped a young
student towards a wider view

To Erika who has continued
that process

FOREWORD

This book took shape during some four years of teaching courses to post-graduate teacher-students on education in China and the USSR. I am grateful to them for discussions which raised new issues and helped to clarify others. Since the concept of education, to include political social-isation, is a broad topic, I hope the book will be of interest to the more general reader as well as to students of comparative and international education.

To many education students, Russian and/or Chinese education is at the same time their introduction to marxism, and many students go no further. This book is an attempt to set the record right by giving a thorough introduction to the writings of Marx himself as they relate to education. It attempts to show what marxism implies for education, as aim, method and content. It then goes on to compare educational developments in the USSR and China in the light of this analysis, attempting to answer the question as to how marxist this has been, in the schools and outside them. Since both countries claim marxist inspiration for what they do I believe that this is a necessary and fruitful approach which can, in turn, throw light upon our own educational problems.

The use of Russia in title and text is a conscious choice since, first, it points to Russian dominance over events in the USSR and secondly, I have not dealt with national minorities in either country except in respect of the problems of language and education which their presence presents.

In addition to my students many others have helped me during the writing of this book. May I specially mention the staff of the Library of La Trobe University who have greatly reduced 'the tyranny of distance', and our Centre secretaries who have helped with typing.

December 1976.   R.F. Price

1 MARX AND EDUCATION

Man, Alienation and the Vision of Communism

While marxism is not a humanism in the sense of assuming the theoretical priority of man over society, its raison d'etre is a concern with man's potential, both as individual and group. In that famous early statement, *The German Ideology*, where Marx and Engels clarified their views in a criticism of the Young Hegelians and contemporary utopian socialists, they wrote:

> The premises from which we begin are not arbitrary ones, not dogmas, but real premises from which abstraction can only be made in the imagination. They are the real individuals, their activity and the material conditions under which they live, both those which they find already existing and those produced by their activity. (*GI*, p. 31)

In everything Marx wrote, whether the early *Economic and Philosophic Manuscripts* of 1844 or the *Capital* (1867) of his maturity, there is protest against the present state of man and affirmation of belief in his future. The object of his prodigious labours was an attempt to understand the world in order to change it.

In a number of famous passages Marx compares man with other animals and brings out his peculiarly human characteristics. In the Feuerbach section of *The German Ideology* he and Engels wrote:

> Men can be distinguished from animals by consciousness, by religion or anything else you like. They themselves begin to distinguish themselves from animals as soon as they begin to *produce* their means of subsistence, a step which is conditioned by their physical organization By producing their means of subsistence men are indirectly producing their actual material life. (*GI*, p. 31)

In the *Economic and Philosophic Manuscripts,* where he used Feuerbach's concept of *species being* to refer to those qualities which were uniquely human (Ollman, p. 84) Marx developed the vision of man as having 'free, conscious activity' as his 'species character', a vision which is important for education. He wrote:

in the first place labour, *life-activity, productive life* itself, appears to man merely as a *means* of satisfying a need—the need to maintain the physical existence. Yet the productive life is the life of the species. It is life-engendering life. The whole character of a species—its species character—is contained in the character of its life-activity, and free, conscious activity is man's species character . . . In creating an *objective world* by his practical activity, in *working-up*, inorganic nature, man proves himself a conscious species being, i.e., as a being that treats the species as its own essential being, or that treats itself as a species being. Admittedly animals also produce. They build themselves nests, dwellings, like the bees, beavers, ants, etc. But an animal only produces what it immediately needs for itself or its young. It produces one-sidedly, whilst man produces universally. It produces only under the dominion of immediate physical need, whilst man produces even when he is free from physical need and *only truly produces in freedom therefrom.* An animal produces only itself, whilst man reproduces the whole of nature. An animal's product belongs immediately to its physical body, whilst man freely confronts his product. An animal forms things in accordance with the standard and the need of the species to which it belongs, whilst man knows how to produce in accordance with the standard of every species, and knows how to apply everywhere the inherent standard to the object. (*EPM*, pp. 75-6)

But labour is not only a process of creation, but of self-creation in which man is also his own educator.

Labour is, in the first place, a process in which both man and Nature participate, and in which man of his own accord starts, regulates, and controls the material re-actions between himself and Nature. He opposes himself to Nature as one of her own forces, setting in motion arms and legs, head and hands, the natural forces of his body, in order to appropriate Nature's productions in a form adapted to his own wants. *By thus acting on the external world and changing it, he at the same time changes his own nature.* He develops his slumbering powers and compels them to act in obedience to his sway. (*Capital* I, pp. 197-8, emphasis added)

In the *Economic and Philosophic Manuscripts* he gives Hegel the credit for this understanding:

Hegel conceives the self-creating of man as a process, . . . he thus grasps the essence of *labour* and comprehends objective man—true, because real man—as the outcome of man's own labour. (*EPM*, p. 177)

In 1845, in the third thesis on Feuerbach, Marx referred specifically to education. The materialism he criticises here is the French variety mentioned in *The Holy Family* (*HF*, pp. 175-6).

The materialist doctrine concerning the changing of circumstances and upbringing forgets that circumstances are changed by men and that it is essential to educate the educator himself. This doctrine must, therefore, divide society into two parts, one of which is superior to society.
The coincidence of the changing of circumstances and of human activity or self-changing can be conceived and rationally understood only as *revolutionary practice*. (*GI*, p. 660)

The same passage in *Capital* quoted above goes on to set man's peculiar creativity in the historical context of nineteenth-century capitalist society. Enjoyment, which as Timpanaro today stresses is 'the basis of all scientific systems of ethics' (Timpanaro, pp. 66, 108) is here posed as problematic.

An immeasurable interval of time separates the state of things in which a man brings his labour-power to market for sale as a commodity, from that state in which human labour was still in its first instinctive stage. We presuppose labour in a form that stamps it as exclusively human. A spider conducts operations that resemble those of a weaver, and a bee puts to shame many an architect in the construction of her cells. But *what distinguishes the worst architect from the best of bees is this, that the architect raises his structure in imagination before he erects it in reality.* At the end of every labour-process, we get a result that already existed in the imagination of the labourer at its commencement. He not only effects a change of form in the material on which he worked, but he also realises a purpose of his own that gives the law to his modus operandi, and to which he must subordinate his will. And this subordination is no mere momentary act. Besides the exertion of the bodily organs, the process demands that, during the whole operation, the workman's will be steadily consonance with his purpose. This means close attention. The less he is attracted by the nature of the work, and the mode in which it is carried on, and the less, therefore, he enjoys it as something which gives play to his bodily and mental powers, the more close his attention is forced to be. (*Capital* I, p. 198, emphasis added)

In the long chapter on 'The division of labour and manufacture' in *Capital* Marx develops his criticism of the crippling effects of the division of labour, quoting numerous previous writers. He contrasts the 'intelligence in production' which is developed in the invention of machines and the organisation of the manufacturing process with the mindless repetitive actions performed by the workers on the bench.

manufacture . . . converts the labourer into a crippled monstrosity, by forcing his detail dexterity at the expense of a world of productive capabilities and instincts . . . (*Capital* I, p. 396)

Machinery is put to a wrong use, with the object of transforming the workman, from his very childhood, into a part of a detail-machine. (*Capital* I, p. 461)

Writing in the *Economic and Philosophic Manuscripts* at a time when the official mores demanded saving and abstinence, Marx's discussion of needs applies even more in today's 'consumer society' with its compulsion to spend.

Under private property . . . the increase in the quantity of objects is accompanied by an extension of the realm of the alien powers to which man is subjected, and every new product represents a new potency of mutual swindling and mutual plundering. Man becomes ever poorer as a man. (*EPM*, p. 115)

Particularly significant is the following condemnation of possession:

Private property has made us so stupid and one-sided that an object is only *ours* when we have it—when it exists for us as capital, or when it is directly possessed, eaten, drunk, worn, inhabited, etc.,—in short when it is *used* by us. (*EPM*, p. 106)

Finally, in considering Marx's conception of man let us turn to some of the passages where he deals directly with the relation between the individual and society. These are of particular interest to us in the USSR and China. In the former 'society' has certainly been 're-establish-ed as an abstraction', and at least from the thirties through to the late fifties youth were forced to participate in artificially collective activities. Activities by individuals or pairs were condemned as anti-social. In China the problem is more that of the persistence of traditional Confucian collectivities which stifle the individual. The first passage comes from the Introduction to the *Critique of Political Economy* (1857):

> Man is in the most literal sense of the word a *zoon politikon*, not only a social animal, but an animal which can develop into an individual only in society. Production by isolated individuals out-side of society . . . is as great an absurdity as the idea of the develop-ment of language without individuals living together and talking to one another. (*CPE*, p. 268)

The second comes from the *Economic and Philosophic Manuscripts*:

> Social activity and social consumption exist by no means *only* in the form of some *directly* communal activity and directly *communal* consumption, although *communal* activity and *communal* consumptio —i.e. activity and consumption which are manifested and directly confirmed in *real association* with other men—will occur whenever such a *direct* expression of sociality stems from the true character of the activity's content and is adequate to the nature of consumption
>
> But again when I am active *scientifically*, etc.,—when I am engaged in activity which I can seldom perform in direct community with others—then I am *social*, because I am active as a *man*. Not only is the material of my activity given to me as a social product (as is even the language in which the thinker is active): my *own* existence *is* social activity, and therefore that which I make of myself I make of myself for society and with the consciousness of myself as a social being.
>
> My *general* consciousness is only the *theoretical* shape of that of which the *living* shape is the *real* community, the social fabric, although at the present day *general* consciousness is an abstraction from real life and as such antagonistically confronts it. Consequently, too, the *activity* of my general consciousness, as an activity, is my *theoretical* existence as a social being.
>
> What is to be avoided above all is the re-establishing of 'Society' as an abstraction *vis-à-vis* the individual. The individual *is the social*

being. His life, even if it may not appear in the direct form of a *communal* life carried out together with others—is therefore an expression and confirmation of *social life.* Man's individual life and species life are not *different,* however much—and this is inevitable— the mode of existence of the individual is a more *particular,* or more *general* mode of the life of the species, or the life of the species is a more *particular* or more *general* individual life.

Man, much as he may therefore be a *particular* individual (and it is precisely his particularity which makes him an individual, and a real *individual* social being), is just as much the *totality*—the ideal totality—the subjective existence of thought and experienced society present for itself; just as he exists also in the real world as the awareness and the real enjoyment of social existence, and as a totality of human life-activity. (*EPM*, pp. 104-5)

The link between Marx's view of man and his concept of communism is the controversial concept of *alienation*, one which perhaps more than any other divides marxists today. Those who have tried to divide Marx into a young humanist and a mature scientist on his use of this concept are clearly factually wrong (McLellan, *Grundrisse,* pp. 13-14; Mandel, 1971, pp. 163-77; Colletti, 1975 (b)). The terms alienation (*Entausserung*) or estrangement (*Entfremdung*) and the related terms, fetishism or reification (*Versachlichung, Verdinglichung*) occur repeatedly in works ranging from the *Economic and Philosophic Manuscripts* and *The Grundrisse,* both, it should be noted, notebooks not intended for publication in their present form, to *Capital* and *Theories of Surplus Value.* Serious argument can therefore only be about their meaning and significance.

In the *Economic and Philosophic Manuscripts* this 'great synthesizing idea', as Meszaros calls it (Meszaros, p. 16) occurs in a variety of forms. Man is separated from his work, from his products and from his fellow men. (Allman pp. 133-4; Walton and Gamble, pp. 14-5.) Meszaros adds alienation from nature (Meszaros, p. 14; cf. Mandel, 1971, p. 165 and his references to A. Schmidt and Marx's concept of nature.) But the seminal idea of human activity becoming separated and appearing as a non-human, natural force opposed to man is perhaps most clearly expressed in *Capital,* vol. 1, ch. 1, sec. 4. Here man's labour is separated from him in the 'fetishism of commoditives' to reappear under the guise of impersonal economic laws and market forces.

There is a definite social relation between men, that assumes, in their eyes, the fantastic form of a relation between things. In order, therefore, to find an analogy, we must have the recourse to the mist-enveloped regions of the religious world. In that world the product-ions of the human brain appear as independent beings endowed with life, and entering into relation both with one another and the human race. So it is in the world of commodities with the products of men's hands. This I call the Fetishism which attaches itself to the products of labour, so soon as they are produced as commodities, and which is therefore inseparable from the production of commod-ities.

. . . the labour of the individual asserts itself as a part of the labour of society, only directly between the products, and indirectly, through them, between the producers. To the latter, therefore, the relations connecting the labour of one individual with that of the rest appear, not as direct social relations between individuals at work, but as what they really are, material relations between persons and social relations between things. (*Capital* I, pp. 83-4)

One of the drawbacks of using the concept of alienation is that it has been used by different writers in widely different ways. (cf. Schacht and Israel.) Too often it has been reduced to a pejorative adjective. Perhaps in its narrow sense of reification it can serve as a reminder that much which we take to be outside our control is in origin 'only human' and thus cap-able of repossession. Certain educational institutions, as we shall suggest later, belong in this category.[1]

Before leaving the concept of alienation another confusion must be dealt with. It is commonly asserted that alienation can never be over-come since it is identical with *objectification*, with man's productive, creative processes. Two passages from Marx's *Grundrisse* dispose of this point.

Individuals with an all-round development whose social relations have been subjected to their own collective control as their own collective relations, are not a product of nature but of history. The degree and universality of the development of the capacities (of the productive forces) which make such individuality possible, pre-supposes precisely production based on exchange values, which pro-duces, along with generality, the alienation of the individual from himself and others, but also the generality and universality of his relations and capacities. At earlier stages of evolution, the single individual seems to be fuller precisely because he has not yet developed the fullness of his relations and because he has not yet opposed them to himself as social forces and relations which are independent of him. Just as it is absurd to desire a return to this original fullness, so it is absurd to believe that we have to remain fixed at this complete void (that exists today). (Quoted in Mandel, *FET*, p. 178, or McLellan, pp. 70-1, Peng. ed. 161-2).

The bourgeois economists are to such an extent prisoners of the concepts of a particular historical phase in the development of society that the necessity of the *objectification* of social labour power seems to them inseparable from the necessity of the *alienation* of this labour power in relation to living labour . . . No special intelligence is needed to understand that, given the free labour that had emerged from serfdom, or wage labour, machines could not effectively *be created* otherwise than as property which was alienated from them (the workers) and which appeared to them as a hostile power, that is, which was bound to confront them as capital. It can be understood just as easily, however, that machines will not cease to be agencies of social production when they become, for example, the property of the associated workers. (Quoted in Mandel, *FET*, p. 179, or McLellan, p. 151, Peng. ed. p. 832)

Meszaros makes the same point:

. . . if it is the *inadequacy* of some forms of objectification that may properly be called alienation, it is not true that objectivity equals 'estranged human relations', although it may be true that the objectivity of civilised society as we have known it so far carried with it estranged human relations. By contrast, an adequate form of human objectification would produce social objectivity as *objectified* but *non-alienated* human relations. (Meszaros, pp. 172-3)

The shift from seeing objectification and alienation as the same to recognising it as historically linked with private property and the commodity exchange economy involved a shift of viewpoint from capital to labour (Meszaros, p. 64 and *Grundrisse*, p. 150, McLellan, p. 731, Peng. ed.). It also made possible the hope that alienation can be overcome in the future and points to the means by which this can be accomplished. However, as Mandel and others have argued, since alienation is a complex phenomenon, involving social, religious, ideological, political and even technical forms, it cannot be abolished easily or by limited measures like the social ownership of the means of production (Mandel, FET, pp. 181-2). Soviet experience confirms this view.

References to communism occur throughout Marx's writings, but as will be obvious from the first quotation below he nowhere does more than point to the most general possibilities. As he and Engels agreed,

> Communism is for us not a *state of affairs* which is to be established, an *ideal* to which reality (will) have to adjust itself. We call communism the *real* movement which abolishes the present state of things. The conditions of this movement result from the premises now in existence. (*GI*, p. 48)

In the previous year Marx had written:

> *Communism* is the necessary pattern and the dynamic principle of the immediate future, but communism as such is not the goal of human development—the structure of human society. (*EPM*, p. 114)

In the same section of these notebooks Marx distinguishes his own conception of communism as the transcendence (*Aufhebung*) of alienation from the views of other communists. After criticising two other forms he came to:

> (3) *Communism* as the positive transcendence of *private property, as human self-estrangement*, and therefore as the real *appropriation of the human* essence by and for man; communism therefore as the complete return of man to himself as a *social* (i.e. human) being—a return become conscious, and accomplished within the entire wealth of previous development. This communism, as fully-developed naturalism, equals humanism; it is the *genuine* resolution of the conflict between man and nature and between man and man—the true resolution of the strife between existence and essence, between objectification and self-confirmation, between freedom and necessity, between the individual and the species. Communism is the riddle of history solved, and it knows itself to be this solution. (*EPM*, p. 102)

Some caveats should be made about this splendid vision. It is to be accomplished 'within the entire wealth of previous development' and not through some return to nature or anti-industrialism such as is popular in many quarters today. 'Fully-developed naturalism, equals humanism' is an affirmation of man as a material being, at the same time natural and human, that is, possessing qualities not to be reduced to the level of other animals. However, as Timpanaro warns, the phrase 'genuine resolution of the conflict between man and nature' must be treated with caution. Sickness, old age, death and other natural calamities may be neither abolished in practice nor in the realm of ideas and to pretend they can is to open the road to 'reactionary scientistic or out-and-out religious ideologies' (Timpanaro, pp. 17, 21).

Marx contrasts his communism as the transcendence of alienation with 'crude communism' and communism where the state continues and man still remains a prisoner of forms conditioned by the as-yet incompletely annulled private property (cf. USSR). In the former there is a levelling down based on envy, an 'abstract negation of the entire world of culture and civilization, the regression to the *unnatural* simplicity of the *poor and undemanding* man who has not only failed to go beyond private property, but has not yet even attained to it' (*EPM*, p. 100). In the *Communist Manifesto* reference is made to early attempts of the proletariat to go beyond the 'economic conditions for its emancipation', a time when 'feudal society was being overthrown'. Marx comments:

> The revolutionary literature that accompanied these first movements of the proletariat had necessarily a reactionary character. It inculcated universal asceticism and social levelling in its crudest form. (*SW* Vol. 1, p. 237)

This is again the point being made by Timpanaro, and is relevant to any evaluation of developments in the USSR and China.

Marx returned to the question in economic terms in his criticism of the Gotha Programme of the German Workers' Party in 1875. Objecting to the programme's use of the phrase 'equitable distribution of the proceeds of labour', Marx wrote:

> Within the co-operative society based on common ownership of the means of production, the producers do not exchange their products; just as little does the labour employed on the products appear here *as the value* of these products, as a material quality possessed by them, since now, in contrast to capitalist society, individual labour no longer exists in an indirect fashion but directly as a component part of the total labour. (*CGP*, p. 11)

Marx went on to distinguish communist society 'as it *emerges* from capitalist society . . . still stamped with the birthmarks of the old society from whose womb it emerges' from a possible later form.

> In a higher phase of communist society, after the enslaving sub-ordination of individuals under division of labour, and therewith also the antithesis between mental and physical labour, has vanished; after labour, from a mere means of life, has itself become the prime necessity of life; after the productive forces have also increased with the all-round development of the individual, and all the springs of co-operative wealth flow more abundantly—only then can the narrow horizon of bourgeois right be fully left behind and society inscribe on its banner: from each according to his ability, to each according to his needs! (*CGP*, p. 14)

Here we find the vision, so exciting for education, of the abolition of the antithesis between mental and physical labour, and the controversial assertion of labour as the prime necessity of life. Leaving the first point aside for the moment, the second relates to Marx's conception of man as a creative species. Ollman points out Marx's use of 'modes of product-ion' to cover religion, family, state, law, morality and science (Ollman, p. 100, Marx, *EPM*, p. 103 A). In the realm of economic production the following passages, written some time before the above, hold the key to Marx's thought on this point:

> Just as the savage must wrestle with nature, in order to satisfy his wants, in order to maintain his life and reproduce it, so civilized man has to do it, and he must do it in all forms of society and under all possible modes of production. With his development the realm of natural necessity expands, because his wants increase; but at the same time the forces of production increase by which these wants are satisfied. The freedom in this field cannot consist of anything else but of the fact that socialised man, the associated producers, regulate their interchange with nature rationally, bring it under their common control, instead of being ruled by it as by some blind power; that they accomplish their task with the least expenditure of energy and under conditions most adequate to their human nature and most worthy of it. But it always remains a realm of necessity. Beyond it begins that development of human power, which is its own end, the true realm of freedom, which, however, can flourish only upon that realm of necessity as its base. The shortening of the working day is its fundamental premise. (*Capital* III, pp. 651-2)

The surplus labour of the masses has ceased to be a condition for the development of wealth in general; in the same way that the non-labour of the few has ceased to be a condition for the development of the general powers of the human mind. Production based on exchange value therefore falls apart, and the immediate process of material production finds itself stripped of its impoverished, antagonistic form. Individuals are then in a position to develop freely. It is no longer a question of reducing the necessary labour time in order to create surplus labour, but of reducing the necessary labour of society to a minimum. The counterpart of this reduction is that all members of society can develop their education in the arts, sciences, etc., thanks to the free time and means available to all. (*Grundrisse,* McLellan, p. 142, Peng. ed. 705)

Labour is not 'merely a joke' but 'damned serious and demands the greatest effort' (*Grundrisse,* McLellan, p. 124, Peng. ed. 611). But it will be performed in understanding of the necessary and the free.

The USSR, China and Communism

The vision of the future communist society held by both Soviet and Chinese Party spokesmen has been drawn from such works as Marx's *Critique of the Gotha Programme, The Communist Manifesto,* or Engels' *Origin of the Family, Private Property and the State.* The *Economic and Philosophic Manuscripts* and the whole discussion of alienation and its transcendence has been ignored.

In the first years of the Russian revolution many held very optimistic ideas on the time required for the transition to communism. Bukharin, in the influential *ABC of Communism* spoke of having to regulate distribution for 'perhaps twenty or thirty years', adding that 'subsequently', when communism was established this would no longer be necessary. Lenin, speaking to the third congress of the Young Communist League in 1920, referred to

the generation of those who are now fifteen years old, and will be living in a communist society in ten or twenty years' time. (OC & CR, p. 145)

But with the failure of the expected European-wide revolution, and the gradual realisation of the difficulties involved, a different time-scale was conceived. Mao Ze-dong warned that it would take at least a hundred years to catch up with the advanced capitalist countries in economic strength and living standards and that the construction of a *socialist* economy, should be envisaged as taking a 'long period' (Schram, 1974, p. 175). Communism would, therefore, take much longer. Under Krushchev there was a spate of optimistic statements about the possibilities of moving into communism by about the turn of the era, but with the accession to power of Brezhnev and Kosygin the question retreated again into the distant, rather misty future.[2]

Turning to the kind of vision of the future portrayed, *The ABC of Communism* placed great stress on the obviously much needed increase in economic production it envisaged.[3] With the abolition of the class struggle, strikes and wars, energy will be freed for production, which will, moreover, be organised and planned (Carr, 1969, pp. 119-21). Classless and free from exploitation, society would become one of comrades (ibid. p. 114). Bukharin takes up a theme from Lenin's *State and Revolution,* suggesting that people will take turns in essential book-keeping jobs required for a planned economy. Participation in discussions and rotation of function will gradually produce a harmonious future where

> just as in an orchestra all the performers watch the conductor's baton and act accordingly, so here all will consult the statistical reports and will direct their work accordingly (ibid. pp. 118, 132, 237-40).

Released from the grind of feeding and clothing himself through this planned plenty man would turn to 'the work of mental development. Human culture will climb to heights never attained before' (ibid. p. 121).

Forty years later *The Fundamentals of Marxism-Leninism* belongs to a different genre.[4] 208 of its 719 pages are devoted to 'socialism and communism' and the final 20 to the future 'communist society' itself. The section headings signal its approach: a society of universal sufficiency and abundance; from each according to his ability; to each according to his needs; the free man in the free society; peace and friendship; co-operation and rapprochement of the peoples; future prospects of communism. Throughout the book there is an emphasis on technology. Consumer goods needed for the good life are even listed, and, ironically, mention is made of 'convenient public transport instead of private cars' (p. 706). The level to which the argument descends is shown in the paragraphs which comment on 'some none-too-clever critics of marxism' who raise 'tricky' questions about distribution under communism:

If all benefits are distributed gratis, will not everyone want to get every day . . . a new automobile? . . . The authors of such absurd suppositions slander the citizens of the future communist society, to whom they ascribe their own failings. The communist system naturally cannot undertake to satisfy all whims and caprices. Its aim, as Engels stressed is the satisfaction of the reasonable needs of people in an ever-increasing measure. (p. 705)

There is emphasis on further free time and the development of man's mental powers. But

communist social relations will educate a man who will abhor depraved tastes and requirements, characteristic of past epochs when possession of things and the level of consumption were primary criteria of man's position in society. (p. 707)

The book ends characteristically with half a page of future scientific marvels, such as living to 150-200 years of age, predicting natural disasters, and producing yet new building materials and fibres. When man returns for the final paean one remains in doubt:

The advance to the shining heights of communist civilisation will always engender in people unusual power of will and intellect, creative impulses, courage, and life-giving energy. (p. 717)

If the *Fundamentals* reads like apologetics, more recent works, with their assumption of the jargon and much of the ideology of contemporary capitalism, read like a masque. An example of this genre is *The Scientific and Technological Revolution and its Impact on Management and Education* by V.G. Afanasyev. He talks about

the saving of working time and the increasing of leisure time and, above all, *the effective use of the latter,* (which) are not only an indicator but also a necessary condition of the formation of the harmoniously developed individual, which is the supreme goal of communism (p. 317, emphasis added)

He goes on to say that 'systems analysis of the means of intensification has today become a most important theoretical and practical problem of communist construction' (p. 318).

It is refreshing to turn from these phrases to some of the pronouncements made in China. Since for Mao Ze-dong communism, like the Hunanese straw sandal, has no pattern, but is to be shaped in the making over a period of 'one to several centuries' it is to be expected that any comments on it will be very general and largely negative.[5] The *Quotations from Chairman Mao* contents itself with the extract from *On New Democracy* where Mao speaks of communism as 'at once a complete system of proletarian ideology and a new social system' (p. 23), and adds that it is 'the most complete, progressive, revolutionary and rational system in human history'. From the *Polemic on the General Line* to some of the textbooks produced in the period of the campaign on the dictatorship of the proletariat (1974-5) for the 'educated youth', stress was laid on measures to facilitate the eventual ending of class differences. Communist society would finally end commodity production and the state. But, as the 'educated youth' textbooks stressed, the absence of classes does not mean that in 'communist society there will be no contradictions, no struggles' (*Zhengzhi jingjixue jichu zhishi*, p. 237):

> At that time contradiction between superstructure and basis, between the relations of production and the forces of production will still continue. Reflecting these contradictions, a two-line struggle of progressive and backward, correct and mistaken will certainly continue to exist. Chairman Mao teaches us: '*Except in a desert, everywhere where there are people, there will be left, centre and right. Ten thousand years in the future it* will certainly be like that'. All these contradictions and struggles push society in a continuous forward development. (*Shehui fazhan shi*, p. 391)

In the next section I shall take up the theory of the transition period. This further distinguishes Mao Ze-dong, both from his opponents in China and from theories held by writers in the USSR.

Historical Materialism—Achieving the Aim

Marx and Engels evolved their political conception of revolutionary socialism, or communism as they called it in 1848, throughout a lifetime of both theoretical studies and practical involvement in working-class politics. Study of history and of political economy was complemented by observation of struggles ranging from that of the Silesian weavers of 1844 to the Paris Commune of 1871. Throughout they strongly opposed what Marx referred to as 'sentimental socialistic daydreams' (*Correspondence*, p. 17), 'playing with fancy pictures of the future structure of society' (*Correspondence*, p. 350), or 'doctrinaire and necessarily fantastic anticipations of the programme of action for a revolution of the future' (*Correspondence*, p. 387). All this he regarded as 'not merely useless but harmful' (ibid.). At the same time he recognised that '*before* the time of materialistic-critical socialism' such ideas played a certain positive role (*Correspondence*, pp. 350 and 387), and Engels enlarged on this in his pamphlet, *Socialism, Utopian and Scientific*.

Engels frequently referred to their views as 'scientific socialism'. In *Anti-Duhring* he attributed this advance to Marx.

These two great discoveries, the materialistic conception of history and the revelation of the secret of capitalistic production through surplus-value, we owe to Marx. With these discoveries socialism became a science. (p. 43)

Further on he showed what he meant by scientific when he wrote:

To thoroughly comprehend the historical conditions and thus the very nature of this act, [proletarian revolution] to impart to the now oppressed proletarian class a full knowledge of the conditions and the meaning of the momentous act it is called upon to accomplish— this is the task of the theoretical expression of the proletarian movement, scientific socialism. (*AD*, p. 391)

Marx himself, in 1843, made the same point in the language of that period:

The reform of consciousness consists *entirely* in making the world aware of its own consciousness, in arousing it from its dream of itself, in *explaining* its own actions to it . . . Our programme must be: the reform of consciousness not through dogmas but by analysing mystical consciousness obscure to itself, whether it appear in religious or political form. (*EW*, p. 209)

In the *Economic and Philosophic Manuscripts* he expressed it even more clearly:

It takes *actual* communist action to abolish actual private property. History will come to it; and this movement, which in *theory* we already know to be a self-transcending movement, will constitute *in actual fact* a very severe and protracted process. But we must regard it as a real advance to have gained beforehand a consciousness of the limited character as well as of the goal of this historical movement —and a consciousness which reaches out beyond it. (*EPM*, p. 124; cf. *PP*, p. 106)

In the *Grundrisse* we find:

> In order to develop the laws of bourgeois economy therefore, it is not necessary to write the *real history of the relations of production*. But . . . the contemporary conditions of production likewise appear as engaged in *suspending themselves* and hence in positing the *historic presuppositions* for a new state of society. (*Grundrisse*, pp. 460-61)

All this is relevant to accusations that marxism is a historicism made by those claiming sympathy with and opposition to Marx's theories. Two passages from *The Holy Family* further show that Marx himself had no such intention.

> Just as according to old teleologists plants exist to be eaten by animals and animals by men, history exists in order to serve as the act of consumption of theoretical eating — *proving* . . . That is why *history*, like *truth*, becomes a person apart, a metaphysical subject of which real human individuals are but the bearers. (*HF*, p. 107)

Such were the views of the 'critical critics' whom Marx was criticising. He goes on to argue that such 'categorising' is only possible until 'man is apprehended as the essence'. Then

> *History* does *nothing*, it 'possesses *no* immense wealth', it 'wages no battles'. It is *man*, real living man, that does all that, that possesses and fights; 'history' is not a person apart, using man as a means for *its own* particular aims; history is *nothing but* the activity of man pursuing his aims. (*HF*, p. 125)

One might ask, if marxism is not a historicism then what about all those phrases claiming that socialism/communism is inevitable? Careful reading of those by Marx and Engels will, I suggest, show that what is expressed is in each case a probable trend, and that only in agitational writings like the *Communist Manifesto* are the qualifications muted.[6] (CM in R. 1848. p. 79)

Let us turn now to the substance of this 'materialistic conception of

history' Key works for this include *The German Ideology,* the *Introduction* to *A Contribution to the Critique of Hegel's Philosophy of Right,*
and Marx's writings on contemporary France. In 1859, in the *Preface* to
A Contribution to the Critique of Political Economy Marx set out 'the
general result of (his) studies' which then served as 'a guiding thread'.
Here we meet the major concepts of historical materialism: *mode of
production* (later in the same preface to be listed 'in broad outlines' as
'the Asiatic, the ancient, the feudal, and the modern bourgeois'); *forces
of production* (*man*, with his skills and experience, and the *instruments
of production*, the tools and machines which he uses); and *relations of
production* (the classes in modern capitalist society). The concepts
structure (basis) and *superstructure*, which have given so much trouble
are also here. The key passage reads as follows:

> In the social production which men carry on they enter into definite
> relations that are indispensable and independent of their will; these
> relations of production correspond to a definite stage of development
> of their material forces of production. The sum total of these relations
> of production constitutes the economic structure of society—the real
> foundation, on which rises a legal and political superstructure and to
> which correspond definite forms of social consciousness. The mode
> of production in material life determines the social, political and
> intellectual life processes in general. It is not the consciousness of
> men that determines their being, but, on the contrary, their social
> being that determines their consciousness. At a certain stage of their
> development, the material forces of production in society come in
> conflict with the existing relations of production, or—what is but a
> legal expression for the same thing—with the property relations with-
> in which they have been at work before. From forms of development
> of the forces of production these relations turn into their fetters.
> Then begins an epoch of social revolution. With the change of the
> economic foundation the entire immense superstructure is more or
> less rapidly transformed. In considering such transformation a dis-
> tinction should always be made between the material transformation
> of the economic conditions of production which can be determined
> with the precision of natural science, and the legal, political, religious,
> aesthetic or philosophic—in short, ideological forms in which men
> become conscious of this conflict and fight it out. (Marx, *SW1*, p.
> 356) (*EW*, pp. 425-6)

In examining actual history a distinction must be made between the *mode of production* and the *social formation*. The former is a theoretical construct and in a particular historical *social formation*, while one mode may be dominant, aspects of other modes are sure to be also present (Amin, 1974, pp. 138-42).

This book is not the place to discuss the problems raised by the following important passage quoted from the above, except in so far as education, regarded as part of the superstructure, is concerned: 'at a certain stage of their development, the material forces of production in society come in conflict with the existing relations of production.' Mao Ze-dong, as we shall see, poses current problems in China in terms of non-conformity/conformity of basis and superstructure and places great importance on the role of education. However, here I shall concentrate on the questions of social class and class struggle, the latter regarded by Marx as the means by which communism was to be realised.

In a letter written in March 1852, Marx noted that the existence of classes had long been described by bourgeois historians and economists. What he did

> that was new was to prove: (1) that the *existence of classes* is only bound up with *particular, historic phases in the development of production*; (2) that the class struggle necessarily leads to the *dictatorship of the proletariat*; (3) that this dictatorship itself only constitutes the transition to the *abolition of all classes* and to a *classless society*. (*Correspondence*, p. 57)

In contemporary Europe, which Marx saw as increasingly dominated by the *capitalist mode of production* the essential social classes of which were *bourgeois* (capitalist), owners of the means of production, and the *proletariat* (working class), owners only of their own *labour power* and the producers of the *surplus value* on which the capitalist class depends. The economic process, now universally becoming one of commodity production and exchange was one which 'produces and reproduces the capitalist relation: on the one side the capitalist, on the other the wage-labourer' (*Capital* I, p. 633). The contradictory nature of capitalist society Marx showed in *Capital* to be embodied in the concept of *a commodity*, at one and the same time *exchange-value* and *use-value*. Its exchange-value is an embodiment of the *generalised* labour necessary to produce it and is the means by which capital makes a profit. Its use-value embodies the *particular* labour which gives it a form useful to its consumer. Exploitation of the workers took place even when the full value of their labour power was paid for, since the normal working day was longer than was required to produce the equivalent of their wages. This difference between the value of what is produced by the worker and the cost of his maintenance is what Marx called *surplus-value.*[7]

In contemporary social formations where the capitalist mode of production is dominant there are, in addition to the essential capitalist and proletarian classes, other classes. Some, like the landowning class or the traditional petty bourgeoisie may be characteristic of a formerly dominant mode of production while others may be new classes. In some social formations, such as France, or the two countries considered here, the peasantry is important. A complete description of the class structure must take into account not only the economic relations of production/exploitation, but also political relations of domination/subordination and ideological relations, also of domination/subordination through the possession and control of knowledge (Poulantzas, 1975, p. 15). Class determination must also take into consideration the marxist distinction between *productive labour* which creates surplus value and *unproductive labour* which, however socially useful or necessary it may be, does not.[8] In contemporary capitalism there has been a proliferation of wage-earners who, unlike the true proletariat, do not produce surplus value. The subject of considerable controversy both within and outside marxist circles, these unproductive wage-earners are probably best described by Poulantzas as 'the new petty-bourgeoisie'. But the problem remains sensitive since it is regarded as a question of identifying the revolutionary class.[9]

Marxism employs the terms fraction and stratum for sub-groups of the social classes. Examples of fractions are the industrial, financial and commercial bourgeoisie, or the artisans and small shop-keepers in the traditional petty bourgeoisie. Poulantzas distinguishes three fractions of the new petty bourgeoisie which in the class struggle are 'polarised in the direction of the working class', i.e. which are likely to adopt a class *position* different from their structural class *determination*: the lower-level commercial and service sector wage-earners; 'the subaltern agents of the public and private bureaucratised sectors' and 'the technicians and subaltern engineers directly involved in productive labour'.[10] Finally, marxism employs the term *social category* to such entities as the state bureaucracy or the intellectuals, the members of which usually belong to different social classes.

Capitalism had for Marx the peculiar property that the proletariat could not liberate itself from its 'wage-slavery' without at the same time liberating the whole of society—except, of course, the tiny minority of capitalists! He saw the proletariat forced by their circumstances to revolt. In 1845 he wrote:

When socialist writers ascribe this historic role to the proletariat it is not, as Critical Criticism [Young Hegelians, especially Bruno Bauer—] pretends to think, because they consider the proletarians as *gods*. Rather the contrary. Since the abstraction of all humanity, even of the *semblance* of humanity, is practically complete in the full-grown proletariat; since the conditions of life of society today in all their unhuman acuity; since man has lost himself in the proletariat, yet at the same time has not only gained theoretical consciousness of that loss, but through urgent, not longer disguisable, absolutely imperative need—that practical expression of *necessity*—is driven directly to revolt against that inhumanity; it follows that the proletariat can and must free itself. But it cannot free itself without abolishing the conditions of its own life. It cannot abolish the conditions of its own life without abolishing all the inhuman conditions of life of society today which are summed up in its own situation. (*HF*, p. 52)

In *Capital* Marx referred to the proletariat as 'disciplined, united, organised by the very mechanism of the process of capitalist production itself' (*Capital* I, pp. 836-7). The important thing is not that the proletariat were poor in material terms, but that they were, and remain alienated and exploited in the abstraction of surplus value over whose disposal they have no control.

Throughout their lives Marx and Engels maintained that 'the emancipation of the workers must be the task of the working class itself'.[11] In September 1879 they threatened to disassociate themselves from the German Social-Democratic Party because it was allowing itself to be swamped with petty-bourgeois people and theories. They stated bluntly:

We cannot ally ourselves, therefore, with people who openly declare that the workers are too uneducated to free themselves and must first be liberated from above by philanthropic big bourgeois and ·petty bourgeois. (*FI & A*, p. 375)

In the same letter they stressed that non-proletarians to be acceptable to a workers' party, to

be of use to the proletarian movement these people must also bring real cultural elements to it . . . Cultural elements whose first principle is to teach what they have not learnt can be very well dispensed with by the party. (*FI&A,* pp. 373-4)

Subsequent events have disappointed those who like Marx and Engels placed their hopes on the proletariat, and social democratic and 'labour' parties have become notorious career arenas for precisely the philanthropic petty bourgeoisie. Nevertheless, the ideas of Marx continue to reassert themselves and the issue of workers' *self*-emancipation and workers' *control* is even more alive today than ever before. Two problems which Marx already raised persist. The first is the welding of the different elements which make up the modern proletariat into a self-conscious, unified body, a 'class *for* itself'. It seems that in a century and a quarter we have advanced only a little from the position described in *The Poverty of Philosophy*:

> Economic conditions had first transformed the mass of the people of the country into workers. The domination of capital has created for this mass a common situation, common interests. *This mass is thus already a class as against capital, but not yet for itself.* In the struggle, of which we have noted only a few phases, this mass becomes united, and constitutes itself as a class for itself. The interests it defends become class interests. (*PP*, p. 146)

The second problem remains to find the right political form, to move from that 'system of socialist sects' to the 'real workers' movement' which Marx noted were always 'in inverse ratio to each other'[12] (*SW* 2, p. 616).

Marx's views on the *dictatorship of the proletariat* were expressed in writings ranging from the *Communist Manifesto* to the *Critique of the Gotha Programme*. He always conceived it as a freeing of the vast majority of the population who would have to dictate to only a few, a very different situation from that pertaining in the countries considered here. The experience of the Paris Commune enabled Marx to suggest some essential features for any successful transitional stage to communism.

> The Commune was to be a working, not a parliamentary, body, executive and legislative at the same time . . . Instead of deciding once in 3-6 years which member of the ruling class was to misrepresent the people in Parliament, universal suffrage was to serve the people, constituted in Communes, as individual suffrage serves every other employer in the search for the workmen and managers in his business. (Draper, pp. 73, 74)

Marx stressed the importance of such things as recall of *delegates* and their responsibility to those who elected them, a very different concept from that of *representatives* who 'raise themselves above real society'. In order to discourage the formation of such professional misrepresentatives functionaries would be paid a workman's wage (Draper, p. 200).

At the beginning of his career Marx had written illuminatingly about that modern scourge, bureaucracy, which now afflicts all walks of bourgeois society from trade unions to 'Multinationals' (not to mention the two countries considered here). He wrote:

> The bureaucracy appears to itself as the ultimate purpose of the state. As the bureaucracy converts its 'formal' purposes into its content, it comes into conflict with 'real' purposes at every point. It is therefore compelled to pass off form as content and content as form ... The universal spirit of bureaucracy is *secrecy*, it is mystery preserved within itself by means of the hierarchical structure ... Openly avowed political spirit, even patriotic sentiment, appears to the bureaucracy as a *betrayal* of its mystery. The principle of its knowledge is therefore *authority*, and its *patriotism* is the adulation of authority ... As for the individual bureaucrat, the purpose of the state becomes his private purpose, *a hunt for promotion, careerism.* (*EW*, pp. 107-8)

This characterisation, further developed in his writings on France, anticipated, as Avineri notes, the 'managerial revolution' (Avineri, pp. 48-52).

The other major political concept which Marx introduced was that of *permanent revolution.* This was taken up by Trotsky and emerges again today in Mao Ze-dong (who, however, distances himself from Trotsky, retaining Stalin's interpretation of Soviet history). In the *Address to the Central Council of the Communist League* (1850), it is treated as follows:

> While the democratic petty bourgeoisie wish to bring the revolution to a conclusion as quickly as possible and with the achievement at most of the above demands, it is our interest and our task to make the *revolution permanent*, until all more or less possessing classes have been displaced from domination, until the proletariat has conquered state power, and the association of proletarians, not only in one country but in all the dominant countries of the world, has advanced so far that competition among the proletarians of these countries has ceased and that at least the decisive production forces

are concentrated in the hands of the proletarians. (*SW* 2, p. 161, emphasis added)

A second passage, in *The Class Struggles in France*, links the concepts of permanent revolution and the dictatorship of the proletariat and stresses the intended goal, the abolition of classes and the revolutionising of man's ideas:

> This socialism is the *declaration of the permanence of the revolution, the class dictatorship* of the proletariat as the inevitable transit point to the *abolition of class differences generally,* to the abolition of all the production relations on which they rest, to the abolition of all the social relations that correspond to these relations of production, to the revolutionising of all the ideas that result from these social connections. (*SW* 2, p. 289)

Historical Materialism in Russia and China

Lenin and the Bolsheviks seized power in October 1917 in the belief that the proletariat of Europe would follow suit, and that united they would be able to create socialism. Stalin's policy of 'socialism in one country' was, if not in the final form, forced upon them as an alternative to retreat. The Chinese Communist Party's road to power and its expectations were different. Upholding a model of 'joint dictatorship of several revolutionary classes', the 'new democracy' outlined by Mao Ze-dong in a pamphlet of that title in 1940, the CCP sought allies among the small anti-Guomindang political parties and organisations, and with the national capitalists whose interests were not bound up with foreign capital (Mao, *SW* 2, p. 350). Significant here, however, is the common belief of both Communist Parties that following their different revolutions their countries were embarked on a period of transition to socialism whose fundamental features had been outlined by Karl Marx.

The Communist Party, regarded by both Russian and Chinese communists as the vital instrument of this transition, and of the further transition to communism, evolved in the long struggle to seize power, when it was the Russian Social Democratic Labour Party (from 1903). Its essential features during the period of this study were described by Stalin in his lectures to the Sverdlov University known under the title of *Foundations of Leninism* (1924). They were:

1. The Party is the 'vanguard of the working class', absorbing their

best elements and through possession of revolutionary theory able to 'see farther' and lead them.

2. The Party must be organised, with subordination of lower to higher bodies, minorities to majorities, and with every member bound by discipline.

3. The Party must be recognised as 'the highest form of organisation of the proletariat', exercising leadership over all other organisations, such as trade unions, co-operatives, and cultural organisations.

4. The Party is incompatible with factions. Stalin admits the need for 'criticism and contest of opinion within the Party', but argues that once 'a decision has been arrived at' iron discipline and unity is required.

These principles, widely described as *democratic centralism*, have been embodied in the Party Rules. Those of 1961 read as follows:

1. election of all leading party bodies, from the lowest to the highest;
2. periodical reports of party bodies to their party organisations and to higher bodies;
3. strict party discipline and subordination of the minority to the majority;
4. the decisions of higher bodies are obligatory for lower bodies (Lane, p. 129).

The organisational principles of the CCP are formally similar, with numerous provisions which guarantee the power to the highest central body, but at the same time all the revisions of the last three decades (1945, 1956 and 1973) give slightly greater attention to democracy than do their Soviet counterparts. The latest Chinese version, that of 1973, is remarkable for its incorporation of many of Mao's particular formulations. These include:

Article 5 . . . leading bodies of the Party at all levels shall be elected through democratic consultation in accordance with the requirements for successors to the cause of the proletarian revolution and the principle of combining the old, the middle-aged and the young . . .

Leading bodies of the Party at all levels shall regularly report on their work to congresses or general membership meetings, constantly listen to the opinions of the masses both inside and outside the Party and accept their supervision . . . If a Party member holds different views with regard to the decisions or directives of the Party organisations, he is allowed to reserve his views and has the right to bypass the immediate leadership and report directly to higher levels . . . It is essential to create a political situation in which there are both central-ism and democracy, both discipline and freedom, both unity of will and personal ease of mind and liveliness. (*The Tenth National Congress*, pp. 67-8)

Soviet Party rules aimed at dealing with 'the cult of the individual and the violations of inner-Party democracy' are formal limitations on length of committee membership (Article 25) with loopholes for officials with 'generally recognised prestige', or such declarations as that 'free and business-like discussion . . . is the inalienable right of every Party member' (Article 27, Lane, p. 524).

The Party Rules reflect what is increasingly becoming recognised as a fundamental difference between the functioning of the Soviet and Chinese Parties. At the centre of this is the distinction between leader-ship styles. The USSR increasingly strengthens bureaucratic-managerial leadership with its emphasis on technological and organisational rules and norms. China, from the *zhengfeng* movement of 1942-4, has develop-ed the cadre style, with the emphasis on human solidarity, commitment to change, and combining redness with expertise. While the bureaucrat-manager has what Brugger terms 'an excessive concern for status and hierarchy' (Brugger, p. 10) the cadre is both leader *and* participant in work and combines mental and manual labour in the process (Selden, p. 215).[13] The cadre leadership style is embodied in what the Chinese refer to as the *mass line*. This Mao expounded in several works in 1943. Essentially it is that

in all the practical work of our Party, all correct leadership is necessar-ily 'from the masses, to the masses'. This means: take the ideas of the masses (scattered and unsystematic ideas) and concentrate them (through study turn them into concentrated and systematic ideas), then go to the masses and propagate and explain these ideas until the masses embrace them as their own, hold fast to them and translate them into action, and test the correctness of these ideas in such action. (Mao, *SW* 3, p. 119)

The intimate connection of education with politics is here clearly expressed as a two-way process of mutual education of leaders and led. It is also involved in the principle to which Mao often returned: 'no investigation, no right to speak' (Mao, *Quotations*, p. 230). A particularly lively exposition of all these questions is Mao's speech to the '7,000 cadres conference' in January 1962 (Schram, 1974, pp. 158-87). It was here that he made the point that 'in the beginning truth is . . . in the hands of a minority' and argued that because of this people should be allowed to reserve their opinions when unconvinced by persuasion (ibid. p. 183).

It was Lenin who first used the notorious phrase, transmission belt, to describe the relation between the CP and the trade unions. In a CC resolution on the 'role and functions of trade unions' he likened relations between the Party and the masses to a factory.

> Just as the very best factory, with the very best engines and first-class machines, will be forced to remain idle if the transmission belts from the motor to the machines are damaged, so our work of Socialist construction must meet with inevitable disaster if the trade unions—the transmission belts from the Communist Party to the masses—are badly fitted or function badly. (Lenin, 1947, 2, p. 766)

Stalin developed this idea. In 1926 he described the 'mechanism' of the dictatorship of the proletariat. The Party was to be the 'directing force' while the mass organisations, the trade unions, Soviets (significantly placed second), the co-operatives and the Young Communist League were to be the 'transmission belts' and 'levers' of the mechanism (Stalin, pp. 136-9). Whether the mass line theory in China offers a more satisfactory alternative has yet to be proved. To date the mass organisations appear to have been either rather ineffective, or bureaucratised 'transmission belts' for Party policy very similar to those in the USSR. Discussion has been more on direct Party-mass relations than on the role of other organisations. It is significant that in the new state Constitution of 1975 the leadership role of the CP is laid down. Article 2 begins: 'The Communist Party of China is the core of leadership of the whole Chinese people. The working class exercises leadership over the state through its vanguard, the CCP.' Except for the system of People's Congresses and similar state bodies, the PLA and people's communes, no other organisation is named in the Constitution.

Perhaps the most significant difference between Soviet and Chinese theories of the transition to socialism concerns classes and class struggle. Before the adoption of the 1936 Constitution in the USSR Stalin referred to the class struggle becoming 'fiercer' under the dictatorship than it had been before (Stalin, p. 253). The desired classless society was to be achieved by 'strengthening the organs of the dictatorship of the proletar-

iat [i.e. the security police and organs of terror], by intensifying
the class struggle' (Stalin, p. 499). Then in his speech outlining the new
constitution in 1936 Stalin declared that following the economic
changes which had taken place the class composition of the USSR had
changed and that dividing lines, economic and political contradictions
between the working class, peasantry and intelligentsia were 'declining
and becoming obliterated' (Stalin, pp. 543-6). While in practice the
terror increased, in theory class struggle would seem to have diminished.
But it remained for Stalin's successors to enshrine this in the 1961
Party Programme:

> Having brought about the complete and final victory of socialism—
> the first phase of communism—and the transition of society to the
> full-scale construction of communism, the dictatorship of the pro-
> letariat has fulfilled its historic mission and has ceased to be indis-
> pensable in the USSR from the point of view of the tasks of internal
> development. The state, which arose as a state of the dictatorship of
> the proletariat, has, in the new, contemporary stage, become a state
> of the entire people, an organ expressing the interests and will of the
> people as a whole. (*Fundamentals*, p. 595)

On classes the textbook emphasises:

> Since all classes and sections consist of working people, since all are
> connected with property of the same type, socialist property, the
> relationships between them are free of any antagonism . . . Thus,
> socialism replaces the age-old struggle of classes by solidarity and
> unity arising from the community of aims, ideology, and ethics.
> (*Fundamentals*, p. 594)

Mao Ze-dong sees it very differently. His view that class struggle
would continue under socialism, expressed in numerous writings since
1949, was finally embodied in the Party Constitution in 1973.

> Socialist society covers a considerably long historical period. Through-
> out this historical period there are classes, class contradictions and
> class struggles, there is the struggle between the socialist road and
> the capitalist road, there is the danger of capitalist restoration and
> there is the threat of subversion and agression by imperialism and
> social-imperialism [i.e. the USSR]. These contradictions can be
> resolved only by depending on the theory of continued revolution

under the dictatorship of the proletariat and on practice under its guidance. (*The Tenth National Congress* . . . , p. 62)

Here also is the marxist concept of *continuous revolution* (buduan geming) which was a constant theme of Mao's, though he did not often label it (cf. Schram, 1974, p. 94). Mao's last great political education campaign, that on the dictatorship of the proletariat, opened in the national press with the publication of pages of quotations on the subject by Marx, Engels and Lenin. These were prefaced by 'important instructions on the question of theory' from Mao himself. Among them was this one:

Lenin said: 'small production engenders capitalism and the bourgeoisie continuously, daily, hourly, spontaneously, and on a mass scale.' This also occurs among a section of the workers and a section of the Party members. Both within the ranks of the proletariat and among the personnel of state organs there are people who follow the bourgeois style of life. (*Peking Review*, 1975, p. 5)

The contrast is complete. In the one case problems are smoothed over and minds closed. In the other people are urged to think about conflicts of interest, differences and difficulties. It is clear which theory is the more educational.

Consciousness and Ideology

In the last section we encountered the much quoted and often misunderstood sentence: 'It is not the consciousness of men that determines their being, but on the contrary, their social being that determines their consciousness' (*EW*, p. 425). In the *German Ideology* Marx and Engels had developed this idea as follows:

The production of ideas, of conceptions, of consciousness, is at first directly interwoven with the material activity and the material intercourse of men, the language of real life. Conceiving, thinking, the mental intercourse of men, appear at this stage as the direct efflux of their material behaviour. The same applies to mental production as expressed in the language of politics, laws, morality, religion, metaphysics, etc., of a people. Men are the producers of their conceptions, ideas, etc.,—real, active men, as they are conditioned by a definite development of their productive forces and of the intercourse corresponding to these, up to its furthest forms. Consciousness can never be anything else than conscious existence, and the existence of men is their actual life-process. If in all ideology men and their circumstances appear upside-down as in a camera obscura, this phenomenon arises just as much from their historical life-process as the inversion of objects on the retina does from their physical life-process. (*GI*, p. 37)

This poses the problem of the relation between basis and superstructure, between the 'economic structure of society' and politics, laws, morality, religion, etc., which was not discussed in the last section. It also raises the controversy over marxism, especially in its Leninist and Stalinist varieties, as a *reflection theory* of ideas.

The first of these problems is discussed by Engels in the fourth section of his essay on Ludwig Feuerbach (1888), and in the 'self-critical' letters to J. Bloch (21 September 1890) and L. Schmidt (27 October 1890). In the first letter he wrote, against the economic determinist epigones of Marx's theories:

> According to the materialist conception of history the determining element in history is *ultimately* the production and reproduction in real life. More than this neither Marx nor I have ever asserted. (*SW* 1, p. 381)

In a letter to H. Starkenburg (25 January 1894) Engels put the relations as follows:

> Political, juridical, philosophical, religious, literary, artistic, etc., development is based on economic development. But all these react upon one another and also upon the economic base. It is not that the economic position is the *cause and alone active*, while everything else only has a passive effect. There is, rather, interaction on the basis of the economic necessity, which *ultimately* always asserts itself. (*SW* 1, p. 392)

In the *Ludwig Feuerbach* essay Engels discusses the force of 'ultimately', or as it is often put, 'in the last instance'. He argues that while 'each person follows his own consciously desired end' (ibid. p. 457) history up to the present has, through a clash of wills and actions, been a realm of necessity. The economic base has ultimately asserted itself through the operation of the class struggle, a struggle which is essentially political (ibid. p. 461).

Timpanaro makes the point that the relationship between the differ-

ent levels of structure and superstructure can 'only be resolved by spec-
ifying, through a series of empirical observations, what is meant by the
relative autonomy of the superstructure' (Timpanaro, p. 114) and he
goes on to criticise the anti-Engelsian position adopted by certain marxist
writers today.[14] This area is, of course of particular importance for
education since it poses the question of the effect of education as a conscious process on the social consciousness of men, and the place of
education as institutions of various kinds in the whole interacting totality.

A number of critics of marxism have objected to what they regard
as a passive reflection theory of ideas.[15] This is often based on too simple
a reading of Lenin's *Materialism and Empirio-criticism* (e.g. p. 128). But
it is hard to see where such critics get the impression of passivity since
certainly all mention of the term 'reflection' in Marx' and Engels' writings
is in a context where the active role of the subject is being stressed.
Furthermore, in the *Economic and Philosophic Manuscripts* Marx draws
attention to the way in which the various senses, the basis of all sciences
(*EPM*, p. 111), are formed by man's past and his immediate present,
and therefore to varying degrees 'see' what they expect to 'see'.

> Not only the five senses but also the so-called mental senses—the
> practical senses (will, love, etc.)—in a word, *human* sense—the human-
> ness of the senses—come to be by virtue of its object, by virtue of
> *humanized* nature. The forming of the five senses is a labour of the
> entire history of the world down to the present.
>   The *sense* caught up in crude practical need has only a *restricted*
> sense. For the starving man, it is not the human form of food that
> exists, but only its abstract being as food; . . . The care-burdened
> man in need has no sense for the finest play; the dealer in minerals
> sees only the mercantile value but not the beauty and the unique
> nature of the mineral . . . (*EPM*, pp. 108-9).

The nature of class divided society, with its various forms of alienation, distort the senses to produce *ideology*, or *false* consciousness.
Speaking in *Capital* of man's religious ideas, Marx says:

> The religious reflex of the real world can, in any case, only then
> finally vanish, when the practical relations of everyday life offer to
> man none but perfectly intelligible and reasonable relations with
> regard to his fellow men and to nature.
>   The life-processes of society, which is based on the process of

material production, does not strip off its mystical veil until it is treated as production by freely associated men, and is consciously regulated by them in accordance with a settled plan. This, however,
demands for society a certain material groundwork or set of conditions of existence which in their turn are the spontaneous product
of a long and painful process of development. (*Capital* I, pp. 91-2)

However, Marx and Engels had already, in the *German Ideology*, made
clear that they expected the proletariat, because of its special position
as the exploited class, to strip off at least part of the mystical veil,
especially in the process of making revolution. They were conscious that
they and other non-proletarians might achieve the same through 'con-
templation of the situation of this class' (*GI*, p. 86). This process of
interaction of theory and practice, a topic to which we must return
below, is described in a passage important for the way it sums up the
essence of their views:

Both for the production on a mass scale of this communist consciousness, and for the success of the cause itself, the alteration of men on
a mass scale is necessary, an alteration which can only take place in
a practical movement, a *revolution*; this revolution is necessary,
therefore, not only because the *ruling* class cannot be overthrown in
any other way, but also because the class *overthrowing* it can only in
a revolution succeed in ridding itself of all the muck of ages and
become fitted to found society anew. (*GI*, p. 87)

Ideology for Marx is a question of the expression of the special
interest of a particular class as the general interest of society as a whole.
In modern bourgeois society the interests of the bourgeoisie are so
presented by what Marx referred to as the ruling class ideology:

The ideas of the ruling class are in every epoch the ruling ideas: i.e.
the class which is the ruling *material* force of society, is at the same
time its ruling *intellectual* force. The class which has the means of
material production at its disposal, has control at the same time over
the means of mental production, so that thereby, generally speaking,
the ideas of those who lack the means of mental production are subject to it. The ruling ideas are nothing more than the ideal expression
of the dominant material relationships, the dominant material relationships grasped as ideas; hence of the relationships which make the one
class the ruling one, therefore, the ideas of its dominance. (*GI*, p. 61)

It should be noted that while Marx and Engels often attacked the 'thinkers of the class' who 'make the perfecting of the illusion of the class about itself their chief source of livelihood' for resorting to a form of apologetics, they did not regard 'false consciousness' simply as conscious falsehood. Engels, in a letter to Mehring in 1893, remarked:

Ideology is a process accomplished by the so-called thinker consciously, indeed, but with a false consciousness. The real motives impelling him remain unknown to him, otherwise it would not be an ideological process at all. (*Correspondence*, p. 511)

Only in times of crisis may the deception become deliberate:

The more the normal form of intercourse of society, and with it the conditions of the ruling class, develop their contradictions to the advanced productive forces, and the greater the consequent split within the ruling class itself as well as the split between it and the class ruled by it, the more untrue, of course, becomes the consciousness which originally corresponded to this form of intercourse (i.e. it ceases to be the consciousness corresponding to this form of intercourse), and the more do the earlier traditional ideas of this intercourse, in which actual private interests, etc., are expressed as universal interests, descend to the level of more idealising phrases, conscious illusion, deliberate hypocrisy. But the more their falsity is exposed by life, and the less meaning they have for consciousness itself, the more firmly are they asserted, the more hypocritical, moral and holy becomes the language of this normal society. (*GI*, pp. 323-4)

Poulantzas, attempting to develop Marx's and Engels' analyses of French and German society in relation to *Political Power and Social Classes,* makes the following general points:

Ideology is present to such an extent in all the agents' activities that it becomes indistinguishable from their *lived experience.* To this extent ideologies fix in a relatively coherent universe not only a real but also an *imaginary relation*: i.e. men's real relation to their conditions of existence in the form of an imaginary relation . . . Precisely because it is determined by its structure, at the level of experience the social whole remains *opaque* to the agents. (Poulantzas, pp. 206-7)

Its social function is, he notes, 'to insert (people) as it were into their practical activities supporting this structure' (Poulantzas, ibid.). Poulantzas, following Gramsci, emphasises that ideology is not 'scattered elements of knowledge, notions, etc., but also the whole process of symbolization, of mythical transposition,. of "taste", "style", "fashion", i.e. of the "way of life" in general' (Poulantzas, p. 208). He makes the important point that ideology can be divided into various *regions*, such as moral, juridical-political, aesthetic, religious, economic, or philosophical, and that 'in the *dominant ideology* of a social formation it is generally possible to decipher *the dominance of one region of ideology over the others*' (Poulantzas, p. 210). Poulantzas illustrates this briefly with discussions of feudal Europe and modern capitalism.

> In the capitalist mode of production and in a capitalist formation, where the economic generally plays the dominant role, we see the dominance of the *juridico-political region* in the ideological. But in particular at the stage of state monopoly capitalism, in which the dominant role is held by the political, it is the economic ideology (of which 'technocratism' is only one aspect) which tends to become the dominant region of the dominant ideology. (Poulantzas, p. 211)

He goes on to emphasise:

> In short, everything takes place as if the centre of the dominant ideology is never in the place where real knowledge is to be sought; as if it carried out its masking role by altering the position, i.e. by deforming the object of science. (ibid.)

In the course of his analysis Poulantzas argues against too close an identification of an ideology with a particular class. Proponents of a one-to-one fit neglect the influence of one class ideology on that of another which succeeds it, e.g. in Britain, where the ideology of the dominant bourgeoisie contains elements of the former aristocratic one (Poulantzas, pp. 203-4). This question is related to that of the origin of class consciousness-ideology and theories of *spontaneism* which, for example, divided Rosa Luxembourg from Lenin.

E.P. Thompson gives a splendid account of just this complexity of the problem in *The Making of the English Working Class*, in his chapter, 'The transforming power of the cross'. He shows how Methodism served both as 'ideological self-justification for the master-manufacturers' and as the religion 'of wide sections of the proletariat' (p. 391). Not only did it uphold discipline and order, as Puritanism had done before it, but it provided 'some kind of community to replace the older community-patterns which were being displaced' (p. 417). Thompson adds 'direct indoctrination' and 'the psychic consequences of the counter-revolution' as reasons why 'so many working people were willing to submit to this form of psychic exploitation' (pp. 411-12).

Ernest Mandel discusses what Poulantzas refers to as the dominant region of the dominant ideology of today's monopoly capitalism in his recent *Late Capitalism* (Poulantzas, p. 211; Mandel, 1975, pp. 500-22). He lists a number of theses 'common to most, if not all, the proponents of "technological rationality"'. These stress the 'autonomous power' of science and technology; that 'emergent problems can only be solved by specialist functional treatment'; that satisfaction of needs and increasing consumption 'increases popular consent to incorporation and subordination'; and that a 'bureaucratic state that is neutral between groups or classes and is organized on technical principles' has replaced 'traditional class rule' (p. 501). Specially relevant to education is Mandel's comment that 'the real idol of late capitalism is therefore the "specialist" who is blind to any overall context' (p. 509). These two widely different examples of ideologies must serve to illustrate what remains a huge problematic. Not least important, and especially for educators, is the role that ideologies play in shaping men's practice. For marxism this remains an open question, the answer to which is largely empirical.

Since religion has been, to a different extent, an important ideological question in both Russia and China, I will introduce here Marx's major writings on this question. As David McLellan so interestingly describes, Marx evolved marxism in the course of a deep study of both philosophy and religion, partly guided by his friend and teacher, Bruno Bauer.[16] Against his friend's advice he included an open declaration of atheism in the introduction to his doctoral thesis:

> Philosophy makes no secret of it. The confession of Prometheus: 'In simple words, I have the pack of gods', is its own confession, its own aphorism against all heavenly and earthly gods who do not acknowledge human self-consciousness as the highest divinity. It (philosophy) will have none other beside. (*Collected Works* 1, p. 30)

Two years later, in 1843, Marx wrote his most extended and famous passages on religion, in the Introduction to his *Contribution to the Critique of Hegel's Philosophy of Right*. It began:

For Germany, the criticism of religion has been largely completed; and the criticism of religion is the premise of all criticism. (Marx and Engels, *OR*, p. 41, trans. that of McLellan, YH & KM, p. 79)

It went on later:

The task of history, therefore, once the world beyond the truth has disappeared, is to establish the truth of this world. The immediate task of philosophy, which is at the service of history, once the saintly form of human self-alienation has been unmasked, is to unmask self-alienation in its unholy forms. Thus the criticism of heaven turns into the criticism of the earth, the criticism of religion into the criticism of right, and the criticism of theology into the criticism of politics. (Marx and Engels, *OR*, p. 42, italics omitted.)

In the *Economic and Philosophic Manuscripts* of the following year Marx, the socialist, denied the need for atheism:

Since the real existence of man and nature has become practical, sensuous and perceptible—since man has become for man as the being of nature, and nature for man as the being of man—the question about an *alien* being, about a being above nature and man—a question which implies the admission of the inessentiality of nature and of man—has become impossible in practice. *Atheism*, as the denial of this inessentiality, has no longer any meaning, for atheism is a negation of God, and postulates the existence of man through this negation; but socialism as socialism no longer stands in any need of such a mediation. (Marx, *EPM*, pp. 113-14, some italics omitted)

In a manuscript written in 1845 or 1846 Marx wrote: 'Religion is from the outset consciousness of the *transcendental* arising from a *real* necessity.' Years later, in *Capital*, he repeated this: 'The religious world is but the reflect of the real world' (Marx and Engels, *OR*, p. 134).

At the end of 1843 Marx wrote *On the Jewish Question*, a critique of two articles on the subject by Bruno Bauer. Here he develops the argument that it is not religious or even political emancipation which man needs, but human emancipation. This is required by both Christian and Jew alike.

As soon as Jew and Christian recognize their opposed religions as merely different stages in the development of the human spirit, as

different snake skins that history has cast off and recognise man as
the snake that used the skins for covering, then they will no longer
be in religious opposition but only in a critical, scientific, human
opposition. (McLellan, *ET*, p. 87)

Marx recognised the class bias of organised religions, and in an early
polemic comments:

The social principles of Christianity justified the slavery of Antiquity,
glorified the serfdom of the Middle Ages and equally know, when
necessary, how to defend the oppression of the proletariat, although
they make a pitiful face over it.
The social principles of Christianity preach the necessity of a ruling
and oppressed class, and all they have for the latter is the pious wish
the former will be charitable. (Marx and Engels, *OR*, p. 82)

Criticising the drafters of the Gotha Programme for not including any
statement of intent to 'endeavour . . . to liberate the conscience from
the witchery of religion', Marx was certainly also aware that direct
attacks would not necessarily promote the first task, that of liberating
man from bourgeois rule. Engels made the point a number of times that
the use of the gendarme would only help religion 'to martyrdom and a
prolonged lease of life' (Engels, *AD*, p. 435; Marx and Engels, *OR*, p.
142).
It is important to note that while Marx considered religion super-
seded already in theory, he was by no means unaware of its positive
role in the past, nor was he advocating stripping people of comfort
before there was something to put in its place. Both these points appear
in the famous passage from the *Introduction*:

. . . the struggle against religion is indirectly the struggle against that
world whose spiritual aroma is religion.
Religious suffering is at the same time an expression of real suffering and a protest against real suffering. Religion is the sigh of the
oppressed creature, the feeling of a heartless world and the soul of
soulless circumstances. It is the opium of the people.
The abolition of religion as the illusory happiness of the people
is the demand for their real happiness. The demand to give up the
illusions about their condition is a demand to give up a condition
that requires illusion. The criticism of religion is therefore the germ
of the criticism of the valley of tears whose halo is religion.

Criticism has plucked the imaginary flowers from the chains not
so that many may bear chains without any imagination or comfort,
but so that he may throw away the chains and pluck living flowers.
The criticism of religion disillusions man so that he may think, act
and fashion his own reality as a disillusioned man come to his senses;
so that he may revolve around himself as his real sun. Religion is only
the illusory sun which revolves around man as long as he does not
revolve around himself. (Trans. McLellan, *EW*, p. 116)

To end this section let us consider briefly the role of *practice* in Marx.
This is currently much spoken of in Euro-American marxist circles in
its German form, *praxis*, though not, as Timpanaro warns, always very
usefully (Timpanaro, p. 56). Moreover, at least two aspects of the concept must be distinguished: more or less passive experience of life against
which ideas may be tested by observation; and action, activities in which
both actor and acted upon may be changed.

In the *Introduction* to the *Critique of Hegel's Philosophy of Right*
Marx wrote:

As the determined opponent of the previous form of *German* political
consciousness, the criticism of the speculative philosophy of law
finds its progression not within itself but in *tasks* which can only be
solved in one way—through practice (*Praxis*).

Further on he added:

Clearly the weapon of criticism cannot replace the criticism of
weapons, the material force must be overthrown by material force.
But theory also becomes a material force once it has gripped the
masses. Theory is capable of gripping the masses when it demonstrates
ad hominem and it demonstrates *ad hominem* as soon as it becomes
radical. To be radical is to grasp things by the root. But for man the
root is man himself. (*EW*, p. 251)

Marx's whole life demonstrated the seriousness with which he took his
early epigram: 'The philosophers have only *interpreted* the world, in
various ways; the point is to *change* it' (*EW*, p. 423). But this, as Avineri
points out (p. 13) depends precisely on a combination of correct theory
and practice which it was Marx's aim to provide.

The marxist concept of practice must be distinguished from that of
pragmatism. The latter was expressed by William James, author of

Pragmatism, as: 'Truth *happens* to an idea. It *becomes* true, is *made* true by events' (Cornforth, 1950, p. 158). As Kolakowski describes it, pragmatism holds that 'truth is not correspondence between our statements and the way things are, but between our statements and the possible gratifications we may experience' (Kolakowski, p. 190). Schmidt, commenting on the post-Leninist formulations 'according to which historical practice is the basis of knowledge and the criterion of truth', makes the point that

> it must not be forgotten that the epistemological role of practice is not exhausted by its retroactive determination of the agreement or disagreement of thought with the Object . . . practice in general can only be the criterion of truth because—as a historical whole—it *constitutes* the objects of normal human experience, i.e. plays an essential part in their internal composition. (Schmidt, p. 119)

Returning to Marx for the last word, here is how he expresses his hope that in their coincidence of being and acting the proletariat would unite theory and practice and fulfil its historic task.

> Not in vain does [the proletariat] go through the stern but steeling school of *labour*. The question is not what this or that proletarian, or even the whole of the proletariat at the moment *considers* as its aim. The question is *what the proletariat is*, and what, consequent on that *being*, it will be compelled to do. Its aim and historical action is irrevocably and obviously demonstrated in its own life situation as well as in the whole organization of bourgeois society today. There is no need to dwell here upon the fact that a large part of the English and French proletariat is already *conscious* of its historic task and is constantly working to develop that consciousness into complete clarity. (Marx, *Holy Family*, pp. 52-3)

One hundred and thirty years later the process of clarification continues, and also the confusing, since the school of labour is a complex one and the demonstrations are not yet obvious enough.

Consciousness and Ideology in Russia and China

The concept of a vanguard party, described in the last section, has been underpinned by a theory put forward by Lenin in 1902 in *What is to be Done?* He argued that Social-Democratic consciousness could not arise among the working class itself, out of its own experience, but must be brought to it from outside.

> The theory of socialism, however, grew out of the philosophic, his-
> toric and economic theories that were elaborated by the educated
> representatives of the propertied classes, the intellectuals. (Lenin,
> 1947, 1, p. 170)

According to this theory the workers could only produce trade union
consciousness. This theory was taken up by Stalin and widely incorporated into official marxism.[17] *The fundamentals* . . . repeated the same
themes in the 1960s:

> the scientific world outlook of the working class must become the
> possession of the masses of the workers. Hence the need for introduc-
> ing this scientific wo ld outlook into the working-class movement
> *from outside* the economic struggle and the sphere of relations
> between the workers and their employers. This task is performed by
> the Marxist-Leninist party. (p. 167)

That, as Antonio Carlo shows, Lenin adopted '*a series* of complex and
contradictory positions' on this question throughout his life is important
in the history of marxist thought, but it does not alter the nature of the
communist parties or their relations with other organisations and
groups[18] (Carlo, p. 40)

Denied a creative role in theory as well as in practice, it is not surprising that Soviet marxist writing has been barren of interest concerning
the relationship between man's social being and his consciousness.
Stalin's writings provide some typical passages where Marx has become
cliche, and others illustrating the mechanistic approach widely discern-
able in Soviet writings. An example of the latter is in the essay, *Dialectical and Historical Materialism*, where after advocating study of 'the
laws of development of the productive forces, and of the relations of
production, the laws of the economic development of society' (Stalin,
p. 585), rather than what is in 'men's minds', their 'views and ideas of
society', Stalin goes on to say:

> changes and development [of production] always begin with
> changes and development of the productive forces, and in the first
> place, with changes and development of the instruments of product-
> ion. (ibid.)

In China Mao Ze-dong's stress on class struggle, noted in the last section, has brought questions of ideology and different class interests to the fore. Moreover, two works widely studied in the mass political education movements deal with questions of consciousness. These are *On Practice* (1937) and *Where do Correct Ideas come from* (1963).

On Practice states on its opening pages: 'Marxists regard man's activity in production as the most fundamental practical activity, the determinant of all his other activities' *(Four Essays*, p. 1). It goes on to elaborate on social practice. By 1963 the formulation had become: 'correct ideas come . . . three kinds of social practice: the struggle for production, the class struggle, and scientific experiment' (ibid. p. 134). It is these kinds of social practice which are 'the criterion of the truth of man's knowledge of the external world' (ibid. p. 3).

Mao separates man's acquisition of knowledge into two stages: the perceptual stage, and the stage of rational knowledge. In the first stage man 'sees only the phenomenal side, the separate aspects, the external relations of things' (ibid. p. 4). After a time the accretion of percepts brings about a change of quantity into quality and concepts, judgements and inferences are formed. This is the rational stage (ibid. p. 5). What appears to be missing from all this is recognition of the role of previously formed concepts on the process of perception. But this is hinted at when Mao writes: 'Our practice proves that what is perceived cannot at once be comprehended and that only what is comprehended can be more deeply perceived' (ibid. pp. 6-7). However, Mao's focus of interest is on arriving at correct political practice through the spiral process he set out in the last paragraph of *On Practice*: 'Practice, knowledge, again practice, again knowledge. This form repeats itself in endless cycles, and with each cycle the content of practice and knowledge rises to a higher level' (ibid. p. 20). In *Correct Ideas*, where he divided cognition into a stage leading from 'existence to ideas' and one 'from consciousness back to matter' he wrote:

Then comes the second stage . . . in which the knowledge gained in the first stage is applied in social practice to ascertain whether the theories, policies, plans or measures meet with the anticipated success. Generally speaking, those that succeed are correct . . . (ibid. p. 135)

Returning to *On Practice* we find the important statement that

perception only solves the problem of phenomena; theory alone can solve the problem of essence. The solving of both these problems is not separable in the slightest degree from practice. Whoever wants to know a thing has no way of doing so except by coming into contact with it. (ibid. p. 7)

But he then admits that 'one cannot have direct experience of everything' (ibid. p. 8) and that 'as a matter of fact, most of our experience comes from indirect knowledge' (ibid.). This leaves a number of problems, important for education, unsolved. Perhaps Mao would say that these can only be solved in practice![19]

Before closing this section it is, perhaps, pertinent to note that both Russian and Chinese marxism put tremendous stress on propaganda and study. In China this comes in the wake of centuries of Confucian moralising. In Russia it follows a century in which liberal democrats preached the importance of secular, scientific thought. In a later chapter I shall return to this question and ask in other terms just what is the relation between theory and practice, between what we are taught, whether through propaganda or in school, and what we learn in the process of living. I will close this section with a final quotation from *The ABC of Communism* where the authors express a view which seems to typify communist thought on this question:

Communist propaganda has become a necessity for the whole society now undergoing regeneration. It must accelerate the inevitable process of transformation . . . The State propaganda of communism becomes in the long run a means for the eradication of the last traces of bourgeois propaganda dating from the old regime; and it is a powerful instrument for the creation of a new ideology, of new modes of thought, of a new outlook on the world. (Carr, 1969, pp. 296-7)

Dialectical Materialism and the Methodology of Marx

The term *dialectical materialism* is not found in the writings of Marx and Engels, though the latter comes near to it, e.g. in speaking of 'materialistic dialectic' in his essay on *Ludwig Feuerbach* (Marx, Engels, *SW* 1, p. 453). Marx, in his early writings, often referred to his own views as naturalism.[20] He was concerned to distinguish his position from that of previous materialists on the one side and from various idealists on the other. *The Holy Family* (1845), in which he and Engels distanced themselves from some of their contemporaries, gives examples of both distinctions while the *Theses on Feuerbach* concentrate on problems of materialism. Engels, who in *Anti-Duhring* looked forward to 'each special science' making 'clear its position in the great totality of things and of our knowledge of things' and with that the end of a philosophy standing above the separate sciences (*AD*, p. 40), over-simplified in *Ludwig Feuerbach*. There he wrote:

> the materialist standpoint . . . was resolved to comprehend the real world—nature and history—just as it presents itself to everyone who approaches it free from pre-conceived idealist fancies. (*SW* 1, p. 451)

In Engels' writings the theme is almost always the distinction between mechanical and dialectical materialism and, perhaps because, as he wrote, 'we, at that time, were all materialists' (*SW* 1, p. 398), he never produced a succinct definition of materialism itself. The following, by Stalin, summarises ideas scattered through Engels' works:

> . . . Marxist materialist philosophy holds that matter, nature, being, is an objective reality existing outside and independent of our mind; that matter is primary, since it is the source of sensations, ideas, mind, and that mind is secondary, derivative, since it is a reflection of matter, a reflection of being . . . [21] (Stalin, pp. 575-6)

Timpanaro, in an important essay, formulates the marxist position as follows:

> By materialism we understand above all acknowledgement of the priority of nature over 'mind', or if you like, of physical level over the biological level, and of the biological level over the socio-economic and cultural level; both in the sense of chronological priority . . . and in the sense of the conditioning which nature *still* exercises on man . . . Cognitively, therefore, the materialist maintains that experience cannot be reduced either to a production of reality by a subject (however such production is conceived) or to a reciprocal implication of subject and object. We cannot, in other words, deny or evade the element of passivity in experience; the external situation which we do not create but which imposes itself on us. (Timpanaro, p. 34)

It is sometimes objected that the terms *materialism* and *matter* imply a limited tangibility excluding many of the essential entities of modern science. For this reason many prefer the term *realism*. But both terms can equally be used in the way indicated by Keat and Urry in the following quotation, and marxist materialism certainly is.[22]

> . . . for the realist, one objective of science is to discover the often
> unobservable structures and mechanisms which causally generate
> the observable phenomena. Thus the realist is perfectly prepared to
> regard terms such as 'election' or 'molecule' as referring to real entities
> in the world, in much the same way as non-theoretical terms do—such
> as 'iron', 'wood', 'red', etc. (Keat and Urry, p. 17)

For purposes of distinction, however, the term *materialism* is to be preferred since, as Timpanaro points out, *realism*, in the sense of 'the affirmation of the existence of a reality not reducible to thought' would include
Plato, St Thomas and many others certainly not materialists. Timpanaro
stresses that

> materialism is not just 'realism'; it is also recognition of the physical
> nature of the subject, and of the physical nature of his activities trad-
> itionally regarded as 'spiritual'. (Timpanaro, p. 80)

Contrary to those European marxists desperately anxious to prove that
their views are not 'crude', this is the real position of Marx and Engels[23]
(Timpanaro, p. 32).

We will now turn to *dialectics*, that view of the material world, both
man and nature, by which Marx and Engels distinguished themselves
from other materialists. Bertell Ollman, one of those who rejects
attempts to divide Marx and Engels on this question (Ollman, p. 52),
sees dialectics as (i) a way of seeing things; (ii) an approach to the study
of problems; and (iii) a method of exposition, (ibid.). Emphasising that
'for Marx the basic unit of reality is not a thing but a Relation' (p. 71),
he shows how Marx used dialectics to clarify the internal relationships
of that which he was discussing:

> Each subject is dealt with from many different vantage points, and
> second, that each subject is followed out of and into the particular
> forms it assumes at different times. (Ollman, pp. 67-8; see also pp.
> 62, 66)

At its most general dialectics is the comprehension of the world as a
'complex of processes'. Engels, in *Ludwig Feuerbach* described this as
follows:

The great basic thought that the world is not to be comprehended as a complex of ready-made *things*, but as a complex of *processes*, in which the things apparently stable no less than their mind-images in our heads, the concepts, go through an uninterrupted change of coming into being and passing away, in which, in spite of all seeming accidents and of all temporary retrogression, a progressive develop-ment asserts itself in the end—this great fundamental thought has, especially since the time of Hegel, so thoroughly permeated ordinary consciousness that in this generality it is scarcely ever contradicted. But to acknowledge this fundamental thought in words and to apply it in reality in detail to each domain of investigation are two differ-ent things. If, however, investigation always proceeds from this stand-point, the demand for final solutions and eternal truths ceases once for all; one is always conscious of the necessary limitation of all acquired knowledge, of the fact that it is conditioned by the circum-stances in which it was acquired. On the one hand, one no longer permits oneself to be imposed upon by the antitheses, insuperable for the still common old metaphysics, between true and false, good and bad, identical and different, necessary and accidental. One knows that these antitheses have only a relative validity; that that which is recognised now as true has also its latent false side which will later manifest itself, just as that which is now regarded as false has also its true side by virtue of which it could previously have been regarded as true. One knows that what is maintained to be necessary is com-posed of sheer accidents, and that the so-called accidental is the form behind which necessity hides itself—and so on. (*SW* 1, pp. 453-4)

Engels also wrote, in *Anti-Duhring*:

cause and effect are conceptions which only hold good in their application to individual cases, but as soon as we consider the indiv-idual cases in their general connection with the universe as a whole, they run into each other . . . so that what is effect here and now will be cause there and then, and vice versa. (*AD*, p. 36)

The question for us is how useful is such a view today? Is metaphysics, in this sense, still with us? My own view is that it is. However, there is the problem that such a definition of dialectics

remains at an extremely general level, a kind of Heraclitanism which does not do justice to the specificity of Marxism in relation to all other theories which do not deny the historicity of reality. (Timpan-aro, p. 91)

Marxism, as Lenin reminds us, is 'the concrete analysis of concrete conditions'. The degree to which such a general framework as that outlined above is helpful remains an open question (see Timpanaro, p. 89).

More specifically Engels attempted to define dialectics in terms of general laws analogous to the laws of the natural sciences to which both man and nature were thought to conform. In *Dialectics of Nature* he gave two formulations of these of which the following is one:

transformation of quantity and quality; mutual penetration of polar opposites and transformation into each other when carried to extremes; development through contradiction or negation of the negation; spiral form of development. (p. 269, cf. p. 26)

Lenin and later marxists have concentrated on the concept of *contradiction*. Surprisingly, this received relatively little treatment in Engels' writings. In *Dialectics of Nature*, however, he does remark:

Dialectics, so-called objective dialectics, prevails throughout nature, and so-called subjective dialectics, dialectical thought, is only the reflection of the motion through opposites which asserts itself everywhere in nature, and which by the continual conflict of the opposites and their final passage into one another, or into higher forms, determines the life of nature. (Engels, *DON*, p. 206)

Ollman defines contradiction as follows:

'Contradiction' is a way of referring to the fact that not all such developments are compatible. In order to progress further in the direction made necessary by its own links of mutual dependence, a component may require that the probable course of change of another component be altered. The development of the two (as internally related elements in the same covering structure) stand in contradiction, and it is through the working out of such contradictions that the larger entity takes on the form it does . . . Contradiction never completely destroys what is contradicted but merely refashions it to suit new ends. Naturally, the way in which this process occurs varies considerably from case to case. As Engels says, 'Each class of things . . . has its appropriate form of being negated in such a way that it gives rise to a development, and it is just the same with each class of conceptions and ideas.' (Ollman, p. 57, quoting Engels, *AD*, p. 195)

Mario Bunge, modern physicist and philosopher of science, gives this definition:

the basic principle of dialectics, regarding the 'contradictory' nature of all concrete existents, which may be interpreted as asserting that every material object, however homogeneous it may look at first sight, is actually inhomogeneous in some respect and to some extent, and is moreover composed of mutually opposed or 'conflicting' (that is, mutually disturbing) parts or features, thus being subject to an inner stress that may develop (eventually enhanced by external forces) to the point of producing a radical (qualitative) change in the object concerned. (*Causality*, p. 115)

Marx, in his rare comments on the dialectic, said:

What constitutes dialectical movement is the coexistence of two contradictory sides, their conflict and their fusion into a new category. (*PP*, p. 95)

true philosophical criticism . . . not only shows the contradictions as existing, but clarifies them, grasps their essence and necessity. (*CHPOR*, p. 92)

The use of dialectics in the realm of non-human nature has been violently opposed by a number of prominent marxists ranging from Lukacs (1919) to Alfred Schmidt and Avineri today.[24] This question has formed another excuse to try and set Engels against Marx and make him the scapegoat for the errors of stalinism and what is attacked as 'positivist marxism'. Timpanaro (p. 89) and others deny fundamental differences of opinion between the two founding fathers, while admitting the need for fresh thinking and 'more precise terms and concepts' (Timpanaro, p. 91). Colletti, in an important recent article, calls for a distinction between *contrarieties*, or 'real oppositions', and *contradictions,* or 'dialectical oppositions'.[25] While it is clearly important to distinguish different kinds of contradiction, and perhaps to clarify assertions as to their universality as phenomena it is uncertain at this stage what advantage is to be gained by terminological distinctions. Since the main problem remains 'the liberation of mankind' energy might better be spent in more directly political areas of study.

Over the years official Communist Parties and non-party marxists have agreed on the importance of Marx's *method*, if they have differed widely in what that method was. Attempts have been made to explicate Marx's method from his own explicit statements in the Introduction to the *Grundrisse* (Penguin edition, pp. 100-108), in the already quoted Preface to *A Contribution to the Critique of Political Economy* (*EW*, pp. 424-8) and in various other prefaces, and by a careful study of the employment of his method in his major works, especially *Capital* (cf. Althusser's writings). Superficially this *method* appears to embody something of structuralism, historicism and empiricism, but careful examination shows it to be different from all of these in their more extreme forms.[26]

Marx's basic method is shown in the following two extracts:

Bourgeois society is the most developed and the most complex historic organisation of production. The categories which express its relations, the comprehension of its structure, thereby also allows insights into the structure and the relations of production of all the vanished social formations out of whose ruins and elements it built itself up, whose partly still unconquered remnants are carried along within it. . . . The bourgeois economy thus supplies the key to the ancient, etc. But not at all in the manner of those economists who smudge over all historical differences and see bourgeois relations in all forms of society. (*Grundrisse*, p. 105)

It would therefore be unfeasible and wrong to let the economic categories follow one another in the same sequence as that in which they were historically decisive. Their sequence is determined, rather, by their relation to one another in modern bourgeois society, which is precisely the opposite of that which seems to be their natural order or which corresponds to historical development. (*Grundrisse*, p. 107)

Marx describes his method of comprehending the 'real and the concrete', using as an example the population. He shows that if he were to

begin with the population, this would be a chaotic conception (*Vorstellung*) of the whole, and I would then, by means of further determination, move analytically towards ever more simple concepts (*Begriffe*), from the imagined concrete towards ever thinner abstractions until I had arrived at the simplest determinations. From there the journey would have to be retraced until I had finally arrived at the population again, but this time not as the chaotic conception of a whole, but as a rich totality of many determinations and relations. (*Grundrisse*, p. 100)

The concrete is concrete because it is the concentration of many determinations, hence unity of the diverse. It appears in the process of thinking, therefore, as a process of concentration, as a result, not as a point of departure, even though it is the point of departure in reality and hence also the point of departure for observation (*Anschauung*) and conception. (ibid. p. 101)

When it finally came to the method of exposition Marx departed from the scheme he had outlined in the Introduction to the *Grundrisse*. There he had suggested proceeding from the 'simple, general, abstract relations towards complex particular wholes' (Nicolaus, *Grundrisse*, p. 38). Instead he chose 'to climb from particular up to the general' (ibid.), and began with an analysis of the commodity, which is, as Nicolaus describes:

at once concrete, material, almost tangible, as well as historically specific (to capitalist production); and it contains within it (is the unity of) a key antithesis (use value v. exchange value) whose development involves all the other contradictions of this mode of production. (*Grundrisse*, p. 38)

In this concentration on the synchronic interrelations of the categories Marx's method appears to be a structuralism. But what was said above about historical materialism will have shown how wrong it is to ignore the historical element in Marx. As Timpanaro comments, Marx was 'looking for an abstract model which would help him to understand that *transient* socio-historical formation which is capitalism' (Timpanaro, p. 195).

Similarly, Marx's materialism brings his method to share features with other empiricisms while at the same time remaining distinct from them. Colletti reminds us, the 'economic categories are only the theoretical expression, the abstractions of the social relations of production'[27] (Colletti, *EW*, p. 24). Not only do they derive from the external, objective world, but are reshaped and modified through a continuing process of *observation-induction* and *hypothesis-deduction*[28] (Colletti, 1972, p. 8). It is the hypothesis-deduction element of the process which prevents the method from being simply an empiricism, one which 'stops at appearances' (Timpanaro, p. 194).

This section cannot end without some comment on the relationship between marxism and positivism, since, as Timpanaro notes, anti-positivism has become *de rigueur* (Timpanaro, p. 122). In order to do this it will be convenient to note the most important positivist 'rules and evaluative criteria referring to human knowledge' as set out by Kolakowski in his critical study, *Positivist philosophy* (pp. 11-18). The first rule, of phenomenalism, denies any real difference between essence and phenomenon. The rule of nominalism states that 'we may not assume that any insight formulated in general terms can have any real referents other than individual concrete objects' (Kolakowski, p. 13). Keat and Urry, discussing this rule, comment on 'the positivist suspicion of theoretical entities' (p. 89). Then there is the rule which 'refuses to call value judgements and normative statements knowledge' (Kolakowski, p. 16). Finally, of less interest to us here, is the variously interpreted rule of the 'essential unity of the scientific method' (ibid. p. 17). It should be clear that marxist materialism differs from each of the first three rules, and no more than a few brief comments will be made here. On the first rule, one is reminded of Marx's comment in the third volume of *Capital*: 'all science would be superfluous if the appearance and essence of things were wholly identical' (*Werke*, 25, p. 825). On the second, Marx clearly regarded valid 'general terms' and 'theoretical entities' as real, material entities, as corresponding to objective reality. On the third, many writers have shown that 'value judgements are inevitably present in scientific research itself' and that the way in which Marx '*inextricably* united in his work statements of fact and value judgements' was, as Colletti argues, 'its most profound originality and its strongest element'[29] (Colletti, 1972, p. 76).

To end this discussion of Marx's method I would like to return to Timpanaro. Criticising both attempts to see marxism as a 'dogmatic-encyclopedic' *Weltanschauung*, or simply as a limited 'revolutionary sociology', he asserts:

> not only must the problems of theoretical critique and practical, revolutionary supersession [transcendence] of bourgeois society be placed *at the centre* of things; it is also necessary to re-examine all the other fields of human culture and all aspects of man's place in the world, using this centre as one's point of departure. One could say, therefore, that Marxism is a dynamic *Weltanschauung*. (Timpanaro, pp. 241-2)

Dialectical Materialism in Russia and China

The 'world outlook' of the Soviet Communist Party, known in its short-ened form as *diamat* was succinctly described in Stalin's essay, *Dialectical and Historical Materialism*, to which I have already referred. Published in 1938 as part of the *History of the CPSU (B), Short Course*, and in the collection, *Problems of Leninism*, it was translated into many languages, including Chinese. Lenin's *Materialism and Empirio-criticism*, the first edition of which appeared in 1908, appeared in a second edition in 1920. This was concerned with such questions as 'did nature exist prior to man' and 'does man think with the help of the brain', that is, questions of materialism, and dialectics was ignored in it. His much more impres-sive *Philosophical Notebooks* were not published until 1929, and had little impact on official ideology. Diamat, as presented in a succession of monographs and textbooks for use in tertiary school courses lost the critical edge which it had for its founders and became, as Colletti called it, a 'cosmological romance' (Colletti, 1973, p. 178). Marcuse rightly comments:

> while not a single of the basic dialectical concepts has been revised or rejected in Soviet Marxism, the function of dialectic itself has under-gone a significant change: it has been transformed from a mode of critical thought into a universal 'world outlook' and universal method with rigidly fixed rules and regulations, and this transformation des-troys the dialectic more thoroughly than any revision. (Marcuse, 1958, p. 137)

The chapter headings of two textbooks used in tertiary institutions at widely different times will illustrate these last comments. They can be supplemented by the relevant chapters of the more easily available *Fundamentals of Marxism-Leninism* which follows a similar approach. Both textbooks employ an abstract approach, drawing examples from the history of philosophy, the natural sciences and history itself, often at second hand from the writings of Lenin, or Marx and Engels. This academic approach is very different from recent campaigns to study philosophy in China where, however simple the concepts may appear to be, they are related to actual problems.

The first book, *A Textbook of Marxist Philosophy*, was selected for translation into English in 1944 by the Society for Cultural Relations in Moscow. They regarded it as 'the best example they could find of the philosophical teaching (then) being given' (Lewis, p. 5). Omitting the added English historical introduction the contents include:

Section 2: *Unity and the strife of opposites.*
1. The law of the unity and conflict of opposites.
2. The division of unity, the disclosure of the essential opposites.
3. Mutual penetration of opposites.
4. Analysis of the movement of the contradiction of a process from its beginning to its end.
5. The relativity of the unity of opposites and the absoluteness of their conflict.
6. Theory of equilibrium.
Section 3: *The law of the transition of quantity into quality.*
1. From naive dialectic to the metaphysic of properties.
2. From the metaphysic of properties to the metaphysic of relations.
3. Quality and the self-movement of matter.
4. The relativity of qualities and universal connection of things.
5. The dialectic of quality and property.
6. The transition of quantity into quality.
7. Contradiction and the evolutionary leap.
8. The dialectic of the 'leap'.
9. The transition of quality into quantity.
10. The problem of 'levelling down'.
11. The nodal line of measurements.
Section 4: *The law of negation of the negation.*

The second book, *Dialectical Materialism* (in Russian), by M.N. Rutkevich was published as a course of lectures for natural science faculties in 1960. It contains the following chapters:

Dialectical materialism: the unity of the scientific world view.
The materialist world as a whole.
Matter and consciousness.
Perception of the world.
Dialectics as science and the method of thought.
Quantity and quality.
Progressive development and its regularity.
Unity and struggle of opposites.
Some categories of dialectics: origin and consequence;
necessity and change;
possibility and actuality;
essence and appearance: law;
content and form.

L. R. Graham, in a 500-page study of the major fields of Soviet natural science, concludes that while it has not been of 'immediate utilitar-
ian value to scientists' diamat has had 'important educational or heurist-
ic value' (Graham, p. 430). Among the 'quite reasonable principles and
opinions' which he sets out as basic to it, Graham includes definitions
of matter and materialism, and statements of the ubiquity of change.
He also notes the important concept of *level of organisation*, or 'integrat-
ive level', as Joseph Needham calls it (Needham, 2, pp. 412, 416, etc.).
This concept, essential if one is to avoid reductionism, he describes as
follows:

> The laws of development of matter exist on different levels correspond-
> ing to the different subject matters of the sciences, and therefore one
> should not expect in every case to be able to explain such complex
> entities as biological organisms in terms of the most elementary physio-
> chemical laws. (Graham, p. 63)

This might be better expressed: while phenomena on one level (e.g. biological) are determined by the laws governing level below them (e.g. chemical) they can only be fully described by concepts applicable to their
own level alone. It must be noted that in researching the relation between
diamat and Soviet science Graham

> rarely found pertinent items of interest in newspapers, popular
> political journals or textbooks of Marxism-Leninism; instead (he)
> looked to the serious monographs and journal articles of Soviet
> scholars . . . (Graham, p. 434)

It is also noteworthy that throughout his study it is principles of materialism rather than dialectics which appear to have been significant,
whether the field was quantum mechanics or human psychology.

Turning to China, we find a tradition in which dialectics has been
more strongly developed than in Europe, and it is tempting to speculate
on the influence this might have on current thinking.[30] What is not in
doubt is that Mao Ze-dong is a major exponent of dialectics and that
through his writings it is being advocated on an unprecedented scale. I
shall examine here two of the major texts, *On Contradiction*, written in
1937, and *On the Correct Handling of Contradictions among the People*,
written in 1957. More recently the unofficial *Wansui* materials have
reached us, showing us dialectics applied to a wide variety of subjects,
including political economy. The criticism of the Russian textbook of

political economy is a particularly striking example of dialectics as a critical tool.[31]

Mao opens *On Contradiction* by quoting Lenin: 'Dialectics in the proper sense is the study of contradiction *in the very essence of objects*' (Mao, *Four Essays*, p. 23, quoting Lenin, *CW* 38, p. 253). Further on he quotes Lenin to illustrate 'the universality of contradictions', and like Lenin does not comment on this rather ill-chosen set of examples:

> In mathematics: + and −, differential and integral;
> In mechanics: action and reaction;
> In physics: positive and negative electricity;
> In chemistry: the combination and dissociation of atoms;
> In social science: the class struggle.
> (Mao, ibid. p. 32; Lenin, 38, p. 359)

Mao moves from the universality to 'the particularity of contradiction'. Stressing that in any 'major thing' there are many contradictions in the course of its development (*Four Essays*, p. 39) he says:

> In order to reveal the particularity of the contradiction in any process in the development of a thing, in their totality or interconnections, that is, in order to reveal the essence of the process, it is necessary to reveal the particularity of the two aspects of each of the contradictions in that process; otherwise it will be impossible to discover the essence of the process. (ibid.)

He then goes on to develop the concepts of principal contradiction and the principal aspect of a contradiction.[32] He writes:

> In any contradiction the development of the contradictory aspects is uneven. Sometimes they seem to be in equilibrium, which is however only temporary and relative, while unevenness is basic. Of the two contradictory aspects, one must be principal and the other secondary. The principal aspect is the one playing the leading role in the contradiction. The nature of a thing is determined mainly by the principal aspect of a contradiction, the aspect which has gained the dominant position. (ibid. p. 54)

> But this situation is not static; the principal and the non-principal aspects of a contradiction transform themselves into each other and the nature of the thing changes accordingly. (ibid.)

Later on Mao makes the significant point that in the contradictions productive forces/relations of production, practice/theory, and economic base/superstructure, while the first is normally the principal aspect and plays the principal and decisive role ('whoever denies this is not a materialist'—ibid. p. 58) yet

> it must also be admitted that in *certain conditions*, such aspects as the relations of production, theory and the super-structure in turn manifest themselves in the principal and decisive role. (ibid., emphasis added)

Mao adds:

> we also—and indeed must—recognise the reaction of mental on material things, of social consciousness on social being and of the superstructure on the economic base. This does not go against materialism; on the contrary, it avoids mechanical materialism and firmly upholds dialectical materialism. (ibid. p. 59)

Quoting Lenin on unity of opposites being conditional and struggle absolute, Mao continues: 'All processes have a beginning and an end, all processes transform themselves into their opposites' (ibid. p. 66). In this connection it should perhaps be noted that the examples of contradictions which Mao discusses tend to be those where the change *occurs over time*, one aspect changing *into* its opposite. Examples given include the proletariat changing from ruled to ruler; the Guomindang changing from being counter-revolutionary to anti-Japanese, or peasants who 'once lost their land' acquiring it again in land reform (ibid. pp. 62-3). Examples of contradictions such as that between the thermal agitation of water molecules and their molecular attraction, disturbance of which leads to a change of state such as freezing or boiling (Bunge, p. 19), or the contradiction between the forces of production and the relations of production, contradictions in which the two opposites exist *simultaneously* in time and through their antagonism bring about a new state of affairs are not discussed.

Holubnychy notes the way in which Mao links the law of contradiction with that of change of quantity to quality in the following passage:

> There are two states of motion in all things, that of relative rest and that of conspicuous change. Both are caused by the struggle between

the two contradictory elements contained in a thing. When the thing is in the first state of motion, it is undergoing only quantitative and not qualitative change and consequently presents the outward appearance of being at rest. When the thing is in the second state of motion, the quantitative change of the first state has already reached a culminating point and gives rise to the dissolution of the thing as an entity and thereupon a qualitative change ensues, hence the appearance of a conspicuous change. . . Things are constantly transforming themselves from the first into the second state of motion; the struggle of opposites goes on in both states but the contradiction is resolved through the second state. That is why we say that the unity of opposites is conditional, temporary and relative, while the struggle of mutually exclusive opposites is absolute. (ibid. p. 67; cf. Holubnychy, p. 34, who uses a slightly different translation).

Here mention is made of contradictions in which the opposites are present simultaneously, and it is clearly these which are concerned in the final consideration.

In the final section of *On Contradiction* Mao discusses 'the place of antagonism in contradiction' and argues that there are antagonistic and non-antagonistic ones. In certain circumstances one form can change into the other, and he cites the example of the contradiction between town and country, antagonistic in capitalist countries and in Guomindang areas of China, but becoming non-antagonistic under socialism (ibid. p. 71). This concept was taken up in the second essay in 1957 when the contradictions were 'between us and the enemy' (antagonistic) and 'those among the people' (non-antagonistic) (ibid. p. 81).

In *Contradictions among the People* Mao dealt with a number of important points which must be briefly mentioned here. He listed some of the contradictions between the People's government and the people: among the interests of the state; of the collective and the individual; between democracy and centralism; between the leadership and the led; and as a result of bureaucracy.[33] He stressed 'freedom with leadership . . . democracy under centralized guidance, not anarchy' (ibid. p. 84) and warned against the kind of events which were then recently taking place in Hungary. To solve non-antagonistic contradictions among the people Mao urged criticism, persuasion and education. The formula was to be 'unity, criticism, unity' and 'learn from past mistakes to avoid future ones and cure the sickness to save the patient' (ibid. p. 88). In discussing the slogan: let 100 flowers blossom, let 100 schools of thought contend, Mao emphasised that

ideological struggle is not like other forms of struggle. The only
method to be used in this struggle is that of painstaking reasoning
and not crude coercion. (ibid. p. 116)

He laid down six guidelines for distinguishing flowers from weeds (pp.
119-20). Discussing the disturbances caused by 'some bad people' he
quoted Laozi, the ancient Daoist, who said: Good fortune lies within
bad, bad fortune lurks within good (p. 126). Finally he went on to discuss the very great contradiction: that China is a big socialist country,
but is economically backward and poor, and he recommended that this
could only be resolved by strict economy.

Considerable effort is being made to encourage dialectical thinking
in China and a number of works exist, some in translation, which
enable us to make some evaluation of the results. In 1966 articles from
a special edition of the philosophical journal *Zhexue yanjiu* (No. 2,
1966) were reprinted in Peking Review (Nos. 17 and 21-5, 1966). Except
for examples of class conflict no convincing examples of contradictions
were given, though the term was employed to cover a number of
problems and difficulties. In pamphlets like *Philosophy is no Mystery*
(1972) and *Serving the People with Dialectics* (1972) the term contradiction was used in a similar way. In an article on growing peanuts,
where the author described contradictions between different parts of
the plant during development, and between the results of different
kinds of planting methods, the usage did not appear to conform with
either Mao's or Marx's usage (*Serving the People with Dialectics*, pp. 1-
9). At this stage it would seem that the value of Mao's writings on dialectics is to help people treat their problems 'as something which it is
in their power to solve' (Jonathan Ree, *Radical Philosophy* 1, 1976, p.
23).

Finally, mention must be made of the periodical, *Ziran bianzhengfa*
(Dialectics of Nature), the first number of which was published in Shanghai in 1973. This is a so far unstudied collection of articles on topics
ranging from the mathematics of computers to animal evolution which
might throw light on an interesting aspect of current Chinese education.

Marxism and Education

From the preceding sections it should be clear that one should not
attempt to set out the implications of marxism for education in abstract
terms. Marxism is essentially the 'concrete study of concrete conditions'.
Instead, these implications will be made clear through a detailed examination of education in Russia and China. However, a few preliminary

comments are necessary.

First of all a definition of education must be attempted in order to indicate the scope of the study. To limit the term to school systems, as is too often done, is far too narrow and leaves out many of those learnings which marxists regard as fundamental. To extend it to all situations in which learning occurs makes it so wide as to seem unmanageable. But marxists, being concerned above all with 'seeing the world as it is in order to change it' regard as education those processes which contribute to the formation and changing of a person's consciousness and character. Consciousness involves world view, while character determines how a person behaves in relation to that view and to the stresses and demands of society. In this marxists combine something of orthodox sociology's definitions of education and socialisation, at the same time imparting to them a critical aspect.[34] While marxism agrees that the individual learns values and symbols it requires of him that he adopt a critical attitude to them in the light of marxist goals.

While the most obvious agent of education is the school, many who are not marxists have also come to doubt whether the really important learnings do take place there. Other agents include the family, youth organisations, religious institutions, trade unions and political parties. The armed forces are also important in a number of ways and their study as educators has been unjustifiably neglected. Educative agents like the family are usually classified as socialising agents, a term which covers peer groups, the mass media and others listed above. Work is probably the single most important socialising agent for those who perform it. At this point in time neither marxism nor orthodox sociology can offer more than partial indications as to the role of these various agents in the total process, and school teachers persist with surprising faith in their own significance.

Marx's vision of communism as the transcendence of alienation and thus of a period when man will become increasingly self-conscious and self-determining has manifold implications for education. It is both a criterion for judging current efforts—to what degree do they contribute to this end—and a guide to the defining of aims and methods. But since communism is 'the *real* movement which abolishes the present state of affairs' it also implies the activity of both teacher and pupil in the process throughout. It is not simply that 'the educator must himself be educated' (Marx, *SW* 1, p. 472). It is that, as Engels wrote in the 1895 Introduction to Marx's *Class Struggles in France*: 'Where it is a question of a complete transformation of the social organisation, the masses themselves must also be in it. . . ' (*SW* 2, p. 187). Education, as Marx noted

during a discussion of the topic by the General Council of the First
International (August 1869), was peculiar in that

> on the one hand a change of social circumstances was required to
> establish a proper system of education, on the other hand a proper
> system of education was required to bring about a change of social
> circumstances. (Marx, GC1868 p. 140)

He added significantly that 'we must therefore commence where we
were'! All of this implies that the major concern of education should be
moral-political, the development of socialist consciousness as it is
phrased in Mao's China. If that is right then other problems can be
correctly tackled. It should not require saying that such an education
would be very different from the moralising slogan-mouthing which has
in many places passed for it.

Meszaros draws attention to an important implication of Marx's view
of man as he is under capitalism, and as he may develop. In the former
his senses are restricted, and moreover 'in place of *all* these physical and
mental senses there has therefore come the sheer estrangement of *all*
these senses—the sense of *having*' (Marx, *EPM*, p. 106). Consumerism has
taken the place of active expression, of that full, creative production
which for Marx is an essential characteristic of humanity. Overcoming
this, developing a truly 'aesthetic education is therefore only possible in
a genuine socialist society' says Meszaros, and he adds that attempts to
do so under present conditions are 'condemned to hopeless utopianism'
(Meszaros, pp. 292-3).

Orthodox sociology has, over the years, paid considerable attention
to the implications for education of the division of society into social
classes. Marxism implies more than recognition of inequalities, or the
desire for 'equal opportunities for all' in the social rat race. Not social
mobility, but the abolition of classes is the aim, facing the marxist
educator with a different set of priorities from that of his liberal
colleagues. At times their efforts may overlap, and at others they will
diverge. Efforts to raise the general level of understanding of the 'lower
classes' will be seen at times by some to be a 'lowering of standards' and
a 'holding back' of the 'more able'.

Still an important problematic is the relations of the individual, his
social class, and the ideology he adopts. To emphasise the fundamental
importance of social class, as marxism does, is not to assert that an
individual automatically adopts the ideology of his class. But it is probably true that in stable times and for those who do not change their

social class the ideas of the class play a dominant role in shaping those
of its individual members. The problem is complicated, particularly for
the 'socially mobile' new petty bourgeoisie, by possible conflicts of
value between the class into which the individual is born and the class
in which he later finds employment. School is often the agency within
which the conflict of class values is worked out. Gordon White has
recently described the confusion in the Chinese GPCR over class origin
and the class position adopted by youth there. At this stage of the argument there are few firm conclusions to inform education. Major ideological positions reflect major class interests. The ruling ideology, which
consciously or unconsciously permeates the school system is a reflection
of the interests of the dominant class but is also accepted by wide
sections of other classes. One might hypothesise that the less this is true
the more the ideology will be explicitly stressed in the schools and other
agencies of political education.

An implication of marxist theories on the dialectic between social
consciousness and social being is the suggestion to link education with
productive labour. This appears in various places in Marx's writings,
particularly in *Capital* and in materials prepared for the First International. In the former, in the course of a discussion of the English Factory
Acts and the experiments of Robert Owen at New Lanark Marx wrote:

From the factory system budded, as Robert Owen has shown us in
detail, the germ of the education of the future, an education that
will, in the case of every child over a given age, combine productive
labour with instruction and gymnastics, not only as one of the
methods of adding to the efficiency of production, but as the only
method of producing fully developed human beings. (*Capital* I, pp.
529-30)

In the International materials the formulation was:

We consider the tendency of modern industry to make children and
juvenile persons of both sexes co-operate in the great work of social
production, as a progressive, sound and legitimate tendency, although
under capital it was distorted into an abomination. In a rational state
of society *every child whatever*, from the age of nine years, ought
to become a productive labourer in the same way that no able-bodied
adult person ought to be exempted from the general law of nature,
viz.: to work in order to be able to eat, and work not only with the
brain but with the hands too. (Marx, *The General Council*, p. 344)

Productive labour, the necessary basis on which any realm of freedom must depend, is an essential school for members of a future classless society. Here they learn the moral-political truths of membership of the working community as well as certain intellectual insights into the processes of production. Combining it with education in a real interrelationship of theory and practice will help to form that socialist consciousness which alone can ensure a mass demand for the acquisition of all-round skills and knowledge. But present-day attempts to provide work experience in a capitalist society which has no use for the labour of many of its citizens, and only occasional need for that of many more, is grasping at straws. Employers will only support it if it promises a more docile and exploitable workforce. Any signs that it is linked with wider social issues will lead to its suppression and the denunciation of the teachers concerned as 'subversive'.

It was in the course of discussing the combination of education with productive labour that Marx defined education as follows:

Firstly: *mental education.*
Secondly: *bodily education,* such as is given in schools of gymnastics, and by military exercises.
Thirdly: *technological training,* which imparts the general principles of all processes of production, and, simultaneously initiates the child and young person in the practical use and handling of the elementary instruments of all trades.[35]
(Marx, *The General Council*, p. 345)

This technological, or polytechnical training, as it is more usually referred to, is clearly different from the combination of education and productive labour referred to elsewhere. Marx makes this clear in the same text where he continues:

The combination of paid productive labour, mental education, bodily exercise and polytechnic training, will raise the working class far above the level of the higher and middle classes. (ibid. p. 346)

Polytechnic training is a cognitive activity centred on an interaction between man and non-human nature. The combination of productive labour and mental education is primarily social, an interaction of man with man. Marx saw working together on a meaningful task as potentially humanising. The young, brought up to take their place in 'the great work of social production' learn to play their part. In *Capital* he wrote:

Moreover, it is obvious that the fact of the collective working group
being composed of individuals of both sexes and all ages, must necessarily, under suitable conditions, become a source of *humane development*; although in its spontaneously developed, brutal, capitalistic
form, where the labourer exists for the process of production, and
not the process of production for the labourer, that fact is a pest-
iferous source of corruption and slavery. (*Capital* I, p. 536)

As we shall see in Chapter 7 educators in the USSR have concentrated
attention on the concept of polytechnical education while Mao in China
has developed the idea of combining education with productive labour.

Marx's concepts of the dictatorship of the proletariat and permanent
revolution have profound implications for education. Democracy can
only be learnt through the practice of democracy, and this must apply
to schools as well as all other sectors of society. The rotation of positions
of responsibility and control is essential if people are to learn to exercise
power. The spread of information in open government, and the discussion
of matters *before* policies are formulated are both education and execut-
ion. The performance of ordinary, manual labour by government and
industrial leaders, as has been advocated in China, is an essential educational process, but the converse, government and management by the
masses, is also essential if society is to become really classless. For this
education, practice and increasing time free of backbreaking and mind-
deadening toil is required, things within the reach of advanced capitalist
countries today, but perhaps more difficult in countries still largely
agricultural and poor.

Finally, the marxist concept of ideology and the production of consciousness have implications in the area of curriculum. Claims for value-
free subject matter must be rejected, but this does not mean the impos-
ition of narrow, dogmatic material in its place. The major question, the
rejection of the capitalist system based on the production of exchange
values, will be regarded as closed. But since the aim is self-conscious and
self-determining human beings the widest discussion and freedom of
access to information of all kinds must be encouraged. Any dogmatism
or techniques of indoctrination can only be self-defeating, a guarantee
of the 'withering away' of marxism itself.

Marxism is both a critical tool to be employed in the examination of
current education and a set of principles to be used in the guidance of
change. As a critical tool it raises a host of questions: about the role of
the different educating and socialising agents and their interrelations;
about the relation between an individual's ideology and his actions;

about the suitability of different kinds of schools, and about the desirability of compulsory schooling itself; or about the nature of the knowledge transmitted in education and its suitability for young people at different stages of emotional and intellectual development.[36] The literature of marxism is relatively poor on such topics, but since their relevance to the major political questions is becoming clearer it is likely that this will change.

Notes

1. But, more substantially, Colletti has tried to show that in Marx's theory 'alienation and the theory of contradiction are now seen as a single theory' Colletti, 1975 (b).
2. Compare the *Party Programme* of the 22nd CPSU Congress with the *Fiftieth anniversary survey* of July 1967.
3. Written in what S.F. Cohen calls 'the heroic period' of the Bolsheviks by Bukarin and Preobrazhensky, *The ABC of Communism* went through numerous editions and translations in the ten years following its appearance in 1920. It was a popularisation of the March 1919 Communist Party programme, and 'its novelty lay in its chronicling of almost every Bolshevik assumption in the year 1919' (Cohen, p. 84).
4. This book, which discusses the 1961 Programme of the CPSU, which it describes as the 'most complete expression of modern Marxist ideas of communism', was widely distributed in translation and used at home by propagandists and in many tertiary school politics courses.
5. Reference to the straw sandals comes in Mao's speech to the Supreme State Conference in January 1958, (Schram, 1974, p. 94) while the comment on 'one to several centuries' is to be found in the 9th comment of July 1964, *On Khrushchev's Phoney Communism*, in the *Polemic on the General Line*, p. 472.
6. Numerous attacks have been made on marxism for being a historicism, most notably by Karl Popper in *The Poverty of Historicism*, 1961, and *The Open Society and its Enemies*, 1962. For an orthodox Communist Party refutation of Popper see M. Cornforth, *The Open Philosophy and the Open Society*, 1968. More recently B. Hindess and P. Q. Hirst, *Pre-capitalist Modes of Production*, 1975, have put forward a form of structuralism in opposition to historicist tendencies which they perceive even in marxists like Althusser, who himself denounces historicism (pp. 8-9). The passage quoted from the *Grundrisse* (pp. 460-61) is worth studying in context in this connection, preferably in the original German. McLellan's translation is here significantly different from Nicolas' (McLellan, p. 108).
7. For a simple account of basic concepts see Marx's *Value, Price and Profit*. Accounts which relate Marx's concepts to modern conditions include E. Mandel's, *Marxist Economic Theory*, 1968, and *Late Capitalism*, 1975. A helpful discussion of the way the total social product is divided is to be found in Marx's *Critique of the Gotha Programme*, FI&A. pp. 344-5.
8. Marx, 1976, p. 1038: 'the only productive labour is that which is directly consumed in the course of production for the valorization of capital'.
9. The lessons of the Chinese revolution do not seem to have been learnt here! Poulantzas (1975) discusses various theories about the non-productive wage-earners, including that of the 'middle class', pp. 193-204. Braverman devotes ch. 18 to 'The "middle layers" of employment' and ch. 19 to 'Productive and unproductive labour'. He undermines the distinctions he makes about 'powers of decision and

command' by stressing that the 'proletarian form begins to assert itself and to impress itself upon the consciousness of these employees' (pp. 407-8), and perhaps too hastily to conclude that 'the two masses of labor . . . form a continuous mass . . . which . . . has everything in common' (p. 423). E.O. Wright, in an important critique of Poulantzas, prefers to include many of the lower fractions of the unproductive workers in the proletariat. He refers to 'contradictory locations'.
10. Poulantzas, 1975, pp. 316-27. Here and on pp. 214-5 Poulantzas appears to mistake the force of Marx's comments on service workers. In *Results of the Immediate Process of Production* Marx notes that a gardener can be either productive or unproductive depending on whether he is employed by a capitalist to produce surplus value or directly by the consumer (Marx, 1976, p. 1045); cf. the case of teachers in schools run as capitalist enterprises who are productive labourers for their employers (Marx, *Theories of Surplus Value*, pt. 1 pp. 410-11).
11. This opening line of the Provisional Rules of the First International (FI&A. p. 82) was repeated by Engels in his preface to the German edition of the Communist Manifesto in 1890.
12. The problem of the relationship between trade unions and political parties and Marx's ideas on this has recently been posed in an interesting way in S. Mallet's *Essays on the New Working Class*, 1975, pp. 188-99. Important Marx texts here are the *Instructions for delegates to the Geneva Congress of the First International*, Marx's letter to Bolte, 23 November 1871, and Engels' comment on the Gotha Programme in his letter to Bebel, 28 March 1875.
13. Fundamental for a study of this question are Schurmann, *Ideology and Organisation*, especially pp. 162-7; Selden, *The Yenan way*, especially ch. 6, and Brugger, *Democracy and Organisation*.
14. See Althusser, *For Marx*, pp. 117-28; Colletti, *From Rousseau to Lenin*, pp. 62-72; and Timpanaro, *On Materialism*, pp. 113-19.
15. Avineri, p. 66; Petrovic, pp. 62-3 and 190-98; cf. J. Hoffman, ch. 5.
16. See both McLellan, *The Young Hegelians and Karl Marx*, pp. 69-81, and *Marx before Marxism*, pp. 64-71.
17. Stalin, pp. 26-9; Gouldner, A.W., 'Prologue to a Theory of Revolutionary Intellectuals', *Telos* 26, 1975-6, pp. 3-36 supports this, p. 16.
18. Carlo draws attention to Lenin's position in his letter to Novaya Zhizn, in *State and Revolution*, and his speech to the 2nd Congress of Trade-unions, in all of which it differed considerably from that put forward in *What is to be Done*. In *State and Revolution* he adopts many of the workers' control-type positions similar to those put forward in China by Mao.
19. Other writings important for understanding Mao's ideas on ideology include *On Correcting Mistaken Ideas in the Party*, *Combat Liberalism*, and *Rectify the Party's Style of Work*.
20. In the *Economic and Philosophic Manuscripts*, e.g. pp. 102, 156.
21. L.R. Graham, p. 40, wrongly attributes this statement to Engels. Stalin, ibid., goes on to quote Engels on the same point.
22. Keat and Urry prefer to describe Marx as a realist and avoid the term materialism throughout their book.
23. Timpanaro notes that in continuing to oppose 'vulgar materialism', the traditional 'enemy', European marxists have not only ended in rejecting materialism, but have failed to answer the real modern trends in bourgeois culture: (i) historicist and humanist idealism, the ideology of the older style bourgeoisie; and (ii) empiriocriticist and pragmatist idealism which is the philosophy of the modern technocrats (Timpanaro, pp. 31-2).
24. Famous scientists who have written in defence of a dialectics of nature have included J.B.S. Haldane, J.D. Bernal, Marcel Prenant—who described Mendelian genetics as dialectical before the Lysenko controversy developed—and Joseph Needham.

25. 'Contradiction and Contrariety', *New Left Review* 93, 1975, pp. 3-30.
26. The account here is based on discussions by M. Nicolaus in his foreword to the *Grundrisse*, L. Colletti's Introduction to Marx's *Early Writings*, and his *From Rousseau to Lenin* and *Marxism and Hegel*, and comments by Timpanaro in his *On Materialism*. The discussion between S. Meikle and D. Ruben, *Critique* numbers 6 and 4 also proved helpful.
27. Quoting Marx, *PP*.p. 92. Marx adds: 'these ideas, these categories, are as little eternal as the relations they express. They are *historical and transitory products.*'
28. See Mao Ze-dong's *On Practice* for his concept of knowledge through a constantly progressing spiral of theory-practice-again theory-again practice.
29. An example of the obscurities to which the anti-positivist debate can descend is the debate in Germany translated recently in English as Adorno, Habermas, *et al., The Positivist Dispute in German Sociology*.
30. Price, 1970, pp. 55-9 outlines this tradition. Needham, vol. 2, is the best full exploration.
31. The article by Richard Levy, *China Quarterly* 61, 1975, pp. 95-117 is a splendid introduction to this material. He compares Mao's writing with that of Marx in the *Grundrisse*.
32. Althusser comments on the un-Hegelian nature of these and other maoist concepts of contradiction (*For Marx*, p. 94, note 6). His remarks in *Reading Capital*, pp. 32-3, I find 'opaque'.
33. Mao on *20 Manifestations of Bureaucracy*, JPRS.49826, 12 February 1970, pp. 40-43.
34. Halsey defines education 'sociologically as the formal transmission of culture' (Mitchell, p. 199), while socialisation is

> the life-long process of inculcation, whereby an individual learns the principal values and symbols of the social systems in which he participates and the expression of those values in the norms composing the roles he and others enact, (Mitchell, p. 194)

35. Wittig draws attention to the problem of whether Marx himself used the now familiar term *polytechnical* education in place of *technological* in this passage. No draft in Marx's writing is extant to decide the question. But since the concept is so clearly expressed the question is of academic interest only. See Wittig, 1964, ch. 8, and 1968, pp. 262-7.
36. A classic study of the interaction of personality and environment which was to some extent informed by marxism is Adorno, *et.al., The Authoritarian Personality*, 1950. A.F. Baum's article, 'The corpus of knowledge', where he compares Descartes', Hobbes' and Marx's attitudes to knowledge is an example of the confusion Marx still seems to arouse in the academic mind. See M.F.D. Young, (ed.), *Knowledge and Control*, pp. 117-31.

2 THE SCHOOL SYSTEM: PART ONE

Structure and Influences

In this and the next chapter I shall discuss those institutions which are conventionally regarded as comprising the education system. These range from pre-school classes through to various forms of education for adults. The backbone of the system is formed by the full-time day (FTD) schools which are here divided into first, second and third level institutions. Other schools come into the categories part-time, spare-time or part-work. These are to some extent modelled on and organisationally related to the FTD system.

While my main aim is to evaluate the post-revolutionary school system of the USSR and China from a marxist point of view, it is necessary to consider briefly the pre-revolutionary systems and the various other influences within and outside the two countries which have shaped their schools. If these are not understood and borne in mind much that results from their influences can be misinterpreted.

When the Bolsheviks came to power in 1917 the educational climate in the world was very different from that of 1949 when the Chinese Communists set up government in Peking. Schooling was a privilege rather than a right. For the majority everywhere it went little further than the rudiments of reading, writing and arithmetic. By the end of the Second World War 'secondary education for all' was on the agenda for the richer countries, and there was widespread acknowledgement of the right of every human being to an education suited to his personal needs and abilities. The Bolsheviks were thus forced to be pioneers, while the Chinese could have been content to remain imitators.

The pre-revolutionary Russian school system, descendant of an Austrian pattern imported by Catherine the Great, was highly stratified. There were separate schools for boys and girls—with insignificant exceptions. Gymnasia led to the universities, while a variety of other schools prepared pupils for trade and the middle and lower ranks of industry and agriculture. The different tracks were isolated from each other and transfer between them was difficult to impossible.

The pre-1949 Chinese school system had taken shape in the traumatic struggles of that ancient civilisation to come to terms with repeated military defeat by the European powers. Turning first to Japan and then mainly to the USA, educators had by 1922 evolved a six-year primary school, followed by a secondary school divided first into four and two, and then three and three years of junior and senior high school. There were kindergartens for some pre-school age children, mostly in the larger towns. At secondary level there were various vocational schools, including some for teacher training. In addition to universities a variety of institutions existed at the tertiary level. As in Russia, the various tracks within secondary and tertiary education tended to be isolated, though not to the same extent.

The first steps in the reform of education in Russia took place amid indescribable privation, with the First World War turning, through Revolution, into the Civil War which lasted until 1920. The Bolshevik leaders responsible for education had in the main lived in exile in western Europe and were strongly influenced, not only by the Russian nineteenth-century liberal-democratic tradition, but also by American and German education and such individuals as John Dewey and Kershensteiner. Typical of these Bolsheviks was A.V. Lunacharsky, the first Commissar of Education, who on 29 October 1917 announced that 'the labouring masses thirst after education'. He proposed a minimum of central direction, believing that 'the people themselves, consciously or unconsciously, must evolve their own culture'.

A new system of schooling was set out in a decree of the All-Russian Central Executive Committee of Soviets on 16 October 1918. Tracking was abolished for the lower levels and a comprehensive system was declared under the title of the United Labour School. This was to embrace all children, girls as well as boys, and those of varying social background. In theory this principle of comprehensiveness has been maintained and even strengthened in Russia, and subsequently after its establishment in China. But in practice in both countries it has been limited by differences in the quality of schools, especially between urban and rural areas, and by factors which have limited the number of children able to progress to the upper levels of the school system.

Under the 1918 decree the United Labour School was to include primary and secondary courses for a combined total of nine years, and was to be compulsory. This last, as we shall see, was to remain a dream for decades. At the secondary level alternative tracks were envisaged: schools for peasant youth; factory schools in which, according to Nearing, students spent 'four hours of each day in the school and four in the factory' (Nearing, p. 25); and 'professional schools' which Nearing compares with 'American technical high schools' of the period (ibid.). The pattern was slightly modified by the law of 18 December 1923, which allowed for 7-year and 9-year schools in which primary and secondary

Figure 1: System of Education in Russia before the Revolution

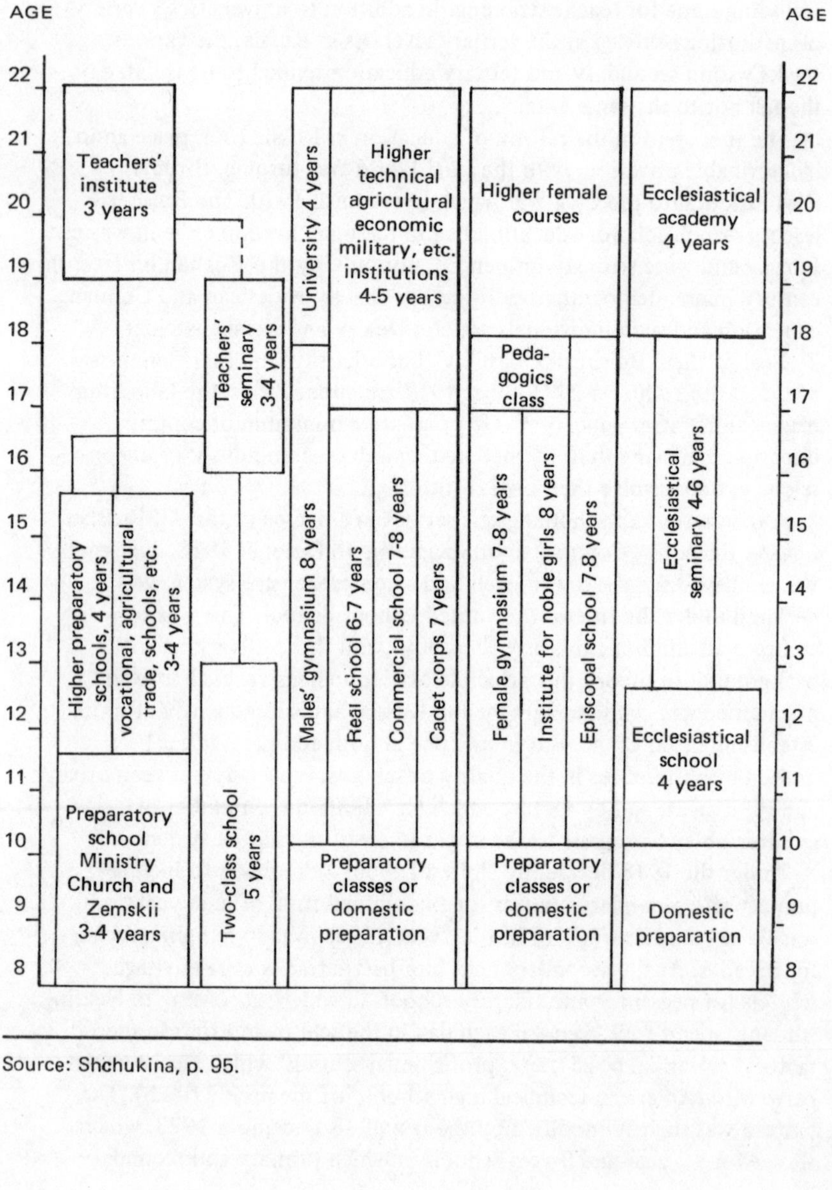

Source: Shchukina, p. 95.

Figure 2: System of Education in Russia in 1919

Institutes, 4-5 years	Technicums, 3 years
United labour school stage 2 4 years	Professional school 4 years
United labour school, stage 1 5 years	
Kindergarten	

Source: Shchukin, p. 100.

Figure 3: System of Education in the USSR in 1935

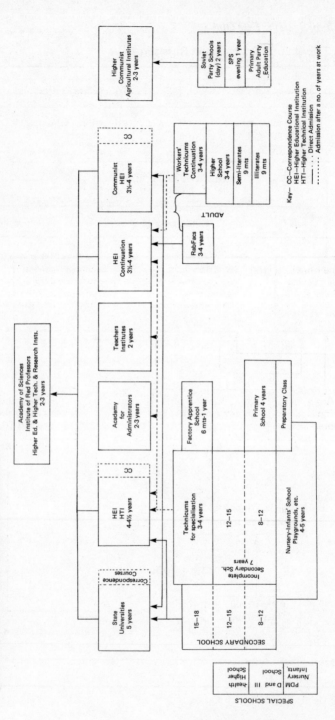

Source: B. King, 1937, p. 53.

Figure 4: School System in the USSR Established by Law 24 December 1958

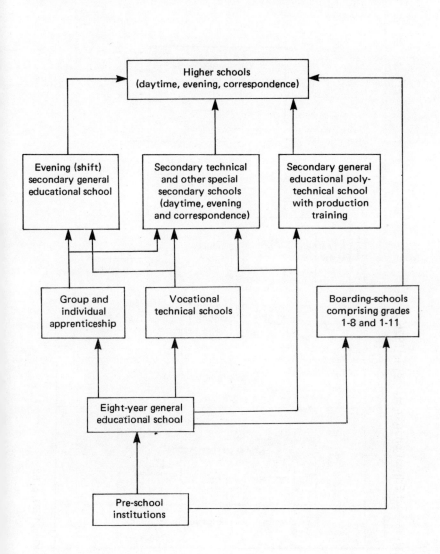

Source: Deineko, p. 30.

Figure 5: System of Education in China, 1922

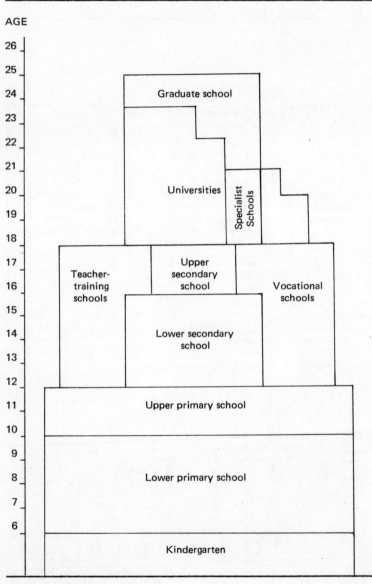

Source: Chen Qing-zhi, p. 715.

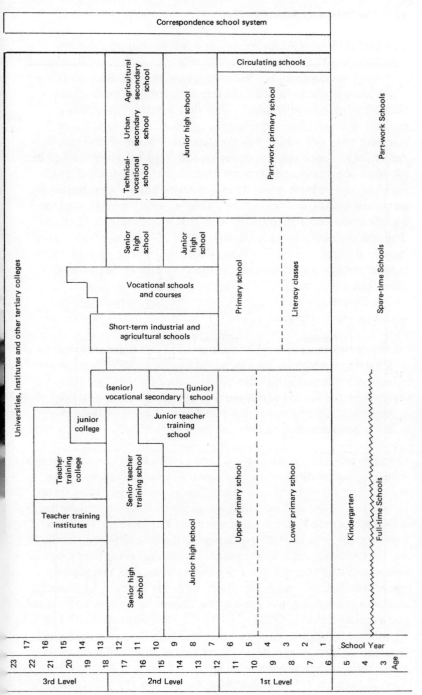

Figure 6: Chinese School System in the Mid-1960s

grades would be combined. Primary grades were reduced from five to four, i.e. age 9-12 inclusive.

The reforms at the end of the twenties and early years of the thirties which saw a return to many of the formalities of the Tsarist school affected content more drastically than they did structure. Primary grades now began earlier, covering the age range 8-11 years, and the complete secondary school now embraced ten instead of nine years. Pre-school provision aimed to cover the age range 3-7 where it could be provided. Schools as separate institutions housed on individual sites were basically of three types: 4-year primary schools; 7-year incomplete secondary schools; and ten-year complete secondary schools. (See the decrees of the CC CPSU(B) of 25 August 31 and 25 August 32 which deal with the curriculum and conduct of the schools, and the Soviet of People's Comissars of the USSR and CC CPSU(B) of 15 May 34 which outlines the new school structure in *Narodnoye obrazobaniye v SSSR: Sbornik dokumentov, 1917-1973 gg,* pp. 156, 161 and 167.)

The Khrushchev reforms of 1958 introduced a compulsory 8-year school aiming to provide:

> an incomplete secondary general-education polytechnical industrial school(ing), which should give pupils a sound foundation of general and polytechnical knowledge, foster a liking for work, inculcate a readiness for socially useful activity, and provide for the moral, physical and aesthetic training of children. (Law of 24 December 1958, Shapovalenko, p. 379)

Complete secondary schooling was to be provided by (1) evening (shift) schools; (2) secondary, general, polytechnical schools with industrial training; and (3) by technicums and other specialised secondary institutions. The second of these forms was to last three years, bringing the total length of the FTD schooling up from 10 to 11 years. The extra time was said to be needed to make up for the time to be devoted to the trade training which was to result in graduates having both a matriculation and a trade certificate. For a variety of reasons, ranging from opposition from the aspiring intelligentsia to the difficulty of providing suitable work training, the thrust of the Khrushchev reform was blunted, and a decree of the CC CPSU of 12 August 1964 restored the 10-year school except for those national republics where Russian is the second language. These may operate an 11-year school to allow for the extra time devoted to the national language.

In China since 1949 the basic American pattern of 6:3:3, primary followed by junior and senior high school, has been basically maintained. From the beginning attempts have been made to shorten the primary school to five years. A 9-year school combining the primary and junior high school grades was tried for a time by the school attached to the Peking Teacher Training Institute (GMRB, 10 June 1960). The Hunan Teacher Training High School and other schools in Jilin, Shanxi and Gansu experimented with a secondary course of only five years (GMRB, 3 July 1960). But only since the Cultural Revolution of 1966-9 have such attempts been maintained. Primary school now appears to be universally five years, with 7- and 9-year combined primary and secondary schools in some places, while in others there are experiments at reducing the length of high school courses to four years.

Any consideration of equal provision of education, or of attempting to abolish class differences comes up against the enormous gulf between the urban and rural areas in both Russia and China. Numerous accounts testify to the brutality of many Russian villages where even cases of cannabalism were witnessed in the famines of 1921-2 and 1933-4. In 1925 Nearing compared 'the ordinary village school' with that of rural USA more than twenty-five years previously and added:

> Village communities are largely illiterate. Children of school age are always wanted to run some errand or to do some chore. These home demands come first, and school duties take second place. During the harvest time it is practically impossible to keep the village children in school. (Nearing, p. 33)

Some forty years and the Second World War later, in 1967-8, half the rural families still had no electric light (cf. Lenin's famous formula: soviet power + electricity = communism; Carr, *Bolshevik Revolution* 2, p. 370), two-thirds of the families baked their own bread and milked their own cow. In the 'small, scattered settlements so typical of Soviet rural areas' the school was typically still an all-age one with one or at most two teachers (Matthews, pp. 260-1).

Conditions in Chinese villages varied greatly before Liberation, and still do, if at a much improved level (Myrdal's and Jack Chen's books are essential reading here). Edgar Snow reports how Xu Te-li, famous teacher and Commissioner of Education in Yan'an, one day complained of some of the difficulties which the communists faced in bringing enlightenment to the villages. Describing how much worse conditions were in the north than in Jiangxi where they had been previously, he said:

This is culturally one of the darkest places on earth. Do you know the people of north Shenxi and Gansu believe that water is harmful to them? The average man here has a bath all over only twice in his life—once when he is born, the second time when he is married! They hate to wash their feet, hands or faces, or cut their nails or their hair. (Snow, pp. 240-1)

The Chinese response to village problems has been to adapt schools to these problems and to the needs and way of life of the peasants. To the horror of traditionally-minded teachers and education bureaucrats who condemned such schools as 'irregular', children have been allowed to attend as and when family and farm duties allowed. Teachers have gone to village houses to coach girls unable to attend school because of having to look after baby siblings, or such girls have been allowed to bring the babes to school with them. Children in tiny hamlets or isolated in the summer camps of pastoral Mongols or Uighur peoples of Xinjiang have been taught by teachers who have circulated from settlement to settlement, teaching a day here and then going on. Since the Cultural Revolution the number of 'irregular schools' has greatly increased, making a big contribution to the universalising of schooling. At the same time rural schools have tended to adapt their timetables to the agricultural calendar, thus avoiding the situation in Russia described by Nearing above.

Recent Soviet attempts to improve rural schooling have followed the typical European pattern of closing small, one-teacher schools and transporting children to larger schools some distance from home. The aim, as an article in the *Teachers' Gazette* described it, is large secondary schools with hostel boarding and well-equipped classrooms and workshops. But they admitted that progress in that direction was 'too slow' (6 August 1970, quoted in SE/71/XIII/5-6).

1. Secondary Vocational and Technical Schools

These schools are normally terminal, leading directly to middle strata jobs as skilled worker or member of the petty bourgeoisie. Persons destined for the upper classes of society do not normally take secondary vocational-technical courses, but proceed via the academic high schools to some form of tertiary schooling. This remains as true for the USSR and China as it does for any capitalist country, whatever provision particular schools may have made for pupils to acquire academic training alongside the technical, and however possible further study may be. (In both countries the CP acts as talent spotter, sending promising

people to tertiary schools for further training, and these may have
initially come up through secondary vocational schools. In capitalist
countries the big enterprises act similarly, of course.)

In the early post-revolutionary period in the USSR there was a conflict between supporters of prolonged general education in the United
Labour School (notably, Lunacharsky and Krupskaya) and those who
wanted early vocational-technical training to man the factories. This is
documented by S. Fitzpatrick (pp. 59-68) and O. Anweiler (pp. 147-9,
etc.). In China this does not seem to have been such an issue, the lines
having been drawn rather between supporters of the Euro-American
style academic schools and forms of 'irregular schooling'. This may
reflect a lower demand for industrial labour. However, the whole
question of secondary technical schooling in China requires further
study, and only a few comments can be made here.

In the USSR the initiative came from the Komsomol in 1920 to set
up factory apprentice schools (FZU–*fabrichno-zavodskoye uchenich-
estvo/uchilishche,* sometimes translated 'factory-plant school', or factory
training school (cf. Medynsky, p. 35; King, pp. 172-3; Tandler, p. 86).
Similar schools for peasant youth were also envisaged. Courses lasted
three years, half the time being spent on general education and half on
industrial training. Initially pupils were accepted with only two years of
primary education, but as school attendance and standards were raised
so entrance requirements for the factory schools were also raised. In
1933-4 the system was reformed. For such trades as plasterers, carpenters
and joiners courses might last only 5-12 months. For lathe operators,
steel smelters' helpers, engine drivers' helpers on the railways, and
other more complex trades courses lasted 2-3 years. The time devoted
to general education was greatly reduced, though in the longer courses
it might, with physical education, still occupy 25 per cent of the time
(Medynsky, p. 35).

An important form of vocational-technical training has been the
technicums, or specialised secondary schools. Continuing a form already
existing before the revolution, the technicums were expanded in scope.
Normally small in size, taking 175-200 students each, the schools initially
demanded completed primary school of their entrants. Courses lasted
for 4 years and combined general and specialised training. Graduates
had to pass a state examination or submit a thesis. In the early years
many graduates of the FZU entered technicums.

Between 1926 and 1933 there was an Industrial Training School
(FZS–*Fabrichno-Zavodskoya Semiletnaya Shkola,* i.e. a factory-plant
7-year school).

An important form of worker education between 1919 and the end of the thirties was the *Rabfac*. The name, Workers' Faculty, implies their function, that of preparing workers as rapidly as possible to enter the ordinary faculties of the university. The first Rabfac was set up on student initiative at the Plekhanov Commercial Institute in Moscow on 2 February 1919. Others rapidly followed. Some were attached to universities, where they met considerable opposition, not to say sabotage, from staff and other students. Some worked during the day, while others were evening institutions. Courses in the latter extended over 3-4 years. The kind of preparatory training provided depended on the institution with which the Rabfac was linked. Though in theory students were expected to go on from the particular Rabfac to the linked higher institution the number of vacancies in the latter was often over-subscribed, and students had to shop around. Some Rabfacs were concerned with teacher training (cf. Tandler for a full account).

On 2 October 1940 a system of Labour Reserve Schools was established by order of the Praesidium of the Supreme Soviet. Male youths between the ages of 14 and 17 were drafted into courses lasting from 6 months to 2 years, after which they had to work 'at regular wages' for a further 4 years. During this time they were deferred from military service. Quotas for districts were laid down, and during the war and just after the system was extended to girls. Zhamin quite incorrectly refers to the setting up of these schools as 'marking the beginning of the vocational-technical education of today' (Zhamin, p. 62).

The situation today is outlined in section 6 and 7 of the *Fundamentals of Legislation of the USSRR and Union Republics on Public Education*, 1973. Vocational training schools are dealt with in the former. They are intended to train 'harmoniously developed, technically well-educated, and cultured young well-qualified workers with professional skill' (art. 31). Graduates will receive 'a corresponding qualification (rating, class, category) in accordance with (their) profession' (art. 34). Section 7 describes the specialised secondary schools, or *technikumi*. These are to train 'qualified specialists' who will receive 'a diploma and badge of an established standard' on successful completion of their course (arts. 36, 39). Technicums may be day, evening or correspondence schools, and, like the vocational schools, they take students in with either an 8-year or full 10-year secondary schooling.

In China secondary vocational-technical schooling has been developed in both FTD schools as well as by the trade union run spare-time system set up in June 1950. During the middle sixties many of the FTD technical schools changed over to part-work schooling and new schools were established on this pattern. Following the Cultural Revolution tertiary institutions have run short courses (*duanxun ban*). (A number of these are described in *Ba wuchanjieji jiaoyu . . .* , pp. 165-94.) The position appears still to be very fluid, with the 'overlapping between regular and spare-time programs, on-the-job training, and work and study programs' which Richman noted in 1966 (Richman, p. 148).

2. Tertiary Level Schools

Tertiary schools under capitalism have in the main been institutions for training members of the bourgeoisie, together with supporting technical experts and ideologues for the ranks of the new petty bourgeoisie. The attitude of communists to these institutions has been ambivalent. In 1918 Lunacharsky commented:

> The university as it has been up to this time does not exist as a learned institution. It is a 'diploma factory', necessary for the careers of future state *chinovniki* who are educated there. (Fitzpatrick, p. 75)

The ABC of Communism admitted the difficulty of foreseeing 'precisely what character the higher schools for specialist training will assume under communism', but was 'perfectly sure that the universities in their present form, with their present professorial staffs, have ceased to be servicable institutions' (Carr, 1969, p. 290). It looked to changes of staff and student social composition and outlook to 'expel bourgeois culture from its last refuge'. In a period when optimists were talking of opening the doors of the universities to everybody who wanted to enter, the possibility that institutions of this form might be inseparable from the fostering of class differences was probably inconceivable. But Mao Ze-dong, with the advantage of some fifty years of Soviet experience, and seventeen years of experience of Chinese institutions modelled on them behind him, was certainly conscious of this possibility. He expressed his doubts and the basic lines of his solution in the statement which headed a report on a new form of workers' college established in July 1968:

> It is still necessary to have universities; here I refer mainly to the need for colleges of science and engineering. However, it is essential to shorten the length of the schooling, revolutionize education, put proletarian politics in command and take the road of the Shanghai Machine Tools Plant in training technicians from among

the workers. Students should be selected from among workers and peasants with practical experience, and they should return to practical work in production after a few years' study. (*Peking Review* 31, 1968, pp. 3, 9)

No such doubts assail contemporary Soviet leaders, and changes in China have not proceeded long or far enough for any conclusions to be drawn there.

Beginning in 1918 the USSR began to lay down the pattern of tertiary schools which was later to be copied by China. A large number of mono-technical institutes were set up in addition to polytechnical institutions and multi-faculty universities. The Moscow Academy of Mining was set up in 1918. New universities were started at Mizhninovgorod (now Gorky), Dnepropetrovsk, Voronezh, Irkutsk, and Tbilisi, all in 1918; one in Azerbaizhan and one in Latvia in 1919; the Erevan and Urals universities in 1920; and one in Belorussia in 1921. By the school year 1922-3 there were 248 VUZi, compared with 105 in 1914-15 (*Ped. Ents* 1, p. 466). A number of institutes, like the Railway Engineering Institute (1828) and the Forestry Institute (1802) in St Petersburg, had existed before the Revolution. In January 1924, Nearing gives a total of 912 'higher technical schools' (i.e. institutes), divided into six main groups: medicine, 66; pedagogy, 331; agriculture, 152; industry, 219; economics and social science, 53; music and art, 92 (Nearing, p. 63). Since then the number and variety of institutions has increased. In 1970-71 the total number of VUZi was 805, of which 50 were classified as universities; 228 were technical institutes; 98 were agricultural colleges; and 90 were medical schools (Zhamin, p. 77; *USSR Ed.* pp. 72, 81).

In pre-Liberation China there were 207 'institutions of higher learning' (Cheng, p. 39), including 20 foreign-subsidised Christian colleges, and Qinghua University, set up with Boxer money to train Chinese for higher studies in the USA. By 1953 these had been re-organised in the Soviet, rather than the Euro-American pattern. Peking National University (1898) absorbed Qinghua's colleges of arts, science and law, and the liberal arts programme of Yanjing (Yenching) University, the Christian university into whose campus it moved. The Roman Catholic University, *Fu-ren* (1925) became the Peking Teacher Training Institute. Many science faculties were combined to form institutes. Of the 182 institutions in 1953, 14 were comprehensive universities; 39 were polytechnic and engineering institutes; 31 were teachers colleges; 29 were medical and pharmacological colleges; 29 were agriculture and

forestry colleges; and there were smaller numbers for such areas as
political science, economics and the fine arts (Cheng, pp. 39-40; cf. Lutz,
C&CC for amalgamations, pp. 473-82). At the outbreak of the GPCR
the number of institutions had risen to 663, of which 21 were universities, and 15 were polytechnic universities, of which Qinghua
University in Peking is the most famous (Tsang, 1968, p. 193 and
Barendsen, 1973, quote *Tsu Kuo*, nos. 11 and 12, 1965; see also Cheng,
pp. 40-53).

While there have been differences over time, and also between the
USSR and China, the tertiary institutions of both countries have exhib-
ited a marked hierarchical structure. This has been most obvious in the
system of academic ranks and degrees. In the flush of revolution, on 8
October 1918, these were abolished by the young Soviet government.
But in March 1938 they were restored and from then on have helped to
make Soviet academics again highly status-conscious. In 1938 the Supreme
Attestation Commission, VAK, was set up with power to approve tertiary institutions for advanced training in research, the granting and con-
firming of advanced degrees, the appointment of all senior academics
and the ratification of the appointment of junior academics (deWitt,
1955, p. 190; OECD, 1969, pp. 300-1). Soviet academic ranks were
specified as professor (*professor*), assistant professor (*dotsent*), and
instructor-lecturer (*asistent-prepodavatel'*).

The Soviet diploma (*diplom*) is granted to those who pass a public,
oral examination, set on the entire course of study. It states the graduate's speciality and the grade given, not only in the final examination,
but also in all the examinations taken during the course. Chinese graduates receive a similar diploma (*biye zhengshu*), stating the specialisation
and the number of years of study completed. In the USSR there are
two higher degrees, the Candidate of Sciences (*kandidat nauk*) and the
Doctor of Sciences (*doktor nauk*). The Candidate degree requires at
least 3 years of full-time study, the passing of certain examinations and
public defence of a thesis. The Doctor is only awarded to Candidates
or professors (in special cases) after public defence of a thesis or on the
basis of specially meritorious work. The difficulties which candidates
for these two qualifications undergo are discussed in Zaleski (pp. 335-45,
esp. sections 842-4 and 848). In China, in 1955, the State Council
authorised the Chinese Academy of Sciences to establish a higher degree
with the title Associate Doctor (*fu-boshi*). Intended as the equivalent of
the Soviet *kandidat* degree, the term of study was laid down as 4 years.
However, though the first batch of students completed their course of
studies no degree was ever awarded. Cheng attributes this to the 'short-

age of qualified teachers and the failure to devise a workable system'
(Cheng, p. 56). But it is more likely to have been because of the opposition of Mao and his supporters to badges of rank. There is no lack of
evidence that skilled researchers are being trained in research institutes
and other places, and there is also plenty of evidence outside China to
suggest that the kind of exercises which make a good academic thesis
are often contrived and of little practical value.

A major feature of tertiary study in both countries is the high degree
of specialisation. Subject matter is divided into specialities, themselves
further subdivided into specialisations closely related to the divisions of
the economy (deWitt, pp. 106-7). This has resulted in, for example,
engineers expert in either bridge design or road construction, but not
both. This narrow training began in the USSR in the 1930s and remains
in both countries today in spite of frequent criticisms (deWitt, pp. 108-
9; Cheng, pp. 98-104). From a marxist point of view what is required is
an education which would provide understanding of the social implications of scientific and economic projects as well as the skills to control
them. Fragmented studies would certainly seem to make for the narrow
social view. But experience elsewhere suggests there is no simple connection between breadth of study and social awareness either. I shall
return to this question in the section on compulsory political studies
during tertiary schooling.

A characteristic feature of Soviet higher education, and to a lesser
but growing degree in China, is the high proportion of students who
obtain their training in their spare time. DeWitt notes that extension-
correspondence (*zaochnyye*) training institutes and other alternative
equivalent training facilities 'emerged only after 1917' (1955, p. 93).
Gradually these have developed until in 1972/3 some 2,382,000 of the
4,597,000 tertiary students were enrolled in evening and correspondence
courses (*USSR Ed.* pp. 94-6). There were 11 evening and 19 correspondence institutes in 1962-3, and over 1,000 evening and correspondence
departments of the FTD tertiary schools (Deineko, p. 192). Some of the
special institutes are large and well organised. The USSR Polytechnical
Institute, offering correspondence courses in chemical engineering, mining, metallurgy and other specialities, had 32,700 students in 1958/9
(Yelyutin, p. 43). It had branches or consultation centres then in 31
cities. Other big institutes are the USSR Institute of Economics, offering correspondence courses in industrial and agricultural management,
statistics, etc., with 9,434 students, and the USSR Law Correspondence
Institute, offering a 5-year course to 12,820 students (Yelyutin, p. 43).
In China spare-time training has been run by the FTD tertiary institutions,

by individual or groupings of factories or enterprises, or by local government bodies. Famous universities like Qinghua, Tianjin and Nanjing (Nanking) all run evening departments in which the normal faculty teach (Cheng, p. 59). Factory colleges were reported in Shanghai, Wuhan, Harbin and other places in the early sixties (Cheng, p. 59). The 21st July Workers' Colleges set up in increasing numbers after 1970 on the model of that run by the Shanghai Machine Tools Factory are short-term rather than spare-time. A group of workers is taken off production and trained, for example, to make a new gear-cutting machine, over a period of perhaps two years. Study is closely linked with current production needs and students remain in the factory which trains them.

In both countries special provision is made for helping part-time students. In the USSR this includes the provision of textbooks, time off for preparation and the taking of examinations, and travelling expenses (see Troitsky, p. 30; Yelyutin, p. 44, and Price, 1970, pp. 200-202). In spite of this there are indications that part-time students find it as difficult to pursue their studies as similar students in other parts of the world. Of the large numbers who start a high proportion either do not finish, or extend their studies long beyond the set time (deWitt, p. 95). For the marxist, of course, the question is not simply one of efficiency or economy of training, though these are important. The major question is whether full-time or part-time study contributes best to producing what Mao calls 'workers with socialist consciousness and culture'. The answer would seem to depend on the nature of the course and its duration, and also on what time of life it is pursued. A situation where all workers could take a 'sabbatical' is rather different from that where there are only some 600,000 FTD tertiary students in a population of 800m.

3. Boarding Schools

In both Russia and China boarding schools have existed both before and after the revolution. At one end of the social scale were the expensive schools for the upper class children, such as the Noble Cadet Corpus founded in 1731 at St Petersburg, or the Smolny Institute for young ladies (1764). At the other end were various orphanages and institutions for the care of children in special need. In China a majority of secondary and tertiary schools maintained boarding facilities for students from out of town, though often these would board with relatives when possible. The attitude of communists to the boarding principle has probably rather favoured it, since the total control over the students' time would permit a more thorough inculcation of communist values, and the elim-

ination of parental values considered backward. This view was stressed
by certain Soviet educators during the twenties (cf. ch. 8) and came to
the fore again when boarding schools were established on a bigger scale
again in 1956. In the official euphoria which led up to the acceptance
by the 22nd CPSU Congress (October-November 1961) of a 'programme
to conclude the building of communism in our country' (Afanasenko and
and Kairov in Redl, 1964, p. 197) many no doubt looked to boarding
schools as necessary hasteners of the process (cf. *Programme CPSU,*
1961, p. 125(b)). In China the matter does not appear to have caused
much serious discussion until the GPCR, when the Mao line was clearly
against them in principle. Experience in the preceding period was taken
as showing boarding as reinforcing the academic nature of the schools,
further contributing to the 'three separations' which Mao Ze-dong
deplored. Hence the move to transfer rural schools 'down' from the
commune level to that of the production brigades, bringing schooling
wherever possible within walking distance of the home. Of course, in
both countries economic considerations are also involved: in China,
the need to provide cheaper schooling on a mass scale; in the USSR, on
the one hand, economic recovery after World War Two made possible
increased provision of expensive schooling, while, on the other, the continued relative poverty, would not allow too great a development.

The decree of April 1957 governing the Soviet boarding schools,
translated in Redl, sets out in detail how they should be run (Redl, 1964,
pp. 167-76). It gives priority to orphans, children of war or work
invalids and various other categories in need of care. Stressing that enrolment by parents is 'entirely voluntary' it then asserts the authority of
the school, through its director, over the parents:

> art. 14. Parents who place their children in boarding schools must
> cooperate with the educational collective by raising the child in a
> correct way while he is in the family. Parents visit their children
> during days designated by the director.
>
> At the request of parents or guardians, the director of the school
> permits the students home visits on Sundays, holidays, and during
> vacations. (Redl, 1964, p. 169, translation amended)

Afanasenko and Kairov, summing up the experience of five years, write
enthusiastically about the 'limitless opportunities' for the close co-operation of parents and school (Redl, 1964, p. 205). Nevertheless, it would
seem that the majority of children in these schools are precisely those
for whom this would be most difficult to fulfil.

It would appear that considerable efforts have been made to keep academic standards in these schools comparable with other, non-boarding schools. Like all soviet schools, they have been encouraged to develop strong links with the surrounding society through productive and social work by the students, and through parents' and community organisations' committees. A limited number of day students are allowed on the proviso that they will be thoroughly integrated into the activities of the boarders.

With the demise of Khrushchev little more has been heard of these schools. The *Fundamentals of Legislation* group them under article 23 with the much more popular and long-standing institutions, the pro-longed-day schools. According to the *Pedagogicheskaya Entsiklopedia* (vol. 4, pp. 714-7) the latter began in Petrograd in 1919 and ever since have provided a service for working mothers. Many of these operate for 9-12 hours a day and provide two hot meals for the children. But the *Fundamentals* sees their functions as much wider than baby-minding. It speaks of 'broadening social upbringing' and 'creating *more* favourable conditions for the all-round development of pupils' (emphasis added). At the same time it defines the purpose of boarding schools as serving 'the same purposes' for children 'lacking the necessary conditions for upbringing in the family', a phrasing which reflects what observers have judged to be the current climate of opinion (Dodge, 1966, p. 98; Mat-thews, 1972, p. 273). Statistics also confuse boarding and prolonged-day schools and it is therefore impossible to judge just how much the former system has been expanded. Afanasenko and Kairov give figures for the RSFSR. In 1956 there were 184 schools with 35,000 students. In 1961 this had shot up to 1,000 schools with 350,000 students (Redl, 1964, p. 199). Matthews quotes *Uchitelskaya gazeta* of 3 December 1968, which gave a figure of 1.6m students in 1968-9, or less than 4 per cent of the general school contingent (Matthews, 1972, p. 273). The *USSR in figures for 1973* has the unhelpful footnote:

> The number of schools and groups of prolonged day has been steadily growing. At the beginning of 1973/74 school year there were 7.2 million pupils in the schools and groups of prolonged day and in boarding schools. (p. 208)

The 1971-7 plan for economic development foresee further growth. 'The number of pupils in prolonged-day schools and groups in 1975 is to be 132.5 per cent of the 1970 level' (Zhamin, p. 58). But though the com-bined total of pupils for 1970-1 was given in the previous sentence as

6.1m there is no forecast of growth for boarding schools. Why? It would be interesting to know more about the attitudes of different social groups to them. Are they seen as too expensive for those wanting an elite schooling for their children? (Dodge gives data which show a monthly charge of 56 r/pupil for parents with incomes of 200+ r/month, p. 88.) Or are they, or are they seen to be, schools for the deprived and the difficult, leading only to the factory bench? There is certainly a hint of the latter fate in the emphasis of article 28 of the 1957 Decree, though one should remember that this was framed around the time of the general school reform of Khrushchev, with its emphasis on the training and encouragement of skilled workers, and its de-emphasis on further academic studies.

For marxists the question must be whether boarding schools are a form which, at the present time, or in the foreseeable future can contribute to a more communal life style, to ending the narrowness and exclusiveness of family-based life. Can they help children to develop understanding and control over themselves and their environment more quickly and easily? Experience to date is not hopeful, though one must remember this in a context of family life as the highly visible norm. There is also the possible danger of creating further and perhaps enduring gulfs between age groups when the more desirable goal would seem to be to bring them together into a new harmony.

Students: Numbers, Composition and Selection

Marxists share with liberals and others a belief in universal basic schooling as a necessary foundation for modern society. In both the USSR and China the Communist Parties have from the start made this their aim. However, poverty has in both countries proved a big obstacle and though growth in school attendance at all levels has been impressive by previous standards when measured as a proportion of the school-age cohort the gap between aim and achievement becomes clear. Lack of basic data, as much as any desire on the part of officials to disguise the facts, has probably made such figures hard to come by. An alternative gauge is declarations of intent to universalise, a recurrent Soviet theme as I shall proceed to show.

The Soviet Census of 1926 revealed that at that time only 60 per cent of the age cohort was at school. A recent Soviet writer traced progress from then through to the sixties:

The Soviet Union achieved compulsory elementary education in 1932, 7-year schooling in 1952, and 8-year compulsory education in 1962.

The process of transition to universal compulsory 10-year education
has been successfully developing since 1966. (Zhamin, pp. 18-19)

Anweiler, however, points out that it was only in 1940 that 4-year
schooling became universal, and then only in the RSFSR (Anweiler,
1964, p. 356). In 1955 *Uchitel'skaya gazeta* admitted that 'many children still receive no instruction, and the number of children who leave
school is still extremely large' (30 November 1955, in CDSP, vol. VII,
no. 50, p. 32). The 19th CPSU Congress held in 1952 had already set
the aim of universal 10-year schooling, in urban areas by 1955 and in all
areas by 1960. The more realistic 20th CPSU Congress in 1956 altered
this to 7 years of schooling plus 3 years of vocational training (Korol,
p. 4). The *Fundamentals of Legislation* of 1973 still claims only the 8-
year school as compulsory and speaks of 'the introduction of universal
secondary and higher education' (art. 3). Anweiler notes that in 1970
some 6.4 per cent of students in the 8-year school, or 354,000 students
in all, left without completing their studies and did not appear subsequently to have completed through evening school. He adds that the
greatest numbers were to be found in the national republics of Kazakhstan, Tadzhikstan and Azerbaidzhan (Anweiler, 1973, p. 103).

For China figures are very difficult to obtain after 1958, except for
particular *xian* or communes. National figures conceal wide differences
between isolated rural areas, where until very recently school attendance
may have been close to zero, and the urban centres where from the
fifties it has probably been in the nineties per centually. The following
estimates for primary school attendance include 'irregular' schools from
1958 onwards, and, since the total number in the age-cohort is uncertain, can only be taken to indicate the trend:

1949	22%
1958	80.3%
1962	56.1%
1966	84.6%
1975/6	93%

The 1958 and 1962 figures were given in the *Guangming Ribao*, 18 July
1968.

Figures for attendance at vocational-technical schools and tertiary
schools require careful and difficult evaluation. Some comments will
be made in the section on 'Education and the economy' below. I will
only say here that too often the easily counted years of attendance are

mistaken for learning acquired, or the written syllabi and textbooks are assumed to have been thoroughly digested.

Turning to the social composition of students, there is again considerably greater information for the USSR than there is for China, in spite of the unhelpful over-simplification of class classification which is almost mandatory, and the suppression of sociological studies during the thirties, forties and early fifties (cf. Matthews, 1972, ch. 2, esp. pp. 44-5). In the twenties much emphasis was placed on the growing number of worker and peasant children attending secondary and tertiary schools. The following figures for tertiary school come from deWitt (1961):

	1928	1930	1932	1934	1938
Worker	25.4	35.2	58.0	47.9	33.9
Peasant	23.9	20.9	14.1	14.6	21.6
Other	50.7	43.9	27.9	37.5	44.5

It should be noted that the fall in the proportion of peasant students partly reflects a fall in this category throughout the population during this time. But in 1938 peasants still formed 46 per cent of the population.

Matthews describes two investigations carried out during the burst of interest in sociology in the mid-sixties. One of these compares the social class background of students in a 4th grade with those of students of the 10-11th grades. The school was in the Gorki *oblast*, in 1964.

Table 2.1

Fathers' occupation	% of all children	
	4th grade	10/11th grade
Specialist	25.8	42.8
Skilled labourer	43.6	23.1
Unskilled labourer	6.6	1.5
Pensioner, invalid	4.6	7.9
No father	13.4	16.6

Source: Matthews, p. 265.

The first three categories speak for themselves, but the last two are unexpected. They could reflect privilege because of war service, or, as Matthews comments, 'have come from the more opulent groups in society' (Matthews, 1972, p. 266).

The second investigation compares the social position of children with that of their fathers. The category 'intelligentsia' may include being a student at a VUZ. The data was gathered from graduates from

Table 2.2

Social groups	Fathers	Social position (%)		
		Children		
		All	Sons	Daughters
Intelligentsia	62	73	68	79
Workers (industry)	10	18	22	13
Workers (service industries)	11	8	8	8
Agricultural workers and peasants	17	1	2	—

Source: Matthews, 1972, p. 266.

the 10-year schools of Novosibirsk *oblast* in 1963.

More recent studies have confirmed this picture and added further details (Avis in Anweiler, 1975). They document the current state of a trend which, in spite of intentions and attempts to alter it, has operated much as it does in countries which have quite other social aims. For an earlier period, when no such questions could be asked in the USSR itself, the Harvard Project on the Soviet Social System has some interesting comments (this Project, carried out in 1950, questioned 3,000 former Soviet citizens on a variety of topics):

> our data indicates: (1) Education is highly correlated with one's self-elected social group, and with one's occupation. (2) The explicit policy of the Soviet regime to favour with superior educational opportunities those in the labouring classes and to impede the opportunities of members of the 'former exploiting classes' may have *inhibited* slightly the educational chances of this latter group. However, it did not offset to any *appreciable* degree the tendency of the children of the upper classes to secure superior access to higher education. Abolition of the regime's policy of discrimination during the mid-thirties has probably produced even stronger stratification. (3) The broad expansion of Soviet education has clearly had major results not only in upgrading the average, but also in putting a floor under the level of education received by the children of all social groups. (Inkeles and Bauer, 1959, p. 144)

In the sample questioned, 'among older children of the intelligentsia and white-collar families 20 per cent were in college, whereas among those of manual origin only 7 per cent were able to attain that level' (ibid.).

In China, following the revolution there was an attempt to give preference to children of workers and peasants and those who had suffered under the Guomindang. Nevertheless, available figures, not to mention the torrent of complaint during the GPCR, testify to the familiar story, that the children of the educated have an advantage in any system of academic selection. The official statistical summary *Ten Great Years* claims that the percentage of students of worker and peasant origin attending tertiary schools rose from 19.1 per cent in 1951 to 48.0 per cent in 1958 (p. 200). Tsang gives a figure of 54 per cent for tertiary graduates of such origin in 1963 (Tsang, p. 200). No figures are available for the post-GPCR period when students have all worked for some two or more years before attending tertiary school. But one can expect some confusion to arise from this since students will probably be classified according to their own rather than their parents' occupation.

We will now turn from the results of the selection process to the process itself. To begin with, there is an interesting contrast between the attitude of the Bolsheviks in 1918 and student radicals in Peking at the outbreak of the GPCR in 1966. A decree of the Council of People's Commissars of 2 August 1918 declared:

> Any person irrespective of class or sex, of not less than sixteen years of age, may enrol as a student in any tertiary institution without producing a diploma, a certificate or proof of having completed secondary school or any other school. (Trans. from Anweiler and Meyer, pp. 65-6)

Students from two Peking high schools wrote to Chairman Mao Ze-dong demanding:

> 1. Immediately abolish entrance examinations to higher educational institutions.
> 2. Senior high school graduates must first of all go out among workers, peasants and soldiers to temper themselves [in work] . . . and receive from them 'ideological diplomas'. (*Peking Review* 26, 1966, p. 21)

Both statements express a concern for social justice, but while the former reflects a totally unreal optimism about possibilities and takes the stand of the individual, the Chinese statement recognises that selection is inevitable at the present time and takes the stand of society. It demands only a different form of selection which it hopes will better serve society.

Before describing particular forms of selection there are three general questions which need stating. First, the place at which selection is made depends on the point at which provision of places cannot meet the demand for them. In both the USSR and China this has gradually moved up through the school grades. But it is not quite so simple, for while in many countries students have been expelled for failing examinations during their tertiary schooling this has apparently been rare in the two countries considered here. Once granted entry to tertiary school every effort is made to help students through. (There have been exceptions to this policy at different times, see Korol, pp. 192-7 and *CDSP* 20, 48, 1968 for recent reports of first-year attrition.) Secondly, there is the question of what Richman refers to as high-talent manpower (Richman, pp. 201-2). The problem is its definition and the amount required by the economy. Richman compares the percentage of tertiary graduates in industry in China, the USSR, the USA and India. He assumes that more is better, and that the proportion in the USA is nearest to the ideal. But it is increasingly clear that this is problematic. Recent attention, focused on just what use is made of knowledge and skills acquired at school (Gorz, 1972), and the factors which go to make successful innovation in industry (Langrish, p. 18), suggests the need for caution in coming to conclusions in this area. It seems likely that traditional respect for universities, vested interests of tertiary staffs, and the pressure of would-be tertiary graduates are all significant factors, however irrelevant they may be to the question of technical-economic need.

Thirdly, there is the vexed question of standards. Tertiary institutions are frequently judged by the quality of publications of staff and research students, rather than by the more difficult to measure criterion of teaching quality. Since these institutions can select most stringently they get able students who then are a credit to them whatever the standard of teaching. Teachers' standards, whether in research or teaching depend to varying degrees on the support they receive in the way of research assistance, secretarial help, libraries and equipment. But above all they require time, and peace, to think. Promotion struggles and a hierarchical system which gives research assistance and opportunities to travel and meet colleagues in one's field disproportionately to the higher, professorial ranks would seem to be designed to discourage the raising of overall standards. In this connection it is interesting to note Cheng's measurement of standards in China in 1955 by the number of holders of high rank (Cheng, p. 79). The question is highly problematic and even the assumption of a positive correlation of quality with years of experience is hardly generally agreed.

In the USSR, after a period in the twenties when they experimented with tertiary school entrance on the recommendation of some labour or political organisation (Nearing, 1926, p. 64), the Soviet authorities returned to a system of examinations. King gives an optimistic description of the system as she found it in the thirties, in which she claims that, different from 'the old-type examination' tests were 'to find out whether pupils have really covered the syllabus and whether they have intelligently acquired the knowledge demanded by the authorities' (King, 1937, pp. 122-8 and 123). Korol describes the system for the fifties in detail, with its exemptions for gold and silver medallists, and preferences given in certain institutions to those with particular work experience (Korol, 1957, pp. 167-208). In China in the years 1950 through to 1966 there was a similar system of nationally organised examinations combined with examinations and other methods of selection organised by the individual schools (Price, 1970, pp. 165-8). In both countries there is considerable evidence, freely expressed in the press, of the tensions and stresses created by the system, including occasional outright abuses (for USSR see, e.g. *CDSP* 18, no. 29, 1966; for China, *SWB* 4509, 4527, 4534 and 4538, all of 1974).

Following the GPCR discussions on selection the Chinese have instituted a selection procedure which in some ways is similar to that tried in the USSR in the twenties. In an attempt to find students 'from among workers and peasants with practical experience' who would 'return to production after a few years of study' the following general procedure has been adopted. The individual must first apply to go to college. His application is then discussed by the army unit, factory workshop, office, or commune production brigade where he is working. It is one of the criteria that applicants will all be working for 2-3 years between school and tertiary institution. If the application is approved by this basic work unit it is forwarded to the local, and then provincial Party committee for further selection and endorsement. Finally, the school to which application has been made carries out a final selection. In 1972 and 1973 examinations were reintroduced to supplement the character reference originally demanded by the high school students in 1966 (*Peking Review* 24, June 1966, p. 19). This has caused further protest (cf. campaign associated with Zhang Die-sheng, SCMP, 5442, 1973) but since one of the criteria is a level of schooling equivalent to that of junior high school or above it is hard to see what alternative could be used which would be better. So long as more people want to go to college than there are places for them, someone is going to be deprived. Only long-term socio-economic change can alter that situation, by providing more places and through rotation of jobs and less emphasis on formal qualifications, perhaps, reducing the pressure of applicants.

While the discussion in China during the past few years has centred on questions of attitude to study and how to select those who will be better able and more willing to serve the community, in the USSR attention has been centred on students' knowledge and intellectual calibre. Typical of the arguments was an article by Academician M. Lavrentyev (*Izvestia*, 25 May 1969) who called for earlier specialisation in the 7th and 8th grades of the secondary school. It is, he said 'unnecessary to strive to give everyone a standardised fund of knowledge, to teach everyone on the basis of a single syllabus' (*CDSP* 20, no. 21). At the same time aptitude and achievement testing appears to be winning considerable support among specialists (*CDSP* 21, no. 5). If this trend is continued it will be a further step away from the ideal of the all-round, free man which Soviet writings still pay lip-service to.

Administration and Financing

The marxist principle of workers' control implies an administrative system which gives power to those doing the work, in the case of education mainly the teachers, but also other concerned groups like students, parents and non-teaching personnel working in the schools. At the same time marxists recognise the need for some degree of centralised decision-making and for such things as help to and subsidies of poorer areas by the richer in particular circumstances. In the USSR and China a committee structure has been established on the representative principle which has clearly been an improvement on previous systems. But the degree of centralisation and the dominant role of the Communist Parties have precluded the growth of more democratic, local control patterns.

In both the USSR and China overall administration of education has been carried out by a central ministry connected with education departments at the lower levels. In both countries there has been a separate ministry for tertiary and specialised secondary education for part of the time. These organs have been responsible for establishing schools, providing most of the finance, appointing staff, laying down curricula and approving textbooks. In both countries other ministries, e.g. Health, Agriculture, or one of the industrial ministries, have also had certain responsibilities for education, often the running of particular tertiary institutions.

The role of the CP as initiator of all major policies in education, as in everything else, is central to an understanding of the system. Represented officially on various school councils in both the USSR and China, it has played a gradually more dominant role in school affairs. In the USSR Party members with university education were less than 1 per cent of members until after 1927. It was therefore impossible for them until then even to begin to dominate internal institution meetings, though measures adopted by the Party at national level already dominated school decision-making in major areas. The Party also began to control the employment of university graduates after 1926 through a commission set up by the Secretariat (Schapiro, 1963, p. 343). Party members were appointed to positions of director and vice-director of institutions from the beginning, often meeting with open or hidden hostility (e.g. Fitzpatrick, 1970, p. 65). By 1936 it was possible to rule that only persons possessing tertiary education should be eligible for appointment to these posts (Korol, 1957, p. 152).

In China the role of the CCP as the leader of educational effort was especially stressed in the Directive of the CC CCP and State Council of 19 September 1958, at the time of the Great Leap Forward (Fraser (2) pp. 554-66). Party-building among teachers was to be further encouraged, and 'all educational administrations and schools should be led by the Party committees' (Fraser (2) p. 559). Many reports attest to the authority attached to the Party member, although he might occupy a lower position in the school hierarchy (e.g. MacFarquhar, 1960, p. 67). Party branches, which could be established where 3 or more Party members worked in the same school, meeting separately to discuss and decide on matters of policy cannot fail to have been a basis for suspicion and in some cases hostility. Whether the CCP will be able, as the result of the Cultural Revolution, to evolve a more open and democratic style closer to the theory of the mass line remains to be seen.

Patterns of management within the schools have, at least until the Cultural Revolution in 1966, been very similar in the two countries. The leadership group of a primary or secondary school depends on size. The Head Teacher (Director) is appointed by the local authority and is assisted by one or more deputy-heads. Next there is a director of studies, or teacher in charge of curriculum. The Head is responsible to the local authority for administration, academic and social matters. In large schools, especially at secondary level, there are administrative offices with clerical staff, and teachers may be grouped under a responsible teacher according to subject taught. Chinese secondary schools may have an Office of Studies.

Each school normally has a School Committee or Council, and a Parents' Committee. Nearing describes a number of school committees in the schools he visited in the USSR in 1925, and visitors since then have confirmed the pattern. The Pokrovsky Elementary School, Rostov, with 1,100 pupils, had a committee of 72 persons. Presided over by the school head, it included 25 representatives of the pupils drawn from each class, 3 members of the parents' organisation and representatives of the city council, the workers in the school, a nearby factory and a trade union. In China, school councils similarly include representatives from the commune labour brigades, factories or sometimes the street committees. School Councils discuss matters of administration, discipline, and the provision and maintenance of buildings and materials. They can act as a link between the school and the wider community, and can organise aid for the school. Soviet schools often maintain close links with a particular factory or enterprise which assists the school in various ways. This relationship is referred to as *sheftsvo*.

Schools in both countries normally have parents' committees. Chaired by the head, the committees may meet as frequently as monthly, and deal with all kinds of school problems. Problems with individual children are normally handled between the parents of the child concerned and the class teacher, who is expected to visit the parents in their home at regular intervals. But where this fails the matter may be discussed by the parents' committee. King describes how in the thirties in the USSR an Assistance Committee, set up by the parents, helped organise school meals, raise finance for extra activities, organise summer camps, find clothes for needy pupils, and sometimes accompany children to the theatre or cinema (King, 1937, p. 145). In China parents, either through the parents' committee or other forms of organisation, make furniture for the school, organise extra-class activities, and often participate in political and labour education.

In both the USSR and China great importance is attached to students assuming responsibility and organising themselves. In addition to the youth organisations there is usually some organisational framework of students within the school and class.

At the tertiary level the pattern of administration does not differ greatly from the pre-revolutionary Russian pattern. Each institution has at its head a Rector (universities) or Director (institutes) appointed by, in the more recent period, the Ministry of Higher Education. The Ministry also appoints a deputy director in charge of scientific and educational matters, and a director's assistant in charge of administration and plant management (Korol, 1957; cf. Price, 1970, pp. 147-8). Institutions may be divided into faculties, each under a dean, and these in turn are divided into chairs, each with a professor in charge. In China the term teaching-research group (*jiaoyanzu* or *jiaoyanshi*) is used for chair.

Minister of Higher Education of the USSR, Yelyutin, writing in 1959, described the system as one-man management combined with collective management (Yelyutin, p. 29). King, in 1937, emphasised the Director's 'sole responsibility for the academic, adminsitrative, and economic life of the university or institute' (King, 1937, p. 188). As a means of dealing with 'students' slackness, or any behaviour which interferes with the institute's regime' he can warn, fine, or ultimately, expel (ibid).

Within the various faculties courses are grouped into specialities, or major options, and specialisations. Teaching staff are grouped around these specialities and specialisations and in China at least these form the basis for small group activities.

An important organ of collective management is the Academic Council (Korol, p. 163). This body consists of the director, who is chairman; the deputy directors; deans; professors in charge of chairs; and representatives of various non-academic organisations (the CP, Komsomol, the trade union, etc.). The extent to which junior staff and students have been represented in the USSR is not clear. In China provision is certainly made, though their influence has in the main probably been slight (Belyayev, *JPRS*, 1176). The functions of the Chinese organ, known as the school council (*xiaowu weiyuanhui*), is also probably rather wider than its Soviet counterpart. Korol quotes a 1938 charter which laid down the duties of Soviet Academic Councils:

> to discuss and consider the semester and annual plans and reports on the work of the institutions, its faculties, and chairs, and to generalise their experiences; to consider methodological questions of teaching and of topics for research; to discuss and propose individuals for the academic titles of docent and professor; to grant the academic title of *assistant* (lowest academic title) and to grant academic degrees of *kandidat* and of *doktor* of sciences. (Korol, 1957, p. 164)

The degree of freedom of appointment of staff would appear to differ between China and the USSR. In the former the appointment of the director of studies (*jiaoyu zhuren*) and the director of administration must be approved by the Ministry of (Higher) Education, but other staff can be appointed on the authority of the Director of the institution. King suggests a similar situation in the USSR (King, 1937, p. 188), but Korol notes that while the initiative for appointment comes from the institution, 'the final decision rests with the Ministry' (Korol, p. 284).

Since the Cultural Revolution in China, in an attempt to bring about 'proletarian leadership' in the school, the former leadership has been replaced by a system of Revolutionary Committees and Workers' Mao Ze-dong Thought Propaganda Teams. In addition the Communist Party organisations have been revived and meet separately as well as having places on the Revolutionary Committees. While there appear to be local variations, the Revolutionary Committees consist of representatives of teachers, cadres and workers, the last usually being members of the Propaganda Team in the school. Students appear not always to be represented. The Revolutionary Committee is responsible for running the school in much the same way as the former School Committee was, but presumably with the Party again taking the major decisions.

The Propaganda Teams are a most interesting new organ, originally set up to restore order in the schools in 1968 (see Mao's statement in *Peking Review*, 30 August 1968, in Chen, p. 260). Members are chosen by the factories, or in the village by the 'poor and lower middle peasants'. Recently in the cities a local authority committee has coordinated appointment to individual schools. Team members sit on the Revolutionary and other committees of the school while at the same time meeting by themselves. They appear to organise school workshops and to liase between factories, communes and the school, as well as sometimes teaching political or technical classes. It will be interesting to see how they develop and what their relations with the Party will be in the future. They appear to be potentially a grassroots democratic force and for this reason are probably vulnerable in any return to a more authoritarian pattern.

Financing is obviously of major importance in any discussion of democratising the schools. First a word on costs to the students. The 1919 programme of the CPSU promised the Russian people not only free education up to the age of 17, but also 'supply to all pupils, at the cost of the State, of food, clothing, footgear, and scholastic requisites' (Carr, *Bolshevik Revolution* 3, p. 444). The realities of the immediate post-revolutionary period and the Civil War turned this dream into a nightmare. In the autumn of 1921 the central government withdrew its responsibility for financing the educational system, and then, first in practice and later officially, it allowed school fees to be reimposed (Fitzpatrick, p. 288). Only under the new Constitution of 1936 did schooling again become free, and then the pressure of war forced a reintroduction of charges for tertiary schooling. Charges of 300-500 r/year were made according to location and field of study, Moscow, Leningrad and the fine arts charging the most. These charges remained in force from 1940 through to 1956-7, when schooling was yet again made free. Throughout the whole period from 1917 until today pupils have been expected to provide their own textbooks, writing materials and other simple necessities.

China, whether from the principle of self-reliance or simply from realism, never made any promises of free education, though the small costs can only have been a deterrent to the very poorest, many of whom have been able to get help one way or another. Schools have charged small tuition fees and pupils have been expected to provide their own textbooks and writing materials. As in the USSR, grants and scholarships have been available to help a proportion of the students.

Schools in both countries have been financed by a combination of central and local funds. The exact expenditure is not always clear from budget figures since education may be combined with scientific research or 'culture' (Donnithorne, p. 367; Davies, 1958, p. 296; Richman, p. 128). Both countries also rely on various other funds such as trade union, and those of individual factories which have connections with particular schools (Noah, p. 53). Goncharov gives figures of 18 per cent for non-state funding in the USSR in 1956 and 1959 (pp. 29, 34, 35).

In China *minban* (people managed) schools are important, especially in the rural areas. A variety of financial arrangements have been made. A report from a *xian* in Shanxi Province in 1965 shows the range of possibilities. 175 primary schools, or 62.2 per cent of the total, were state supported. 39 schools, 13.9 per cent, were state run and aided by the collective. Some teachers were paid by the brigade. 44 schools, 15.6 per cent, were jointly run. Mostly 2-class, 2-teacher schools, the teachers were partly paid by the state and partly by the collective. 20 schools, 7.2 per cent, were described as collective managed and state aided, but no details of the aid were given. Finally, 3 schools, 1.1 per cent, were wholly supported by the collective, the teachers also being the production brigade accountant, teaching during the day and doing his accounts in the evening. (*Gengdu xiaoxue* . . . , p. 48). It is significant that it is this type of school which has had most freedom in planning its own curriculum and choosing its own teachers, but whether this is from principle or necessity is a question only time will answer.

3 THE SCHOOL SYSTEM: PART TWO

Pre-school Education

From the early days of the socialist movement thought in this area has been divided between liberating women from the burden of child care, with its emphasis on the mothers, and on the care and proper upbringing of the children themselves. As in many non-socialist countries, there have been those who have seen the provision of child-care services as necessary when the demands of the economy required mothers to work (as in many countries during World War Two), while retaining traditional ideas about the place of women in the home and the family as the best child educator during its early years. *The ABC of Communism* (section on the family) expresses these various attitudes, arguing that since 'the faculty of educating children is far more rarely encountered than the faculty of begetting them' the 'parents' claim to bring up their own children' should be 'laughed out of court' (Carr, 1969, p. 285). It goes on to speak of the millions of mothers who will be

> freed for productive work and for self-culture. They will be freed from the soul-destroying routine of housework, and from the endless round of petty duties which are involved in the education of children in their own homes. (ibid.)

Recognising the inadequacies of current institutions which acted as a deterrent to parents sending their children to them, the book urged parental involvement and control through parents' organisations.

Vera Fediaevsky, writing for a foreign audience in 1936, described how in November 1917, immediately after the Revolution, a special Department for the Protection of Motherhood and Infancy had been set up in the Commissariat of Health. Concerned at first to deal with the the appallingly high infant mortality rate, it gradually widened its scope to 'embrace the whole social and economic life of women' (Fediaevsky, pp. 3-4). Later she defined the objectives of the creches which were set up as:

> 1. To liberate woman from the care of her children while she is working or studying and to enable her to take part in the social and political life of the country. The relation of creches to the economic

plan of the country is of great importance and must ever be kept in mind.

2. To give children a communist educational foundation.

(Fediaevsky, p. 31)

Immediately after Liberation in China the aim of the expanding pre-school institutions was mainly on releasing mothers for work and there was little if any of the early Russian expression of hostility to family care for the pre-schoolers. It may be argued to what extent this was the result of poverty which made even the economically desirable provision of child care impossible. There appears to be a consistent belief in the minds of many Chinese communists, Mao amongst them, that salvation will not come through mechanical divisions of society into, e.g. children and adults. Even in emphasising class struggle there is the hope that the great majority of the former exploiting class can be won over through education and remoulding. All of which is not to say that in China pre-school education is not seen as an important means of education. It is.

Provision

Pre-school institutions can be divided into the usual creche (in Russia *yasli*; in China *tuo'er suo*) catering for the nurslings—often looked after separately in a nursing room—and babies up to 3 years, and kinder-gartens (in Russia, *detski sad*; in China, *you'er yuan*) for the age range 3 to 7 years. Provision in both the USSR and China has always been better in the cities than the countryside. Factories and big offices have often run splendidly equipped institutions, many with facilities to board the children where the parents' work made this desirable. At the other end of the scale, village creches and kindergartens have often been organ-ised temporarily, to enable the mothers to join in the harvesting. As in other spheres, it is difficult to estimate true demand for pre-school places, since demand is partly a function of supply. But only in the major cities of the USSR can provision be said to be adequate (Institute of Education 70, p. 12, 30 per cent attended the creche and 85 per cent the kindergarten in one of the Moscow estates visited).

In the USSR provision of institutions and places has grown as shown in Table 3.1.

Ministry of Education figures for 1 January 1963 showed a total of 5,600,000 children attending creche and kindergarten, while the London Institute of Education report speaks of an expected population of 12m for 1970-71 (Institute of Education 70, p. 4).

Table 3.1

	Creche	Kindergarten	Children
1917	14	285	5,000 (in two combined)
1921	668		
1924-5		1,139	60,196
1939		23,123	1,039,000 (c. 6% of age cohort)

Source: Medynski, 1952, in D.L. Meek, p. 5.

In China, Tsang points out, the nursery school grew out of the need to provide child care for working mothers, while the kindergartens were an extension of school to the 5-7 year olds from the wealthier families (Tsang, p. 165). Before 1949 there were very few of either institution. C.K. Yang gives some figures for expansion during the first decade (Table 3.2).

Table 3.2

1951	15,700 creche/kinders = 9 x pre-1949 fig.	520,000 children		in cities
1952	4,300 neighbourhood nurseries			in cities
1955	4,000 nurseries	127,000 children	manuf/mining ent.	
	687 neighbourhood nurseries	38,000	in 60 cities	
1956	6,000 nurseries		indus/commerc/ govt/edn. estab.	

Source: Yang, p. 150.

Yang cites Peking to show growth against need. Before Liberation there were 11 nurseries. In February 1951 there were 65, 47 attached to public offices. But there were 400 offices, 800 schools and 30 medium to large factories whose workers could be regarded as needing such a service (Yang, p. 150).

Pre-school Programmes

(1) In China: the most recent account and, surprisingly for such an important topic, one of the fullest, is that of US social worker, Ruth Sidel (1972). She reports on nursing rooms, 4 nurseries and 7 kindergartens which she visited in 1971. She sums up her impression of nurseries as follows:

Our impression was that the nurseries in the urban areas were more concerned with teaching ideology than those on the communes, which seemed more like co-operative baby-sitting enterprises. In both locales, however, for this young age group, personnel are recruited far more on the basis of personality characteristics than of any kind of formal training, and we had the feeling that the Chinese consider a warm motherly type with common sense the best sort of person to care for small children. This anti-expert bias is, of course, reflective of what is going on in society at large. (Sidel, p. 126)

This last comment is contradicted by the description of the Ten Mile Inn brigade kindergarten, reported in Isabel and David Crook's book. But this might apply to the older age range, where more complicated skills are required. There young women in their early twenties were selected and sent for special training to the regional capital (Crook, p. 160).

In the nursing rooms described care was purely physical. Mothers appeared to feed their babies at regular intervals. Few toys were in evidence, except at the Shanghai Machine Tool Plant (p. 97).

In the nurseries/creches there was an organised routine (see pp. 113-14, below) in which meals and rest periods were divided by periods for physical exercise, games, and also 15 minutes of political education. This last includes repeating some of Chairman Mao's directives, the *Three Old Articles* (p. 122) and stories about PLA heroes such as Lei Feng. At the Chao Yang Workers' Village nursery, Shanghai, they mentioned using the 15 minutes for 'military training', but unfortunately no details were given (p. 113).

When one of the teachers was asked about labour she replied that at this young age the only labour required of the children was such tasks as learning to dress themselves and feed themselves (pp. 114-15). In addition to this there is great stress on helping each other. R. Sidel records:

> We were told repeatedly that if a child falls down, other children are taught to help him up. The teacher does not run to him but encourages the other children to go to him and help him. . . At the beginning it is under the instruction of the teacher; but then it gets to be a habit. (p. 122)

The children are also encouraged to help each other with such difficult operations as buttoning up jackets which have the buttons at the back.

Yung Ping, nursery worker in Shanghai, expressed the view that there should be more 24 hour nurseries because 'she feels, children progress more quickly in a nursery'. They become 'accustomed to mass activity' and have 'a regular life and regular activities, get more education, exercise and training' (p. 117). This view was shared by 'all the people' with whom R. Sidel talked. Discussing the problem of separation from the parents for six days of the week, Yung Ping commented:

> The first three months the children think about their parents, as they are not used to living apart from them. Sometimes after they have been home with their parents for a day (Sunday) and a night they will come back in low spirits, but after a while they get used to living in the nursery and are not sad any more. (Sidel, pp. 117-19).

For those who continue with a full 24 hour kindergarten there is a break at 7 years when they return home to live and go to a day primary school, but according to Yung Ping this change is quickly adjusted to since contact with the parents has been maintained all along and school, after all, occupies 6 hours a day, 6 days a week (Sidel, pp. 119-20).

Already in 1960 Felix Greene reported on his visit to Bei Hai Kindergarten that the Principal had stated:

> Our children . . . when they grow up, will take their place in the country's work—they will be children trained in communist ideals. They will love labour. They will respect people. . . These principles are taught according to age levels, in conversations, songs, nursery rhymes, art and games! (Quoted in Sidel, 1972, p. 77).

In 1972 teacher Gao at the Yu Yao Road Kindergarten, Shanghai, was stressing ideological education and criticising former methods for lacking 'any class feeling or class sympathy' (Sidel, p. 77). She alleged it had all been 'education of a mother's love'.

Consistent with the more advanced age range, the timetable includes longer periods of more formal study, and also some genuine productive labour. A typical day's activities, given during a visit to the Yandun Road Kindergarten, Guangzhou in May 1975, is as follows:

0730 hrs.	Children do exercises on arrival. Have breakfast then perform free activities.
0830	Classes: 15-20 minutes duration for younger groups. 30 minutes for 5-6 year olds.

Play activities outside.
1100   Lunch.
1200   Sleep.
1500   Various activities, depending on the weather. Stories,
          dancing, both collective and individual.
1700   Children collected by parents.

From Sidel's and my own observations I have compiled the following notes on the formal lessons which take place in kindergartens in the seventies. Areas of work include language, mathematics, art, music, dancing and productive labour. Language work is mainly oral. It is expressly forbidden at the present time to teach reading, though characters which appear regularly in slogans, such as Chairman Mao, the Communist Party, worker, peasant, are taught for recognition only. Story telling is important, often from pictures pinned to the wall. In Yandun Road Kindergarten I saw pupils stand formally at the board and repeat memorised sentences. How much free expression is encouraged is not apparent. In this case the children, whose native speech was Cantonese, were using *putonghua* (Mandarin) for story telling, which may account for the memorisation. Sidel reports a lantern lecture on Norman Bethune for six year olds, after which pupils were expected to answer questions on the moral of the story. The only books which Sidel mentions, or which I saw, were *lianhuanhua* (picture-story books), suspiciously new and unfamiliar to the children. Sidel wrongly identifies them as 'kindergarten readers' (pp. 135, 196-201).

Mathematics classes observed were the normal number concept kind, complete with felt boards and cut-out animals and farm implements and crops. Six-year-olds at the kindergarten of the Jilin Automobile Plant were demonstrating equations using this apparatus with cut-out numbers to show, e.g. $5 + 4 = 9$ (May 1976). Art lessons included copying from model drawings provided by the teacher and using coloured pencils, to folding coloured paper to make aeroplanes, tractors and other objects, again from models. Singing and dancing reaches high standards, judging from the performances given to foreign visitors, and the children obviously thoroughly enjoy it. But one is left wondering about those who may never be chosen to perform. Also in all these performances the children act adult parts and are thus often the objects of fun, a role which is not necessarily consistent with the dignity of independent human beings. These are questions on which it would be interesting to have discussions with Chinese colleagues, but which conditions of the Education Tour at present seem to preclude. (The fault is not wholly on the Chinese side!)

Productive labour takes the form of assembling cardboard boxes for a local crayon or cigarette factory, sorting small items of scrap and other jobs which at the same time train in manual dexterity. Labour is of short duration, but regular, and children appear to enjoy it. Other labour performed is of the 'socially useful' variety: sweeping and tidying, or tending plants in the grounds.

One noticeable feature of Chinese kindergartens is the absence of 'mechanical toys, blocks or other building equipment, stuffed animals or live animals' which are such a feature of kindergarten in other countries (Sidel, p. 133). When I visited the Viet Nam Friendship Commune, Peking (16 September 1966) where the kindergarten was housed in a single northern-style house with a big play-yard there were the following toys on a table at the back of the room: 15 small model animals; 2 wooden brick sets, small; 2 buckets and spades; 1 model truck and 1 model boat. The room was bare of plants and had few paper decorations. At the Railway Workers' Estate in Taiyuan (4 August 1966) there was a kindergarten for 210 children, 78 of them boarders, set up in 1955. I noticed two-seater baby rockers, several 3-wheeled horses; a large model boat in which numerous children were playing, and 4 tricycles. It was clear that in both of these, and at the kindergarten at the Longjiang Tea Commune, Hangzhou (March 1967), that no use was made of play apparatus for concept formation or stimulating the imagination and that nature was studied, if at all, *in situ* rather than in the classroom. Whether Ruth Sidel is right in what she implies by the following remark is another of those interesting problematics with which our study is leaving us: 'This paucity of equipment adds to the impression that teaching and learning in China are a people-to-people phenomenon' (Sidel, p. 134).

(2) In the USSR: English readers are fortunate in having two invaluable sources on this subject, one dating from 1936 and the other one originally published in Russian in 1962 (revised 1965) and translated in 1969. These enable one to gain a very detailed grasp of Soviet ideas, and to compare them over time: Vera Fediaevsky and Patty Smith Hill, *Nursery School and Parent Education*, 1936, and Henry Chauncey (ed.), *Soviet Preschool Education* (2 vols. 1969). The first book was written expressly to give foreigners information on Soviet work, while the second, therefore much more detailed, is a manual for training Soviet pre-school personnel.

A number of themes stand out in both books: the importance of routine, of a regime; the necessity for guided play and the role of the teacher as stimulator; training a collective; the importance of work. David Rosenhan, in a preface to *Soviet Preschool Education* describes the programme as 'sensible' and adds:

> It is . . . tailored to the infant's capacities with considerable leeway given to individual differences. But its most striking hallmark is *its emphasis on precocity*: that which will be learned inevitably ought to be learned early. (Chauncey 2, p. vi, emphasis added)

It is interesting to compare the political aims mentioned by the two books. Fediaevsky mentions 'a communist educational foundation' as the aim at the beginning of her section on creches. In an appendix an educational poster is quoted, saying: 'Labour is the basis of communistic education' (Fediaevsky, p. 248). Together with this goes collectivism:

> Group consciousness and association are considered essential factors in all educational processes in the USSR and so co-operative play and work are stimulated very early in life. The teacher tries to make the *relationship between children co-operative rather than competitive.* (Fediaevsky, p. 101, emphasis in original)

Directly political education takes the form of making the children 'acquainted with the achievements of their great leaders of the working class' and celebrating 'revolutionary anniversaries and festivities' (ibid.). Early contact with the Young Pioneers is advised in order to stimulate 'a desire for good organization and a tendency to work diligently' (Fediaevsky, pp. 101, 250).

In the later book the rhetoric of class struggle and proletarian socialism is replaced by such passages as the following:

> National holidays, in which the patriotism of the Soviet people, their feelings of international solidarity, and their pride in Soviet achievements in all fields of life are all strongly reflected, are triumphantly celebrated in the kindergarten as well. The deep patriotic feelings which are experienced by adults enter into the consciousness of children through happy experiences linked with preholiday activities and with the special day itself. (Chauncey, p. 196)

Fediaevsky speaks of the all-round development of the child, 'education of the *whole* child, of the personality of the child' (p. 83), and often mentions the importance of encouraging the imagination and creative abilities of the child (e.g. p. 88). *Soviet Preschool Education* goes much further and lays down lists of virtues to be acquired:

> Such personal moral qualities as humility, modesty, truthfulness, diligence, sociability, goodwill, co-operativeness, thoughtfulness, and cheerfulness form the foundation of a child's moral being. (Chauncey, p. 141)

Speaking about celebrations of festivals it says:

> The contents of a programme and the level of the performance must correspond to the objectives of a communist education: to awaken in the children good feelings towards people, to teach them to value the beauty of labour, to engender in them a love for what is dear to the Soviet people (nature in their homeland, songs and literature), and to develop *good taste* and a sense of humour. (Chauncey, p. 198, emphasis added)

It also speaks a number of times of independent thought and the importance of creativity, but the methods advocated would often seem to be in conflict with this aim. A good example of this is on page 192. In the first paragraph it says: 'To teach children to think independently is the most important objective of the teacher.' But while admitting the difficulty of this task it returns to conformity in the next paragraph:

> Children must be taught to start and finish their work on time (that is, to work at approximately the same speed), to carry out exactly the teacher's instruction, to work on their own without disturbing others, to evaluate their own work and the work of others *from the viewpoint of the instructions given* by the teacher and the results achieved. (Chauncey, p. 192, emphasis added)

Other examples of this conflict are in the sections dealing with training in the graphic arts. Describing work with 3-year-olds, exercises which facilitate control of the pencil are advocated:

> Following instructions and demonstration of an adult, he draws a number of dots representing either snow or rain; he makes circular movements, drawing smoke rings, balls and marbles; he makes so-called unidirectional movements, either horizontals (paths, rulers)

or verticals (sticks). (Chauncey, p. 121)

The teacher not only guides the children in techniques (necessary and helpful), but also inculcates a particular style.

> Such specialists as N.P. Sakulin stress the importance of an encouraging attitude toward these drawings and attempts to find likenesses between the drawings and some real objects. It is proper for the teacher herself to help the child to see some kind of resemblance in what he has drawn. (Chauncey, p. 121)

This question is also treated in Miriam Morton's *The Arts and the Soviet Child* (e.g. pp. 15-6). She argues that

> The emphasis, the frequent overemphasis, on realism has its roots in Russian social history, tradition, and national temperament, as well as in Soviet-socialist doctrine. (Morton, p. xix)

Whatever the truth of this is, there is little doubt of the contradiction between teacher guidance and pupil initiative, nor the fact that both are necessary. The problem for education is to find the balance.

Especially for the creche-age infant, the importance of a strict regime is emphasised in similar terms in both books. In 1936 Fediaevsky wrote:

> The strict observation of the daily routine has two chief purposes in view; in improvement of children's physical health and the establishment of right habits of health and general conduct. (Fediaevsky, p. 48)

Soviet Preschool Education states:

> Strict adherence to a schedule is a necessary condition for ensuring the proper growth and development of infants. If the life of children is regulated by a fixed schedule, if every day they eat, sleep and are kept awake at definite hours of the day, this will help to raise the children to be healthy and psychologically well balanced. (Chauncey, p. 13)

Fediaevsky follows the above sentence with:

> Dinner and breakfast periods are looked upon, not only as means of

meeting nutritional requirements, but as genuine 'learning situations'. Here children have opportunities for acquiring hygienic and cultural habits, such as learning to wash their hands before meals. Also habits of social service are acquired through helping each other. Customs of courtesy and politeness are emphasized. (Fediaevsky, p. 48)

Sleep sessions are also to be regarded as 'learning situations for self help and *social* help' (pp. 48-9, emphasis added). Efforts are made to carry these routines into the home.

It is important that the schedule and diet established at the kindergarten be also observed at home. To that aim, the nurse confers with the parents, makes clear to them the importance of a unified schedule for both home and school. (Chauncey, p. 15).

And again, speaking of the regime for the 3-year-old:

The parents must be acquainted with the schedule set up for the group, and they must be counseled as to the best means of co-ordinating the home and school life of their child. (Chauncey, p. 79).

Recommendations for integrating the individual in the group, developing collective habits are particularly significant. At the same time these are based on strict *mutual* respect between adult and child. In *Soviet Preschool Education* there are some striking passages in this connection. For example:

While washing the children, the adults talk to them and encourage their actions. . . Many small children do not like to have someone wash their face; therefore this must be done gently and carefully with appropriate remarks made to encourage the child. (Chauncey, p. 12)

Forcing a child to eat if he refuses to do so is useless and may even bring about aversion to food. (Chauncey, p. 17)

The child's restlessness must be taken into account, as well as their spontaneity and ability to imitate. It does happen that these traits are mistaken by the teacher for naughtiness. For example, during speech exercises, Dima (2 yrs 2 mths) picks up a marble which he just rolled and announces in a loud voice, 'I have a marble'. Immediately Lara raises her work and says, 'I have a drum'. These examples are followed by Kolya, Sasha, and so forth. The teacher is displeased and reprimands the children because they disturb the quiet atmosphere. However, the teacher in this case is quite wrong. (Chauncey, p. 108)

A comfortable routine helps to control the child's behaviour, to stabilize his nervous system, and to regularize his activity. . . It is useless to keep the children waiting in line or for their turn, and in fact it can be harmful. (Chauncey, p. 135)

To readers weighed down by Russian (and Chinese) love of precept the *Soviet Preschool Education*'s acknowledgement that 'it is impossible to develop morality through words, lectures, and instructions alone' comes like a breath of fresh air. It goes on:

Kind feelings and proper moral conduct result from training and a very sincere example. Teachers must think ahead and plan good deeds for the group as a whole and for each child . . . (Chauncey, p. 142)

Activities suggested range from comforting a sick fellow-pupil, defending someone who is weak, to the giving of a present 'so as to give pleasure to someone' (ibid.).

Methods of encouraging collective feelings and activities include 'the wholesome "give and take" in daily living with other children' (Fediaevsky, p. 98), playing games 'side by side' at an age when 'they do not always share a single conception of the intent or contents of the game' (Chauncey, p. 95), and the use of language which stresses sharing (Bronfenbrenner in Chauncey, p. 4, where a teacher says: 'Children, here is our dolly. Vanya you give our dolly to Katya, Katya, pass it to Marusya: now Marusya and Petya swing our dolly together'). Another activity encouraged for the same purpose is watching older children at play (Chauncey, p. 124, Fediaevsky, p. 88). This is especially important for the younger groups. As the children get older more stress is placed on work as a social activity. Fediaevsky writes:

Step by step the child is led from self-help to help in and for his group. He learns to button the clothes of his younger playmate; he wipes off the table; carries the cups and spoons to the sideboard. Through these social activities he feels himself a member of the group. (Fediaevsky, p. 101)

Outlining the aims of 'labour education' Fediaevsky stresses that work should be suitable for the children's physical and mental development and should be 'work, the usefulness of which they understand'. She adds such activities as washing toys and tools, watering flowers, feeding pets and clearing paths through the snow (Fediaevsky, pp. 96-7). Observation of adult work is also encouraged (Fediaevsky, pp. 95, 100). *Soviet Pre-school Education* repeats the stress on 'work training which is interesting in nature and appropriate to the children's stage of development' (Chauncey, p. 131). It gives such examples as making toys and simple objects for use in the kindergarten, washing doll's clothing and other objects, and caring for plants and animals.

It is in the use of toys and equipment for play that the USSR would appear to be ahead of China, and one wonders why this long-stressed facet of child education was not copied more widely in the latter during the period of Soviet influence in the fifties. Mentioned throughout, Fediaevsky has two special chapters devoted to the subject (pp. 125-79). Special equipment begins with the furniture of the creche, where, e.g., the playpens are raised off the floor on legs to bring about eye-level interaction with adults (Chauncey, p. 4) and reduce fatigue through bending on the part of the teacher (Fediaevsky, p. 135). Ladders and slide, and other 'gymnasium apparatus' is provided indoors and out, not only for muscular development, but also 'for the development of the child's personality and character traits'. It 'stimulates the child's bold, daring, adventurous, self-reliant, and resourceful activities' (Fediaevsky, p. 138). Read in the 1970s this does not sound very new, but when the USSR began widespread experiments on these lines in the twenties and thirties it was among the pioneers in the field. Materials which are now found in every baby-goods and toy-shop throughout the world were still unfamiliar to the average Russian mother in the thirties, and remain so to millions in China today, if not in their pure play forms, then certainly as serious educational materials. Fediaevsky wrote:

> Blocks and other building materials contribute to the development of children's creative capacities through the opportunity which they offer for invention, originality, ingenuity and habits of industry. They lend themselves to the children's native constructive needs and interests.
>
> Dolls and toy animals are used to supplement the blocks and thus enrich children's dramatic play. They appeal to their interest in animals and people's relation to animals.
>
> Coloured collapsible toys, multi-coloured beads, mosaic stones or

cardboard tiles and diminutive musical instruments are selected for use in nursery institutions to foster sensory and motor development.

Builder-boards develop exactness in handling, sharpness of vision, quickness of the hand and eye co-ordination and sagacity and interest in techniques and skills. (Fediaevsky, p. 87)

In *Soviet Preschool Education* the language of modern psychology is added, the same toys being advised for the development of 'concept formation'. At the same time the importance of natural materials like sand and water are discussed (Chauncey, pp. 104-7).

Teachers

Concepts of the Teacher

For something like two and a half thousand years the concept of teacher and scholar have been closely linked in China. For much of this time school teachers were drawn from the same pool as the ruling scholar-bureaucrats and rehearsed the same moral-political themes on which they had been reared. At the same time, setting an example of and often sermonising on, the Confucian ethic was part of the duty of the non-teaching official. In the fourth century BC Mencius expressed the ideal:

> There are three things in which the Superior Man delights, and to be a sovereign of the empire is not one of them. That his parents are both living and that his brothers are upright, is one delight. That he can look up to heaven with a clear conscience, and look out upon men without shame, is his second delight. That he can obtain the young men of finest talent in the empire and educate them, is his third delight. (*Mencius*, 7.1.20, quoted in Galt, p. 98)

Mao Ze-dong expressed the same attitude in his last interview with Edgar Snow, when he said that it was as a teacher that he hoped to be remembered (*Life*, LXX, No. 16, 30 April 1971). With the rise of European-type schooling in the late nineteenth century other concepts of the teacher developed.

In Russia the concept of the teacher was first shaped by the Christian Church. Then with Peter and especially Catherine II there began the state system of schools in which the modern secular teacher took shape. By the beginning of the nineteenth century, 'teaching was now recognized as a profession which accorded special, even though flexible, civil rank to a young man or woman' (Johnson, p. 72). With the possibility for suitably qualified gymnasium teachers to become instructors in the universities (Johnson, p. 73) the status distinction between *prepodav-atel'* (university-gymnasium teacher) and *uchitel'* (primary school teacher), a distinction which persists until today, hardened. The well-known nineteenth-century educationist, K.D. Ushinskii rubbed home the difference when he advocated a different training for primary school teachers from that given to teachers of higher grades.

> He thinks that too much study for the former can actually be harmful, in that it might lead to radical ideas concerning politics, morals, or religion which would be unbecoming in a village teacher. (Johnson, p. 244, cf. B. King, 1937, p. 205)

A teacher anywhere is inevitably more visible than most other roles. Since he is expected to be a model for his students it is not surprising to find continual reference to both his on-duty and off-duty behaviour. In 1624 the Rules of the School of the Lutsk Brotherhood at Kiev began:

> The 'Didaskalos', or teacher, of this school must be devout, judicious, humble, gentle, continent, not a drunkard, nor a fornicator, nor a usurer; not irascible, envious, ridiculous, nor foul-mouthed; not a sorcerer, nor a liar; not a party to heresy, but a promoter of piety, at all times conducting himself as a model of religious behaviour. For the pupils will be imbued with the same virtues as their teacher. (Johnson, p. 11)

In the nineteenth century Ushinskii made a similar point:

> it is only fair to require of the public school teacher . . . that his life not only offer no grounds for scandal, not only subvert respect for him on the part of parents and children, but, on the contrary, that [his life].serve as an example to them as well as to others, and not contradict his school precepts. Only under such conditions can he have an ethical influence on the children, and his school work be truly effective. (Johnson, p. 244)

In the Soviet period M.I. Kalinin, who referred to teachers as 'engineers of the human soul' (Kalinin, p. 93), often spoke on this theme in his addresses to teachers. At a conference in December 1938 he said:

> Of course, a teacher's main work is to teach his particular subject,

but apart from everything else he is copied by his pupils. That is why the teacher's world outlook, his conduct, his life, his approach to each phenomenon, affect all his pupils in one way or another. . . It can be safely said that if a teacher enjoys great authority, some people will bear traces of his influence throughout their lives. (Kalinin, p. 76)

In post-revolutionary Russia and China the new requirement for teachers to exemplify the communist way of life both in and out of class added new strains to an already exacting career.

Quotation from two documents of the last decade will round out the official concept of the teacher, in each case specifically the full-time secondary school teacher. First, the Temporary Work Regulations, published by the Chinese Ministry of Education in 1963 (translated by Susan Shirk, *China Quarterly* 55, 1973):

Since teachers bear the glorious responsibility of rearing a new generation of students for our fatherland, they must continuously improve their own political, cultural, and professional level and strive to become both red and expert. (p. 529.4)

The fundamental task of teachers is to teach the students well. Teachers should warmly love the cause of education and strive to fulfill their educational tasks. The basic requirements for teachers are:

Teach good lessons. Study the teaching material, improve teaching methods, and raise the quality of teaching to a high level. Take loving care of the students. Show warm concern for the students, patiently educate them, put strict demands on them, guide and help them develop their intellectual and physical capacities, and raise their ideological consciousness. Serve as models. In thought and behaviour try to become examples for the students. Study assiduously. Be concerned about politics, and study Marxism-Leninism and the works of Mao Ze-dong. Study very hard in one's profession, and strive to be expert in the specialised knowledge of one's subject. Continuously raise one's political, cultural, and professional level. (pp. 537-8. 35)

The second document is the Regulations of the Secondary General Education School adopted by the USSR Council of Ministers in

September 1970:

32. The leading place in the school belongs to the teacher. He performs the honorable and important governmental task of providing instruction and communist upbringing for the young generation.
35. The teacher's basic duties are:
to provide pupils with a firm knowledge of the foundations of science, to instil in them a communist world view, and to develop the cognitive interests and abilities of schoolchildren;
to imbue pupils with the spirit of communist morality;
to be concerned with protecting the health of pupils, to study their individual characteristics and living conditions;
to maintain ties with parents or parent substitutes and with the community; to disseminate pedagogical information;
to systematically improve his ideological-theoretical level and pedagogical qualifications.
The teacher is responsible for the quality of instruction of pupils, for the level of their knowledge and their upbringing.
The teacher is called upon to set an example in his work, in his daily life, in his conduct, and in his observance of the rules of socialist life in the community. (*Soviet Education*, XIII, 3-4, 1971, pp. 110-11)

In the Chinese document work with parents is treated in paragraphs 22 and 23. Home visiting is a requirement for the class teacher in both countries. (This is discussed by Marie Sieh, p. 189, and described fictionally by F. Vigdorova, e.g. pp. 99-108.)

Teacher Style

While there have been notable exceptions, it is a fair generalisation to say that the typical teaching style has been authoritarian and formal. The teacher stands at the front of the class and explains the textbook, brings pupils to the black-board to answer questions, assigns reading and hears memorised passages. The teacher possesses the knowledge which his students are to acquire. Other models in which learning has been conceived as a more mutual process have been put forward by Tolstoi, Shatskii, John Dewey and others. Dewey was not only known in both countries at second hand through his writings, but himself visited them. His lectures in China, where he spent from May 1919 to July 1921, have just been translated back from Chinese to English (Clopton and Ou, 1973). As noted elsewhere, attempts to develop new styles in the USSR were abandoned in the thirties because of the CPSU's concept of leadership, the chronic shortage of trained teachers, and the physical shortages which made individualised learning methods and 'learning by doing' almost impossible. Dewey was attacked in the USSR, and later in China, more because he was an American liberal than because of his particular educational ideas, but in the process the latter were also attacked.

In the past decade there has been a renewed stress on creative methods in teaching in the USSR, but this has not yet affected the fundamental professional style of the teachers, a style which has come under attack in China during and since the Cultural Revolution of 1966-9. The impetus for the attack came from Mao Ze-dong, whose brief utterances on the subject were copied on to *dazibao* and plastered over the walls of college campuses throughout China and have reached the rest of the world through Red Guard materials brought out of China. Part of a general attack on what Mao and his supporters see as the bureaucratic style, criticisms are based on the failure of the previous 17 years to provide sufficient trained teachers, and especially to heal the urban-rural gap. Rather the contrary: the schools were seen as exacerbating it, and teachers were models for the urban white-collar worker, when what Mao wanted was a model of the 'well-educated worker imbued with socialist consciousness', willing and able to live in the rural areas and contribute to their development.

It is important not to mistake Mao Ze-dong's strictures on bureaucracy and 'bourgeois experts' as attacks on expertise. Quite the contrary. Expertise is an essential quality to be nurtured, but always to be combined with redness. By redness is meant concern for and understanding of the 'why' and 'for whose benefit' questions which professionals wrapped up in problems of techniques so often ignore. W. Brugger put the distinction as follows:

> What is to be criticised is not expertise per se but *professionalism*. I define a professional here as not only someone who knows his job and is committed to its values but a person who also evaluates the *rest of society* according to the values of his job. The professional defines a layman in pejorative terms as one who lacks those values to which he the professional is committed. What is promoted according to current Chinese thinking is not esprit de corps but service to the community. (Brugger, 1973, p. 27)

Mao Ze-dong's concept of teacher style has to be seen in the context of his view of education as problem-solving. The teacher's job is to help the student to solve problems himself. Talking to his nephew Mao Yuan-xin in 1964, Mao Ze-dong advocated the distribution of lecture notes and less talk:

> The question of teaching reform is mainly a question of teaching staff. The teachers are of limited competence and they can do nothing without their notes. Why can't they give you the notes and study problems *together with you?* When students in higher classes ask questions, the teachers can answer 50% of them, but are ignorant of the others, and have to discuss them with the students. This is not bad. One should not put on airs to frighten people. (*CB*, 888, p. 14, emphasis added)

Speaking to a delegation of educators from Nepal in the same year Mao commented:

> in order to be a teacher, one should first be a pupil. No teacher is not a pupil first. Furthermore, after becoming a teacher, one also must learn from the masses in order to understand the conditions of his own pupils. (*CB*, 888, p. 15)

At the Hangzhou Conference in 1965 Mao added another thought:

> If a university course takes five years to complete, one should work at the lower levels for three years. Members of the faculty should also go along, working and teaching at the same time. Isn't it possible to teach philosophy, literature, or history at the lower level? Must they teach in tall, modern buildings? (*CB*, 891, p. 53)

The problem of teacher authority, whether 'putting on airs to frighten people', or simply being stiff and formal through fear of losing control, also involves student attitudes to their work and in many of the reports during and since the Cultural Revolution this has been recognised. In 1967 press comments on the reluctance of teachers to face classes which had humiliated them, while urging teachers to 'unite with their students' and 'discard self interest', at the same time call on the students to 'respect their teachers' and 'actively help them, develop their achievements' and 'improve their work' (*SCMP*, 4063, Nov. 1967). In the campaign sparked off by the publication of 12-year-old Huang Shuai's letter, first in the *Peking Daily*, and then the *People's Daily* in December 1973, criticisms of authoritarian behaviour of the teachers was coupled with discussions by staff and students of various schools on 'what is a good pupil?' Answers were predetermined by the widespread slogan: 'study well and make progress every day'. The descriptions given (e.g. *China Reconstructs*, August 1974) must be judged against the highly authoritarian society of a still very traditional China, and not read as if they applied to schools and teachers as known in the West European and North American countries. In that context the following extracts are the more remarkable. The first describes Huang Shuai's teacher in the Peking suburban primary school, following her criticisms:

> When the new school year began Ji Hong-ru faced a new class of 5th-graders. Instead of tersely announcing his disciplinary rules as he used to, he asked the children to talk it over and work out their own rules. In class he tried to get them to think independently and to give their own views on the content of the lesson. (*China Reconstructs*, August 1974, p. 5)

The other reveals teacher fears and the hoped-for outcome:

> At first one teacher who could not understand why the newspapers published Huang Shuai's letters said: 'Well, Huang Shuai's won this round.' But what happened afterwards changed his mind. 'Huang Shuai won all right', he said, 'but so have the teachers. We teachers and pupils are comrades-in-arms in the same trench fighting together to sweep away the remnant influence of the revisionist line in education. We won this round together. And we'll face future battles together, too.' (ibid.)

Another aspect of the Cultural Revolution teaching reform which could have perhaps even greater significance if it were persisted with is the increased involvement of non-teachers in the schools. Since 1949 the shortage of suitably qualified teachers has forced the Chinese government to encourage large numbers of Party officials, skilled technicians, workers and peasants to engage in part-time teaching. But during the Cultural Revolution and since the emphasis has begun to change into seeing this as virtue rather than necessity. One of the first references was in the report of the Shanghai Institute of Mechanical Engineering which recommended that skilled workers should become part-time teachers, while the full-time teachers should mainly play a co-ordinating role between the factory schools and the FTD colleges (*Peking Review* 37, 1968, p. 17). In August of the following year an investigation report of the Peking Electrical Engineering School also recommended that skilled workers should become part-time teachers. But they added that full-time teachers should institute a '3-step rotation system' whereby while one group was teaching another would combine study with working in a factory to gain further experience, and a third group would go to the rural areas and PLA units for re-education (SWB, 3150,B, p. 5). This idea received considerable publicity but was probably doomed as a general principle by teacher shortages and by the opposition of more conservative elements among both teachers and factory management.

Another potentially significant outcome of the Cultural Revolution in China has been the establishment of a corps of 'worker-teachers' in the FTD general schools. Workers are seconded to a school where many teach the natural sciences and technical subjects. At present details of how long they remain in teaching and how many are involved are not revealed and the whole programme is obviously experimental. (Seybolt, pp. 155-65, has an article on the matter from Jiangsu Province. In a discussion with representatives of provincial education authorities in Shenyang and Tianjin in 1976 no information on worker-teachers was volunteered and time did not allow questioning on the matter.)

In accordance with the general injunction to link education with productive labour in China, teachers are being called on to take a regular part in production of various kinds. This is in marked contrast to the emphasis of the 1963 Temporary Work Regulations (Shirk, p. 539, sec. 40). Another way in which an attempt is being made to bring teachers closer to people in other walks of life is the introduction of payment in kind, as a share of the harvest. This was brought in for rural teachers in 1968-9, bringing them in line with other commune members (*RMRB*, 6 February 1969 and 6 January 1969).

Supply and Conditions

The problem of the supply of teachers involves not only numbers in relation to that of children to be taught, but also that elusive factor, quality. Recent developments in China have introduced new dimensions to this. Conventionally, for want of a more genuine measure, it has been stated in terms of length of training, the type of training institution and, sometimes, the length of teaching service. The fallacies involved in such measures appear to be unavoidable, though development of teacher and school collectives along lines begun in China, and to some extent earlier in the USSR, may make the question redundant through an ongoing attention to quality.

In the USSR pupil-teacher ratios fell from 34.4 in 1914 to 19.0 in 1966-7 overall, while the ratio for tertiary institutions in the latter year was 17.0 (calculated from figures given in the *Pedagogicheskaya Ent-siklopediya*, vol. 4, p. 67; see also deWitt, 1955; the *International Yearbook of Education*, 1969, and *Science Policy in the USSR*, pp. 176-7). In China comparable figures are available for 1948 and 1965. These show changes in the pupil-teacher ratio from 30.3 to 50.0 for primary schools, 13.0 to 38.0 for secondary schools, and 7.7 to 4.8 for tertiary schools. The worsening ratios in primary and secondary schools are due to the enormous increase in student numbers for these grades in a period too short to train sufficient teachers (for data see *Ten Great Years*; Richman, p. 164; Orleans in EPMC, p. 511).

In both countries the greatest difficulty is to obtain teachers for the rural areas. In 1970 the Minister of Education for the Russian SFSR announced that in the previous five years more than 120,000 tertiary graduates had been sent to teach there, bringing the number of tertiary qualified teachers of the 5-10th grades to about two thirds of the total. In future, he added, about 90 per cent of teachers graduating would go to the rural areas (*CDSP*, 23, 3, p. 21). The problem will remain, however, how to keep them there. For China, at a much earlier stage of development, the problem of finding rural teachers is also very difficult and it is not yet a question of tertiary graduates for the most part. No data are available, but newspaper articles have frequently described how members of the 'educated youth', that is, the secondary school graduates sent down to the rural areas, have been persuaded to become primary school teachers in the communes.

Turning to conditions of work, one must beware of the difference between those laid down by statute and the real situation, which is often very different. Work norms are in both countries very reasonable in theory, but the shortage of educated people, especially in the rural areas, and the low wages both encourage the performance of extra work. In the USSR this multiple job-holding is widespread among the better qualified, and is known as *sovmestitel'stvo*. Elaborate rules and regulations exist in an attempt to regulate it (Korol, pp. 297-300). Less is known about this practice in China, and references to 'other work that teachers do in addition to teaching' (1963 Temporary Work Regulations, section 37) do not necessarily refer to paid employment.

In the USSR work norms take account of the grade and subject, with lower contact teaching for teachers of secondary subjects which require written work to be marked. In the thirties B. King notes that primary teachers were expected to teach 96 hours a month compared with only 48 hours a month for secondary teachers (King, p. 207). More recently the norm has been given as 4 hours a day or 24 hours a week for teachers of grades 1-4 and 3 hours a day or 18 hours a week for teachers of grades 5-11 (*Ped. Enc.* 2, p. 95; cf. Grant, pp. 143-4). While similar norms probably exist for Chinese teachers I have been unable to trace them. Rather, one comes across complaints of overwork and pleas for sufficient time for academic work, as compared with political and other duties (Chen, p. 32). The 1963 Temporary Work Regulations call for 'having at least five-sixths of their working-time for professional work', confining 'political study and Party, League, and Union meetings and social activities' to the other sixth (Shirk, pp. 538-9).

While school students have vacations of two weeks duration during winter and spring and a further three months in the summer in the USSR, teachers officially only receive 48 working days paid holiday (King, 1937, pp. 220-21 and 311; *Ped. Enc.* 3, p. 237; Section II.8, 1970 Secondary School Regulations, *Sov. Ed.* p. 103). During the remainder of the time Soviet teachers are expected to prepare lessons, attend conferences and do other work in and around the school. In China the 1963 Work Regulations specifically state that

> Except for important activities uniformly laid down by the school, both recreation and vacation time should be the concern of the teachers themselves. (Shirk, p. 539)

Han Ying-lin made the same point to Jan Myrdal during an interview in the autumn of 1962:

> The teachers [of the Liu Lin Primary School] are quite free during the holidays. They can go home if they wish [since some come from outside the village], they can go away somewhere, they can do further study or anything else they like. (Myrdal, p. 373, additions in parenthesis)

Salaries in the USSR have, since the thirties, included differentials for qualifications and grade of teaching. B. King comments: 'This is to encourage teachers to improve their qualifications and their work' (1937, p. 208). In addition to a basic wage for the number of hours worked, teachers are paid for leading circles after school, being a class teacher, or for other duties involving extra time. In the thirties salary increases were given for every five years service after the first five years, amounting to 72r/year for those with university or special training, and 60r/year for other teachers (King, 1937, p. 207). Salaries in 1935 were:

Primary teacher (Moscow), 171 r/mth
(provinces), 133 r/mth
Secondary teacher (Moscow), 307 r/mth
(provinces),   261 r/mth

('average salary', King, 1937, p. 208). Teachers received a pension of
50 per cent of the average of their monthly salary for the last year of
service if they had given 25 years service, but this must not exceed 150 r
(ibid.) Table 3.3 shows the order of wages in the 1960s.

Table 3.3

Level of work	Period of service (years)			
	To 5	5-10	10-25	Over 25
Tertiary	80	90	100	137
Teachers' Institute or equivalent	72	77	83	128
Secondary special	67	72	77	111
General secondary	60	65	72	111

Source: Ped. Enc. 2, p. 95.

Comparisons must be made with the wages of other workers at the
same period, and between different types of teachers. Inflation and
revaluation of the ruble makes comparison between the thirties and
sixties more complex than can be attempted here, nor is it germane to
the argument of this book. The planned average wage for large-scale
industry was to be 66.90r in 1927-8 and 98.28r in 1932-3, but wages in
'census industry' reached 123r in 1932 (Nove, 1969/70, p. 199). Before
the reform of October 1931, a foreman of the metallurgical industry
received 225-230r/month whereas a highly skilled worker under him
might be earning 300r (Webbs, p. 714). (For a discussion of prices,
taxes and purchasing power at that time see Nove, 1969/70, pp. 201-
8.) Wages for the sixties are given in Lane, who cites an average figure
of 113r for manual and non-manual workers in 1968. (Lane, pp. 398-
404 includes a useful summary of policy on differentials. Details
of teachers wages in 1971 are given in *Sov. Ed.* 71.13.7, p. 42.)

   B. King comments that pay was a 'serious grievance. It was', she
went on, 'very low, and in the early years was rarely, if ever, paid regularly' (1937, p. 206). China did rather better during the early years of
its revolution, ending a long period when conditions resembled those
which B. King describes. Immediately on liberation wages were stabilised

in terms of basic grain. Following a 32.8 per cent increase for primary
teachers, providing a minimum of about 20 ¥/month in 1956 a scale
depending on qualifications was introduced (Table 3.4).

Table 3.4

Qualification	Minimum	Maximum
	yuan/month	
3 years junior teachers' training school or equivalent	20	26
2 years senior teachers' training school or senior high school	24	31
Graduate of 2-year college course	34	44
Graduate of 4-year college or institute course	40	52

Source: Chen, p. 33, quoted in Price, 1970, p. 224.

During and since the Cultural Revolution there has been a move to pay
rural teachers in kind, similarly to other commune members, with state
subsidies where this would involve a loss of earnings. By contrast, university teachers, especially those eminent before 1949, continue to receive
high salaries, but it is believed that these will die with the death of this
generation. Wages range from 50-90 ¥/month for an assistant (*zhu-jiao*)
to 260-380 ¥/month for a professor (*jiaoshou*) (Cheng, pp. 151-2).

In addition to the hierarchy of training, position and salary Soviet
teachers are also awarded medals (of K.D. Ushinskii and A.S. Makarenko,
Ped. Enc. 4, p. 443), or the special title of *Otlichnik narodnovo pros-
veshchenia* (Excellent worker in people's education, ibid., and 3, p. 235
cf. Grant, pp. 149-50). According to Medynsky, over 100,000 Soviet
teachers had been so decorated by 1950 (Medynsky, p. 47). In China
any tendency to set up a similar system has given way to local appraisal
of teachers qualities, such as is described for Yangyi Commune Secondary
School by the Crooks. There, in 1960, teachers were rated for 'selfless
communist character, good work style, good attitudes to manual labour,
good ideology, concern for the masses' (Crooks, p. 176). Rating was
performed monthly or fortnightly 'in the school', but the authors do
not make clear by whom or how it was done. At the Guangdong Teacher's College in 1971 visitors were told that they aimed to be 'four-good
companies and five-good soldiers' (private communication). Though
not specified the criteria were presumably similar to those described by
Dai Xiao-ai. Borrowed from a similar movement in the army the four

were: good in politics, studies, relations with classmates, and in labour; while the five were: good in politics, study, labour, daily life and personal cleanliness (Bennett and Montaperto, p. 240).

The heavy work programme which both Russian and Chinese teachers have borne in addition to normal teaching duties was described in the thirties by B. King.

> Conscientious Soviet teachers at present have very little leisure. Their free time is not given up only to self-improvement. They are expected to interest themselves in the children's out-of-school activities. They have to take an active part in the political and social life surrounding them. This is particularly the case in the village, where the teacher is the starting-point and centre of all the cultural activities. They are often called upon to volunteer to teach the illiterate or semi-literate in factory or farm. Usually these extra services are paid for, but sometimes they are regarded as the social obligation of the teacher, and are unpaid. The teachers have to help to initiate libraries, reading-rooms and Red Corners for the adult population. Once a month the class teacher is expected to visit the homes of the younger pupils. . .
> (B. King, 1937, pp. 219-20)

Section 38 of the 1963 Temporary Work Regulations, in its prohibition of 'drawing teachers into participation in work outside school' without permission from the educational administrative department, and plea for 'stabiliz(ation) (of) teachers work' is one admission of the problem. Chen gives other examples, though he fails to allow for the element of exaggeration which is often present in complaints of this kind (Cheng, *TTCC*, p. 32).

With the general increase in educational levels, the development of library and other cultural facilities, pressure of outside duties in the USSR has probably diminished over the years, and teachers have defined their role in more specialised terms. In China there has been a continuing conflict of the two concepts, with the wider one, associated with the Mao proletarian line in the recent Cultural Revolution, currently winning the day. Integration with the workers and peasants, combining teaching with labour and practising 4 or sometimes 5 togethers (studying, fighting, working, labouring and carrying out recreational activities together, as one Peking secondary school listed them in 1967, cf. *SCMP*, 4063) are the slogans of this type of teacher. One should not forget that the conflict has not been always a peaceful one. During the anti-Rightists movement in 1957-8 and particularly during the Cultural Revolution

many teachers were humiliated, and in a few extreme cases driven to
suicide by attempts to 'remould' their *sixiang* (thought). Hinton, in his
account of the struggles at Qinghua University, gives some examples of
the depths to which the Red Guard struggles descended (pp. 199 and
221). More typical of what teachers suffered is the account by Dai Xiao-
ai:

> The struggle was always very intense. We forced the teachers to wear
> caps and collars which stated things like 'I am a monster'. Each class
> confronted and reviled them in turn with slogans, accusations, and
> injunctions to reform their ways. We made them clean out the toilets,
> smeared them with black paint, and organized 'control monster teams'
> to see that it was done properly. We would charge them with specific
> mistakes and not relent until they admitted they were true. It took
> nearly a week of constant struggle to make the man admit he had
> said 'Mao was wrong' in a conversation with one of his fellow teachers.
> They had little rest and were forced to sleep apart from their fellow
> teachers. We would join into informal groups, raid their quarters, and
> begin to work on them again. They could not escape us. (Bennett and
> Montaperto, p. 41, referring to treatment of two teachers, selected by
> the Party leadership for struggle in the 'White Terror' part of the
> movement)

It is the more remarkable that some reports testify to an easier relation
between teacher and student in the post-Cultural Revolution period.
(Andrew Watson, *China Now* 16, 1971, p. 6. My own discussions with
teachers and others on subsequent visits to China suggest conditions are
both better and worse.)

Teachers and the Communist Party

One of the most significant things which divides teachers in the USSR
and China is probably membership of the Communist Party. Especially
perhaps in China, where in 1958 and again since the Cultural Revolution,
the leadership role of the Party group within each school has been
affirmed, non-Party teachers have been confirmed as the more power-
less. It remains to be seen whether the more open practice of the mass
line proclaimed during the Cultural Revolution will become the rule,
and whether this will compensate for the inegalitarian nature of the
Party/non-Party division.

The exact structure and functioning of Party organs concerned with
education in both the USSR and China remains uncertain. The 1969

OECD report on *Science Policy in the USSR* writes that 'sections for Science and Culture or Science and Educational Establishments *probably exist* in all Republican and Regional Party Committees' (p. 50, section 53, emphasis added). Certainly there is a Department for Science and Establishments of Higher Education of the Central Committee. The Agitation and Propaganda Department of the same body has also certainly played an important part, but most of the direct leadership of teachers has come through the general Party committees. In the larger schools and institutions Party organisations of teachers and other Party members (workers or students) have been the final link (see *Science Policy* . . . , p. 308 for chart showing Party control of tertiary schools; Fraser, pp. 559-60 gives the 1958 CC/SC directive re. Party control in China). One view of such a school Party organisation is given by Dai Xiao-Ai:

> It is meaningless to talk of any relationship between students and the Party. We had no relations with the Party. We all thought of it as a powerful but secret organization. I knew that certain teachers were Party members but I had no idea of what went on in meetings or how the Party worked. (Bennett and Montaperto, p. 21)

Such a view would not be surprising for an ordinary student, but Dai was a highly self-conscious student leader, preparing himself for future leadership, and almost certainly, Party membership. The views of non-Party teachers were openly expressed during the 100 flowers (1956-7) period and certainly reflect the view of the older professionally-minded teachers (MacFarquhar, *HF*, pp. 100ff). Dai confirms the resentments expressed:

> Party members, of course, had great prestige throughout the school. In fact, this led to friction among the teachers. Many teachers who had had good training and experience but who were not Party members were not promoted, while Party members were. The teachers who were not Party members resented this. When these tensions came out during the Cultural Revolution, I was amazed that they were so deep. (Bennett and Montaperto, p. 21)

One wonders whether a system of rotation of posts, not involving 'promotion' would not avoid these difficulties—difficulties which in one form or another seem to be universal. But with power held by the self-chosen few conflict would seem to be inherent, however benevolent the guardians.

It is not easy to discover what proportion of teachers are Party members. Apart from obvious questions of regional differences, data is given in terms of Party composition, not that of different trades and professions. Thus the Soviet Party census of January 1927 revealed that 67,001 members worked in educational establishments, approximately 17 per cent of the total of 1,147,074 members (Carr, 1971, p. 101). In 1973, 2,042,577, or 13.8 per cent of the members worked in health, education, science or the arts. For the more recent period data exists, showing that by 1968 some 25 per cent of teachers had become Party members (Matthews, p. 220, quoting *Kommunist* 16, 1969, p. 17). In tertiary education in the USSR 34.4 per cent of all teachers were Party members in 1947, but this figure disguised wide discrepancies between fields of study. 91.5 per cent of teachers of the socio-political and philosophical subjects were members, compared with 26.9 per cent for physics and mathematics, and 31.5 per cent for technology (Korol, p. 292).

In China the Party has been conscious of the value of recruiting teachers, especially in the villages, since long before liberation (Townsend, p. 45, referring to a resolution of July 1926 on the peasant movement). On the other hand there have been complaints that 'admission to the Party is more difficult than entering heaven' (Jiangxi Ribao, 24 June 1956, quoted in Chen, p. 38). In 1960 a report in the *Renmin Ribao* from Shanxi said that 15 per cent of all primary and secondary teachers in the province were Party members and that there were Party branches in all secondary schools, including teacher training ones, and also in some primary schools. (SCMP. 2329, RMRB. 22 August 1960). Earlier, in 1956, the *Renmin Shouci* admitted that only 170,000 of the 220,000 *xiang* had a Party organisation (Schurmann, p. 131). At the Yangyi Secondary school described by the Crooks there was a policy of recruiting teachers already Party members, and in July 1960 membership, including an unspecified number of students, was 13 in a school of 726 students and 53 teachers (Crooks, pp. 176 and 172). At the Liu Lin primary school described by Myrdal the Headmaster, the teacher in charge of the Pioneers, and the Deputy Head were Party members, a total of 3 out of 9.

Teacher Training

In both the USSR and China teachers have throughout been trained in schools both at the secondary and tertiary levels, the former for primary teachers and the latter for secondary teachers. In the thirties the former were known as technicums. They took students of 15-16 years and trained them for three years (King, 1937, p. 215). Otherwise Soviet teachers were and are trained in special Pedagogical Institutes, or in the ordinary universities (Deineko, pp. 48-54; Grant, 1964, pp. 132-9 and 1969, pp. 52-92).

Table 3.5. USSR: Teacher Training Curricula by Subject Areas

Pedagogic Institute:	Length of course	Teacher Training Subjects	Political Subjects	General Education Subjects	Specialist Subjects	Elective Subjects, etc.	Total hours
Primary teaching	4	1522	390	380	1068	364	3724
		40.9	10.5	10.2	28.7	9.8	100%
Foreign Languages (2)	5	474	544	140	3504	544	5206
		9.1	10.4	2.7	67.3	10.4	100%
Maths. and Physics	5	504	480	380	3376	—	4740
		10.6	10.1	8.0	71.2	—	100%
Mathematics	4	364	390	380	2212	260	3606
		10.1	10.8	10.5	61.3	7.2	100%
Russian Lang. and Lit.	4	364	390	380	1860	580	3574
		10.2	10.9	10.6	52.0	16.2	100%
University:							
Russian Lang. and Lit.	5	240	520	690	2620	280	4350
		5.5	12.0	15.9	60.2	6.4	100%
Mathematics	5	214	480	440	2672	660	4466
		4.8	10.7	9.9	59.8	14.8	100%

Source: Grant, 1969, pp. 71-3.

Table 3.6. USSR: Pedagogic School Curriculum (Primary Teaching)

Year:		I		II		III		IV		
Semester:		1	2	3	4	5	6	7	8	Total
I General Subjects										
1. Social study								2	3	81

Year:	I		II		III		IV		
Semester:	1	2	3	4	5	6	7	8	Total
I General Subjects (cont.)									
2. Mathematics	2	2	2	3	3	3	3	4	398
3. Physics (+astronomy)	2	2	2	2	2	2	2	2	294
4. Chemistry	3	2	3	2					194
5. Econ. geography								4	60
6. Biology							2	2	66
7. Foreign language	3	2	2	2					175
8. Scientific atheism								1	15
Total Group I	10	8	9	9	5	5	9	16	1283
II Specialist Subjects									
9. Russian lang. methods	3	3	2	4	4	3	4	3	479
10. Literature	4	2	3	2	3	2	3	3	403
11. Arithmetic + methods	4	4	4	2	2	2			344
12. Nature study + methods		2	2	3					138
13. History + methods	3	2	2	2	3	2			266
14. Anatomy, phys., hygiene	2	2							78
15. Psychology		4							80
16. Pedagogy			5	4	2	2			247
17. Singing + methods	2	2	2	2	2	2	2	2	294
18. Drawing and modelling + methods	2	2	2	2	2	2	2	2	294
19. Theory and method of PE					2	2	1		90
20. Educational materials	1			1		1	1	4	134
Total Group II	21	23	22	22	20	18	13	14	2847
III Physical education	2	2	2	2	2	2	2	2	294
Civil defence							1	1	33
IV Practical training									
1. School workshop, tech. drwg., etc.	2	2	2	2	2	2	2	2	294
2. Agric. studies, etc.	1	1	1	1	1	1	1	1	147
3. Technical media						2	2		70
4. Teaching practice					6	6	6		324
Total hours	36	36	36	36	36	36	36	36	5292

(Plus optional subjects)

Continuous teaching practice and pioneer camp practice—10 weeks.

Source: ibid.

Table 3.7. USSR: Pedagogic Institute Curriculum (Primary Teaching)

Year:	I		II		III		IV		
Semester:	1	2	3	4	5	6	7	8	Total
1. History of the CPSU	3	4							120
2. Marxist-Leninist philosophy			4	3					120
3. Political economy					2	0/4			80
4. Scientific communism								4	70
5. Foreign language	3	3	2	2	3				240
6. Physical education	2	2	2	2					140
7. Psychology	4	2	2						150
8. Pedagogy		2	2	2	2	0/2			170
9. Anatomy, phys., hygiene	4	2							112
10. Russian or mother tongue		3	3	4	3	0/2	3	4	366
11. Intro. to linguistics	2								38
12. Children's lit. elt. lit. theory						0/3	3	4	160
13. Russian (native lang.) methods				3	4	5/3			182
14. Mathematics	4	4	4	4					280
15. Arithmetic methods					3	4			110
16. Natural science	2	2	2						112
17. Geography & regional study	2	2	2						112
18. Nature study methods			3						58
19. History methods						2/4			66
20. Drawing & methods				2	2	0/2	2	2	160
21. Singings, music & methods		2	2	2	2	0/2	2	2	234
22. Theory & method of PE					4	0/2			100
23. Workshop & labour trg. method				3	4	0/4			190
24. Special course, elective pract.						5/2	2	8	214
25. Course determined by rep. or VUZ	4	2	2						150
Total hours	30	30	30	30	30	12/30	12	24	3734

(Plus elective courses)

Practice: (1) Nature study & regional study—3 wks. (semester 2)

(2) Pioneer camp practice   —6 wks. (semester 4)

(3) Continuous school practice   —5 wks. (semester 6)

19 wks. (semester 7)

Total   33 wks.

Source: ibid.

Table 3.8 China: Timetable for Senior Teachers' Training Schools, 1957-8

Subjects	Weekly hours by year and term					
	1		2		3	
	1	2	1	2	1	2
Language and literature						
Chinese language	2	2	2	2	2	2
Literature	4	4	4	4	5	5
Teaching methods	—	—	—	—	2	2
Mathematics						
Arithmetic	—	—	2	2	—	—
Algebra	3	3	—	—	—	—
Geometry	2	2	2	2	2	—
Teaching methods—arithmetic	—	—	—	—	2	3
Physics	2	2	3	3	2	—
Chemistry	3	3	—	—	—	—
Human anatomy and physiology	2	2	—	—	—	—
Geography						
Physical geography	2	—	—	—	—	—
Chinese geography	—	2	2	—	—	—
Foreign geography	—	—	—	2	—	—
History						
Modern world history	2	2	—	—	—	—
Chinese history	—	—	3	3	3	3
Politics	2	2	—	—	—	—
Psychology	—	—	2	1	—	—
Education	—	—	2	2	3	3
Physical activities	2	2	2	2	2	2
Music	2	2	1	2	1	2
Drawing	2	2	2	1	1	2
Practice teaching	—	—	1	1	3	4
Total	30	30	28	27	28	28
Weeks per term	18	17	18	17	18	13

Source: Chen T.H. p. 18, based on timetables published in the *Jiaoshi Bao (Teacher's Newspaper)* 23 and 26 July 1957, quoted in Price, 1970, pp. 230-1.

In China, at the tertiary level there is a distinction between a *Shifan Xueyuan* and a *Shifan Daxue*, the former taking students from and returning them to the locality, while the latter recruits from and trains for the whole country. I have used the terms teachers' training college and teachers' training institute respectively. Both employ curricula similar to those of the Soviet pedagogical institutes (Price, 1970, p. 228). American writers prefer the old-fashioned term, normal college.

The heavy nature of the curriculum, and the similarities between the two countries can be seen from the specimen curricula above. Much of the similarity stems from Soviet influence in China during the fifties (Price, 1970, pp. 102-4). In the Cultural Revolution teacher training came in for considerable criticism, not least for reliance upon Soviet textbooks, such as that by Kairov on education. Attempts to reform training methods have involved sending teams of students and teachers into the countryside to engage in in-service training of rural teachers, studying conditions in the rural schools and preparing special teaching materials to suit their needs (*Honggi*, 6, 1971. pp. 84-8, quoted in Seybolt. pp. 166-77).

Curriculum and Methods

Marxism as a theory of social change brought about through understanding of reality by, and mass action of the working people themselves has profound implications for school curricula and methods. It immediately focuses attention on mass, general education rather than selective or specialised higher studies. Then understanding requires both accurate information, of the right scope and quantity, as well as the theoretical tools with which to handle it. This implies some sort of core course of studies and systematic knowledge. At the same time, since the object is practical and marxism emphasises the combining of theory and practice this knowledge must at the same time be linked with work and social problems. There is to be no pretence that subject matter is value-free. On the contrary, a major part of the requirement is the criticism of different value positions in regard to various kinds of information. While the stress will be strongly cognitive marxist emphasis on all-round development and the broadening of freedom through knowledge and a variety of skills will require encouragement of affective (aesthetic) and of physical education as well.

So far as teaching methods are concerned, the problem will be to develop critical thought and independence. This implies abandonment of authoritarian methods of teaching and study. Since the aim is to raise *mass* standards attention would have to be given to *compensatory* teaching and special methods for those who find particular subjects and skills difficult, in order to give to as many as possible real freedom of choice.

It is against these sorts of criteria that Soviet and Chinese curricula and methods will be judged here. Since the subject is vast I shall concentrate on only four topics which will serve to bring out the major problems.

Language and Literacy

The USSR and China are multi-lingual countries. This adds considerably to the problems of class and regional dialects which, since the work of Bernstein and others, educators are beginning to recognise in countries which are regarded as mono-lingual (see Lawton, 1968; Levitas, ch. 7; and Rosen, 1974). As well as educational these problems are political and economic.

The first political problem is that of choice of a national language and perhaps other official languages in which the business of government is to be conducted, here Great Russian on the one hand and a dialect of Chinese known as *putonghua* (common speech) on the other. Then comes the choice of language for the various levels of the school system, which also involves education and economic problems. In both the USSR and China recognised minorities have the right to instruction in their mother tongue. Language is such a basic human activity that it easily becomes a focus for social and political discontents, especially where there is a history of racial or national oppression (Fishman, 1972). In poor countries this may be exacerbated by the cost of producing books and translating documents into a variety of languages and it may be difficult to judge this against the political, educational and human costs of not doing so.

In this web of interlacing problems what is the marxist position? The right of self-determination for nations defended by Lenin, and honoured in the breach by his epigones, can be of help only where a language, like those of the Baltic nations, or Cantonese and the other major coastal dialects in China, is spoken by so many people over a linguistically uniform area as to make self-determination meaningful. The problems are more difficult when the population is a small minority, scattered, when the language has no written form, or when there are doubts as to whether it is capable of survival without special measures. The use of the terms language and dialect here is fluid. Properly it is better to restrict language to those dialects which are separated by national frontiers, such as German and Dutch. (cf. Chao, pp. 132-3.) Here the basic marxist principle of concrete investigation of concrete situations, cited by Lenin in the same article on national self-determination (Lenin, 1947, 1, p. 568), combined with the principle of opposition to oppression in any form, is the only guide. So long as there are class differences and major differences of wealth and culture between groups of people speaking different dialects there is a fertile field for conflicts and no simple rules can be applied to spirit them away.

Language policies in the USSR have varied over the past sixty years. While China may have been more consistent this is perhaps a factor of shorter time, the much smaller population of 'national minorities', and the overwhelming weight of the Chinese cultural tradition expressed in the writing system. Before reviewing these policies the range of languages and language families should be noted. The accompanying table shows the variety of these for the two countries, together with estimates of the numbers of people for whom they are the mother tongue.

In Imperial Russia the policy was unequivocal. Minister of Public Education, Admiral Shishkov, declared in 1824: 'the education of all people throughout our whole Empire, notwithstanding diversity of creed or language, shall be in Russian' (Johnson, p. 98, cf. B. King, p. 279). In Imperial China in the same period, as for centuries previously, ruling Manchu families, Chinese, or members of the various other nationalities alike had, if schooled, to learn the artificial *wenyan* and *guanhua,* respectively the written and spoken form of classical Chinese which, like Latin in medieval Europe, served as the language of the small official class and the medium of almost all written communication. With the Russian Revolution of 1917 the policy changed. On 31 October 1918, a decree of the People's Commissariat of Education gave all minority nationalities the right to instruction in their native languages in all schools and universities, and the right to maintain separate public schools. Various institutions were set up to help make this a reality, such as the Leningrad Institute of the Northern Peoples, and the Moscow Committee of the North. Many non-written languages were supplied with alphabets and serious efforts were made to encourage those in danger of dying out. The major languages were, of course, already written, those whose people were Muslim using the Arabic script. During the twenties this was changed to the Latin alphabet, partly to break the hold of the religion, and then in 1939, again largely for political reasons, the Latin alphabet was replaced by the Cyrillic (Winner, 1952; Bennigsten and Quequejay, 1961). The major Russian dialects, Ukrainian and Byelorussian, also suffered political oppression. After about 1928 fears of separatism led to a reimposition of russification and suppression of any signs of cultural pluralism (Shimoniak, pp. 219-26).

Increasingly over the years until the sixties the non-Russian languages became the medium of instruction in schools for the minorities through-

Table 3.9 Distribution of Languages/Dialects in the USSR and China

Language/dialect	Language group	Number of speakers (millions)
In USSR		
Armenian	Armenian/Indo-Eur.	3.2
Estonian	Finnic/	0.96
Lithuanian	Baltic/Indo-Eur.	2.6
Latvian (Lettish)	Baltic/Indo-Eur.	2
Georgian	Circassian	9
Uzbek	Turkic/Altaic	9
Kazakh	Turkic/Altaic	5
Kirghiz	Turkic/Altaic	1.4
Azerbaijani	Turkic/Altaic	4
Mongolian (9 or 4 major dialects)	Mongolian/Altaic	3 (USSR/China)
Various	Manchu-Tungus/Altaic	(USSR/China)
In China		
Wu (Shanghai etc)	Chinese/Sino-Tibetan	46
Xiang (Hunanese)	.. .. ..	26
Gan (Jiangxi)	.. .. ..	13
Kejia (Hakka)	.. .. ..	20
Yue (Cantonese)	.. .. ..	27
Min (Fukienese)	.. .. ..	22
Tibetan	Tibeto-Burman/Sino-Tibetan	6
Lo-lo	.. .. ..	n.a.
Thai	Sino-Tibetan or Malayo-Polynesian	n.a.
Miao	Mon-Khmer (?)	n.a.
Yao	Mon-Khmer (?)	n.a.

For Russian see Soviet Census, 1970. For other languages see Chao Yuen-ren, 1968, pp. 93-7; Kratochvil, 1968, pp. 16-17; and Forrest, 1965, pp. 94-5.

out the USSR, usually for grades 1-4, but in some cases to 7th or even to 10th grade. But legislation in 1959, repeated in 1973, making the choice of the language of instruction optional for parents appears to have put the official seal on the decline of all but a few languages (see art. 11 of the *Statute on the 8-year school*, in Shapovalenko, p. 393, and art. 20 of the Law of 19 July 1973 in *Fundamentals of Legislation*, p. 18). The minority languages of the RSFSR have shifted from being the medium of instruction to being taught as a separate subject (Silver, p. 33). In Republics like the Tartar ASSR, Dagestan ASSR, and probably in Kazakhstan and Uzbekistan native-language schools have recently been confined to the rural areas (Silver, p. 38). If this becomes an established trend it could add a new dimension to a persistent social and educational problem.

In China after 1949 a similar policy of encouraging the non-Chinese languages has been pursued. Mongolian still employs the old Uigur script, while Uigur itself, as well as Zhuang and a number of other small languages have been given Latin alphabets. There is too little information available at present to judge the degree of sinification which is taking place, and just how much the mother tongue is employed in the schools. Throughout the Chinese-speaking territory official policy is to use *putonghua* as the medium of instruction. While there is no question of the local dialects being weakened there is a body of testimony to the effectiveness of this policy in popularising the national speech among the young.

Turning to the problem of literacy, this was a problem which faced both Russia and China at the time of their Revolutions, and one which they both tackled with determination. The extent of literacy is difficult to determine anywhere because of definition and detection, and in places where statistical records are poor the figures given are often no more than inspired guesswork. The Russian census of 1897 gives the literacy in European Russia as 32.6 per cent; in the S. Caucasus as 24.1 per cent; and in W. Siberia as 17.0 per cent (*Ped. Ents.* 1, p. 612). For Central Asia the same source gives a figure of 6 per cent, while Barnes quotes a figure of 1.5 per cent for males only in 1913 (Barnes, p. 209, cf. Shimoniak, pp. 458-61). Various estimates for China in the early fifties put the overall literacy figures at from 10-15 per cent, but the figure in the cities must have been considerably higher than this (Price, 1970, p. 202).

The methods employed to eradicate illiteracy included special schools for adults, the enlisting of every literate to teach at least one illiterate (cf. the 1919 decree calling on all literates to help with similar campaigns in China in the 1950s), and special materials written in simple language, but with an adult content, to encourage adults to read. In the USSR by 1939 it was claimed that 87 per cent of the population was literate, including 82 per cent of women. By the 1959 census figures for literacy range from 93.2 per cent for women in Turkmenistan to 99.8 per cent for men in Estonia. For China there are still no overall figures and perhaps the best evaluation of the tremendous efforts which have been made there which can be made is to suggest that those who have to read and write for their work can do so, but that for others, especially villagers, there is still a long way to go.

A major difference between the problems faced in eliminating illiteracy in the two countries stems from the nature of their writing systems. In the USSR, whatever the language, they use an alphabet, each symbol of which corresponds more or less closely to the phonemes of the language. In the case of Russian the Cyrillic alphabet is the result of special invention to suit the Slavonic languages. (It was invented by the Greek monks, Cyril and Methodius and first adopted by Bulgaria in *c.* 885 AD. See Evans, pp. 42-3 and deBray, pp. 1-3, 193.) In its modern form a mere 33 symbols are required to write any word in the language. With Chinese the problem is very different. There the script is morphemic, each symbol representing a larger element of sound than a single phoneme (roughly, a syllable) to which meaning, either lexical or grammatical is in every case attached. To reach tertiary school level of literacy requires the knowledge of perhaps as many as 6,000 symbols, or characters. In the literacy campaigns the aim has been to teach peasants 1,500 basic characters, and workers 2,000, a situation suggesting the basically undemocratic nature of the writing system. Special materials have been published using these basic vocabularies, but probably in insufficient numbers to encourage literacy.

In the late fifties many of the characters were simplified, making them easier to write if not necessarily easier to remember, and at the same time a new alphabet, known as *hanyu pinyin,* was devised. The latter has been used only for teaching purposes, and in dictionaries and for a few other minor purposes. In the post-Cultural Revolution discussions of language reform there have been renewed calls for a wholesale changeover from characters to this alphabet, but this seems unlikely for a variety of reasons, not least being the vested interests of those who have struggled to learn them (see Price, 1970, pp. 73-6; Chao, pp. 101-12; and the fortnightly pages of the *Guangming Ribao* devoted to the language reform, especially 1974 onward).

Relating the Curriculum to Life

In Russia in the 1920s and in China during and after the Cultural Revolution there were attempts to relate school curricula to the life of the family, factory and farm. Both in inspiration and in the concrete proposals which came out of the prolonged discussion there were significant similarities and also differences between the two attempts. The major difference is in the interpretation of Marx's suggestion for linking education with productive labour and his concept of polytechnical education, which was taken up strongly in Russia. These are so important that they will be discussed separately below.

In Russia educators were influenced by Dewey and other exponents of progressive education to attempt to evolve school curricula around problems arising from the world outside the school. These were to be studied practically, in an 'open door' way, as the Chinese would put it today. Pinkevich, a leading educator and President of the Second State University of Moscow, wrote: 'children are not to study verbal descriptions of phenomena and things but rather the phenomena and things themselves' (Pinkevich, p. 302). Finally, in 1923 the new syllabuses were ready, prepared by the State Scientific Council. In addition to special programmes in the Russian language and mathematics the core of the syllabuses was an integrated course around the themes of nature, labour and society. These themes and the teaching method advocated for them were strongly and persistently defended by Lenin's wife, Krupskaya. In 1925 she wrote:

> The aim of the school is to give an understanding of living reality to the child. To achieve this, only those connections which exist among phenomena in practical life and which illuminate those ties in the proper manner, showing how they appear and develop, should be revealed. (Zepper, p. 272)

The same theme was emphasised by another educator, Blonsky, who spoke of giving 'a unified and complete outlook upon the world' and described the complex method as 'the application of the dialectical method in pedagogy' (Pinkevich, p. 304).

In an attempt to emphasise the practical nature of the desired courses the Council put out a list of the 'Minimum labour knowledge and abilities for those who graduate from the Primary School'. But teachers were unprepared for such programmes, and, as Pinkevich complained, publishers stepped in with 'primary readers in which one may learn about everything under the sun'. Thus what was intended to be

practical became again purely a reading exercise (Pinkevich, p. 310).
Krupskaya put her finger on the problem in 1924 when she wrote:

> In essence (the complex method) . . . only introduces the skeleton
> of work which must be somehow clothed with material and the flesh
> of concrete reality . . . Here is a colossal work. If a teacher is not
> politically trained, does not gain an understanding of problems in
> economics, and does not understand natural phenomena, of course
> he will be helpless. (Zepper, p. 269)

Another grave problem was the shortage of even the simplest tools, and
writing materials during those years.

Table 3.10a Programme of the Primary School (Age 8-12)

Grade	Nature	Labour	Society
1	Seasons.	Immediately surrounding labour life of both village and city family.	Family and school.
2	Air, water, soil. Nature and care of cultivated plants and animals which surround man.	Labour life of village or city block in which child lives.	Social institutions of village and city.
3	Elementary observations (information) in physics and chemistry. Nature of local region. Life of human body.	Economics of local region.	Provincial social institutions. Picture of past of one's own country.
4	Geography of Russia and other countries. Life of human body.	State economy of Russian Republic and other countries.	Organisation of state in Russia and other countries. Pictures of past of humanity.

Source: Pinkevich, 1929, p. 305. See also Scott Nearing, 1926, pp. 94-5.

Table 3.10b Programme for the 6th Grade (Children 13—14 years of age)

Nature: its resources and powers.	Man's exploitation of these resources and powers.	Social life.
1. Physics and chemistry in so far as they are necessary for an understanding of (1) life of	1. Mining of ores, minerals, and fuel.	Workers and capitalists. Hired labour and capital. Private ownership at expense of production.

Nature: its resources and powers.	Man's exploitation of these resources and powers.	Social life
animals and man and (2) application of these sciences to industry (machine construction, locomotives, electricity).		Conditions of working class. Union of noblemen and capitalists. Limited monarchy. Republic. Dictatorship of bourgeoisie. Democratic republic. Capitalism. Competition. Chaos in production. Struggle of labour and capital. Chartists. Year of 1848. Communist Manifesto—expression of impulses of working class. International union of workers, 1st International. Attempt of workers to take power into their hands. Paris Commune. 2nd International. Strikes. Organisation of labour. Assimilation into political parties.
2. Ores, rocks, metals, mineral fuel. Deposits in Soviet Union.	2. Chemical and mechanical industry. Trade. Manufacture. Factories. Organisation of labour in trade, mill and factory. Development of various branches of industry in Soviet Union and in other countries. Regional industries of Soviet Union.	
3. Technical plants and animals.	3. Technology of products of village economy.	
4. Man as a member of animal kingdom. Anatomy and physiology of man.	4. Anthropogeography: man and human society; dependence upon natural environment.	
5. Hygiene of physical and mental work. Sound and unsound body.	5. Man as a working power. Organisation of his labour. Protection of labour and health of workers.	Capitalism in Russia. Remnants of serfdom. Autocracy. Struggles of 1905 and 1917.

Source: Pinkevich, 1929, p. 307. See also Scott Nearing, 1928, pp. 95-6.

Table 3.11 Minimum of Labour Knowledge and Abilities for those who Graduate from the Primary School

A. ORIENTATION ABILITIES

1. Orientation in space:
   Ability to find any location either in the city or in the country according to a given plan.
2. Orientation in time.
   Ability to determine the necessary time to cover a certain distance or to execute a simple errand.
3. Orientation in size and quantity.
   Ability to count and measure through use of abacus, scales—simple and decimal, metre, tape measure.
4. Orientation in quality.
   Ability to judge the approximate quality of objects of first importance.

A. ORIENTATION ABILITIES (cont.)

5. Orientation in social and state institutions.
    Ability to make inquiries in a social or state institution.
6. Orientation in all forms and rules of locomotion and transportation.
    Ability to use trams, trains, post office, telegraph, telephone.

B. EXPRESSION ABILITIES

1. Ability to prepare a plan of yard, house, street.
2. Ability to draw simple objects.
3. Ability to prepare a report about completed work.
4. Ability to draw up a plan for some proposed work.
5. Ability to report any event or occurrence.
6. Ability to prepare a budget or specification.

C. HEALTH ABILITIES

1. Ability to take hygienic care of one's self and others, and to render first aid.
2. Ability to ventilate, disinfect, and keep sanitary a building.
3. Ability to repair, cleanse and wash dress and clothes.
4. Ability to prepare an ordinary meal.

D. PRACTICAL ABILITIES

1. Ability to make minor repairs of buildings, furniture, and dishes by means of simple carpenter's and locksmith's tools.
2. Ability to use electricity and irrigation devices.
3. Ability to make minor repairs of the latter wherever possible.
4. Ability to take apart, clean, and assemble simple machines, such as meat-cutter, burner, etc.

E. FARMING ABILITIES

1. Ability to take ordinary care of domestic animals and plants.
2. Ability to work in field, orchard, and vegetable garden according to one's physical and mental development.

F. SCIENTIFIC-EXPERIMENTAL ABILITIES

1. Ability to make systematic and accurate observations of certain phenomena.
2. Ability to gather systematically facts with regard to a given subject.
3. Ability to use dictionary, catalogue, newspaper, journal and directory.
4. Ability to use museum, exhibitions, library and archives.

G. COMMUNITY ABILITIES

1. Ability to participate in and lead general meetings, to take and report minutes, to work as member, president or secretary.
2. Ability to execute individually and collectively various social obligations such as participation in commissions.
3. Ability to organise social undertakings such as circles, troops, co-operatives, clubs, general holidays and recreations.
4. Ability to prepare wall newspaper, volumes, journals.

Source: Pinkevich, 1929, pp. 311-2. See also Scott Nearing, 1926, pp. 96-8.

In China attempts to relate the schools to life have taken place on two occasions, in the period of the Great Leap Forward in 1958, and again during the Cultural Revolution of 1966. On both occasions the organising idea has been the marxian concept of combining education with productive labour, an idea which will be considered in detail in a separate chapter. But other changes to the curriculum have been involved. Some of the most interesting sounding have been in the 'irregular schools' which are not on the tourist circuit, and for which the teaching materials are not available, except in the occasional newspaper article (some details appear in *Socialist Upsurge in China's Countryside*, pp. 415-42). These schools, more than the FTD schools, followed Mao's injunction that

> material of instruction should bear a local character and some more local or indigenous teaching material should be used. Textbooks dealing with agriculture should be compiled by the province concerned. Some indigenous literature should be taught. (Mao, *CB*, 888, 7)

Since the emphasis has been on work the changes have been easy to make in the science area, physics, chemistry and biology becoming more applied, or amalgamating to become basic industrial or agricultural knowledge. The difficult problem has been the humanities, and for this the only guide seems to have been Mao Ze-dong's statement to a visiting Nepalese Education delegation in 1964. There he said:

> it is infeasible to set up workshops in a college of arts, and it is infeasible to run workshops for literature, history, economics or novels. *The faculty of arts should take the whole society as its own workshop.* Its students should contact the peasants and urban workers, industry and agriculture. (Mao, *CB*, 888, p. 15, emphasis added)

Accounts of attempts to translate this into viable courses, especially at tertiary level, and glimpses of the new teaching materials reveal how far there is to go before one can say there is a real advance in relating the humanities to life.

Throughout 1968-9 there was a mass campaign to rewrite the teaching materials and newspaper accounts spoke of groups uniting teachers, skilled workers and peasants, and students producing and testing new materials. Unfortunately there is no indication as to whether the results were incorporated in any of the next textbooks finally officially issued by the provincial authorities when the schools reopened.

In the primary and secondary schools, in addition to pupil participation in both production labour and various socially useful practical activities (helping old people and the handicapped), the world of work seems to have taken an increased part in the reading materials. The following list of chapter headings from recent textbooks is probably typical. The first is from a volume on Industrial Knowledge used in primary schools in Shanxi Province (Shensi):

(1) General economic policy; (2) Industry learn from Da Qing (oil-field complex); (3) Steel—Anshan charter; (4) Coal—mining pre- and post-liberation; (5) Petroleum—drilling and use; (6) Electricity; (7) Lime and cement; (8) Simple mechanics; (9) New industrial achievements.

The second is from a book of Agricultural Knowledge used in primary schools in Jilin (Kirin) Province in 1976:

(1) Agriculture is China's economic base—agriculture study Da Zhai (the model village); (2) Knowledge of meteorology; (3) Soils; (4) Fertilizers, natural and artificial; (5) Plants—life histories; (6) Cultivation of crops: maize, rice, hemp, etc.; (7) Prevention of pests; (8) Forestry; (9) Animal husbandry: rearing pigs, chicken and rabbits.

The second book was 134 pages long, illustrated with clear line drawings.

It is clear that China suffers from many problems similar to those which caused the abandonment of progressive methods in the late twenties in the USSR. A high proportion of primary teachers lack basic knowledge, being in some cases only junior high school graduates. Better-trained teachers lack practical experience and have the wrong social-political attitudes to breathe life into new teaching materials, which is one reason in favour of the worker-teachers. Perhaps it is at least partly for these reasons that no attempt to introduce broad integration of subjects like the Russian *complexes* has been attempted.

The Academic Backlash.

Beginning towards the end of the twenties in the USSR, and culminating in the 25 August 1931 resolution of the CC CPSU (B) 'On the primary and secondary school', there was a strong attack on complexes and all the methods advocated by the leaders of the People's Commissariat of Education. These criticisms were later summed up in the 1953 edition of the *Great Soviet Encyclopedia* in these words:

For the interpretation of the complex theme, material was drawn from various subjects (Russian, mathematics, science, and others), which infringed upon the systematic account of each of them taken separately and did not provide the student with lasting knowledge. Students acquired scrappy, fragmentary knowledge and were not disciplined to work with the textbook and books. The teachers' role in the education process was reduced by the complex system of education. The teacher was emancipated from the responsibility of teaching sequentially the academic subject to the student in a definite and strict system. The system was not conducted with the knowledge which necessarily consolidates acquired knowledge. In the complex system of education, the bond between separate academic subjects took on an artificial and far-fetched character, and their content was illogically determined because of the formal demand for working out this and that complex theme—nature, labour, society. (Zepper, p. 267)

Similar complaints were made in Peking, decades later after the Cultural Revolution. A *Red Flag* article written by a teacher from Peking University complained that it was not sufficient to study theory as and when required by some practical problem. He used the colourful expression: 'stumble across something, then teach it; something missing, then fill it in' to describe what was being done. Vice-Commissar of Education, Epstein, made the familiar criticism:

They could talk about the railway of their district, or the local industry, but could neither write well nor grammatically. Their arithmetic was in an equally bad state. (King, 1937, p. 23)

B. King describes the changes as she saw them then:

They stabilised the changes that had been going on for some time. Dealing with methods, the brigade system was abolished and individual work restored. In schools the class lesson, well prepared, was to be the basic method, but visits to museums, factories, etc., individual work in the laboratory, and, particularly, work with books, were not to be excluded. (King, 1937, p. 23)

Krupskaya, like everyone else was forced to bow to the superior authority of the Party, but she made feeble protests now and then. In 1932 she wrote:

We have changed to the subject system of instruction which gives systematic study to the branches of phenomena, but does this mean that we want to erect barriers between separate subjects? The power which we pursue in our school is to give indispensable knowledge for the reconstruction of life on socialist principles. (Zepper, p. 281)

To illustrate these new programmes I give those of urban and rural schools in 1935, that of 10-year schools after World War Two in the late forties, and that of the 8-year school following the Khrushchev reform. Readers will note slight changes in both subjects offered and hours allotted to them. The conservative nature of such programmes was noted by Hans, who compared the recommendations of D. Tolstoy for 1871 with the project for an 8-year Real School by Count P.N. Ignative (1915), and the curriculum of the 8-year school of 1959. Grouping the subjects, the results are as follows: (in total hours)

	1871	1915	1959
Humanities	154	80	87
Maths, and sciences	47	73	84
Physical culture, practical work and arts	–	34	93

In China in the fifties curricula and methods were strongly influenced by those of the USSR (Price, 1970, pp. 101-4). The programme given here, however, does not differ greatly so far as the actual subjects studied are concerned from that of the Guomindang schools of the previous period (Swetz, p. 98). The difference is more in the content of the syllabuses, for which at present no comprehensive comparative study exists. (Swetz is interesting for mathematics; R.H. Solomon compares childrens' readers of 1922-9 with those of 1960 in respect of attitudes to family, authority, work, etc., in *China Quarterly* 22, April-June 1965; Roberta Martin's 'The socialisation of children in China and on Taiwan: an analysis of elementary school textbooks' in *China Quarterly* 62, 1975, pp. 242-62 is also relevant.)

Table 3.12. Soviet School Programmes, 1935

Urban Schools

					Secondary School					
					Incomplete Secondary					
		Primary								
Subject	Class:	1	2	3	4	5	6	7	8	9	10
Russian language		9	9	6	6	4	3	2	1	—	—
Literature		—	—	—	—	2	2	2	2	3	4
Arithmetic		5	5	5	8	4	1	—	—	—	—
Algebra, geometry and trigonometry		—	—	—	—	1	3	4	4	4	5
Nature study		2	2	2	2	2	2	2	2	2	—
History		—	—	1	2	2	2	2	4	4	4
Geography		—	—	2	2	2	2	2	2	2	—
Physics		—	—	—	—	—	2	3	3	2	2
Chemistry		—	—	—	—	—	—	2	2	2	3
Geology and mineralogy		—	—	—	—	—	—	—	—	—	1
Social science		—	—	—	—	1	1	1	—	—	—
Foreign language		—	—	—	—	3	3	3	3	3	3
Art		1	1	1	1	1	1	—	—	—	—
Handwork and manual work		1	1	1	1	2	2	2	2	2	2
Machine drawing		—	—	—	—	—	1	1	1	1	1
Singing		1	1	1	1	1	1	—	—	—	—
Physical culture		1	1	1	1	1	1	1	1	1	1
Military studies		—	—	—	—	—	—	—	—	1	1
		20	20	20	22	26	27	27	27	27	27

Rural Schools

					Secondary School					
					Incomplete Secondary					
		Primary								
Subject	Class:	1	2	3	4	5	6	7	8	9	10
Russian language		11	11	8	7	5	4	3	2	—	—
Literature		—	—	—	—	3	8	8	3	4	5
Mathematics		6	6	6	7	7	6	5	5	5	6(7)
Nature study		3	3	3(2)	3	3	3	3	3	3	—
History		—	—	1(2)	3	3	3	3	5	5	5

Rural Schools (cont.)

					Secondary School						
					Incomplete Secondary						
			Primary								
Subject	Class	1	2	3	4	5	6	7	8	9	10
Geography		—	—	3	3	3	3	3	8	3	—
Physics		—	—	—	—	—	3	4(3)	4(3)	3	3
Chemistry		—	—	—	—	—	—	2(3)	2(3)	3	4
Geology and mineralogy		—	—	—	—	—	—	—	—	—	2(1)
Social science		—	—	—	—	1	1	1	—	—	—
Foreign language		—	—	—	—	2	2	2	2	2	2
Art		1	1	} 1	} 1	1	1	—	—	—	—
Singing		1	1			1	—	—	—	—	—
Machine drawing		—	—	—	—	—	1	1	1	1	1
Handwork and manual work		1	1	1	1	1	1	1	1	1	1
Physical culture		1	1	1	1	1	1	1	1	1	1
Military studies		—	—	—	—	—	—	—	—	1	2
		24	24	24	26	31	32	32	32	32	32

Source: B. King, 1937, pp. 312-13.

Table 3.13 USSR: School Curriculum of Late 1940s

				Number of hours per week				
Age	7-8	8-9	9-10	10-11	11–12	12-13	13-14	Total
	1st	2nd	3rd	4th	5th	6th		7th hours for
Subject	grade	grade	grade	grade	grade	grade	grade	entire
Russian and reading	15	14	15	8	10[a]	8[a]	6[a]	2,508
Arithmetic	6	7	6	7	7	2	—	1,155
Algebra, geometry	—	—	—	—	—	5	6	362
Natural science	—	—	—	2(3)	2	3	2	314
History	—	—	—	3	2	3(2)	2	314
Constitution of the USSR	—	—	—	—	—	—	2	66
Geography	—	—	—	3(2)	3	2(3)	2(3)	346
Physics	—	—	—	—	—	2	3	165
Chemistry	—	—	—	—	—	—	3(2)	83
Foreign language	—	—	—	—	4	4	3	363
Physical culture	1	1	2	2	2	2	2	396
Drawing	1	1	1	1	1	1	—	198
Draughtsmanship	—	—	—	—	—	—	1	33
Singing	1	1	1	1	—	—	—	132
Total	24	24	25	27	31	32	32	6,435

[a]The course in Russian language in grades five, six and seven covers the systematic study of grammar, spelling and punctuation. Literature lessons acquaint the pupil with outstanding works of Russian letters. These lessons are an introduction to the course in the history of Russian literature which is studied in grades eight, nine and ten.

		Number of hours per week				Total
Age	13-14	14-15	15-16	16-17		hours
	First 7	8th	9th	10th		for
Subject	grades	grade	grade	grade	Total	course
Russian language and recitation	76	—	—	—	76	2,508
Literature	—	5(6)	6	5	16.5	544
Arithmetic	35	—	—	—	35	1,155
Algebra, geometry, trigonometry	11	6	6	6	29	990
Natural science	9.5	2	2	—	13.5	545
History	9.5	4	4	4	21.5	705
Constitution of the USSR	2	—	—	—	2	66
Geography	10.5	3	2(3)	—	16	528
Physics	5	3	3(2)	4	14.5	478
Astronomy	—	—	—	1	1	33
Chemistry	2.5	2	3(2)	4(3)	10.5	346
Foreign language	11	4(3)	3(2)	4	22	726
Physical culture	12	2	2	2	18	594
Drawing	6	—	—	—	6	198
Draughtsmanship	1	1	1	1	4	132
Singing	4	—	—	—	4	132
Total	195	33	31	31.5		9,680

In 1948-49 the teaching of psychology and logic was introduced in 538 secondary schools in twelve of the larger cities; beginning with grade nine, two hours a week are devoted to psychology, and in grade ten two hours a week to logic. In the 1949-50 school term the study of these subjects was extended to another 149 secondary schools in Moscow, and to 2,313 schools in other cities of the RSFSR. In the 1950-51 school year psychology and logic will be taught in 3,192 rural secondary schools, as a result of which the number of class hours per week will increase to thirty-three; the number of hours devoted to physics and chemistry in grades nine and ten will be altered slightly.

Source: Medynsky, pp. 23, 26.

Table 3.14. USSR: Programme of the 8-year School, 1959

Discipline	1st	2nd	3rd	4th	5th	6th	7th	8th
				Hours per week in form				
Russian	12	12	12	10	6	5	3	2
Literature	—	—	—	—	2	3	2	3
Mathematics	6	6	6	6	6	6	6	5
History. USSR Constitution	—	—	—	2	2	2	2	3
Nature studies	—	—	—	3	—	—	—	—
Geography	—	—	—	—	2	2	2	2
Biology	—	—	—	—	2	2	2	2
Physics	—	—	—	—	—	2	2	3
Chemistry	—	—	—	—	—	—	2	2
Draughtsmanship	—	—	—	—	—	—	1	1
Foreign language	—	—	—	—	4	3	3	3
Art	1	1	1	1	1	1	1	—
Singing	1	1	1	1	1	1	1	1
P.T.	2	2	2	2	2	2	2	2
Manual training	2	2	2	2	3	3	3	3
Socially-useful labour	—	—	2	2	2	2	2	2
Total	24	24	26	29	33	34	34	34
Socially-useful production practice								
number of days	—	—	—	—	6	6	12	12
number of hours	—	—	—	—	18	24	48	48

Source: *Public Education in the USSR*, Ministry of Education, Moscow, 1963, p. 36.

Table 3.15. China: The Primary School Timetable

Subjects	1	2	3	4	5	6	Total hours for 6-year period
	Weekly hours by year						
Language	12	12	12	12	10 / 9[a]	10 / 9	2,244
Arithmetic	6	6	6	6 / 7[a]	6	6 / 5	1,224
History					2	2	136
Geography					2	2	136
Natural science					2 / 2[a]	2 / 3	170
Agricultural knowledge					1	1	68
Manual labour	1	1	1	1			136

Primary School Timetable (cont.)

Subjects	1	2	3	4	5	6	Total hours for 6-year period
	Weekly hours by year						Total hours
Physical education	2	2	2	2	2	2	408
Singing	1	1	1	1	1	1	204
	2[a]	2	2				306
Drawing	1	1	1	1	1	1	204
Weekly assembly	1	1	1	1	1	1	204
Total hours	24	24	24	24	28	28	5,032[b]

[a]alternative hours given in *UNESCO World Survey of Education*. I, Primary Education, 1958.
[b]total given in the World Survey, which does not include agricultural knowledge or the weekly assembly.
   Other figures taken from the table in Chen (*China Quarterly*, no. 10), which quotes Ministry of Education figures for 1957-8, taken from the *Jiao-shi Bao*, 12 July 1957.
Source: Price, 1970, p. 117.

Table 3.16. China: The New Curriculum Proposed for 1957-8

Subjects	Junior high school years			Senior high school years			Total number of hours in 6 year course
	hours per week						
	1	2	3	1	2	3	
1 Chinese language	2	2	2	0	0	0	204
2 Literature	5	5	5	5	5	5	1,010
3 Arithmetic	6/5[a]	0	0	0	0	0	187
4 Algebra	0	4	2	4/3	2	2	455
5 Geometry	0	2	3	2/3	2	2	389
6 Trigonometry	0	0	0	0	2	2	134
				Mathematics			1,165
7 History of China	3/2	3	·0	0	3	3	385
8 World history	0	0	3	0	0	0	102
9 New and newest world history	0	0	0	3	0	0	102
				History			589
10 Politics	2	1	1	2	2	2	336
11 Physical geography	3/2	0	0	0	0	0	85
12 World geography	0	2/3	0	0	0	0	85
13 Chinese geography	0	0	3/2	0	0	0	85
14 Economic geography of China	0	0	0	0	2	0	68
				Geography			323

Subjects	Junior high school years			Senior high school years			Total number of hours in 6 year course
	hours per week						
	1	2	3	1	2	3	
15 Botany	3	2	0	0	0	0	170
16 Zoology	0	2/4	2	0	0	0	170
17 Human anatomy and physiology	0	0	0	2	0	0	68
				Biology			408
18 Physics	0	3/2	2	3	3	4	485
19 Chemistry	0	0	2/3	2	2	3	317
20 Foreign language	3	0	0	4	4	4	510
21 Physical education	2	2	2	2	2	2	404
22 Music	1	1	1	0	0	0	102
23 Drawing	1	1	1	0	0	0	102
24 Basic agriculture	0	0	2	0	0	0	68
Weekly load	28/29	30	31	29	29	29	
				Grand total			6,023

V. Klepikov, 1960, p. 73, ex *Renmin Jiaoyu*, undated.
[a]alternative figures refer to differences in the two terms.
Source: Price, 1970, pp. 134-5.

Recent Reforms in the USSR

In the USSR there have for a long time been complaints of lack of training in independent thinking, and in spite of the long-standing emphasis on science, there have been complaints of insufficient knowledge in these areas. From the middle 1950s there has been increasing interest in creativity training and the discovery of talent. In 1952 a group under the direction of L.V. Zankov of the Institute of Theory and History of Education of the APS began working on a new curriculum for the primary school which would be based on sound psychological principles (especially those of Vygotskii and his school) and incorporate thorough experiment in new teaching methods. Further work was done by a group under D.B. El'konin in the Laboratory for the Psychology of Children and School-age Youth in the Institute of Psychology, and by the Department for Primary Teaching in the Institute for General and Polytechnical Education. These exhaustive studies were put into effect in 1966/7 when the new syllabuses were introduced into the first grade and primary schooling was declared henceforth to be reduced from 4 to 3 grades. Gradually new syllabuses were introduced for the whole 10-year grade range. According to V. Zhamin these were

> built on a linear principle, while in the old syllabuses the material was arranged concentrically. In other words, the new syllabuses do away with the old system of repeating study material in successive classes without any significant addition of new data. This led to outdated information being given, while repetition caused a loss of interest in the subject under study. (Zhamin, 1973, p. 45)

This seems a little different from Zankov and the other researchers, who were concerned with such things as raising the level of difficulty of instruction, increasing the tempo of learning, and raising the cognitive level of the material (cf. Schiff, 1972, p. 48). Their interest was in ways of thinking rather than the particular 'information', out-dated or otherwise. This was brought out in an article by Zankov (*Izvestia*, 4 April 1969, CDSP, 21, no. 14), where he criticised both dull, repetitive exercises and pure entertainment, and called for 'intensive mental work' where 'the operation of the memory will combine with the search for ideas'.

At the same time as these new syllabuses were introduced the regulations were relaxed to permit, from the 7th grade upwards, electives. Accounts of permitted time vary, Zhamin giving 3 hours a week each for grades 7 and 8, and 6 hours a week for 9 and 10. *Soviet Pedagogy* gives 6 hours, or 9 per cent of total time, and 12 hours, or 16 per cent respectively, which is different again from Zhamin's 'up to 18 hours a week in the 7th-10th grades' under the 'standard curriculum' (Zhamin, 1973, p. 49; *Soviet Education*, 1969, XII, 2, p. 37). But more important than time is the content, and on this there seems to be a healthy disagreement. Zhamin describes electives as 'one of the flexible forms of acquainting pupils with present-day scientific, technological and cultural achievements', a kind of passive statement typifying so much that is wrong with Soviet education. The *Soviet Education* article describes them as a bridge between general education and the student's future special skill. It would seem that the educational authorities have conceived the electives in the general spirit of the search for and nurturing of special talents, as extensions of the normal lessons to further stretch the chosen few. One of the problems which teachers have faced in creating elective courses is to distinguish them from what is already done in the *kruzhki* or circles and clubs (*Ped. Ents,* 2, pp. 529-30; King, 1937, p. 74). This and other problems were discussed by young teachers in Moscow at a meeting which clearly brought out the conflict between broadening students' interests and deepening the skills of the few (*CDSP*, XXI, no. 1, p. 35).

4 EDUCATION AND THE ECONOMY

This chapter will begin by describing the major features of the economic histories of the USSR and China necessary for a consideration of the interrelations of education and the economy. Growth of production will be described as a measure of increasing wealth, and therefore of the possibilities for providing a richer education. The description of development will outline the economic basis for a change of the social class structure, as well as the technical changes making demands for new skills. I shall try to assess not only the educational requirements of contrasting development policies, but also what lessons such policies may have for those who carry them out. Since much of the detailed information, especially for China, still remains unavailable only rather tentative speculation is at times possible, but this may suggest lines for future enquiry.

A major objective of this chapter is to assess to what extent economic development in the USSR and China have been congruent with or conducive to marxist *educational* goals. This inevitably raises questions about the socio-political nature of their social formations, about their direction of change, and how they should be categorised in marxist terms. In the campaign on the dictatorship of the proletariat in 1975 Mao Ze-dong drew attention to persisting wage systems and commodity exchange 'scarcely different from those in the old society' and claimed only that 'what is different is that the system of ownership has changed' (*Peking Review* 9, 1975, p. 5). Mandel, on the basis of the absence of *fundamental* capitalist economic features described the USSR as having gone beyond capitalism but not having reached socialism, i.e. as a *transitional* society (Mandel, 1968, pp. 560-5). He argued that profit is no longer the economic driving force and that means of production are accumulated as *use*-values (ibid. pp. 568-9). On this last ground he would, presumably, reject application of the following outline of *state capitalism* which, except for the question of surplus-*value* (rather than *product*) appears to describe both countries rather accurately:

> there has been a radical rationalisation and state-ization of the economic sector without the workers themselves having real control of production, and with the state remaining an institution distinct and 'separate' from the popular masses. In cases such as these, the heads

of the state apparatus occupy, by way of the state, the same place of ownership (here state-ized) and possession of the means of production 'separate' from the workers, exercising the powers that derive from this: the exploitation and extraction of surplus-value is shifted towards the heads of the state apparatus itself. (Poulantzas, 1975, p. 189)

(It should be said that Poulantzas does not himself refer to either the USSR or China in this connection, nor does he imply that the heads of state apparatus necessarily extract surplus-value for personal profit.)

In any case let this suffice to remind us that while this chapter concentrates on the economic in reality this cannot be separated from politics, and that this is especially true when it comes to questions of education.

Indices of Growth

The economies which the communist governments inherited and set out to develop were by any criteria backward, predominantly agricultural, and suffering from the effects of prolonged war, external and civil. True, both countries had made some progress in industrialisation, improving agriculture, and building a school system. But compared with such countries as Britain and the USA these gains looked so small as to make talk of socialism seem almost a mockery. (In fact, it was never thought possible by the early Bolshevik leaders without the aid of revolutionary governments in the more advanced European countries. Only when this hope had quite receded could Stalin come forward with his then incredible proposition of 'building socialism in one country'. (Mandel, 1968, p. 548; Carr, 1970).) In both countries much of the industry was owned and developed by foreign capital. In Russia in 1913 it is estimated that about 33 per cent of the capital of private companies was foreign-owned. Foreign capital dominated in the oil industry and was important in metal goods, textiles, chemicals and woodworking (Nove, (1), p. 18). In China foreign firms were largely concentrated in the coastal cities of Shanghai and Tianjin, and in Hankou. They were favoured by tax and tariff concessions, and their foreign staff enjoyed extra-territorial rights in the foreign concessions wrung out of the weak Chinese governments by war and threats. Japan developed some heavy industry in Manchuria, producing 'about half the coal, about 2/3 of the iron, and something like 9/10 of the steel produced in China' (Hughes and Luard, p. 15).

One measure of the state of industrialisation is the size of the industrial working class. In Russia in 1913 less than 10 per cent of the population worked in industry (2-3 million in factories plus 1 million railwaymen and ¾ million miners—Dobb, p. 36). But of these, 53 per cent worked in enterprises with more than 500 workers, a very high figure for the period (cf. USA, 31 per cent in 1914—Dobb, p. 34). However, these workers were still to some extent linked with the village in a way which was foreign to their counterparts in Manchester and Birmingham. In 1910 two-thirds of the Petersburg factory workers still owned some village land and nearly one-fifth of them returned to the village every summer for the harvest (Dobb, p. 36). For China Hughes and Lurad (p. 14) give a figure of 1 m workers in industry and 10 m in handicrafts for 1937, while Emerson gives a figure of 3 m and 5.8 m respectively in 1949 (p. 427). I have not come across any data on concentration, but it would seem likely that this was less than in Russia and that workers were more divorced from farming. (Chesneau discusses the peasant origin of the great majority of workers after World War One, noting their frequent trips back to their native villages—pp. 48 and 51—but long hours and infrequent holidays would seem to have precluded a part-peasant life-style.)

Another important index of growth is that of towns. As we have noted on various occasions Marx and Engels regarded the gulf in cultural standards between town and country as one of the characteristics of capitalism which would have to be overcome under socialism, and both Russians and Chinese have taken up the theme. Nevertheless the growth of cities has probably been generally accepted as good in the USSR while in China it has been strongly resisted. In the USSR the urban population has grown as follows:

1914	24,700,000
1926	26,300,000 (17.9%)
1939	55,900,000
1956	87,000,000 (43.4%)
1971	139,000,000 (57.0%)

Table 4.1. Comparative Industrial Output

	Russia 1913	USA 1913	UK 1913	China best pre-1949
Electricity (milliard Kwhs)	2.0	25.8	4.7	5.9
Coal (million tons)	29.2	517.8	292.0	61.8
Oil (million tons)	10.3	34.0	—	0.3

	Russia 1913	USA 1913	UK 1913	China best pre-1949
Pig iron (million tons)	4.2	31.5	10.4	1.8
Steel (million tons)	4.3	31.8	7.8	0.9
Cotton textiles (milliard metres)	1.9	5.7	7.4	45,008 bolts.

Source: Nove, p. 14.

	Russia 1913	Russia 1921	China Best pre-1949	China 1952	China 1971-73
Coal (000 tons)	29,000	9,000	61,875	63,528	320-390,000
Power (m. Kwh)	2,039	5,200	5,955	7,261	71,000 +
Oil (m. tons)	9.2	3.8	0.32	0.436	36-53
Pig iron (m. tons)	4.2	0.1	1.8	1.9	
Steel (m. tons)	4.3	0.2	0.923	1.349	18(1970)[a]
Mineral fertilizer (m. tons of standard units)	0.089	0.135	0.229	0.181	7.4[b]
Cement (m. tons)	1.777	1.850	2.293	2.861	
Metal cutting lathes (units)	1,800	2,000	5,390	13,734	
Motor tyres (units)	—	85,000	75,000	417,184	
Paper (m. tons)	269.2	284.5	0.165	0.372	
Sugar (m. tons)	11.3	10.1	—	0.249	

[a]Field gives figure from Perkins, p. 158.
[b]Field.
Source: Nove, p. 68, Roger A. Clarke and Hughes & Luard.

In 1956 the USSR was said to have 1,566 towns and 2,723 settlements 'of an urban type' (*USSR, A Reference Book*, p. 6). In 1953 in China there were a total of 5,568 urban areas. Table 4.2 gives some comparisons by size.

Table 4.2

Town and/or town size	Number of such towns China 1953	USSR 1956
Moscow (without suburbs) 4,839,000		
Leningrad (without suburbs) 2,814,000		
Peking, 2,768,149		
Shanghai, 6,204,417		
500,000 to 999,999 persons	16	20

Town and/or town size	Number of such towns	
	China 1953	USSR 1956
200,000 to 499,999 persons	28	40
100,000 to 199,999 persons	49	73

J. S. Aird comments:

At the moment (1967) China appears to be the one major under-developed country of the world in which urbanization is not gaining ground relatively; in fact, the proportion of the total population in urban areas in Mainland China may be smaller today than in 1958. (*EPMC*, p. 378)

A final index, basic to the economies of both countries is that for grain production. Table 4.3 gives some figures for this.

Table 4.3

		Total grain production	Production/ capita	Marketed outside the village
USSR,	1913 (a good year)	82 m tons	580 kg	21 m tons (26%)
	1928	73.3 m tons	480 kg	
China,	1957	163.0 m tons	256 kg	
	1952	—	220 kg	
	1974	274.9 m tons	344 kg[a]	

[a]1974 figure from R.M. Field, *China Quarterly* 63, 1975, p. 97.

Tang, from whom these figures are quoted (Eckstein, p. 466), argues that they gave the USSR a margin of safety in which to develop industry which is lacking in China. Even in the famine year of 1932, he claims, there still remained 375 kg/head of grain on the farm after forced collection (Eckstein, p. 467). A difficulty here is that of the accuracy of population estimates on which per capita calculations are made. Laird also cautions against thinking that such figures mean that the farmers in Russia were ever well fed, and reminds readers that when Russia was exporting grain in pre-revolution times there was 'repeated mass starvation among the peasants' (Laird, p. 76).

Progress in Development

It is important to remember that the Bolsheviks, when they came to power in 1917, had no economic blueprint to follow, or experience to guide them. During the whole first decade there was controversy and much confusion, policies being adopted out of necessity as often as from theoretical considerations as to how a socialist economy should be constructed. This was particularly true of the first period, known as War Communism, when the extreme shortages dictated rationing and money was replaced by barter. This period lasted from the middle of 1918 to the early part of 1921. With the end of the Civil War, a famine in which millions died (Nove, 1969, p. 86), and widespread economic chaos the New Economic Policy (NEP) was instituted which encouraged small-scale capitalist manufacturing, private trade, and even sought the aid of foreign capitalism to restore production of oil and timber (Nove, 1969, p. 89). This policy reached its height in 1925, and there is difficulty in assigning an exact date to its end (Nove, 1969, p. 136). While NEP certainly helped to repair the damage of the first years, investment in industry was still insufficient and in 1923 attention was drawn to the famous 'scissors crisis'. This term was used to describe a diagram of Trotsky's shown to the 12th Party Congress in which the rise in prices of industrial goods was plotted against the fall in that of agricultural goods (Carr, *Interregnum*, p. 29). Following this further troubles were caused by state reduction of prices, when instead of commodities seeking buyers, 'the buyers seek commodities' (Nove, p. 139).

With the new grain crisis of 1928 arguments which had been going on over the economy during the past years were resolved in favour of 'super-industrialisation at the expense of the peasants' (Mandel, p. 553). In 1929 the first Five-Year Plan was launched. Then late in 1929, through to 1934 came the collectivisation of the land which was to scar the Russian experiment in creating socialism as perhaps no other event of the heroic fifty years did. Reacting to the movement which brought the percentage of peasant households collectivised from 23.6 per cent in 1930 to 71.4 per cent in 1934 the peasants slaughtered their animals, reducing their numbers to a level from which the larger kind did not recover till late in the fifties.

Table 4.4

Animal (millions)	1928	Low (year)	Recovery (year)
Cattle	60.1	33.5 (33)	61.4 (57)
Cows	29.3	19.0 (34)	29.0 (57)

Animal (millions)	1928	Low (year)	Recovery (year)
Sheep	104.2	32.9 (34)	103.3 (56)
Pigs	27.7	9.9 (33)	27.6 (41)
Goats	10.4	3.3 (33)	11.0 (39)
Horses	36.1	14.9 (35)	never

Source: R.A. Clarke, pp. 129-34.

The war years, with their loss of perhaps as many as 30 million people, a high proportion of them men, further added to the malaise of the village.

Looking back in 1962 the marxist, E. Mandel commented:

> Thanks to this distinctive structure of the economy and what it implied—overall planning and a monopoly of foreign trade— a remarkable development of the productive forces was achieved. . . the USSR has become, at least as regards overall output, the second industrial power in the world. (Mandel, p. 557)

He went on to examine the failures, in per capita production, in agriculture and consumer goods, and above all in the human relations established. A. Nove, summing up his 370 pages of description, makes similar points from a non-marxist point of view (see Nove, 1969, pp. 372-9).

In China the Communist Party came to power pledged to a programme of national reconstruction. Between 1949 and 1952 order was restored, the currency stabilised and a nationwide tax system introduced, dikes and railways were restored (the former, according to one commentator, equivalent to digging 10 new Panama Canals—quoted, Prybyla, p. 52) and food and clothing were more equitably distributed. During the same period the promised land reform was carried out, the land and tools of the landlords being distributed amongst the other peasants, and those landlords and other elements regarded as particularly oppressive being tried and sentenced by people's tribunals (Prybyla, pp. 42-8).

Between 1953 and 1957 China embarked on her First Five-year Plan. Under Soviet guidance, it was an ambitious attempt to set up a sound industrial base in steel, coal, electric power and other branches of heavy industry. At the same time an attempt was made to develop industry in new centres away from the formerly foreign-dominated coastal cities. Emphasis under the plan was on industries taken over by the state from foreign owners, or the KMT government (largely former Japanese firms), and on a number of new plants to be built with Soviet assistance. A number of private firms came under joint state-private ownership at this time, the former owners being paid as manager or technical advisor and also receiving a dividend (nominally 5 per cent—Donnithorne, p. 147). Slowly over the period, rising to a crescendo in 1956, handicrafts were organised into co-operatives.

In 1958 an attempt was made to crash through the development barrier by means of The Great Leap Forward. The more conservative second Five-year Plan was laid aside in favour of mass initiative and 'boot-strap' local efforts. Peasants flocked to the towns in search of easier conditions, and factories recruited peasants in the hope of substituting labour for scarce fixed capital. Man-made problems were exacerbated by poor harvests in 1959 and 1960. In July 1960 Soviet experts were withdrawn, taking their blue-prints with them, and leaving numerous construction jobs half-completed. There followed a period of slow recovery during which the emphasis returned to managerial-technical expertise, and away from mass initiative. The rural communes which had started in 1958 (Prybyla, pp. 284-93) with grandiose plans for communal feeding and large-scale agricultural planning, settled down to a pattern in which decisions about agriculture were normally taken by those who were most directly affected, the production teams which correspond to the natural villages. These finally became the basic accounting units (Prybyla, p. 293). The production brigades, intermediate between team and commune, generally managed local industries, trade, education and the militia. But the allocation of functions between the three levels has varied over the years, as has the size of the larger units (Donnithorne, pp. 49-51; cf. Chen and Ridley, 1969).

The Great Proletarian Cultural Revolution which broke out in 1966 and raged through to 1969 affected the economy in complex ways. Immediately the effect was largely negative. Zhou En-lai is reported as having said that costs were not as high as those of the Korean War, a comparison which admits their severity (*SCMP*, 4154, 1968). Many observers noted transport dislocation, problems at the docks, and shortages of coal and steel during late 1967 and early 1968 (cf. Prybyla, p. 551). Considerable efforts were made by the leadership to limit the effects of the Cultural Revolution, the slogan 'grasp revolution and promote production' being repeatedly employed. At the same time, discussion of economic problems in the millions of *dazibao* and other published materials was relatively slight. The experience of Da Zhai and Da Qing were cited, and in October 1966 Sun Ye-fang was attacked for putting forward ideas similar to Liberman in the USSR (Grey and Caven-

dish, pp. 238-49). In view of the hoped-for improvement in the economy
from the employment of Maoist ideas such a paucity of discussion is
rather surprising. However, the Cultural Revolution was important in
making clearer basic divisions on certain economic questions among
China's leaders.

China's economy after the Cultural Revolution, despite impressive
gains in industry and agriculture over the previous twenty years, remains
an economy of relative poverty. During 1969 the slogan was 'make
revolution thriftily' and the attack on pollution was at least as concerned with saving useful materials from waste as with health and aesthetic
considerations. By 1970 reports (e.g. FEEcR, February 1972 in 1973
Asia Yearbook, p. 110) spoke of the economy having 'regained ground
in virtually every sector' and moving ahead at impressive speed. The
policy of 'agriculture the basis with industry the leading factor' continued, and there was considerable stress on the continued development
of local industries and small-scale production as part of the 'policy of
walking on two legs'. Official Peking statistics in September 1972
revealed that 40 per cent of all cement and 50 per cent of all chemical
fertilisers were produced by plants 'not attached to the central industrial
departments' (FEEcR 1972 *Yearbook*, p. 145). They also revealed that
80 per cent of all farm equipment was made by mainly small local factories (ibid. p. 151). In 1971, with a grain (plus potatoes) harvest of 240m
tons, food remained the big bottleneck to further development. Vast
increases are needed in productivity, not to feed the population of some
750m people, but to release labour for industry and construction, and
to free land for growing industrial crops (cf. FEEcR 1973 *Asia Yearbook*, p. 128). The weather remains the recurrent threat, and work
continues on water control in an effort to insulate food production
from drought and flood. Another severe handicap is the poor state of
communications, again in spite of considerable efforts. Roads, particularly in rural areas, and the railways are unable to meet modern demands,
in spite of the help given by a widening network of canals river and
coastal shipping routes (FEEcR 1972 *Yearbook*, pp. 153-4).

'Two lines' in Economics

In order to highlight some points of importance for both economics and
education I shall describe, in the manner of the Cultural Revolution
debate, 'two lines' in economics. One of these is the Soviet model which
came into being about 1930 and persisted with modifications even
after the death of Stalin. The other is the economic policy advocated
by Mao Ze-dong, originally in Yan'an, and then with increasing insistance

in the PRC after 1949.

The Soviet model is essentially a highly centralised one with lines of command running vertically. Major industries are run from ministeries in Moscow, or Peking where the system was copied in the fifties. Communication is between each firm and the ministry rather than between firms on the same level (for details see Dobb, p. 343; Nove, 1968, pp. 66-70). Economic planning, organised by a State Planning Committee (Gosplan) at the centre, is by material balances and physical output targets for enterprises (Nove, 1968, pp. 72, 226 and 228). Emphasis is on heavy industry and agriculture is exploited as the main source of capital accumulation. Light industry, domestic trade, services, residential housing construction and maintenance are relatively neglected (Prybyla, pp. 113-14). Finally, the leadership style is that of the *manager*. Schurmann has described this as a preference for rational organisation and for rules which can be used to 'enforce compliance from his workers' (Schurmann, p. 167). Brugger summarises it as 'commitment to change within a network of technological solidarity' (Brugger, p. 259). Inspired by the model of the Ford Motor Company, the USSR evolved a management pattern which Schurmann describes as follows:

> Soviet managers and workers are held individually responsible for work performance. Thus technical management and individual responsibility may be regarded as key characteristics of Soviet industrial management. (Schurmann, pp. 242-3)

The 'Mao line' contrasts with this on each point. Mao's position on centralisation is a recognition of the importance of both central direction and local initiative. In *On Ten Major Relationships* he urged that

> the local administration should be allowed to carry out more things under the unified plan of the Centre. . . To consolidate the leadership of the Centre, it is necessary to pay attention to local interests. (*CB*, 892, p. 27)

Translated into economic administration terms this has meant reducing the powers of the central Ministeries and increasing the powers of intermediate levels: production brigades, counties, and provinces (Bastid, in Schram, 1973, pp. 191-2). Central planning is necessary for overall guidance and it is particularly important for each level to make plans as a basis for checking on progress. But these are not to be regarded as a substitute for initiative or a straightjacket. (See the *Sixty Work Methods*, especially points 4-13. 4 stresses overall planning, checkups and appraisal and comparison as ways of 'bringing achievements into play' and 'rectifying mistakes'.) The policy of 'agriculture as the basis and industry as the leading factor', declared at Party Conferences in 1962 (Domes, p. 128), involves long-standing measures like restricting the state tax on agriculture, and new ones like reducing prices for chemical fertilisers, insecticides and farm machinery. Combined with higher priorities for light industry and various services (rural medicine) these measures are based on the theory that because of quicker turnover it will enable a faster accumulation of capital, and at the same time provide a market for and thus stimulus to heavy industry itself (Gray in Schram, p. 144). These policies involve the question of incentives on which there has been much misunderstanding. (Those who over-stress moral incentives include Wheelwright and McFarlane, ch. 9; J. Robinson, p. 37; Gurley, p. 20.) While Mao has opposed material incentives which would disrupt the solidarity of workers and peasants, and which would encourage private rather than public economic activities, he has consistently supported those which help to increase production, demonstrate the superiority of socialist measures and arouse *mass* enthusiasm. (One example of this is in *CB*, 892, p. 26 where Mao says: 'Unless irresistible natural calamities are encountered, the peasants should be enabled to receive every year an income higher than the one in the previous year on the basis of agricultural production'.) Finally, the preferred leadership style is the *cadre* rather than the manager, one who *participates in* the ordinary labour which he *leads* through politically inspired activism and technical competence. He is the embodiment of redness and expertise, at once worker and leader. His method is the 'mass line' by which grassroots feelings are worked up by the Party into viable policies through an up and down process of listening to and discussing with the working people (Compton, pp. 176-83; Selden, pp. 274-6; Schram, 1973, p. 29).

Education and the Economy

The interrelations between the economy and education will be divided into three groups of problems: what different economic models require of education; what lessons the economy may teach those who work in it; and the more direct relations between the economy and the school system.

Considering first the 'two lines' in economics which I have just described, these require rather different educational policies. The Soviet line being essentially a command economy based on technological considerations requires major attention be given to the training of technical-managerial experts at tertiary level, and to mass training of loyal and well-disciplined technicians and ordinary workers. Except for the highest levels it will be unnecessary, if not actually harmful, for people to be trained to be critical or too 'creative'. A positive attitude to work is essential, and will form a major goal of general education. By contrast the Mao line, with its aim of a greater spread of decision-making and initiative, demands a much greater spread of the information and expertise necessary for this. For this line to become actual and the required enthusiasm and participation to be sustained the real situation would have to reinforce the rhetoric, something for which there is too little evidence up to now. It is not a question of 'selfless' service to the people, but conscious, rational compromise of present and future interests and conflicting interests of urban and rural and other regional divisions. Political economic education is for this essential, but it would need to be rather more sophisticated than any that foreign observers have been allowed to see.

Turning to the question of what the economy teaches people, the most important lessons surely spring from the determination of the social classes which immediately divide people and ensure significantly different experience to different groups. Class membership daily reinforces consciousness, or unconscious acceptance, of relations of dominance and subordination on the political and ideological levels. Determination of the different classes in the USSR and China, as in the capitalist countries, requires consideration of all three levels, the economic, political and ideological. Those mainly non-marxist writers who have discussed the question fail to do this in any consistent way. Matthews, who presents a fairly lengthy discussion of 'the official theory of class and social development' clearly does not himself understand Marx's conception of class (Matthews, p. 33). Like the Soviet authorities he quotes he does not attempt any analysis which would distinguish those people exercising 'real economic control' (Poulantzas, 1975, p. 18), or those exercising supervision and legitimising this control (ibid. pp. 242, 246) from the class identified as 'employees'. When he does give figures for 'the people who, in their working lives, really control the Soviet Union' he mixes up these first two classes (Matthews, p. 143, data from Semenov, in Osipov, p. 132).

Looking at the figures which Matthews gives for changes in the class composition of the USSR between 1913-24 and 1968, the most striking changes are the decline in the peasantry (and its change from private to collective farming) from 75.4 per cent of the population to only 22.3 per cent, and the accompanying increase in the class of workers

and employees from 14.8 per cent to 77.7 per cent. There is abundant
testimony to the lessons involved in these changes! Turning to the figures for the intellectuals and white-collar workers taken by Semenov
from the 1959 census (Matthews, pp. 143-9; Osipov, p. 132), one finds
a figure of 1,347,000 for heads of state administrative bodies and enterprises (0.6 per cent of the population). Adding to these the figures
for key Party officials would give an approximate figure for what,
assuming a definition of the USSR as 'state capitalist', might be called
the 'state bourgeoisie'. On the same assumption, Semenov's data suggest
a figure in the order of 19.8 million (9.5 per cent of the total population)
for the 'new petty bourgeoisie'.

For China available figures are for kind of employment rather than
class, and estimates of the latter are more uncertain than for the USSR.
Comparing 1952 with 1958 (when figures were inflated by the Great
Leap Forward) the numbers working in industry increased from 5.3m
to 23.7m, or from 0.92 per cent to 3.6 per cent of the total population.
Figures for employment in non-agricultural 'material production' changed from 5.2 per cent to 7.3 per cent of the population. The total non-
agricultural employed increased from 6.4 per cent to 8.8 per cent in
the same period. A rough measure for the peasant population in 1970
can be made from Orleans' estimate of the urban population of 125m
plus or minus about 5m. That would give a figure of 85 per cent of
800m for village dwellers, the great majority of them peasants turned
commune members, or collective farmers.

Figures for a possible Chinese 'state bourgeoisie' or 'new petty bourgeoisie' are even more difficult to arrive at. Combining Orleans' figures
for government administration personnel and Richman's figures for
administrative cadres (pp. 756, 757) suggests something in the order of
3-4m 'managers'. The 'new petty bourgeoisie' in the same year, 1958,
might have been in the order of 8m, or 1.2 per cent of the total population (13.7 per cent of the urban population).

It is difficult to go beyond speculation for just what a person's class
position teaches, other than in the area of job opportunities and related
schooling. An important area is that of attitudes and expectations for
self and others. I shall return to this in the final chapter. I will close this
discussion with a few details of schooling and experience of leading political and industrial personnel available in the literature.

For the USSR, *Party Life* (14, 1973, p. 25) gives some interesting
figures for the educational level of local Party secretaries. Between 1939
and 1973 *raikom* and *gorkom* secretaries having a tertiary schooling
increased from 28.6 per cent to 99.2 per cent in the same time. About

Table 4.5. The Class Composition of the Soviet Union

Class	1913	1924	1928	1937	1939	1959	1968
Percentage breakdown							
Employees	3.0	4.7	5.6	45.7	17.7	20.1	22.9
Workers	14.0	10.1	12.0		32.5	48.2	54.8
Collectivised peasants and craftsmen in co-operatives	—	1.3	2.9	48.8	47.2	31.4	22.27
Individual peasants and free craftsmen	66.7	75.4	74.9	5.5	2.6	0.3	0.03
Bourgeoisie, land-owners, traders and kulaks	16.3	8.5	4.6	—	—	—	—
Numerical breakdown (millions)							
Total population	159.2	137.7	150.0		170.6	208.8	236.7
Employees	4.8	5.2	8.4	163.4	30.2	42.0	54.1
Workers	22.3	15.2	18.0		55.4	100.6	129.8
Collectivised peasants and craftsmen in co-operatives	—	1.8	4.4	79.7	80.5	65.6	52.7
Individual peasants and free craftsmen	106.2	103.8	112.3	9.0	4.4	0.6	0.1
Bourgeoisie, land-owners, traders and kulaks	25.9	11.7	6.9	—	—	—	—

Percentage breakdown: *Narodnoe Khozyaistvo SSR v 1961*, p. 27, *Nar. Khoz. SSR v 1968*, p. 35, *Nar. Khoz. SSR v 1969*, p. 30, *SSR i zarubezhnye strany, stat. sbornik*, Moscow, 1970, p. 24.
Numerical breakdown: Total population 1913, 1939 (census of 17 January within existing boundaries), 1959 from *Narodnoe khozyaistvo SSR v 1961*, pp. 7 and 8; 1924, 1928, 1937, estimates and hypothetical figures from F. Lorimer, op. cit., pp. 30, 135; 1968, from Narodnoe khozyaistvo SSR v 1968, p. 7. Other totals calculated. calculated.
Source: Matthews, p. 35.

Table 4.6. Numbers of Intellectuals and White-collar Workers 1959 census

Type of worker	Number
1. Workers in state administration and public organisations including:	2,389,000
(a) heads of state administrative bodies and social organisations and their subdivisions	392,000
(b) heads of enterprises and their subdivisions	955,000

Type of worker	Number
(c) government employees (juridical personnel, inspectors, and so on)	1,042,000
2. Technical-economic intelligentsia including:	4,991,000
(a) engineers and technicians (excluding engineers occupying positions as heads of enterprises)	4,206,000
(b) agrotechnicians	477,000
(c) planning engineers and statisticians	308,000
3. Scientific and cultural workers including:	5,294,000
(a) teachers, educators, scientific workers	2,836,000
(b) medical workers	1,702,000
(c) cultural administrators	462,000
(d) artistic administrators	190,000
(e) professional writers and journalists	104,000
4. Office employees including:	2,912,000
(a) bookkeepers, accountants	1,817,000
(b) cashiers	413,000
(c) clerical personnel	536,000
(d) agents and filing clerks	146,000
5. Transport employees (conductors)	334,000
6. Communications employees (radio-telegraph, telegraph, telephone operators)	476,000
7. Retail trade and catering workers including:	2,452,000
(a) shop assistants, kiosk and snack-counter managers, etc.	1,166,000
(b) waiters	184,000
8. Workers in communal and public service establishments including:	2,307,000
(a) janitors, watchmen	2,030,000

Source: Osipov, p. 132.

Table 4.7. Distribution of Nonagricultural Employment: 1952-8 (population in thousands)

Branch of the economy	1952 number	1952 %	1953 number	1953 %	1954 number	1954 %	1955 number	1955 %	1956 number	1956 %	1957 number	1957 %	1958 number	1958 %
Total	36,752	100.0	39,116	100.0	39,750	100.0	38,864	100.0	39,366	100.0	39,667	100.0	56,867	100.0
Material production branches	30,200	82.2	31,954	81.7	32,310	81.3	31,258	80.4	30,808	78.3	30,953	78.0	47,918	84.3
Handicrafts and carrier services	7,364	20.0	7,789	19.9	8,910	22.4	8,202	21.1	5,780	14.7	6,560	16.5	1,465	2.6
Salt extraction	500	1.4	500	1.3	500	1.3	500	1.3	500	1.3	500	1.3	700	1.2
Fishing	1,336	3.6	1,404	3.6	1,472	3.7	1,540	4.0	1,500	3.8	1,500	3.8	2,000	3.5
Industry	5,263	14.3	6,121	15.6	6,370	16.0	6,121	15.7	7,480	19.0	7,907	19.9	23,734	41.7
Water conservancy	134	.4	198	.5	266	.7	261	.7	409	1.0	340	.9	1,360	2.4
Capital construction	1,048	2.9	2,170	5.5	2,100	5.3	1,935	5.0	2,951	7.5	1,910	4.8	5,336	9.4
Transport, posts and telecommunications	4,655	12.7	4,764	12.2	4,873	12.3	4,876	12.5	4,103	10.4	4,417	11.1	5,823	10.2
Trade and the food and drink industry	9,900	26.9	9,008	23.0	7,819	19.7	7,823	20.1	8,085	20.5	7,819	19.7	7,500	13.2
Nonproductive branches	6,552	17.8	7,162	18.3	7,440	18.7	7,606	19.6	8,558	21.7	8,714	22.0	8,949	15.7
Finance, banking and insurance	351	1.0	396	1.0	632	1.6	704	1.8	677	1.7	621	1.6	400	.7
Services	443	1.2	452	1.2	461	1.2	470	1.2	479	1.2	489	1.2	489	.9
Education	2,005	5.5	2,159	5.5	2,206	5.5	2,168	5.6	2,542	6.5	2,542	6.4	3,127	5.5
Medicine and public health (inc. traditional medicine)	1,041	2.8	1,142	2.9	1,245	3.1	1,347	3.5	1,628	4.2	1,908	4.8	2,160	3.8
Cultural affairs	92	.3	100	.3	108	.3	116	.3	124	.3	124	.3	131	.2
Government administration	1,523	4.1	1,698	4.3	1,598	4.0	1,576	4.1	1,748	4.4	1,698	4.3	1,183	2.1
Mass organisations	1,053	2.9	1,143	2.9	1,090	2.7	1,096	2.8	1,215	3.1	1,184	3.0	1,281	2.3
Urban public utilities	41	.1	69	.2	96	.2	123	.3	133	.3	133	.3	150	.3
Meteorology	3	–	3	–	4	–	6	–	12	–	15	–	28	–

... Nonagricultural Employment in Mainland China 1949-58. US Bureau of the Census, Washington, 1965, p. 128, quoted in

60 per cent of these secretaries graduated in engineering, agronomy or economics. During the same period secretaries of primary party organisations with tertiary schooling increased from 4.7 per cent to 42.1 per cent and those with only primary schooling decreased from 78.8 per cent to 0.6 per cent.

Hough gives information on the education and experience of both Party officials and industrial directors, particularly the 'men of 1938' who replaced those purged in 1936-8. He shows the increasing tendency for industrial ministers (commissars) and Party First Secretaries to have engineering qualifications through the period 1941 to 1957 (Hough, pp. 38-55), and, as one would expect, that the more important posts and most industrialised *oblasti* to have a higher proportion. In the later period many of the Party Secretaries have considerable prior experience in industry (ibid. pp. 52-3).

For China Donnithorne comments on the background of factory directors and deputy directors. In the late fifties and through the sixties many, in joint state-private firms, were former owners, while others were former PLA officers and veteran Communist Party cadres with often little formal schooling. In 1955, she records, 56 per cent of chief engineers were tertiary graduates (Donnithorne, p. 194).

Richman notes (p. 150) that

> since there is a much greater shortage of high-talent [i.e. qualified] manpower in China, it is necessary to utilise most semi-professionals as technicians, supervisors, and even middle- and upper-level managers and engineers in many cases.

Employment by industry of tertiary graduate engineers rose from 32,000 in 1952 through 217,000 in 1961 to about 270,000 in 1964. In addition there were in 1961 over a million semi-professional technical graduates (Richman, p. 170). These form a key part of the 'state bourgeoisie' and 'new petty bourgeoisie' categories. Their distribution among different enterprises varies with the branch and its importance in the national economy (Richman, pp. 195-200). Most were employed, in the firms surveyed, as heads of sections, vice-directors and similar posts. In 1955 only 6 per cent of 'industrial leaders' were tertiary graduates, but Richman found 25-50 per cent of vice-directors of the majority of firms he visited so qualified (pp. 204-5). But only 3 of 36 top directors were. Only one of the 34 enterprise Party Secretaries had had tertiary education.

Related to the class structure of society is the way in which in modern

capitalism, and up to now in the USSR and China, there has been a
steady removal of decision-making from the point of production and a
reproduction of the work process on paper in the office. This has been
accompanied by a growth of certain factions of the petty bourgeoisie.
Associated particularly with the name of F.W. Taylor, this process has
been of much greater significance than the knowledge revolution about
which educators and journalists talk so much, and the new skills which
this has demanded of some workers and technical personnel (major
studies of this question are by A. Sohn-Rethel, and Braverman; E.
Thompson, pp. 395-7 discusses the ideas of Andrew Ure, 1835). Another
phenomenon is the accelerating process of certification, also present in
the USSR, whereby the paper qualifications demanded of jobs have
been raised. This, of course, has little to do with the actual knowledge
or skill required by these jobs, but is rather a factor of the competition
of the schooled for scarce jobs and the vested interests of the educators.

In the USSR there is plenty of evidence of job dissatisfaction on the
part of the workers. This is recorded for the early period by the figures
for labour turnover, and by the penalties in force through the thirties
to the mid-fifties for breach of labour discipline (Nove, 1969, pp. 197,
260-1, 346). More recently dissatisfaction has been confirmed by sociological studies, such as that on a group of young Leningrad workers in
1963 (Osipov, pp. 99-125 and Matthews, pp. 123-5). There is no evidence
here that work conditions are giving the Soviet worker the idea that 'he
both controls and owns a socialist enterprise' (Osipov, p. 122). Quite
the contrary. Nor are current developments in Soviet industry likely to
improve the situation greatly, any more than are attempts on the part
of certain well-known capitalist firms to add job-interest to the building of motor-cars.

One of the lessons which industry is supposed to teach the workers
is co-operation, and no doubt at various levels it does. But it can also
teach competition and be divisive. Carr and Davies describe some of
the divisions among engineers (petty bourgeoisie) during the late
twenties in the USSR (pp. 596-71). The Cultural Revolution revealed
differences between the young workers and the older, skilled workers
in China, reflected in membership and policies of the two major Red
Guard groups, the *Zaofandui* and *Chiweidui*. The Stakhanov movement
appears to have been as divisive as it was helpful to production (Nove,
1968, p. 233; Trotsky, pp. 80-5). One cannot but be doubtful of articles
which claim that such emulation movements and shock workers 'induce
not only these, but also all other workers . . . to live in a communist way',
especially when one reads the accompanying account of the life-style of

two 'leading workers' (Osipov, pp. 173, 178).

A revealing example of the lessons which can be drawn from the economy appeared in the Chinese pamphlet, *Philosophy is No Mystery*. A young woman in a production brigade in Zhejiang Province began weaving cloth and neglecting work on the collective fields. After a time this encouraged others to follow suit. Their motives were given as to 'have nice clothes to wear, pocket money to spend', and a preference for staying indoors rather than getting sunburned working in the fields (*Philosophy*, p. 61). Because of the threat this presented to the collective economy the brigade leadership used persuasion and the reading of Chairman Mao's works, and it is recorded that the girls became convinced of the error of their ways.

Finally we come to the problems of the relation of the economy to schooling. There has been a great deal of discussion of the degree to which economic growth can be attributed to the increased schooling of the population which has accompanied it. A clear answer to this would have been of some use to governments of 'developing' countries faced with the problems of financing schools. Looking back at the industrialisation in Europe J.D. Gould concludes:

> The impression remains that the early industrial revolution was successful in spite of, rather than because of, the educational facilities on which it could draw. (Gould, p. 310)

Significantly, he notes the out-of-school education which occurred in Britain during this period, and he also draws attention to the unsatisfactory nature of measuring education by the number of years of schooling attended (ibid. p. 309). He surveys the different factors which affect industrial output, such as innovations, both technological and managerial, and he distinguishes between inventions and improvements (Gould, table on p. 299; cf. Langrish, 1972; also Gorz, 1972, who suggests a social, class, rather than technical function for vocational training).

The experience of the USSR is inconclusive. There have been constant complaints about the shortage of trained personnel, or, in spite of planning, about the shortage of people with the *right* training. There is more evidence for the way in which the demands of the economy have been translated into the provision of various kinds of training programmes, both in schools and within industry itself. Other evidence shows how the promise of expansion and upward mobility has lured students, and teachers, into directions contrary to those dictated by the real and immediate needs of the economy. B. King describes how factory apprentice schools were used as a stepping stone to tertiary schools until the government stepped in and reduced the length of courses in general education to prevent this (King, 1937, p. 45; Anweiler, 1973, p. 45; *Ped. Ents.* 4, p. 718). Some reports from China suggest that part-work schools in 1958 were seen by some as the only road *out* of the village. The Khruschev reforms of 1958-9 were also in large part dictated by the need of the economy for middle grade technicians and the need to try and stem the flood of students into tertiary schools.

In China the complaint of Mao Ze-dong and his supporters in the Cultural Revolution was that the schools were urban-orientated and were producing graduates unsuited to the needs of a socialist economy in which agriculture was the basis. It seems clear that schools were producing more young people with aspirations for industrial jobs than the economy could provide for, while the village was being denuded of much-needed talent. It seems to be the hope of Maoist educators that by such measures as the linking of education with productive labour and preparing city youth for life in the rural areas while they are in high school, education will play a major role in changing the Mao line in economics from theory to practice.

Another problem is the proportion of trained personnel and their different types of training required by the economy. Richman gives figures for the percentage of tertiary graduates in relation to total employment for China, the USSR, India and the USA (p. 201). In another place he compares the proportion of those classified as Engineering-Technical-Managerial Personnel in the USSR and China who are tertiary graduates (p. 205). But while he compares attitudes to work and some aspects of the qualitative dimension of the matching of education with industrial requirements he seems to miss the central question. This is how one can judge just what kinds of skills are required in what proportions and to what degree various certificates really guarantee these. Too often Richman skips from talking of level of training to the term 'high-talent manpower', which may be quite a different thing. This problem would also seem to be connected with that of whether full-time training is better than some part-work or sandwich-course arrangement. Here, as I have mentioned elsewhere, one has only the hint offered by the study of Queen's Award firms in Britain to suggest that the part-time trained are the ones who have made the key contributions there (Langrish, p. 18). It is possible that if China maintains her present policy of 'open door education' and 'open door research' she may help us to decide some of these problems.

There are a large number of relations between the economy and school which can only be touched on here. Collective agriculture brings with it the need for book-keepers, agricultural specialists, mechanics and electricians which individual peasant agriculture did not have. Industrialisation requires the training of peasants in urban work- and living-habits, not to mention a host of new technical skills. For some of these schools have been provided. For others there has been only the process of socialisation. The enormous growth, especially in the USSR, of managerial personnel has prompted the provision of numerous schools and classes both by the Communist Party and by the formal education system. The match between specialist training programmes and the job profile of society has been the subject of a number of studies (important studies include, for the USSR: de Witt, 1961; Zaleski, *et al.*, 1969; Korol, 1957; and for China: Cheng, 1965; and Wu and Sheeks, 1, 1970). In all these problems the focus for marxists will be to what extent changes facilitate or hinder the development of a more socialist conscious and less class-divided population.

5 LABOUR AND EDUCATION

Clarifying the Concept

As we saw in the section on 'Marxism and Education' above, Marx uses several phrases to express what he called 'the germ of the education of the future':

> This education will . . . combine productive labour with instruction (*Capital* I, 1976, p. 614);
> co-operate in the great work of social production (*The General Council*, p. 344);
> combination of education with industrial production (*The Communist Manifesto, SW* 1, p. 228).

I suggested there that for Marx there were two aspects of the process he was advocating. The one expressed most clearly in his instructions to the General Council under the term technological or polytechnical education is a process of understanding and skill training. The other, underlying all three quotations above, involves the intellect and the emotions in their involvement in the necessary work of society. This is not a process of adjusting the individual to society in a passive, conforming manner, but of forming a critical consciousness based on understanding through participation. Education is here a supplement to living and not, as with most current schooling, a substitute for it.

It should be clear that the use of the term 'productive' labour has nothing to do with the distinction between productive and unproductive labour in the sense of labour producing surplus value. Rather it is in the very general sense of 'purposive activity carried on for the production of use-value' (Marx, 1976, p. 290), or in the more limited sense of the production of objects for the purpose of consumption. Soviet and Chinese educators have made distinctions between productive and socially useful labour, the latter being the performance of services ranging from cleaning the school, through directing traffic, to guiding blind workers to and from work. Since all productive labour is, or at least should, be socially useful, and much service labour clearly produces use-values, though intangible, the distinction is often difficult and may not be justified here. What is required is an understanding of what is learnt from participation in different kinds of labour. Learning may be categorised as *moral-political*, or *intellectual*, a term which will be used to include both the acquisition of understanding and of mental and manual skills. If it could be shown that the learning outcomes were significantly different as between productive and socially useful labour rather than as between, for example, harvesting and making printed circuits, it would be a considerable advance on our present position.

Because of its usage in Soviet and Chinese literature the distinction between *productive* and *socially useful* labour will be retained in the descriptions which follow. The former will be applied to activities of an industrial, agricultural or commercial nature, and the latter to activities of a 'helping' nature (teaching illiterates; helping the aged or the sick). From an educational point of view it appears likely that a crucial distinction may be whether the activities are *simulated* or *real*, the latter being activities which make a contribution to the wider social unit, or the production of use-values which are actually consumed. The making of lamp-holders or coffee tables in the British grammar school woodwork shop is in this view simulated, whereas the Moscow school which produces furniture for sale in the state shops is engaged in real work. Of course there are marginal activities difficult to classify, but these should not be allowed to obscure the distinction.

The term *combining* also requires definition. It involves where the labour is performed, whether *in school* or *outside* it. If it is performed outside it may only be *observation* of other people's labour, as when students visit a gas works or are guided round the offices of the local council, or it may be *participation* in various forms and degrees. Then it may be *linked* or *not linked* with other school studies such as the natural sciences or mathematics. Also important is who organises the labour, *the school teachers*, the administration of *the workplace*, or some *other body*, such as a youth organisation. By organising is meant planning and directing the work, whether consciously as an educative experience or not. Where the work is real this may be done only by the school, or by the work place, or probably more usually some degree of joint direction will be involved.

I mentioned above moral-political and intellectual learning as possible outcomes of the combination of labour and education. Another outcome mentioned in the literature is not learning but *economic profit*. The labour of students has often been suggested as a means of cheaper schooling. On another level the economic advantage to parents of schooling which allows students to continue a high level of participation in the household economy is in some cases the only means of ensuring peasant children getting any schooling at all. Seen as aims of combining education with labour these three categories, the moral-political, intellectual and economic, should shape the form which the combination takes, and there is some evidence that this is so. (In the September 1958 directive of the CC CCP and State Council where these aims are mentioned the phrase *deyu, zhiyu huo tiyu*—moral, intellectual and physical—is a straight quotation from Mao Ze-dong and the reference to physical need not be taken seriously. Though it may have been intended I cannot recall any subsequent mention of it. Chinese text from *Lun jiaoyu yu shengchan laodong xiangjiehe.* For the English translation see Fraser, 1971, p. 558.)

In spite of the considerable body of literature on labour and education there has been little attempt to distinguish the categories involved, much less to compare learning according to any contrasting combinations of them. It is hoped the above discussion may facilitate this. In what follows a classification of school types based on a limited number of combinations of some of these categories will be used. The major divisions will be made on the proportion of time spent on labour and its general type.

1. Traditional academic schools whose pupils join the work force only after leaving school (though some may perform work in their spare time). Time spent studying is comparable to that spent by adults at work.
2. Full-time schools in which simulated work situations occur in workshops and laboratories, and where there may be courses in basic production techniques, or economic production may influence the syllabus of various subjects.
3. Full-time schools which perform real productive work in school workshops or farms.
4. Reduced-time schooling. Students perform work, either within or outside the school, but under the organisational guidance of the school.
5. Reduced-time schooling, enabling students to perform work outside the school which is not related to study within it.
6. Full-time technical schools in which non-technical studies may be absent or minimal.
   (a) Where work is only simulated.
   (b) Where real productive work is performed.

Before discussing what has been done in the USSR and China to practice 'polytechnical education' or to 'combine education with productive labour' I shall examine the ideas of N.K. Krupskaya and Mao Ze-dong. The former is an exponent of a concept of polytechnical education which places the emphasis on the cognitive aspects of schooling. The latter has instead developed the second strand of Marx's thought, the forming of a critical consciousness through participation in social life.

The Ideas of N.K. Krupskaya

Nadezhda Krupskaya (1869-1939) wrote and spoke extensively on the subject of polytechnical education. Volume 4 of her *Pedagogical Works*, a volume of over 600 pages, is devoted to 'work training and polytechnical education'. Born into the Petersburg intelligentsia, Krupskaya gave up her studies for full-time political activities. While her teaching experience seems to have been limited to a Sunday evening school for adults during 1891, she was fully conversant with the latest, not to mention traditional, theory and practice of Europe and North America. What influence she exerted was through her work as a functionary of Narkompros, and through her influence on her husband, Lenin.

In describing the aims of polytechnical education Krupskaya returns again and again to its role in making people 'masters of industry'. In 1918 and 1920 she used the phrase, emphasising the importance of 'broad knowledge' as opposed to 'narrow, purely mechanical skills'. She wrote:

> The aim of the polytechnical school includes the preparation of a new generation of people who would be workers and masters of industry in the complete sense of the word. (Zepper, p. 240)

At a conference on industrial education in FZS schools in 1931 she made a similar point:

> Will the polytechnical school give less theoretical knowledge than there was up until now? No, not less, but more; but the knowledge itself will be *qualitatively different* than that which our old school, so-called 'academic school', gave and which the modern bourgeois school gives.
> . . . [it will give] a whole series of new and very important knowledges necessary to master Marxist-Leninist theory, to master technology, and to become a master of life, citizen of a Soviet country, and a builder of socialism . . .
> . . . However, this is not all: a polytechnical school must not only give knowledge, but teach how to apply it to life. (Zepper, p. 257)

Mastery through understanding, knowledge capable of being applied, and a disposition for change, these were to be the aims. Speaking about the Soviet school to the First All-Union Teachers' Congress in 1925 Krupskaya said: 'It shows the students how to use knowledge for the transformation of life' (Zepper, p. 271). One other advantage of this type of education which Krupskaya mentioned a number of times was that it would, 'as nothing else, reveal youths' physical and intellectual abilities and allow them to choose a conscientious specialty by 16-17 years of age' (Zepper, p. 242).

Krupskaya was at pains to distinguish between polytechnical education (*polytechnicheskoye obrazovaniye*) and technical training (*technicheskoye obucheniye*). Vocational training must 'not begin too early' because

> accustoming a child to this or that vocation from early childhood means that the discovery and development of his creative abilities are prevented and that the spirit within him is killed. (Zepper, pp. 238-9)

Writing some ten years later she commented: 'a 13 year-old child working at a machine for many hours does not get us anywhere'. And significantly:

> Working at a machine from childhood makes man inattentive to his surroundings. Concentrating all his attention on the machine, he only knows how to work under another's order. (Zepper, p. 254)

Interesting when comparing with current experiments in China is the following remark:

> What is to be done in the labour school? Buy chicks and compel children to look after them? Certainly not. It is necessary to profit from the work which children do at home caring for chickens, but an entirely new content must be put into the school. (Zepper, p. 255)

In the preface to a brochure on *Progressive Schools in the Struggle for Polytechnism* Krupskaya, in 1931, attempted to outline the relationship between the factory (here plant = zavod) and the school.

> Schools still face vast work under polytechnical conditions. It is

necessary to establish exactly in what sequence children are evoked
to work at a plant, how they are evoked to study a plant, which
skills are required, how they are to be aroused, and to interpret
their work and the whole labour organisation at the plant. In school
and in the plant, children's work must be co-ordinated in the closest
possible way. It is necessary to reconstruct all curricula, to revise all
schedules, and to rationalise all school work. Interest in technology
and striving to master it must be enkindled in children. (Zepper, p.
253)

Krupskaya distinguished two different stages of the schooling process.
In 1920 she described them as follows:

The first stage of the Unified Labour School (polytechnical school
for children from 7 to 12 yrs old) is only a preparatory stage for
conscious participation in production.
  The task of the first stage in the polytechnical school is to give
children the opportunity to accustom themselves to humanity's
ideas and life through books; to teach them to use a book, the ability
to write, mathematical and graphic competence as work tools; to use
every means of observation, of studying trades, of free creativity to
develop the constructive abilities of children; to acquaint them with
the surrounding life of nature; to teach them to observe and to test
their observations experimentally; to give an idea about nature's
wealth and about the life of the surrounding locality; and to give an
idea about the life of all countries and the whole world.
  But the most important task of the first stage is in training the
ability to live and work collectively (organisation of school life, organisation of collective work, organisation of play). Work at this stage
must be very easy (gathering plants, caring for animals, delivering
letters and notices, tidying up and so on).
  The second stage (from 12 to 16 years inclusive) must be established on participation in production. (Zepper, pp. 240-41)

Consciously and admittedly based on the best experience from Western
Europe and the USA (Dewey, Kilpatrick, etc.), Krupskaya here describes
what goes on in the better primary schools throughout the world today
and it is a little hard to see how to describe this as polytechnical education in any special sense. It is at the secondary stage that the idea
becomes clear. Here Krupskaya recommends exposure of students to the
main branches of the economy: agriculture, the chemical industry and

the technical (mechanical) industry. City and country youth must participate in each alike, and theory must be closely linked with practical experience in each field. The summer months are to be spent practising agriculture, the first year near home, but later farther afield where conditions are different. As always with Krupskaya, she returns to stress the importance of theory:

> It speaks for itself that the basic programme must be accompanied by study of the political economy, cultural history, history of social life, history of the Revolution, etc. Also, skills must be allotted a proper place.
> Attention must be given to the practical and theoretical study of languages. (Zepper, p. 241)

The precise flavour of Krupskaya's thought comes out in her description of teaching sewing. In 1929 she wrote this in order to show that 'training for any work can have a vocational or polytechnical character'.

> Sewing can be taught in a variety of ways. It can teach how to make even stitches, or how to work button holes by the hours. This training will be a handicraft. But it is possible to provide an entirely different training. Sewing instruction can be established so that it would be linked with study of material and tools. This should be done so that it would become clearer to a child that a different instrument is needed for different materials for production in the very same process: one needle is needed to sew muslin, another type for broadcloth, leather needs an awl to sew, it is unnecessary to sew paper together because it is pasted; wood is not sewn but is knocked together, etc. This would be the polytechnical approach to learning sewing. It is not only possible to permit individual work, but collective as well: in two's, three's, in succession—introducing rhythm in work, sometimes retarding, sometimes accelerating, and then performing a series of other movements rhythmically to a song, too. Sewing can be taught differently on a machine: you can show only how to run the whell, insert the shuttle, etc. Or study of the sewing machine can be connected with study of the machine itself and analogous machines. By such methods sewing as a vocation can be taught by combining this training with the analysis of materials, tools, motors, etc.,—this will be polytechnical education. (Zepper, p. 248)

Krupskaya, wrestling to delineate the polytechnical curriculum, touches on the distinction between productive and socially useful work, categories which are not mutually exclusive but do not entirely overlap. Writing in 1931, and in the stress of the time forgetting for a moment her aim of 'mastery', she said:

> Shop work and labour . . . must be linked with the battle to increase conscious discipline, common work, the immediate task, and productivity. Our vocational education is going along these lines now. Of course, this does not exhaust the socially useful work of the school, it is much broader. It would be wrong if vocational training would exclude or take the place of other socially useful work. (Zepper, p. 261)

In 1925, talking of the difficulty of providing suitable work for young city children, a favourite theme, Krupskaya wrote:

> The sections of public education, communal work, sanitation, and others [i.e. of city soviets] should entrust a definite part of the work to children. . . examine in what kind of work children may help so that this work can be connected with studies. (Zepper, p. 274)

In 1936, in a letter to M.P. Malyshev of the Department of Schools of the CC CP(B) she complained:

> . . . it has now turned out to be a *school isolated from life* which makes the organization of *socially useful work* difficult. Now useful labour, productive labour, is reduced to mere production of *useful objects for school studies.* Usefulness of this work is very relative; useful labour should go beyond the school walls, useful things should be made for kindergartens, for neighbourhood organizations—living associations, rest homes for the aged, for libraries, etc.

She goes on to emphasise the educational side of such work:

> *The work plan in shops must be thought through especially from a pedagogical point of view.* It cannot be accidental, it must be particularly *polytechnical.* Here it is especially important to avoid *hackwork.*

Mao Ze-dong and Labour and Education in China

Though trained to be and acting for a short time as a teacher, Mao

Ze-dong has never expressed himself at length on the subject of education. Like his classical forebears, it is clearly close to the centre of his Thought, and there are stimulating, and sometimes startling, passages on it in his writings on China's revolutionary struggles, and in his remarks to political colleagues, Red Guards, and visiting delegations. Many of these have only recently become available (*CB*, 888, 892; *JPRS*, 49826; Schram; *MTTU*). The emphasis is on relating education closely to practical needs and combining theory and practice. Long bookish courses must be shortened and 'stuffing' methods of teaching must be replaced by others which encourage initiative and the ability to solve problems. The concept of polytechnical does not appear, but rather 'the worker with socialist consciousness and culture'. Like Marx before him, Mao is primarily concerned with the smooth and early introduction of the young into the adult-dominated world of work and responsibility, characteristic of the peasant background in which he was himself reared. In the famous letter of 7 May 1966, Mao wrote:

> While (students) their main task is to study, they should in addition to their studies learn other things, that is, industrial work, farming and military affairs. They should also criticize the bourgeoisie. (*CB*, 888, p. 17)

He has frequently complained that, in the words of a current slogan, students suffer from *three separations* (*san tuoli*): separation from proletarian politics, from the workers and peasants, and from production.

The first direct references to linking schools with productive work appear in 1957, though a number of 'part-work' schools had existed in the Yan'an period and Mao had encouraged 'irregular' village schools (*The United Front in Cultural Work*, 20 October 1944, *CB*, 888, p. 6). Recommendations are tentative at first:

> Concerning the question of schools run by communes or brigades those communes or brigades with the necessary conditions should be permitted to run schools.
>
> Materials of instruction should bear a local character and some more local or indigenous teaching material should be used. Textbooks dealing with agriculture should be compiled by the province concerned. Some indigenous literature should be taught, and this also applies to natural sciences. (Summary of talk to heads of education departments and bureaux of 7 provinces and municipalities, 7 March 1957, in *CB*, 888, p. 7)

This immediately followed the famous speech *On the Correct Handling of Contradictions among the People* (27 February 1957) where Mao declared:

> Our educational policy must enable everyone who receives an education to develop morally, intellectually and physically and become a worker with both socialist consciousness and culture. (Mao, *Four Essays*, p. 110)

In January 1958, in the draft of *Method of Work*, Mao went further and advocated

> As far as circumstances permit, all secondary vocational schools and skilled workers' schools should tentatively run factories or farms . . . Apart from carrying out production in their own farms, all agricultural schools may also sign contracts with local agricultural co-operatives for participation in labour, and send teachers to stay in co-operatives for the purpose of integrating theory with reality. . . (*CB*, 888, p. 8)

Universities, secondary and primary schools of all kinds were, circumstances permitting, to engage in production either in their own workshops and farms, or by some system of contracting. These ideas became incorporated in the Directive of the CCP CC and the State Council on Educational Work issued on 19 September of that year.

> The Party line in education work seeks to make education serve the proletariat politically, and to unite education with productive labour . . . Marxist-Leninist political and ideological indoctrination must be carried out in all schools to indoctrinate the teachers and students with . . . the viewpoint calling for the integration of mental labour with physical labour. . . The future direction is for schools to run factories and farms, and for factories and agricultural co-operatives to establish schools. (*Directive*. . . in Fraser, 1971, pp. 554-66)

The document went on later:

> Productive labour must be listed as a formal course in all schools. Every student must spend a certain period of time in manual labour in accordance with the rules. The campaign of hard work and thrifty study has now been universally launched. There are facts to show that provided productive labour is well led, it is of advantage ethically,

intellectually, or physically to the students. This is a correct way of
training new personnel of all-round development. (*Directive*, section
3)

Apart from the reference to 'thrifty study' the document does not
mention the economic aspect of combining labour and education. But
Mao Ze-dong, while he does not rate this as its main function, does not
neglect it. Replying to a request from the Jiangxi Communist Labour
College to commemorate their third anniversary, Mao wrote:

I completely endorse your cause. Part-work and part-study, running
schools through the practice of working while studying, does not
cost the state a cent. There are primary schools, secondary schools
and colleges dispersed in mountains throughout the province, and
there are a few on the plain. Such schools are good indeed. (*CB*, 888,
p. 10)

A majority of Mao's comments on labour and education obviously
refer to the intellectual benefit to be derived from the combination.
Talking to a delegation of teachers from Nepal in 1964 he complained
that 'few people are for the new method, and more people are against
it'. He went on:

Qinghua University has its workshops, and it is a plant of science
and engineering. It won't do for its students to acquire only knowledge from books without working. However, it is infeasible to set
up workshops in a college of arts, and it is infeasible to run workshops for literature, history, economics or novels. The faculty of
arts should take the whole society as its own workshop. Its
students should contact the peasants and urban workers, industry
and agriculture. Otherwise they are not much use on graduation.
(*CB*, 898, p. 47)

Mao repeated the point at the Hangzhou Conference on 21 December
1965:

In order to remould the colleges of arts, students should be sent to
the grassroots level to take up industrial, agricultural and commercial
work. As to the colleges of science, and engineering, things are
different. They have workshops and laboratories, and they work in
workshops and conduct experiments in laboratories. But they also

must contact the realities of society. (*CB*, 888, p. 16)

The previous paragraph of this speech showed the intellectual purpose when Mao referred to the present when

> philosophers are incapable of fostering philosophy, men of letters are incapable of writing novels, and historians are incapable of fostering history. (ibid.)

None of this refers to the moral-political aim of closing the class gap, though the same medicine may produce that result too. The process of integration of study and work described in the same speech would certainly seem to go a long way to closing class gaps.

> On graduating from a senior high school, one should first do some practical work. It will not do to go only to the countryside. One must also go to the factory, the commercial store, and the company unit [of the army]. After doing this for a few years, two more years of study will be sufficient. If a university course takes five years to complete, one should work at the lower levels for three years. Members of the faculty should also go along, working and teaching at the same time. Isn't it possible to teach philosophy, literature or history at the lower level? Must they teach in tall, modern buildings? (*CB*, 888, p. 16)

In all this the aim is clear but the methods are left open for further experiment. This accords with Mao's theory of knowledge, outlined in *On Practice*. There he describes the model: practice, knowledge, again practice, and again knowledge. In this endless dialectic, true for both the individual and for the group, the essential practice is in the real world outside the school, and through this very dialectic itself Mao expects the educators to find the right mix for today, and for tomorrow when it comes.

Finally, in Mao's view childhood, rather than being increasingly prolonged by the extension of schooling and the inability of society to provide jobs, is to be reduced and merged into the *real* adult world as the only way to learn *real* things. As noted above, study is to supplement living, not to substitute for it. Here is the vision of a harmony of young, middle aged and the old, each with something special to contribute to the others, which is so tragically lacking in late capitalism.

The Experience of the USSR

While Krupskaya's writings on polytechnical education have been
singled out for special attention, she was far from alone in devoting
attention to the subject. From casual mention to lengthy volumes, the
term has been explored from 1917 to the present day. Under the guise
of 'the unified labour school' the subject is discussed in the *ABC of
Communism* (pp. 286-9). As in China nearly four decades later,
'labour is necessary', it is stated, 'not only for the healthy physical
development of the children, but also for the proper development of all
their faculties.' The authors, Bukharin and Preobrazhensky, go on:
'Labour should be a need, like the desire for food and drink, this need
must be instilled, and developed in the communist school.'

In the first year of the Revolution, 1918, educators of Petrograd and
Moscow were deeply divided on the nature of the school system to be
set up, and their controversy delayed the opening of the new school
year by one month. The polytechnical aspect of education was only
one of the issues which divided them. The Petrograd group, led by
Lunacharsky and Ludmila Menzhinskaya, acknowledged inspiration
from August Lay (Die Tatschule), John Dewey, Kerschensteiner (the
Arbeiterschule), Ferriere and Montessori, as well as such Russians as
Tolstoy, S.T. Shatsky and Ushinsky. For them polytechnical education
was to be carried out in school workshops, and trade training was to be
postponed to late adolescence (Fitzgerald, p. 29). The Moscow group,
led by V.M. Pozner and P.N. Lepeshinsky, wished to remove the child
from parental influences and conduct education in a school—commune
(shkole-kommuna) throughout the whole year. Labour was to be the
real work of maintaining the school commune. The *Statement on the
United Labour School* presented by Pozner to the First All-Russian
Congress of Education and the State Education Commission advocated:

> Productive labour must serve as the basis of school life, not as a
> means of paying for the maintenance of the child, and not only as a
> method of teaching, but as socially-necessary productive labour. . .
> The school is a school-commune, closely and organically linked
> through the labour process with its environment. (quoted in Fitz-
> patrick, p. 33, from *Direktivy VKP(b) i postanovleniya sovetskogo
> pravitel'stva o narodnom obrazovanii zo 1917-1947 gg*, Mos-Len,
> 1947, pp. 120-7; cf. *Declaration on the United Labour School* in
> Lunacharsky, *O narodnom obrazovanii,* pp. 522-38).

Two quotations will have to suffice to give the atmosphere of those terrible, but inspired early days. Lepeshinsky describes his own school-commune:

> Life *forced* the creation of boarding-schools (because there was no-where to put homeless orphans, children of the streets, or it was not possible to send children from neighbouring villages home in the evening) . . . The building *had* to be cleared of rubbish. Provisions are being given out somewhere: they *must* be brought or dragged home, otherwise in a few hours painful hunger will be felt. It is not very pleasant to lie on the bare floor with nothing to lie on, so beds *must* be set up. Shirts are dirty, insects are nesting on the body, so washing of shirts is *on the agenda*. The school has received cloth, which means great rejoicing and a lot of work: it is *necessary* to sew and sew and sew. There is no wood and the school is freezing—so it is necessary to *drop everything* and mobilize all forces in the search for firewood . . .

Going on, as Fitzpatrick notes, 'to make a virtue of necessity', he adds:

> And in this way the circumstances of the children's psychological rebirth emerge. *Social* labour and *communal* conditions of life are doing their great educative work. . . (Quoted in Fitzpatrick, from *Narodnoe prosveshchenie* Narkompros, Moscow (monthly) 1919, nos. 16, 17, p. 16)

A teacher from the Ranenburgsky *uezd* described labour training in the local school during 1918-20.

> They invited a local villager, usually a joiner or a carpenter, to teach his trade to the children, but the whole equipment of the 'workshop' consisted of a bag containing a plane, saws, an axe and so on which he brought with him. . . (Quoted in Fitzpatrick, from A.S. Tolstoy, 'At work on the organization of the labour school', *Narodnoe prosveshchenie,* 1927, no. 10, pp. 132-4)

Through the twenties the debate on polytechnical education and relating school and work, or school and life, continued. Three groups emerged: Pinkevich and Kalashnikov; Shatskii; and Shul'gin. They were divided on such questions as whether labour should be performed in the community, or in special workshops within the school.

Writing for an American audience in 1930, Pinkevich asserted:

> . . . we are not supporters of the thesis that an existing society can be changed through the school. To make the school the embryo of a future socialistic order is impossible for the simple reason that the school cannot be independent of its environment. (Pinkevich, p. 153)

Similar reasoning made Kalashnikov reject the school as a means of educating people for agricultural communes (Anweiler, p. 413). Pinkevich placed the emphasis on general education, with a socialist bias, and at the upper levels a professional, vocational, training was to be added. 'A man must have an all-round education and at the same time know well some particular specialty', he wrote (Pinkevich, p. 28). This is very different from the 'principles of all processes of production' of Marx. His book describes the ideas of foreign and Soviet writers on labour and education.

Shatskii, long experienced as leader of summer camps for children and other school-communities, favoured the performance of productive work by students, particularly as an organising force within a school-collective. But it should be of a suitable nature, related to current needs and children's interests and possibilities. He was sceptical about the possibilities within an urban, industrial environment (Anweiler, pp. 328-9 and 62-3).

Shul'gin, famous as the exponent of the 'withering away of the school', remarked that 'in reality however men learnt not in school but in life, not only in childhood, but throughout the whole of life' (Anweiler, p. 417). While recognising the importance of spontaneous factors in education, in the factory, courts of justice, or political meetings, he sought to organise and regulate them (ibid. p. 418). About the role of labour he wrote:

> To our mind labour is the best method of so introducing young children to the labouring class and of so merging them with the class-builder that they may not only understand the proletarian ideology, but may actually begin to live, to strive and to build according to that ideology. But this is not all. Labour is to us a means of inducting children into the working world family in order that they may participate in and understand the struggle of the masses, follow the history of human society, acquire working, organizing and collective habits, and come into the possession of the discipline of work. To us labour, because of its superior integrating power, is the best method of teaching children how to live the contemporary life. The

factory is the first and most sensitive plate [?] of modern society.
Since labour, self-government and contemporary life merge into an
inseparable union, the march of economic events calls for school
which will train the warrior and builder of life. (Pinkevich, p. 199)

In spite of all the efforts and all the talk, by the end of the twenties
there was neither clarity, nor any firm practice which might be called
polytechnical schooling (Anweiler, p. 376). Productive labour was either
self-service of the cooking and mending variety, or assisting factories
and farms to fulfil output targets. In both cases education tended to be
forgotten. In 1931 the CC CP stepped in. In the ensuing years experiment was replaced by a centrally directed, uniform school system in
which separate subjects replaced attempts at a complex method, and any
linking with life and with production took place through the textbook,
supplemented by occasional excursions, or practical work in the laboratory or school workshop. The curriculum became weighted towards
the sciences, especially physics and mathematics. The interpretation
to be given to polytechnism henceforth is shown in the following
extract from the CC CPSU statement of 5 September 1931:

Every attempt to disassociate polytechnization of the school from a
systematic and firm mastery of science—especially of physics, chemistry, and mathematics, the teaching of which must be based upon
rigorously defined and carefully worked out syllabi and curricula
and carried out in accordance with a firmly established school calendar—represents a most fundamental perversion of the concept of
the polytechnic school (*Xrestomatia po istorii pedagogika*, p. 497,
trans. in Korol, p. 27)

In the fifties through to the middle sixties there was a fresh wave of
interest in polytechnical education, with the emphasis on vocational
training. It began at the 19th Congress of the CPSU, just before the
death of Stalin, when a resolution on education proposed 'to undertake
the realization of polytechnic instruction throughout the secondary
schools' (Korol, p. 28). Amongst numerous publications on the subject
was a work by five writers entitled *Polytechnic Instruction in Schools
of General Education*, published by the RSFSR Academy of Pedagogical
Sciences in 1953. It stressed the vocational training aspect in these terms:

If the students are to be given only theoretical knowledge of scientific
principles on which productive processes are based at the neglect of

inculcating work skills, then the polytechnic instruction will have
an abstractly-theoretical character and will have poorly prepared
(the students) for work. If only the work skills are inculcated without the theoretical knowledge of productive processes, then the
instruction will not be a polytechnic instruction but a sterile training
in trades—'technicianism'. (Quoted in Korol, p. 28)

It should be superfluous to comment that the *breadth* of training
distinguishes *poly*technical from *mono*technical training, and that
theoretical knowledge of some kind is imparted with almost any *training* programme! For various reasons little progress was made until 1958,
when N.S. Khrushchev took the lead in initiating a new school reform.
At the 20th Congress of the CPSU in 1956 he had complained of 'a
certain rift between our schools and life' and of the slowness of teachers
and the Academy of Pedagogical Sciences to implement polytechnical
education (Korol, p. 32). Beginning at the 13th Congress of the Komsomol in April 1958 and in his Memorandum 'on the strengthening of the
ties of the school with life' of September 1958, Khrushchev put forward
his proposals. In December 1958 and December 1959 laws were passed
by which the compulsory 7-year school was replaced by an 8-year one,
to be followed by a 3-year secondary 'general polytechnical school
with industrial training' (cf. appendices to Shapovalenko). Article 28 of
the December 1958 law included the controversial ruling: 'Preference
for admission to higher educational institutions shall be given to persons
who have experience of practical work' (Shapovalenko, p. 385). It also
said:

Admission to higher educational institutions shall be on the basis of
character references given by the Party, trade-union, Komsomol and
other public organizations, by the directors of industrial undertakings
and collective-farm managers, so that through competitive selection
the most deserving, trained and capable people, who have proved
themselves in production, may be enrolled in higher educational
institutions. (ibid.)

In the curriculum of the 8-year school 'manual and technical training'
and 'socially useful work' together occupied 4-5 hours a week in grades
3-8. In the secondary school 'production training and productive work'
occupied 12 periods a week in each grade. The balance of the curriculum
changed as shown in Table 5.1.

Table 5.1

	1955 Ten-year school	1958 Eleven-year school
Humanities	47.0%	36.0%
Natural sciences and mathematics	37.2%	32.5%
Technical work, production, excursions	7.3%	21.0%
Artistic training and physical culture	8.5%	10.5%

Source: Shapovalenko, p. 104.

Article one of the statute on the secondary school makes clear the trade training aspect of the reform:

> Completion of the course at a secondary general-education labour polytechnical school with vocational training shall qualify young men and women for work in their chosen field and for admission to higher educational establishments. (Shapovalenko, p. 401)

But as subsequent events were to prove, this was hope rather than promise. Freedom of choice would require a variety of factories within reach of the school, and moreover, factories which would subsequently require fresh labour. This was admitted by I.A. Kairov, then President of the Academy of Pedagogical Sciences, in March 1965:

> Experience has convincingly shown that the vocational training of students within the framework of the secondary school has not been successful. In the conditions of our country it proved impossible to bring into harmony the territorial principle of enrolling students in the general educational schools and the planning and organization of vocational training. Thus the needs of particular economic regions for cadres were not accounted for, and the personal interests and inclinations of the students were almost completely ignored. (Trans. from Anweiler, KdS, p. 90)

In August 1964 the 10-year school was restored, and in 1965 and again in 1969 the amount of practical work performed in school was reduced. 'Polytechnical education' returned to being largely subject matter.

Polytechnical Education as Subject Matter

While Marx's concept of polytechnical education was precise and defined, its use in the following examples borders on the magical and is highly misleading.

In an article entitled 'Polytechnical education as illustrated in history and geography teaching' N.G. Dairi and L.I. Samoilov write:

In the reorganization of the schools, substantial improvement in the teaching of history has been brought about through some curtailment of the material relating to the early periods of history and expansion of contemporary history, both Soviet and foreign, making history teaching considerably closer to life. The pupils, including those attending 8-year schools, cover the whole course of world history from ancient times to the present day. They become acquainted with the history of many countries, with various aspects of their societies and with all important events.

All this helps to give the schoolchildren an understanding of history as a process of progressive development of society rather than a haphazard collection of events, and understanding of the objective laws governing that development, a scientific appreciation of past and present events in the life of society and the beginnings of a scientific outlook on the world.

All history courses include a detailed description of the means of production and their progressive development, transmitting to the children a volume of concrete, graphic and colourful factual material as well as general conclusions in a form they can understand.

It teaches the young to hold technical progress in high esteem and gives them a better understanding of the problems in the field of scientific and technical development which the Soviet Union is in the process of solving. It aims at providing pupils with a profound understanding of the social significance of production and labour, the fundamentals of political knowledge and an understanding of their personal duty in the sphere of production. (Shapovalenko, pp. 309-10)

The authors go on to list activities which will further these aims:

(a) participation by senior pupils in production meetings at factories or State farms; (b) study of the history of industrial undertakings and collective farms; (c) lectures and amateur performances organized by schoolchildren for workers and collective farmers; (d) talks and essays at schools on subjects such as 'Why I chose a particular trade' (turner, animal farmer, etc.), 'What I have learnt from my work at the factory (or on the collective farm)', 'My apprentice master', etc. (ibid.).

Korol quotes from a book on *Polytechnic Instruction in Schools of General Education* published in 1953 which lists skills to be taught in mathematics. They include:

> ... rapid mental and written computation; ability to round-off numbers and to check results of operations; ability to use tables, handbooks, abacus, and slide rule; ability in reading formulas, ... ability to formulate and solve equations in working out various technical and economic problems; ability to carry out book-keeping, budgetary, and cost computations, and so forth. (Korol, p. 29)

Commenting on the book as a whole Korol remarks:

> The headings obviously include every known phase, method, and element of the teaching process, and the text throughout exemplifies opportunities for relating theory to practical ends, including industrial application. (Korol, pp. 30-31)

It is as if 'polytechnic' had become a magic word which could transform the most 'bourgeois' of content into a potion which would nourish the 'new socialist man'!

Combining Labour and Education in China

Chinese practice will be discussed under three sub-sections: policies and aims; types of part-work school; and the problems of part-work schooling.

There have been three periods in the history of the PRC when a policy of combining education with productive labour has received particular attention: 1958-60, 1964-5, and the post-Cultural Revolution period, especially 1969-72. In each of these periods new schools have been established, said to exemplify the principle, and other measures have been publicised. In each case the forms encouraged have been the same as, or developments of, those pioneered in Yan'an. In 1958 the stress was on schools at all three levels introducing some form of labour into the curriculum, often in the form of school plots of land or small workshops, and in the rural areas the agricultural high schools were set up. In 1964, after a period of opposition to the policy, during which a majority of the experiments of the 1958 period were abandoned or shut down, the emphasis was divided between primary schooling in the rural areas and technical high schools in the cities. There was also activity at the tertiary level, with some new institutions set up and others converted to a part-work basis. The Cultural Revolution put renewed emphasis on linking labour and education as the only means of nurturing 'red and expert successors to the revolution' and once again an attempt was made to change the nature of the full-time schools through the introduction of courses in labour and the setting up of workshops and farms. But at the same time the setting up of various forms of what the opposition described as 'irregular' schools was renewed in the rural areas, many of which still lacked any educational facilities for their children.

Many of those who supported the setting up of the agricultural high schools in 1958-60 saw them as a means of bringing technical knowledge to the village. Others stressed both the direct contribution to production which school workshops could make, or the indirect contribution through the release of workers from other jobs, e.g. students doing the work of school janitors, etc. (cf. Vogel, p. 244). By 1964, when it was clear that the universalising of schooling was proving an almost intractable problem, numbers of supporters of regular schools were prepared to support the setting up of various forms of irregular primary schools in the rural areas, and also the extension of part-work forms for the training of medium grade technicians. Their attitude was condemned during the Cultural Revolution, one contributor to the *People's Daily* debate describing it as follows:

> Liu Shao-qi's method of simultaneously promoting work-study schools and the full-time schools was the 'double-track' system of the capitalist countries and an educational system instituted for the purpose of restoring capitalism and separating the workers and peasants. (RMRB, December 1968)

It is in the attempt to make schooling universal that the concept of part-work becomes most hazy. Numerous people have praised it as the only means by which to accomplish this aim. But when one examines the various forms of schooling set up it becomes clear that what is being stressed is the schooling, its part-time nature and flexibility, rather than any linking of schooling with labour. The various forms of *xunhui xiaoxue* or circulating schools, where the teacher goes from village to village, or from camp to camp where Mongol or Uighur herdsmen tend their flocks, teaching one day here or two days there, may or may not relate what is taught to some productive activity. But they do enable small groups of children to receive schooling where before they had none. Half-day schooling, adjusting the school calendar to that of agriculture enables children to work outside the school, but it is a moot point whether this is sufficient to include it under the concept of part-work education. For any control over moral-political or intellectual learning to occur productive labour must surely be linked in some way with the school, organisationally and perhaps to its theoretical studies.

One of the benefits frequently mentioned is economic, either for the school, the community which supports it, or for the parents. In the last case some form of irregular school which enables the student to continue to play his part in the household economy is the only type of school which he could attend. In the case of girls who have to look after their younger siblings it has been reported both that the teacher takes the school into the home, and that the girl brings her young siblings to class with her. In neither case should this be regarded as part-work schooling, though it is usually reported under that general heading. The various cases reported where the teacher works outside the school for part of his time are more difficult to classify. Often they are reported as beneficial in reducing the cost of education to the community. At the same time such experience may assist the teacher to be more effective in the classroom, through the respect he will gain from his proven ability in the outside work-world, and because he will have the practical experience necessary to relate theory to practice. It may similarly be argued that work-experience, apparently unrelated to schooling, may give the student confidence in his abilities and a range of experience on which he can draw in various ways within the school situation.

Whatever the benefits, real or hoped for by its supporters, opposition to part-work schooling and 'irregular' institutions has been, and continues to be strong. Some observers suggest the post-Cultural Revolution situation is radically different because the principle has been widely discussed and experimented with, and because of its adoption in some form throughout the FTD as well as other forms of schooling. A more careful look at the conceptual confusion which makes evaluation of experiment impossible, and at counter-attacks by the opposition already apparent by 1972 would suggest a little more caution. Some of the difficulties of an intellectual nature will be discussed in connection with particular forms of part-work below. An organisational difficulty which has received little discussion in Chinese materials to date is the big discrepancy between the number of urban youth and the factories in which they could be given practice. Any attempt to make such practice the norm could result in devastating disruption of the production process. At the same time, the limited development of industry and the shortage of machines and raw materials makes the running of workshops by schools a difficult problem. It must be remembered here that much effort is being put into training urban youth for a future life in the rural areas.

One of the most intractible problems is the real gulf in standards which will persist between the irregular schools and the richer urban FTD schools. Ambitious students and their parents will still look to the latter as the road out of the village, and if means are not found to enable some to travel this road it will only harden the gulf between city and the rural areas. The addition of some form of labour for 33 per cent of the city curriculum will not necessarily alter this problem or bring nearer the wished-for closing of the class gap between intellectual, worker and peasant, between mental and manual work, or between town and country. Current trends are certainly promising, but as the Chinese say, they are only the first step on a 10,000 *li* road. Clarity of theory might speed the journey and ensure the road travelled is the right one.

The Range and Extent of Part-work Schooling

Quantitative assessment of part-work schooling suffers from the usual problem of Chinese data. There are almost no available overall figures, and the many partial reports are non-comparable, or from too limited a sample. Nevertheless, it would seem better to consider what is available than to ignore the problem of quantity altogether.

Barendsen gives the data for agricultural high schools during their first period of foundation (Table 5.2).

Table 5.2

Provinces, etc.	No. of schools	Enrolment	Date
Liaoning	930	n.a.	Aug. 1959
Shanghai (outskirts)	220 (171 Dec. 61)	27,000 (16,000 Dec. 61)	Aug. 1959
Hebei	2,125	230,000+	Nov. 1959
Shandong	1,380	134,000	Nov. 1959
Guangxi Zhuang AR	530	46,996	Nov. 1959
Inner Mongolian AR	400	31,000	Jan. 1960
Jiangsu	2,174 (1,500 Nov.61)	279,890	Apr. 1960
Sichuan	4,640	385,113	Apr. 1960
Fujian	560	41,200+	Apr. 1960

These figures already show a reduction on some published earlier, e.g. for Jiangsu province. In 1960 two different figures were published for the overall national position. On 2 February the *People's Daily* gave a figure of over 20,000 schools with a total enrolment of 2,190,000 students. On 15 March the NCNA gave a figure of over 30,000 schools with an enrolment of 2,960,000. Barendsen points out that the second figure probably includes FTD secondary technical schools, at the junior high school level, though the figure was requoted by the mass media on subsequent occasions without qualification (Barendsen, *CQ*, pp. 109-10).

When it comes to attempting to assess the significance of part-work schools in universalising schooling one is first faced with problems of definition, and then with the data itself. Figures of school attendance are notoriously inaccurate since they are normally recorded at their highest in all countries. There is also a natural desire to emphasise progress and conformity with current policies. Nevertheless, the data shown in Table 5.3 are interesting for the variety of provinces covered.

Table 5.3

Province	Xian population		% of age-range in school now	previously	Date reported
Hebei	Yang Yuan	n.a.	39.5	14.3	1964 cf. 1961
	Zunhua	n.a.	97.0		1971
Shanxi	Chang Zhi	230,000	93.8		1965
	Li Cheng	111,122	94.1		1964
	Jin Nan Zhuan Qu, (29 xian)	4,656,963	92.28		1964
	Xiyang	n.a.	99.2		1971
Shandong	Ning Yang	n.a.	77.7	44.0	1965
Henan	Xinyang diqu	n.a.	78.0	42.8	1965
Jilin	Pan Shi	370,000	87.4	65.0 (vil.)	1964 cf. 1963
Heilongjiang	Ke Shan	300,000	85.0+(v)	76.6	1964 cf. 1963
Inner Mongolia	Keshiketeng Banner		94.0+	27.0	1965
Gansu	Qui Quan		97.0		1971
Qinghai	whole prov.	2,050,000	84.0		1964
Jiangsu	Yi Xing		90.0+	67.9	1965
Zhejiang	Yu Yao (1 Bde)	676	93.8	46.0	1964
	Hangzhou suburb		90.0		1964
Hubei	Yang Xin	390,000	85.8	42.6	1964

Province	Xian population		% of age-range in school		Date
			now	previously	reported
Jiangxi	Yi Huang	107,000	92.0		1964
Guangdong	whole prov.	37,960,000	80.0+		1965
	Hai Kang		Prim. + jun. h. univ.		1971

Source: *Renmin Ribao* and *Guangming Ribao.*

It will be seen that there were no reports from 12 provinces, ranging from Sichuan and Anhui to Xizang (Tibet) and Xinjiang. It could be that richer provinces like Anhui do not require part-work schooling to provide universal schooling, though this seems unlikely, while in poorer areas with a small scattered population, like Xinjiang, the situation is not yet good enough to make reporting possible. In any case, these 20 examples must be seen against a total of some 2,000 *xian*. At the height of the optimism of the Great Leap Forward the State Statistical Bureau was only able to claim universal primary schooling in 1,240 of these (Lu Ting-yi, *EMBCWPL*, p. 1). It is also important that the majority of these 20 examples are of particularly poor areas, with difficult communication. What the figures do show is that there is a widespread appreciation that various forms of irregular schooling enable almost all children to obtain some schooling where conditions previously made school attendance impossible. One should also note that reports are almost always given in such a form as to act as a model.

Types of Part-work School

1. Ban-geng (gong), Ban-du Xiao Xuexiao: Half-cultivate (work) Half-study Primary Schools

There are numerous references to schools under this name in 1965 and again in 1969-72. Those set up in Chang Zhi *xian*, Shanxi, are typical, (*Gengdu xiaoxue . . .* , pp. 108-20). Concerning linking labour (*laodong*) the report (from the *xian* Party Committee and *xian* People's Committee) recommends combining a 'big unity' with a 'little flexibility'. The exact time spent on labour is to depend on the agricultural calendar, and on the availability of labour power locally. The Sha Yu upper-primary schools (48 part-work ones) operate a '5/7 system', five months of work and 7 months of labour. There is a two-month break for the spring planting and 15 days for the summer harvest. In the period of 20 days cultivation the school operates a half day system each of work and study. During the autumn harvest and planting there is another break of half a month. Finally 15 days were left flexible. In Yi Tang Brigade the schools run a '4/3/3/2 system'. From November through to the end of February schooling is full-time. In March, July and August students work two days and study 5 days a week. In April, June and September they operate a half day system. In the busiest months of May and October the school takes a break so all can work in the fields.

The curriculum in these schools consists of language, arithmetic (including use of the abacus and elementary book-keeping and statistics), elementary agricultural knowledge and general knowledge. There is also a weekly meeting. Syllabi are based on the FTD schools, but adapted, with locally written materials for agricultural knowledge and other practical matters. *In Memory of Norman Bethune* and *Serve the People* by Mao Ze-dong are studied. The weekly programme is:

> language, 12 periods; arithmetic, 8 periods; agriculture, 2 periods; weekly meeting, 2 periods; general knowledge, 2 periods; music and physical training, 1 each.

The total study time for the year, 810 periods, is less than the 999 periods for the FTD schools, but there are 27 periods more of language work, and 18 more of arithmetic. The report claims that in two years of study the resulting standards are equivalent.

This type of school appears to conform to type (5) above, but the agricultural knowledge and book-keeping, etc. is obviously related closely to the brigade's practical needs. It is interesting to compare the curriculum with that proposed during the Cultural Revolution by Li Shu xian, Jilin, and widely adopted throughout China (*People's Daily*, 12 May 1969).

2. Fushi Xiaoxue–Combined-class Primary Schools

This is another way in which schooling is made universal. In 1965 the *Wenjiao ju* (Cultural Bureau) of Yang Yuan *xian* reported on various types of *fushi xiaoxue*, or combined-class primary schools in their *xian*. These they grouped as follows:

(i) *Jiaocha jiaoxue:* (alternating teaching) here grades were grouped in various combinations and the teacher moved from class to class. In some cases classes met simultaneously, and in others some grades came in the morning and others in the afternoon.

(ii) *Luntang jiaoxue:* shift-classroom type teaching; here the teacher moves from room to room, leaving a student in charge when he is absent.

(iii) *xunhui jiaoxue:* circulating teaching; students are isolated in small hamlets and the teacher goes from one to the other, teaching for a period of time in each.

In these schools the students normally do 2-3 hours of labour per day in the upper grades, and during the busy season work for half the day. Again the type is (5) of our theoretical scheme, but the form of teaching is independent of any consideration of linking labour and education. It depends rather on teacher shortage, and on the economics of dealing with very small numbers of children.

3. Yilanzi xuexiao—the Village College

This is another type of school widely described in articles on part-work schooling. Again the form has nothing specially to do with combining work and education. Here various forms of school are gathered together under the same roof. The Qi Men Yan Brigade in a commune in Anhui set up a village college in 1964-5 comprising a FTD lower primary of two classes, totalling 85 students; two spare-time study classes, one for literacy and the other an upper primary level class; totalling 90 students; a senior high school correspondence class of 44 students; a club run jointly with the YCL; and groups for the study of literature and the fine arts. Whether the primary students do productive labour appears to depend on their parents' wishes, for the report says only: 'children who are able to study the whole day attend the FTD class; those not able to study the whole day attend the cultivate-study class' (*Geng-du xiaoxue* . . . p. 142). Arrangements for labour depend on the seasons and are such as to rank the school in type (5).

4. Labour in the FTD City School

Two primary schools will illustrate the situation in the FTD schools. The first, Tongyi Road Primary School, Tianjin, began in 1958 by setting up a small workshop, in the open air because of opposition. Under the pressure of the period labour was put into the curriculum as a subject, but this, together with politics, was abolished in the retrenchment in 1962, and was only restored after the Cultural Revolution. Now, they claim, theory classes are closely related to production. Practical work, which began with untying knots in string and wrapping sweets, graduated through producing bamboo instruments for the China Musical Instruments Factory in 1969, to making more than 23 different products in 4 well-equipped workshops, a majority for the motor industry. In addition to doing productive work students also perform social work, especially helping blind workers at a nearby factory, taking them to and from work (*SCMP*, 4711; *RMRB*, 19 July 1970).

The second school is Hangzhou Junlu High School which I visited in May 1975. The school maintains relations with some ten factories and farms in the neighbourhood. In simple workshops the students produce blades for electric fans and carry out electro-plating jobs. There is a school farm of 20 *mu* on which they grow the major crops of the region. In addition students work in adjoining farms. We watched a row of girls transplanting rice under the joint supervision of their biology master and a local peasant, while nearby boys were pulling up rape plants which had seeded. Outside the school a girl student was ploughing a commune field with a walking tractor. Productive work is linked with the other school subjects. We observed a qualified medical doctor explain the life-cycle of *Schistosoma* to a class and then supervise the students practising the subcutaneous injection of saline solution. Both these schools belong to type (3).

5. *Nongye Zhongxue—the Agricultural High Schools*

These schools, type (4) in our classification, were the first part-work schools to be established in 1957-8. For the early years my account is based on that of Barendsen (1964). The schools appear to have had little in the way of special buildings or equipment, and teachers, as will be seen below, were almost all untrained and ill-qualified. Intended at first to train technical personnel for the villages, the schools aimed to parallel the junior high schools and admit students in the age range 12-15. It is unclear both what size the schools were and to what extent they were boarding institutions. Jiangsu recommended a size of 300, but reports spoke of 100 to 600 students. In any case students must have lived away from home, contrary to later experience. In some schools established in Guangdong about 1950, where the aim was both to increase production and to divert pressure away from the FTD school system, they were definitely boarding schools, set up at the sites where the particular labour task was to be performed. But these may have been special cases. Certainly schooling, perhaps because of the near-famine conditions of the time, was perfunctory.

Work schedules in the agricultural high schools varied, starting with a half-day system in most cases, but by 1960-62 the slack-period study system was the norm. Work included both agriculture and industrial work, the latter being mainly producing fertilisers and insecticides. An aim of the schools was to be self-supporting but while significant economies were reported few seem to have achieved their aim.

Studies consisted of the now familiar Chinese language, mathematics, politics and basic agricultural knowledge, and an attempt was made to make the contents practical. History and geography, normally studied in junior high schools, were absent, as was much of the physics and chemistry. Algebra and geometry were replaced by book-keeping and surveying in the mathematics courses.

Some ten years later, in 1968, *Red Flag* reported the setting up of the Wukou Tea Cultivation and Study High School in Jiangxi. Replacing a former FT technical high school, apparently, the curriculum was considerably simplified. Language and literature were replaced by the study of Mao Ze-dong Thought, and 12 subjects concerned with tea cultivation were replaced by two. In addition some mathematics, physics and chemistry were studied. In addition to a special course in labour, students worked in the tea fields and processing plants. In addition to 4 full-time teachers, workers and technicians also taught the students. The school claimed to be 'self-sufficient with some surplus without asking a single cent from the state' (*SCMM*, 634; *Red Flag*, 4, 14 October 1968).

6. Jishu Zhongxue–Technical High Schools

In 1964-5 a number of technical high schools changed over to a part-work system, thus changing from type (6) to type (4). Reports published in a booklet in December 1965 came from 13 provinces and the three cities of Peking, Shanghai and Tianjin, with the majority of examples concentrated in the industrialised provinces of the NE. Industries involved ranged from iron and steel, through radio-electronics, machine-tools, chemicals and railways, to cotton weaving and printing. 10 schools were run by single plants, 2 by a number of small plants jointly, 11 jointly between factory and education office, while two appear to have been only under the city education office. In all cases entrants were expected to be graduates of the junior high school. Courses were normally reported as 4 years, though some were only 3 or 2 years. At the Yang Pu Cotton Printing and Dyeing Mill they began in 1961 with a 3-year part-work school, but extended this in 1964 to take in pupils from the upper primary school, making the course 7 years in all.

The favourite division between work and study was alternate weeks of each, with a few schools preferring a half-day system, or 3 days of work and 3 days of schooling. Jilin reported a total 4-year curriculum of 2,500 hours compared with the FTD total of 3,500 hours. Tianjin mentioned a figure of only 2,200 hours. A textile factory school in Shanxi gave a subdivision of time for the four years: 94 weeks were spent on special theory; 95 weeks on *laodong*, 86 of which were to be industrial experience and 9 weeks agriculture; 3 weeks were spent on political education; and 16 weeks were vacations. A Hangzhou engineering school broke down the curriculum into 13 per cent politics; 30 per cent for specialist studies, practical; 29 per cent for specialist theory, and 28 per cent for language, 3D geometry and triangles, algebra and higher mathematics. In the year there are a total of 20 weeks for study classes and 23 weeks for labour, in addition to which time is allocated for revision, examinations and vacations.

7. Gongchanzhuyi Laodong Daxue—Communist Labour College

Set up in mid-summer of 1958, the Communist Labour College has been the model for subsequent part-work colleges at the tertiary level. It established a central college at Nanchang in Jiangxi Province, and branch schools throughout the province. It has been constantly reported that 'the aim of the main school is to give its students a university-level education and that of the branch schools to provide junior or middle-grade technical personnel' (*China Reconstructs*, September 1972, p. 10), but the term *daxue*, translated both by Chinese media and US sources, as *university* is misleading. Since the education given is mainly of the post-secondary school technician level the word *college* is to be preferred.

Barendsen traces the early history of the college, and its sister college, the *Gongye Laodong Daxue*, or Industrial Labour College, also at Nanchang. Figures for enrolment varied from report to report, but by 1960 about 55,000 seemed to be the overall figure, with 88 branch schools. In 1972 a figure of 130 branch schools was reported (*China Reconstructs*, September 1972, p. 7). According to the same source the original school was founded by 11,000 volunteers, including some from Shanghai and 7 other provinces. Starting on a bare site they built dormitories and classrooms, and went on to open up farms and workshops. The College opened its doors to

> ... all workers, peasants, commune cadres, and demobilized service-men, irrespective of sex, who possess definite production knowledge and have attained *a definite standard* in education, and all students and youths of society, irrespective of sex, who have attained the standard of junior high school, provided they are between 17 and 30 years of age, have a clean personal record, and are physically fit. (Barendsen, p. 44, his emphasis; high school for middle school, my correction)

Various courses have been offered, ranging from 2, through 3 to 4 years. In addition a preparatory course was set up to bring students up to the necessary basic standard where necessary. The division of time between schooling and productive labour has varied. In the 4-year course the division was reported as:

1st year, classroom study: 5 months, productive labour: 6 months
2nd   6   5
3rd   7   4
4th   7   4

Specialties and productive labour are in the areas general agriculture, forestry, animal husbandry and farm mechanics, with forestry the most important. In addition students study Chinese language, mathematics, physics and chemistry, and also politics. Productive activities have included the establishment of grape growing in an area previously thought to be unsuitable, the supplying of improved seeds to a whole county (*xian*), and the production on a commercial scale of insecticide made according to traditional formulae. This and other work has enabled the main school and between 1/3 and 2/3 of the branches to be self-support-ing in food and running expenses (Barendsen, p. 53; *China Reconstructs*, September 1972, p. 7).

In 1965 the NCNA reported a total of 16,000 graduates, 1,300 from the main school, 8,800 from the branches at intermediate tech-nical level, and 6,200 from *xian* schools at primary technical level. In 1972 only the total of graduates since 1958 was given, 120,000.

Chaoyang Agricultural College, after it moved from Shenyang in 1970, is another such college which has become a model (*China Pictorial*, 1976, 3, pp. 10-15).

8. Wuhan University

Reporting in 1971, this university described the way in which it had, beginning in March 1969, attempted to link up with factories and carry out a 'three-in-one combination of teaching, scientific research and production'. Ten small-scale factories were set up within the university, including 'an air battery-cell factory, a transistor parts factory, and a plant for multiple-use of biological resources'. The last began work on extracting chemicals from hog bristles, and finally succeeded in trial production of spinnable viscose fibre and nylon fibre, together with some chemicals of pharmaceutical value. In the course of this work over 300 technical personnel were trained 'for other provinces'.

The university found that for success it was necessary for factories to undertake considerable planning responsibility, since production was continuous and does not normally provide the range of stimulus and variety necessary for good teaching. Under factory direction it was possible to provide workers to ensure continuity of production in some cases when students and teachers moved to other studies, and production jobs were selected which gave suitable stimulus for research and study.

9. Colleges Send out Work Teams into the Villages

Medical colleges and teacher training colleges exemplify another method in which teaching is brought into close contact with the world of practice, though in a service rather than productive sense. The sending of medical teams into the villages has been carried out for some time. Dr Horn describes how his hospital in Peking sent its first team in April 1965. One of its main tasks was the training of medical auxillaries who would remain and work in the villages (Horn, ch. 13). After the Cultural Revolution this practice was extended, with student doctors going along and learning in the course of treating patients in the field. Similarly teacher training colleges have begun to send groups of teachers and students out into the villages to assist the schools there, while at the same time carrying on with their studies in teacher education (Guangdong T.Tr.C. Seybolt, 1973, pp. 166-77).

The Problems of Part-work Schooling

1. In Fulfilling the Moral-political Aim

This has been repeatedly expressed as eliminating the difference between (a) industrial workers and peasants, (b) between town and countryside, and (c) between mental and physical labour (e.g. *People's Daily*, 24 August 1965). It has also been expressed in terms of learning 'the workers' noble qualities: devotion to the public (good); a hard-working spirit; and simple and hard living' (*Red Flag*, 4, 14 October 1968). The first aims require far-reaching changes in society, and any success which part-work schooling has in this area can only be small. It may help to keep educated youth from flocking to the cities, and it may help to raise standards without reinforcing the idea that a city career is the only possible one. At the same time performing hard or dull work can often produce distaste and the desire to escape. Whether an earlier exposure to such risk is worse than a later one remains to be seen. Such negative learning was well described by a Guandong student now in Hong Kong.

> . . . we spent one month of each term on farms where we lived and worked with poor and lower-middle peasants. We were supposed to

learn how they thought so that we could emulate them in our own
work. We did everything from carrying water to tending babies. It
was fun for the first few days each time and a welcome change from
the routine of classes. But after a while we always grew to dislike it.
The peasants were so backward and conditions were so difficult that
it was hard to work. Even the most active students usually were ready
to leave after a week or so. (Bennett and Montaperto, pp. 24-5)

The same student commented on jobs performed on campus:

. . . a schedule of dormitory, classroom, and grounds cleaning for
each class. It is hard to think of scrubbing floors as 'making revolution',
and there was some shirking. (ibid. p. 12)

Such complaints were not limited to students from academic schools for
intending cadres. Some students at the Taiyuan Heavy Machine Works
Secondary Technical School were reported complaining: 'Every day
dirty hands and oily body! It's really depressing' (*Ban-gong, ban-du
zhong deng jishu* . . . , p. 154). Much more than simple exposure to
labour is required if such attitudes are to be changed, and exhortation
will produce only outward conformity.

2. In Fulfilling the Intellectual Aim

The main problems here are that productive work, as pointed out by
Wuhan University, does not necessarily—in fact is unlikely to—raise the
right kind of problems in the right variety and order to conform with
the best teaching sequence. These problems were also raised in articles
in the September 1972 issue of *Red Flag* by Qinghua University and
the Dalian Industrial Institute. They have long been the rocks on which
schemes of linking education with productive work have foundered,
which is not to say that methods cannot be found to overcome them.
The problem is simplest where it is desired only to train students in
fairly simple technical tasks, and most difficult where the aim is a deep
theoretical grasp over a fairly wide range of subject matter.

The practical difficulties of organising productive labour as intellectual
education are greatest where there is some attempt to provide polytechnical rather than monotechnical training. It is rare for there to be a
suitable range of industries within reach of the school. Then, whether
the aim is poly- or monotechnical, there is the problem of accomodating
large numbers of students in the available factories. Successful programmes have often been of a pilot nature, involving rather few students

from a few schools. The Wuhan article hinted at this kind of problem when it said:

> Some leadership comrades of factories also show insufficient concern over educational revolution, welcoming teachers but not students to their factories. They welcomed them to make technical innovations at the factories but did not welcome their teaching lessons there. (*SCMP*, 4935, p. 60)

Nor have factory management the time, or often the expertise, to engage in the necessary detailed planning to make mass-scale working in the factories an educational success.

3. In Fulfilling the Economic Aim

This has proved to be the easiest aim to fulfill, both at the level of the individual family and at the level of state savings. Under the slogan *qínjiǎn bàn xué* (run schools with industry and thrift) there has been a great extension of *minban*, or locally financed schools, or combinations of local and state financing. One example of the latter is the village college at Qian Ku Ling Brigade, Zhejiang, where in 1965 the production brigade found 61.9 per cent of the school finance, fees provided another 21.6 per cent and the state provided 16.5 per cent (*Geng-du xiao*, pp. 134-5). At a similar school in a commune in Anhui work by the teacher and students has enabled the brigade to abolish fees, and even provide a subsidy for students from especially poor families (*Geng-du xiao*, p. 142). Estimates of comparative costs were given by the then Guangdon Provincial Party Secretary, Ou Meng-jue, in 1964. In one *xian* they were: for keeping one student at a

full-time junior high school	76 yuan/year
state-subsidised agricultural high school	6
full-time agricultural technical high school	350
part-time agricultural technical high school	140

In another *xian* the costs were: for keeping one student at

a full-time junior high school	130 yuan/year
a part-time junior high school	14

(*SCMP*, 3333, 1964; *RFP*, pp. 212-3). Barendsen quotes the example of a student whose costs at an agricultural high school were:

Board   33 yuan/year
School fee (tuition)   4
Books   2
                                   39

This student was able to earn 70 yuan during the busy farming season leaving a profit of 31 yuan for the family (Barendsen, p. 34; ex. *SCMP*, 2595, 1961).

Since the Cultural Revolution a number of schools have given figures of their earnings through part-work activities. A Tianjin primary school which began reclaiming land in 1966 and farming it had by 1970 earned a total of 10,000 yuan. They emphasised that students no longer pay fees or buy their own books (*SCMP*, 4725, 1970). The Tongyi Road Primary School, Tianjin, mentioned above, made a profit of 100,000 yuan in their 12 years of productive work. In addition to buying equipment, teaching aids and books they have aided poor students. Another primary school, in Liaoning, also over 12 years, made more than 80,000 yuan 'for the state'. In addition to paying all school expenses they bought a Dongfang Hong tractor for a nearby commune (*SCMP*, 4717, 1970).

For the individual families the economic advantages of the various part-work arrangements are clear. Adjustment of the school calendar ensures that their children's labour is available when it is most needed. In addition, flexible times of attendance during the day allow children to get some schooling where economic circumstances would otherwise make it impossible.

Conclusions

A number of observers have drawn attention to the coincidence of the Khrushchev reforms in the USSR and the development of part-work schooling in China. Some have seen this as a continuation of China's policy of 'Learning from the USSR'. Wittig has even gone as far as to suggest that the Chinese reform preceeded that in the USSR and might have influenced what was done there! (Wittig, 1964, p. 146). In both countries the growth of the school systems had produced a superfluity of secondary school graduates who saw their future in tertiary schooling and then a place in the intelligentsia. Both countries required instead a large number of middle grade workers and technicians. In the USSR the pool of labour from the villages had dried up and factories had to draw on city school graduates for their labour. In China other pressures operated: the desperate need for cheaper schooling, and the desire of the central government to keep its taxes as low as possible so as not to antagonise the provinces and the peasants. These were the pressures which produced, as we have seen, very different solutions, albeit often using the guise of very similar slogans.

Other writers have used the term polytechnical education to describe what has been attempted in China (e.g. Hawkins, p. 110). From the above account it should be clear that this is mistaken. Talking with Chinese educators I have found either that the term, in Chinese, *zonghe jishu jiaoyu*, is either quite unknown, or is understood to describe Soviet 'revisionist' education in a form which the Chinese now reject. In reading Chinese education materials I have only encountered the term in accounts of Soviet education during the fifties, or in translations of Soviet educators, or the works of Marx.

Turning to more general questions, the long experience in the USSR has demonstrated many difficulties encountered with attempts to combine education and labour in various forms. The Khrushchev reforms have shown particularly clearly the opposition of the schooled and aspirants to the intelligentsia to such measures. Such opposition is also clearly present in China. Then there is the opposition of factory managers, and even workers, who see the invasion of school students as a disruption of production and a threat to their jobs. When the aim is vocational training the difficulties experienced in the USSR in matching training and job experience with final job placement is also instructive.

Finally, this chapter has argued that in the USSR the term polytechnical education has lost any special sense and is now applied to both general, academic education and to purely vocational training. In China the concept of combining education with productive labour has been advanced as the germ of a socialist education in which living and learning will not be separated. Mao looks forward to an integration of the experience of young, middle aged and old people, and of work, learning and leisure. Classes are to be abolished, not as suggested in recent decades in the USSR through the steady increase in the number of graduates from 'special secondary and tertiary schools', but through forms of workers' control of the political economic process in which learning is an ongoing and integral activity.

6 EDUCATING THE NEW, SOCIALIST MAN

Aims and Claims

The marxist aim of creating a human society under man's collective control involves a rejection of a static human nature, whether 'fundamentally' good or bad. It conceives man shaped by and shaping the human and non-human environment in an ongoing dialectic. Clearly, then, the attempts to define a list of qualities, inevitably abstract and largely static, of some 'new man' are unmarxist. But they have been and continue to be a feature of much writing on both the USSR and China.

The ABC of Communism spoke of 'communist consciousness', 'a proletarian mentality', and said it was the task of the new school 'to train up a younger generation whose whole ideology shall be deeply rooted in the soil of the new communist society' (Carr, p. 284). Lenin, talking in 1920 to the 3rd Congress of the Komsomol, said members should train themselves to be Communists. Embracing a morality which 'serves the purpose of helping human society rise to a higher level and rid itself of the exploitation of labour' they should devote their efforts to the task. Through devoting their efforts to the common cause they would become 'real Communists'. They should display initiative and enterprise, and set an example of training and discipline (Lenin, 1947, 2, pp. 661-74). Here was a vision of an activist, but not a frozen list of supposed virtues, such as was to follow a decade and a half later.

Jean Riappo, Vice-Commissar of Public Instruction in the Ukraine, talking to the American teacher, Scott Nearing in 1925, said: 'We are trying to combine the knower and the doer in one person' (Nearing, p. 142). Pinkevich wrote, in 1930:

> We dream of a man fully equipped with all the knowledge of the present day and to whom all that is truly beautiful is dear; we dream of an active, strong man, struggling through the revolutionary classes of contemporary society for a realization of ideals which throughout the world will bring peace and happiness to all mankind. (Pinkevich, p. 28)

Dreams, certainly, but still open and developmental.

In the following decade, at the 10th Komsomol Congress of 1936, the same year that Stalin proclaimed the new Soviet Constitution with its assertion that 'our Soviet society has already, in the main, succeeded in achieving Socialism' (Stalin, p. 548), one of the Komsomol leaders spoke enthusiastically about the supposed new man:

> People are growing up who are strangers to national differences, strangers to bourgeois individualism and selfishness, people in whom internationalism and comradeship are innate qualities. (Muskin, quoted in Fisher, p. 199, cf. pp. 226-7)

An indefatigable exponent of the new Soviet man was the old Bolshevik and President of the Praesidium of the Supreme Soviet, M.I. Kalinin. At a conference of 'best urban and rural schoolteachers' in 1938 he said:

> The new Socialist man is in the process of creation in our country. This new man must be imbued with the very finest of human qualities.

He then went through them:

> They include, firstly, love, love for one's own people, love for the working masses. Man should love his fellow-men . . . Secondly—honesty. . . Thirdly—courage. . . Fourthly—a comradely team spirit. . . Fifthly—love for work. One must not only love work, but also be honest in one's attitude to it, with the thought firmly engraved in one's mind that a person who lives and eats without working, lives on the work of others. . .

He added:

> One could continue the list of the qualities of the new human being, but I shall limit myself to these. They are the qualities of the Marxist-Leninist. . . Discipline goes without saying—it follows from the qualities I have enumerated above. (Kalinin, pp. 73-5)

These words, coming after the horrors of the collectivisation and the period of trials and mass denunciations, make it seem as if incantation was necessary to dispel the reality and conjure up the new by the very familiarity of the cliches. Which is not to decry the thousands of soviet people who gave their health and often their lives to serve the cause in which they believed.

The tone set in the thirties has persisted. In 1961 the Vice-president of the Academy of Pedagogical Sciences said, in addressing an International Seminar:

> A new and superior morality has grown and developed in the process
> of building a new society. . . The following traits are characteristic of
> the Soviet man: Soviet patriotism and Soviet humanism, collectivism
> and internationalism, new communist attitude to work and public
> property, a developed sense of discipline and organization, truthful-
> ness and honesty. (Goncharov, pp. 9-10 English translation)

In 1974 the Novosti Press pamphlet, *The Most Human World*, by Mike
Davidow continues with such phrases as:

> Enthusiasm for work is characteristic of Soviet people. Congeniality
> and a genuine group spirit are typical of Soviet people.
> Soviet man and woman are the most morally clean people we have
> ever met. (Davidow, pp. 4, 6, 12)

A more realistic note was struck by Stalin in two speeches to Soviet
managers and business executives in 1931. He looked forward to one-
man management of economic enterprises as soon as sufficient Bolsheviks
had mastered technology and economics (Stalin, p. 355). At the same
time his appraisal of the 'old' man among Soviet workers was shown by
his recommending wage differentials and other capitalist management
techniques (Stalin, pp. 359-77). In general Party policy has assumed
this view of man while the 'new man' image has been reserved for the
rhetoric.

In China it is hardly surprising to find repeated moralising about
the 'new man' and campaigns to study the latest living, or more usually
dead, exponent of his virtues. In addition to 'learning from Soviet
experience' China has suffered some 2,000 years of Confucianist moralising from which it is clearly hard to escape. (In the *Zhou li* of the minus
third century one finds the *six duties*: filial reverence; sincerity in friendship; kindliness; love of kindred; faithfulness; sympathy/charitableness;
and the *six virtues*: knowledge; benevolence/humanity (*ren*); reverence/
wisdom; uprightness; moderation; harmony/peace. See Mayers, pp. 342,
347, and Galt, pp. 127-8.)

Much of the moralising extols virtues which it is hoped will be adopted
by the ordinary working people. An example is Article 42 of the Common
Programme adopted by the Chinese People's Consultative Conference in
1949:

> Love of the fatherland and the people, love of labour, love of science,
> and the taking care of public property shall be promoted as the public
> spirit of all nationals of the People's Republic of China. (Fraser, 1, p.
> 83)

Much of Mao's writings in this vein concerns the behaviour of cadres but
the *three old articles* (*Serve the People*, 1944; *In Memory of Norman
Bethune*, 1939; and *The Foolish Old Man who Removed the Mountains*,
1945) were intended more generally. They extol serving the people;
absolute selflessness; persistence and hard work; and modesty and the
ability to learn from others.

In the late fifties the discussion was couched in terms of fostering
'for the working class tens of millions of intellectuals who are red and
expert' (Fraser, 2, p. 554). The CC CCP and State Council directive of
September 1958 which set education this aim, later defined the required
'new man':

> A new man of all-round development in the communist society is
> one who has both political consciousness and culture, and is capable
> of taking up both mental and physical labour. He is not the bourgeois
> intellectual of the old society who is only vocationally proficient but
> not red, and alienated from productive labour. The call of the Party
> for 'the fostering of workers with socialist consciousness and culture'
> correctly interprets the meaning of 'all-round' development. (Fraser,
> 2, p. 557)

In the following year Zhou En-lai told the National People's Congress
that measures to link the schools with productive work were making
possible 'training new men with a communist outlook' (Fraser, 1, p.
311). However, by the mid-sixties, while expert-training appeared to be
proceeding there were grave doubts about the red part, and numerous
articles began to appear discussing ways of ensuring the training of
'successors for the revolution'. One of these listed the 'requirements for
successors to the revolutionary cause of the proletariat' as follows:

(1) They must be genuine Marxist-Leninists.
(2) They must be revolutionaries who whole-heartedly serve the
    overwhelming majority of the people of China and the whole
    world.
(3) They must be proletarian statesmen capable of uniting and work-
    ing together with the overwhelming majority. Not only must they

unite with those who agree with them, they must also be good at
uniting with those who disagree and even with those who formerly
opposed them and have since been proved wrong.
(4) They must be models in applying the Party's democratic centralism, must master the method of leadership based on the principles
of 'from the masses, to the masses', and must cultivate a democratic style and be good at listening to the masses.
(5) They must be modest and prudent and guard against arrogance
and impetuosity; they must be imbued with the spirit of self-
criticism and have the courage to correct mistakes and shortcomings in their work. (*Training successors* . . ., pp. 12-13)

It is clearly inappropriate to attempt empirically, as some have done,
to either confirm or refute such claims as have been made here, and the
following sections of this chapter will rather only survey the major
agents responsible for promoting these moral-political qualities.

Methods of Education Employed

1. Educating the Leaders

Immediately in the wake of the revolution the CPSU began establishing
special institutions to train Party members and other people who were
to occupy leading state positions. The first such organisation, the Sverdlov University in Moscow, opened in 1918 and produced its first graduates in 1923. The most important institution training higher party
workers, it enrolled 900-1,500 students a year and included Lenin,
Bukharin, Pokrovsky and Stalin among its occasional lecturers. It was
there that Stalin delivered his lectures on *The Foundations of Leninism*
in April 1924. In 1921 the Zinoviev University opened in Leningrad,
then Petrograd, with more than 800 students. In the same year two
other institutions were set up: the Communist University of Toilers of
the East, and the Communist University of National Minorities of the
West (Carr, 1970, 2, p. 205), each with about 1,000 students. The former
was said to have students from 57 different nationalities at the end of its
first year, with branches in Turkestan, Baku and Irkutsk (Carr, 1966, 3,
p. 270). The latter enrolled Lithuanians, Jews, Poles, White Russians,
Germans, Estonians and Finns. Both schools had four-year courses,
alternating periods of 8-9 months study with shorter periods of field
work as propagandists. Opening its doors on 1 September 1925 was a
slightly different institution, the Sun Yat-sen University of Toilers of
China. With Radek as first president this university aimed to produce

'staff officers of the Chinese revolution' (Carr, 1970, 3, pp. 746-7 and
n. 5). With 280 students, including 46 women, in 1926 it offered a 2-year
course with lectures in Russian, German, French and English. Many of
its students were members of the Guomindang, whose support the
Soviet Union sought. Some students also attended from India, Japan
and Korea (Harper, p. 286). Between 1921-4 a number of communist
universities were set up in such places as Kharkov, Kazan, Tiflis, Tashkent. Schapiro gives the totals as 10 schools with 6,000 students in
1924 and 19 schools with 8,400 students in 1928 (Schapiro, p. 343).

Other early foundations served different purposes. The Institute of
Red Professors, set up in 1921, trained teachers for higher educational
institutions. Pokrovsky was its first president. Planned to have one
branch in Petrograd, only the Moscow branch eventuated, and because
of involvement in inner-party struggles enrolment remained low (Carr,
1970, 2, p. 206). The Socialist Academy of Social Science, established
by a decree of 25 June 1918 began as a 'free association of persons having
for its purpose the study and teaching of social sciences from the stand-
point of scientific socialism and communism' (Webbs, p. 966). In 1923
it became the Communist Academy and in 1926 its functions were
redefined as:

> (a) elaboration of problems of Marxism and Leninism; (b) combating
> of bourgeois and petty-bourgeois distortions of Marxism-Leninism;
> and (c) rigid advocacy of the standpoint of dialectical materialism
> both in the social and the natural sciences, and repudiation of the
> survivals of idealism. (Decrees of TSIK of All-Union Congress of
> Soviets, 26 November 1926, quoted in Webbs, p. 967)

Originally in competition for many functions with the non-communist
Academy of Sciences, the Communist Academy eventually closed and
merged with the latter in 1936 (Schapiro, p. 470). Two important
research institutes established were the Marx-Engels Institute and the
Institute of Lenin, both of which collected documents and published
writings and comments.

The various communist universities were closed down in the late
thirties. It is not clear whether this was because many of their leading
personnel were involved in the various oppositions within the Party, or
whether the leadership of the Party felt their functions could now be
assumed by the ordinary state universities. In any case, after World War
Two the Party operated only one tertiary education institution, the
Higher Party School (de Witt, p. 17; Mickiewicz, p. 6). The Party also

operates an Academy of Social Sciences of the CC CPSU with a 3-year course for party members with tertiary education, and there are a number of Republic Higher Party Schools and 4-year 'inter-oblast' schools which do not rank as part of the general education system (Mickiewicz, pp. 5-6).

In these various schools, only the Sverdlov University had exclusively Party students, and in the early years there was difficulty in finding Party members to staff them. In 1924 60 per cent of the staff remained non-party (Carr, 1970, 2, p. 205). In the twenties and thirties these schools performed the functions of ordinary tertiary colleges in addition to their specialised political function, training some 60,000 specialists, mainly for managerial roles. Data are not available after 1938, except for occasional references to numbers graduated in particular years (de Witt, pp. 93, 298-9; Mickiewicz, p. 6; and Churchward, p. 43).

In China there is one Higher Party School in Peking, first headed by Yang Xian-zhen who became famous in the controversy over 'one divides into two'. (He emphasised the unity of opposites, rather than their division and conflict.) For training political cadres the Chinese People's University was set up in Peking in 1950 and gradually evolved over 15 years into a school with 10,000 students and more than 1,600 staff. Quoting An Zi-wen, Schurmann suggests that people's universities were set up in numbers to parallel the regular universities, but this is not so (Schurmann, p. 169). Cadre departments existed within the regular tertiary institutions, and numerous 'red and expert colleges' and May 7th Cadre Schools have been organised on a long- and short-term basis, but it is probably true that none of these attempted the same level of work as the two major institutions first mentioned. It is significant that the Peking People's University closed during the Cultural Revolution and to date (1976) has not reopened. (For a study of this university see C.T. Hu, 1973).

The formal schools which have been described above cater for only a small minority of Party members and a few high non-party cadres. But education is no less important a duty of all Party members, self-education in the principles of marxism in order to exercise leadership better and to transmit Party policy. The Rules of the CPSU adopted at the 22nd Congress in 1961 put it as follows:

> It is the duty of a Party member . . . (d) to master Marxist-Leninist theory, to improve his ideological knowledge, and to contribute to the moulding and education of the man of communist society. To combat vigorously all manifestations of bourgeois ideology, remnants

of a private-property psychology, religious prejudices, and other survivals of the past; to observe the principles of communist morality,
and place public interests above his own;

(e) to be an active proponent of the ideas of socialist internationalism
and Soviet patriotism among the masses of the working people. (Lane,
p. 518)

The latest Constitution of the Chinese CP, adopted at the 10th Congress
in 1973 states succinctly: 'Members . . . must: (1) Conscientiously study
Marxism-Leninism-Mao Tsetung Thought and criticize revisionism' (10th
NC docs. p. 65). Previous Party constitutions in both countries had
similar injunctions, though the phrasing has varied over time. Likewise
the emphasis given to organised study and the degree to which this has
been together with or separate from non-party people has also varied.
Describing the situation in the late twenties in the USSR, Harper states
that 'about 15% of the enrolment' in party and Komsomol schools 'is
non-party' (Harper, p. 276). Four decades later, in 1966, according to
A. Dmitriuk, deputy director of the Department of Propaganda and
Agitation, party members made up about 75 per cent of the enrolment
(9m in total of 12m, Mickiewicz, p. 13).

The term *politgramota,* or political grammar, was applied in the early
Soviet period to elementary political education, and after 1924 attendance
of Party and Komsomol members at a widespread network of schools
and classes was expected. The degree of compulsion has varied with
time and place, but continued membership and even more, promotion in
the organisation, has generally been dependent on at least some study of
politics (Harper, p. 276, Webbs, p. 398). While the purpose of all this
political schooling has been

the intensification of the ideological tempering of communists, of
leading cadres, the formation in them of firm Marxist-Leninist con-
victions, the developing of the ability to understand the laws of
social development, to apply the theory and principles of scientific
communism in practice (M. Semichaevsky, quoted in Mickiewicz, p.
13)

it has also served a general educational function. Reading political texts
has taught and confirmed simple literacy at a time when the bulk of the
Soviet, and more recently Chinese, population was illiterate. However,
at times political classes were deserted in favour of others concentrating
purely on general education. This occurred in 1926, when students turned

to the Schools for the Semi-literate, which numbered more than 3,000, 800 in Moscow itself (Harper, p. 280). Classes in agriculture and technical subjects were also competitors at this time (Harper, p. 282), and reports of attitudes to political studies in such books as *The New Class Divided* by Parry suggest this has continued.

Mickiewicz gives a detailed description of the institutions which have provided political education in the post-Stalin period. At the bottom of level is the *politshkola*, or political school. It aims to cater for those 'who do not have sufficient education and preparation for independent study' (Mickiewicz, p. 63). Teacher and students usually meet for 75 to 95 minutes, two or three times a month (ibid. p. 64). Lecturing is avoided and attempts are made to relate classes to problems in the work place, students being assigned simple investigations or tasks connected with increasing production through the practice of economy (ibid. pp. 72-3). Next in the hierarchy is the study circle, sometimes referred to as the school of the fundamentals of Marxism-Leninism. These normally cater for middle-aged or elderly people with not more than some high school education. While some concentrate on policy documents of the CC CPSU and government, most study the history of the Party, fundamentals of Marxism-Leninism, Marxist-Leninist philosophy or political economy. In 1963 an article in *Party Life* suggested:

> In the mass political circle, in our view, it is not necessary to give a strictly fixed plan. The real, inspiring propagandist—this is the chief thing for such a circle. And themes: today—the international situation, next time—problems of literature and morality, then talk about cost and price formation, and then perhaps, popular colloquy about necessity and accident. And without fail—argument, discussion, and persuasion, and not learning by heart. (N. Gents, quoted in Mickiewicz, p. 86)

Circles usually meet once a fortnight for two hour sessions. In an 8-month year they probably meet about 19 times in groups of 10 to 25 persons (ibid. p. 90). Current politics circles may meet through the summer. An important function, and one apparently difficult to sustain, is that of encouraging the art of discussion. Teachers are also expected to train students in methods of study, such as serious reading and the making of outlines and summaries (ibid. p. 99). The subject matter of circles for teachers is expected to feed through into their classes in the primary and secondary schools (ibid. pp. 113-4). At the apex of this hierarchy are the institutions called Evening Universities of Marxism-Leninism.

Catering for the 'party, soviet and economic *aktiv* and the intelligentsia' (Mickiewicz, p. 52), evening universities have included history, philosophy and economics faculties, the last added after 1956. Formerly courses ran for 3 years with a total class time of 468 hours (about four hours a week), but this was cut back to 2 years with 312 hours (still about four hours a week) in the mid-sixties.

In China political education for party members and cadres takes place in groups within the work place. Doak Barnett's informants describe meetings of the Party branch, held of an evening or a Saturday afternoon once a week for two hours. In addition to information and instructions from the higher Party authorities and criticism and self-criticism sessions, time was set aside for study (*xuexi*). Study materials ranged from CC directives, or editorials in the *People's Daily*, to Mao's writings *On Practice, On Contradiction* and other themes (Barnett, *CBPC*, pp. 25-6, 161-5; Richman, *ISCC*, p. 764). In addition to Party branch meetings cadres often attend other political study sessions, both during working hours and in their spare time. During major political campaigns or movements such as the Great Leap Forward, or the Cultural Revolution a very high proportion of their time may be so occupied (for a brief description of the major movements see Tsang, pp. 218-35; M.K. Whyte is another analysis of refugee materials, chapter 5 concerning cadre political education).

2. Educating the Masses

In both Russia and China moral-political education is explicitly conveyed by the mass media, the press, radio, television, through libraries, museums and public lectures of various kinds, and also through the arts, especially literature, cinema and theatre. Theoretical justification is provided by citing works of Lenin and Mao Ze-dong. Hopkins emphasises Lenin's influence on the Soviet press (p. 53), but his remarks on 'party organization and party literature' have been widely generalised to cover other media and the arts. A famous quotation from this pamphlet, written in 1905, and cited by Mao Ze-dong (Mao, *SW* 3, p. 86) is:

> . . . the socialist proletariat must advance, develop fully and completely and translate into life the principle of *party literature.* . . Literature must become *part* of the common cause of the proletariat, 'cog and wheel' of a single, great Social-Democratic mechanism brought into motion by the entire politically-conscious vanguard of the entire working class. Literature must become a component of organized, planned and integrated Social-Democratic party work. (Lenin, *What*

is to be Done?, p. 21)

He went on to make clear

> . . . we are discussing party literature and its subordination to party
> control. Everyone is free to write and say whatever he likes, without
> any restrictions. But every free union (including a party) is also free
> to expel members who use the party's platform to advocate anti-party
> views. Freedom of speech and the press must be complete. . . (ibid. p.
> 24)

But practice has been otherwise.

The seminal text of Mao Ze-dong is his *Talks at the Yan'an Forum on
Literature and Art* (May 1942, in *SW* 3, pp. 69-98). There he argued
that

> in the world today all culture, all literature and art belong to definite
> classes and are geared to definite political lines. There is in fact no
> such thing as art for art's sake, art that stands above classes. . . (Mao,
> *SW* 3, p. 86)

Speaking of the work of writers in the anti-Japanese struggle, he said:

> The purpose of our meeting today is precisely to ensure that literature
> and art fit well into the whole revolutionary machine as a component
> part, that they operate as powerful weapons for uniting and educating
> the people and for attacking and destroying the enemy, and that
> they help the people fight the enemy with one heart and one mind.
> (ibid. p. 70)

Later he commented:

> We are proletarian revolutionary utilitarians and take as our point
> of departure the unity of the present and future interests of the broad-
> est masses, who constitute over 90 per cent of the population. (ibid.
> p. 85)

Discussing the problem of whether to attempt to raise standards or concentrate on popularisation Mao Ze-dong said what was needed was not
'more flowers on the brocade' but 'fuel in snowy weather'(ibid. p. 82).
But this did not mean that higher standards should not be also required

(ibid. p. 83). The important thing was to start from the people, their needs and current standards: 'We must popularise only what is needed and can readily be accepted by the workers, peasants and soldiers themselves' (ibid. p. 80). Mao returns to the educational role of writers and artists again and again, and makes the point which Marx made in the Feuerbach manuscripts. For example at the Propaganda Conference in 1957 he said:

Our writers and artists, our scientific and technical personnel, our professors and teachers, all are educating the people, and training our students. Because they are educators and teachers, they have the prime duty of being themselves educated. (Mao, *Selected Readings*, p. 484)

In *On the Correct Handling of Contradictions Among the People* (1957) Mao discussed Party policy towards non-Marxist ideas. He wrote:

As far as unmistakable counter-revolutionaries and saboteurs of the socialist cause are concerned, the matter is easy: we simply deprive them of their freedom of speech. (Mao, *Four Essays*, p. 117)

Recognising the difficulty of 'unmistakable' and the dangers inherent in stifling freedom of discussion Mao went on to lay down six criteria for distinguishing 'fragrant flowers from poisonous weeds'. These were:

(1) Words and actions should help to unite, and not divide, the people of our various nationalities.
(2) They should be beneficial, and not harmful, to socialist transformation and socialist construction.
(3) They should help to consolidate, and not undermine or weaken the people's democratic dictatorship.
(4) They should help to consolidate, and not undermine or weaken, democratic centralism.
(5) They should help to strengthen, and not discard or weaken, the leadership of the Communist Party.
(6) They should be beneficial, and not harmful, to international socialist unity and the unity of the peace-loving people of the world. (ibid. pp. 119-20)

In giving such a list Mao was certainly aware of the difficulties of judgement in each case, and of such problems as *who* should judge (the Party, the masses, 'experts', or even the police) in which particular instance. But he would have regarded it as in the nature of the problem that only such general criteria are possible. The application of these criteria would be an educative process for those concerned. They were anyway, he added, only the political criteria, 'applicable to all activities in the arts and sciences'. They were necessary, but not sufficient, for 'naturally, in judging the validity of scientific theories or assessing the aesthetic value of works of art, additional pertinent criteria are needed' (ibid. p. 120). Above all 'what is needed is scientific analysis and convincing argument. Dogmatic criticism settles nothing' (ibid. p. 118).

CPSU policy towards the arts evolved during the stormy period of the twenties when the majority of the intelligentsia were hostile to communism. Lunacharsky, poet, playwright and critic was Commissar of Education. Trotsky, ex-Minister of War, wrote *Literature and Revolution* (1924), and gave qualified support to the Party's right to 'interfere' in 'the field of art' (Trotsky, Ch. 7; Deutscher, 1959, ch. 3; Fitzpatrick, ch. 5, 6). *Proletkult* was organised in Petrograd and Moscow for 'the elaboration of a strictly class ideology and purely proletarian culture' (Fitzpatrick, p. 93) and struggled with *Narkompros* for hegemony in the cultural field. In 1925 the CC CPSU resolved that: 'in a class society there is and can be no neutral art' (quoted in Struve, p. 89). But it remained hesitant before the complexities of the problem. It was only in the following decade that hesitations vanished and the dogma of *socialist realism* was proclaimed.

The term socialist realism was said to have been coined by Stalin (Struve, p. 256). It was defined by Maxim Gorky, Zhdanov and others at the Moscow Congress of the new Union of Soviet Writers in August 1934 (Gorky, pp. 133-40; Struve, ch. 21; Zhdanov, pp. 9-18). Struve summarises its positive and negative features. On the one hand it attempted to shift the focus of literature back from machines and processes to human beings. On the other hand, emphasising the task of portraying 'the new Soviet man' in an ever positive light it opened the way to a new formalism of cardboard characters. It also justified a rigid conservatism and restraint on experiment (Struve, p. 259).

In China the political problems concerning revolutionary romanticism, revolutionary realism, or the treatment of positive, middle or negative characters are compounded by problems of the highly conservative Chinese traditional forms and the degree to which they should be influenced by Euro-American forms. This particularly affects opera, music and painting.

It might be noted at this point that communists have not been alone in feeling concern for the moral-political influence of the creative arts. The Roman Catholic Church has long exercised censorship and maintained an Index (Manhattan, Ch. 4). Parents widely believe certain information and entertainment 'unsuitable' for 'children'. The mass media are increasingly being investigated to try and ascertain their effect (A.J. Jenkinson is an early study).

Another problem which can only be mentioned does not concern the moral-political nature of the arts directly. This is the relationship between professional and amateur, artist and public. The relegation of the vast majority of the population to the role of passive spectators is surely a form of alienation for which neither the USSR nor China really recognise nor provide a solution. The competitive pressures, particularly in the USSR, especially on the young to get into special schools and circles is quite anti-socialist. The encouragement of amateur performances, considerable though it is, does not really touch the problem. During the Cultural Revolution in China the problem surfaced, but rather in sport where the slogan became: friendship first, competition last. But in China the pressures for professionalism are strong and persistent. (Some of these questions are treated in Mackerras, 1973, pp. 35-7; Jiang Qing (Chiang Ching) pp. 60-1; and Vasquez, 1973, especially ch. 17, 19).

Literature and the arts are too complex a matter to do justice to here. All that will be attempted is to give a brief account of the structure and functioning of the major mass media. To estimate their real educative role, the question which really interests us, requires research that has hardly begun. The only aspect of the problem which can directly be studied from the outside is content analysis of materials, such as has been done for Khrushchev's agricultural policy by Ploss (1965), or for nuclear war strategy by Kintner and Scott (1968). It is also possible, at least for the USSR, to follow discussion in newspapers and journals of both approaches and perceived responses. This is often surprisingly frank. One can, and should, also always estimate the exposure of different sections of society to different media. At the simplest level: Chinese newspapers are not likely to be found circulating at village level even today; while in the USSR the huge figures for circulation do not guarantee that particular articles are read, much less uniformly understood. Then there may be important changes over time. Hough recently noted some shift in the USSR from oral agitation at the work place to the mass media (Hough, pp. 126 and 136), and there is no doubt that with the further development of television other changes will occur.

Prime place in both the USSR and China is held by the press, both the newspapers and periodicals. Playing an important role as 'collective propagandist and collective agitator' and 'collective organizer' in Russia before the Revolution (Lenin, 1947, 1, pp. 256-71), it continues to be given major place today. Newspapers and journals are published by various organisations. The CC of the Communist Party has its daily: *Pravda* (Truth) in the USSR and the *Renmin Ribao* (People's Daily) in China. The praesidium of the Supreme Soviet of the USSR publishes the daily, *Izvestia* (News), for which there is no direct equivalent in China. Other important Russian newspapers include *Komsomolskaya Pravda*, published by the CC of the Komsomol, *Trud* (Labour), organ of the CC of Trade Unions, *Literaturnaya Gazeta* (Literary Gazette), published by the National Union of Writers, and, interesting for our purposes, *Uchitelskaya Gazeta* (Teachers' Gazette) published bi-weekly for educators. In China the second national newspaper is the *Guangming Ribao* (The Illuminating Daily). This and the *Renmin Ribao* can be obtained abroad on subscription. Other major Chinese newspapers are the *Gongren Ribao* (Workers' Daily), organ of the All-China Federation of Trade Unions, the *Jiefang Ribao* (Liberation Daily, Shanghai) and the *Wenhui Bao* (Shanghai). Journals, other than the central Party journals which publish important policy statements and discussion documents, are too numerous to mention. These Party journals are *Kommunist,* founded as *Bolshevik* in 1924 and renamed in 1952, in the USSR, and *Honggi* (Red Flag) in China. Both can be obtained abroad. (Some information on the working of the *Renmin Ribao* and *Jiefang Ribao* is given by MacFarquhar, following a visit to them in 1972. See also Cheng, 1965, p. 5 and Yu, 1964.)

The circulation of newspapers and their readership has risen since the revolution. In the USSR 889 newspapers were published in 1918 with a total circulation of 1.7m. In 1953 the numbers were 7,754 and 44.2m (Hopkins, p. 93). The figures for journals were 753 in 1918 and 1,614 in 1953, with an annual circulation of 267.1m copies. Comparable figures for China are not available. In 1959 the then Minister of Culture said there were 1,884 newspapers, but Hong Kong analysts suggested only about 800 would have a wide circulation (Yu, p. 108). In any case, what is important is the readership, and the influence exerted, both of which are difficult to determine. There is no doubt that in both countries readership greatly exceeds publication figures, especially for those articles which are used in political education groups. Newspapers are displayed in various places publicly (picture, Hopkins, p. 324), read to groups of illiterates and others, and excerpts are copied on to the ubiqitous chalk-board 'newspapers' in China. At the same time, even

today in Russia, and even more in the Chinese village, there are shortages, in the latter case chronic.

Any discussion of the press in the early years in the USSR or in China
today must take account of the problem of mass illiteracy. Hopkins
quotes Russian sources for the twenties warning:

> The local press, because it circulates among the most uneducated,
> was to keep in mind that the masses, 'almost everywhere are barely
> literate and even illiterate. . . Articles and news items must be short,
> written clearly and accurately. . . Editors must be certain that every
> printed line, every word in the newspaper neither is incomprehensible
> nor bewildering in the most distant, most remote village.' (Hopkins,
> p. 85)

The morphemic Chinese script must make the problem even more
difficult and may account for the highly repetitious form of many of
the articles (cf. Schumann, pp. 60-2).

The question of participation in the press is, I believe, of fundamental
importance for the development of genuine consciousness, and may be
taken as a barometer for other aspects of society. Writing in 1969 about
Khruschev's attempted reforms Hopkins remarked:

> The Soviet press, he (Khruschev) argued, must be a 'true people's
> forum', aiding the party and the masses in the creation of a Communist
> society. This was, of course, no more than had been said for nearly
> half a century in the Soviet Union. But circumstances had changed.
> By Khrushchev's twilight years, the Soviet media had become a giant
> industry. True, letters to the editor were counted as evidence of a
> people's press. So were articles in local and central newspapers by
> factory foremen, peasant milkmaids, or young Komsomols. But these
> were mechanical gestures to an ideal that had ossified. The press
> by the 1960's not only was entrenched in the party bureaucracy,
> but was in the hands of professional political journalists. Like their
> foreign colleagues, they were not inclined to draw the unskilled
> masses into editorial work. That wispy vision of little knots of
> common men producing their own newspapers had been made obso-
> lete by industrialization if nothing else. (Hokins, pp. 105-6)

The institution of the *rabselkor*, or worker-peasant correspondents,
which began largely spontaneously immediately after the 1917 Revolution,
was one which in different circumstances might have developed 'that

wispy vision' into flesh-and-blood participation. (Hopkins makes the mistake, so common today, of confusing *industrialisation* with the forms capitalism has so far given it.) Conceived as standing somewhere between the masses and the Party, the *rabselkor* was to bring to public attention the problems as seen from the factory floor and village field. A majority has always been workers and peasants, with an emphasis on poor peasants in the early years before collectivisation, though some teachers and doctors in the rural areas became correspondents. Organisation has been by the editorial offices of the big newspapers, rather than the Party, and in the twenties efforts were made to limit the control of the latter over their correspondent members in order to ensure genuine representation of mass views (Harper, p. 99). Correspondents were nevertheless often seen by the masses as spies of the Party and during the early years numbers were attacked and even murdered (Harper, pp. 99-100; Hopkins, p. 87). With the change of emphasis from the expression of local news and views to being 'threads' of the Party which 'should run from the Party through the newspaper to all the working-class and peasant districts' (Stalin, *Works* 5, p. 288) the element of participation was lost. (See Stalin, *Works* 6, pp. 274-5, where he opposes election of correspondents by workers' meetings in favour of choice by newspaper editors, and hence by the Party.)

The *rabselkor* grew slowly until 1924, when there were some 100,000 of them. By 1928 the number had risen to 500,000 and in 1930 to 3m (Hopkins, pp. 87, 97). After Stalin's death there was an attempt to revive the organisation. The CPSU published a decree in August 1958, ordering local branches to establish training schemes for correspondents and to hold public meetings to explain their function to workers and peasants (Hopkins, p. 297). A further decree in June 1960, when the number of worker-peasant correspondents was said to be more than 5 million, encouraged the spread of amateur participants to other media (ibid.). About this time 'raids' on factories and other institutions, investigating their activities, were encouraged (ibid. pp. 298-9).

Less is known about worker correspondents in China. At the *Wenhui Bao*, which I visited with a delegation in August 1975, they have 2,000 'distributed in all walks of life'. They are organised by subject (health, industry) and regionally. Regular twice weekly meetings are held with the regular journalists attached to the group, and there are periodical full meetings. MacFarquhar notes 'a system of workers acting as stringers in factories' for the *Jiefang Ribao* (p. 151), but for the *Renmin Ribao* he says only that a majority of articles are written by non-journalists. He cites a 'maoist dictum that the whole Party should take a hand in writing papers' (pp. 146-7).

Another practice, common to Russia and China, is the wall newspaper. As originally conceived this was a vehicle for local, general expression. Harper describes it as he knew it in 1926:

The wall newspaper has become itself an institution of practically all Soviet institutions, at least in the more politically active urban centres. On entering a bank, commissariat, factory, or club, for example, one finds in the corridor or some similarly prominent place the wall news- paper of the 'collective' of the institution. In the villages, where the wall newspaper has also penetrated, it will be found in the Cantonal Soviet headquarters, or in the village reading-room, and perhaps even in the village school. Some of these wall newspapers are quite elabor- ate in their makeup; even the most modest are neat and attractive in appearance. Some are written by hand in printed characters, but the majority are typewritten; none are printed by press. (Harper, p. 96)

Hopkins, writing in 1969, comments that they are 'the most pervasive, albeit not the most influential' of the country's newspapers. He com- pares them with personal columns of American weeklies, and their incidental news notes (Hopkins, pp. 204-6). He suggests that they normally appear about twelve times a year, especially appearing for such events as November 7th, Women's Day or New Year's Day, though a few are weekly.

Harper notes that while the CP, Komsomol and Young Pioneers were expected to take a leading role in the production of wall newspapers the paper was 'supposed to be the organ of the whole group'. He goes on:

The problem of exercising the leadership expected of the Communist element, while at the same time avoiding the exercise of a kind of tutelage with respect to the mass, is present even in this primary form of Soviet civic activity. (Harper, p. 96)

As with the *rabselkor*, the function of transmitter gradually took over from that of representative of the masses, though the latter function probably never got completely lost. Harper is among observers who have commented on how 'unusually frank in their criticism' the wall news- papers can be (Harper, p. 97). It would be interesting to know how many are critical of the bureaucracy, and how many concentrate on the sins of fellow workers, like that pictured in Hopkins (p. 205) pillorying drunkards (in a cardboard manufacturing plant in Bratsk, Siberia). Many are probably of the bland variety which Hopkins saw at Leningrad University and the Leningrad Academy of Sciences library (Hopkins, pp. 204, 206). Certainly criticism must be difficult when guidelines like this are to be followed:

> The wall newspaper may not carry articles directed against decisions of the party bureau. . . The primary party organization directs the wall newspaper, the party bureau must direct and control it, and not the reverse. If the wall newspaper comes out against decisions of the party bureau, it contradicts the party bureau of which it is an organ, and subsequently violates statutes of the CPSU. (Ilin, quoted in Hopkins, p. 206)

Hopkins attempts to gauge the participation in wall newspapers. Assuming 10 persons per issue of the some 500,000 papers gives a total of some 5m people 'enlisted in ferreting out deficiencies, restating national policy, promoting increased production, and the like' (p. 206). But he concludes correctly

> Certainly, the wall newspapers are not the voice of labour, or of the students, or of farmers. As party organs, they preempt and substitute for what originally in the 1920's were to be the common man's spontaneous outpourings. (Hopkins, p. 207)

In China an interesting and effective extension of the wall newspaper has been developed known as the *dazibao*, or big character poster (sometimes a *xiaozibao*, written in smaller characters, often distributed as a leaflet or small pamphlet). These were used extensively in the hundred flowers movement of 1957, during the Cultural Revolution of 1966-9, and again during the 'criticize Lin (Biao), criticize Confucius' movement of 1973-4. *Dazibao* differ from wall newspapers in being produced by individuals as well as groups (e.g. Red Guard groups), and in normally being concerned with a single topic and special occasion (Schurmann, p. 317, makes the mistake of confusing the two by his unfortunate translation). While there is evidence that the Party organisations attempted to censor *dazibao* during the Cultural Revolution by covering or removing offending items, there is no doubt that this device is a powerful vehicle for conveying information (often misinformation!) and comment. While considerable use has been made of those *dazibao* which became available outside China there has been no study of them as a means of democratic expression. This would probably require field work which is currently impossible.

Radio and television now play an important role in both Russia and China, though both countries have been hampered by poverty and technical backwardness. In spite of the invention of a device for radio transmission by A.S. Popov in Russia in 1895, regular broadcasting did not begin until October 1924. By 1928 there were some 70,000 radio receivers and 22,000 loudspeakers connected by landline (Hopkins, p. 90). Receiving an enormous setback during World War Two, it has only been in the last decade that radio reception has become really universal in the USSR (Hopkins, pp. 246-7). Television, a later and yet more expensive invention, began with an experimental transmission in the USSR in April 1931. Some programmes were broadcast in 1939 in Moscow, and by 1941 400 TV sets were available. But again the war delayed development and it was not until the sixties that both transmitters and receivers had been constructed in quantities sufficient for a mass audience (Hopkins, p. 250).

The PRC, beginning already in the era of television, has been able to make faster progress in spite of initially greater poverty. Concentrating initially on the cities, attention was turned to the villages in 1955, when in December the third National Conference on Broadcasting Work in Peking put forward plans for some 900 line-broadcasting stations with 500,000 loudspeakers, 80 per cent of them to be in the village. Television has been confined to the bigger cities, but radio production has expanded into the transistor field and in the post-Cultural Revolution period visitors report that land-line radio reception is being increasingly supplemented by the pocket transistor receiver. In addition to central and provincial broadcasting stations there are local networks in the communes. This allows the broadcasting of very local news and information and involves local personnel in selection and transmission.

Like the newspapers, the tone of Russian and Chinese broadcasting is serious and didactic. Harper describes the early programmes on Moscow radio (pp. 325-6). An analysis of Radio Moscow in the early sixties gave: 55 per cent music; 16 per cent news; 10 per cent social-political information; 9 per cent literature and drama; about 7 per cent to youth; and the rest a mixture (Hopkins, p. 239). A similar analysis of TV gave: 22 per cent films; 10 per cent literature and drama; 18 per cent music; 17 per cent news; 14 per cent for youth; 8 per cent social-political information; and 2 per cent miscellaneous (ibid.). The content of Chinese broadcasts can be judged from a study of either the BBC Summary of World Broadcasts, or from the US equivalent (Fraser, 1965, p. 419). Hopkins' summary of the characteristics of the Soviet mass media probably applies reasonably well to China:

> What perhaps gives the Soviet mass media distinguishing character-
> istics are the omissions. Every subject, attitude, and style of writing
> in the Soviet mass media has its equivalents in the American press,
> but the reverse is not true. The conscious purposefulness of
> information eliminates facts and opinions that, while trivial, could
> lend depth to an individual's awareness of the world around him.
> Information unfavourable to the Soviet state seldom reaches the
> Soviet public, or does so in diluted form. (Hopkins, p. 178)

But there are regrettably few studies of the treatment of issues by Soviet media, and none comparing Soviet and Chinese media. (Schurmann, pp. 62-8, gives a brief account of the major types of articles in the Chinese press and their role in 'what the Soviets call *agitatsiia*, agitation'.)

One of the essentials for any system of education is a good library service. It was Lenin's opinion that 'the library and reading room would for a long time be the main source of political education for the masses and almost their only school' (Krupskaya in Simsova, p. 10). Himself a model library user (ibid. p. 8), Lenin did much during the first few years of the Soviet Republic to lay the basis for a genuine people's library system. He attempted to mitigate the ravages of war and conserve stocks of books and other printed matter for *public* use. (Compare Simsova, p. 39 with Horecky, p. 1, where the latter mistakenly accuses Lenin of nationalising private *libraries*. Lenin mentions stocks and excepts libraries.) He set as the ideal for Soviet libraries to follow the principles he had seen operating in the libraries of 'western countries', stressing particularly mass accessibility, even for children (Simsova, p. 15; Horecky, p. 1). Developments since Lenin's time have both realised his vision, and to the extent that censorship operates, denied it. In his careful and critical study Horecky notes that while libraries collect and preserve with great care they at the same time restrict access to their collections (p. 150). Among the special features which he pays tribute to are:

(1) a deposit system whereby publishers/printers must supply certain libraries with a specified number of copies of everything they print;

(2) Resources are marshalled in support of industry and scientific research. This includes the abstracting, translating and listing of foreign publications.

(3) Reading rooms in the major libraries are widely stratified accord-

ing to materials and readers' educational background.

(4) General libraries make available extensive services for children and young people. (Horecky, pp. 152-3)

In China, as in the USSR, the library system can be divided into various sections. These include the public libraries under the Ministry of Culture or equivalent local Departments; university and school libraries under the Ministry of Education and local departments, the Chinese Academy of Sciences Institute Libraries; specialised Government libraries; Labour union libraries and reading rooms; and libraries of the armed forces. The National Library at Peking, originally founded in 1912, is the national deposit library. One copy of all Chinese publications must be deposited there within three days of printing. Besides housing former imperial collections and other rare works it concentrates on the social sciences. The Peking Library is also responsible for exchanges with foreign countries. Like the other designated national library, the Shanghai People's Library, it is a centre for bibliography and library science research. Other major libraries are at Wuhan, Shenyang, Nanjing (Nanking), Guangzhou (Canton), Chengdu, Xi'an (Sian), Lanzhou, Tianjin (Tientsin) and Harbin. In an attempt to co-ordinate the work of libraries in helping scientific research a Book Selection Committee, having advisory powers only, was established in 1957. Another important body is the Institute of Scientific and Technical Information of China. It engages in acquisition of domestic and foreign materials, and in publication, including, because of the shortage of foreign currency, the reprinting of foreign books and periodicals (*Directory of Selected Scientific Institutions in Mainland China*, p. xvi).

It is very difficult to judge the degree to which the libraries serve the various needs of the community, in the USSR, China, or indeed anywhere. Horecky discusses some of the problems, such as the difficulties of quantitative estimates for library holdings. These are inflated by duplicate copies, or by counting volumes instead of titles (Horecky, pp. 27-9). Librarians often count it good that there is a high turnover of borrowings, but this can mean that no one can keep a book long enough to make real use of it. Qualitative questions are perhaps even more difficult. Both Soviet and Chinese libraries make great efforts to provide materials suitable for different kinds of readers, but both indulge in a similar form of censorship (details of the Chinese methods are not well described, but it is known that there are special collections, and that access is restricted. Some light on this is thrown by Schwarz's study of the *Ts'an-k'ao Hsiao-hsi*; see also Nunn). Any evaluation of library services should also take into account book and journal publication.

Both Russia and China have made great efforts to expand these services and to provide them cheaply. Both the type of book and the quantity is relevant to their value in mass education. (For China see Nunn, and more recently, E. Wu.)

Museums, exhibitions and excursions have formed an important element of political education since the early days of the Russian revolution. Reading the 12-page chapter which Harper devotes to the subject (1928) reminds one of similar accounts in present-day China. There are the old palaces to remind one of the 'bitter past and the sweet present' and the sweat wrung out of the skilful workers who built them. The following extract from a guide to the estate of Tsaritsyno near Moscow gives the flavour:

> One has only to note the manner of life of the Russian autocrats, the kind of people who surrounded them, the ways in which they spent their time, and their tastes, pleasures, and thoughts, and immediately it will be clear that this rule was alien to the toiling masses, resting, as it did, on the class regime of the landlords and building its welfare on the exploitation of the labour of the people. A trip to Tsaritsyno will make these statements clear to you. (Quoted in Harper, p. 217)

Reading captions on an exhibition of archaeological find in the Imperial Palace, Peking, during a recent visit I encountered almost identical phrases. Lessons about the bad times are supplemented by the museums of the revolution, like that in Moscow, with their photographs and documents, or the Lenin museum and its numerous smaller counterparts scattered through the land. In China there is the impressive Museum of the Chinese Revolution on Tian An Men Square, opposite the Great Hall of the People. Also in Peking is the People's Revolutionary War Museum. Throughout the USSR and China there are similar museums and collections. Places associated with Mao Ze-dong's leadership, such as the places where he worked in Yan'an, Jingganshan where he set up his first revolutionary base, and the Institute of the Peasant Movement where he trained peasant cadres in 1926 in Guangzhou, have, especially since the Cultural Revolution become places of revolutionary pilgrimage, visited by millions. At them exhibitions and guides tell of their revolutionary significance.

Harper describes how in the twenties the schools, youth organisations and trade unions organised visits to museums, promoting an interest which is sustained to today. Then the Cultural-Education Section of the Moscow Soviet of Trade Unions, for example, had organised excursions advertised in clubs and public institutions by big black and red posters: 'The Trade-Union is the school of communism'; 'The Workmen's Club is the forge of proletarian consciousness.' Visits were recommended to the Museum of Trade Unions to study trade union history, or to the Polytechnical Museum and the Psycho-Technical Laboratory of the Commissariat of Labour to study 'the scientific organization of labour' (Harper, pp. 211-3).

With the growing up of new generations and the distancing in time of the events portrayed in the museums from the crowds that observe them the problem of communication increases. The peasant and worker masses who first surged through the great palaces of the Tsars or the Forbidden City in Peking will have experienced quite different emotions from the relatively wealthy Young Pioneer of Moscow or Leningrad of the seventies, or the Hongxiaobing of today's Peking. To be effective as political education exhibitions and excursions must change to meet this problem. In both Russia and China attempts have utilised the living to convey the reality of the past. Heroes of the revolutionary and patriotic wars tell their stories, Mrs Kosmodemyanskaya tells about her children (Zoya and Shura), as does the mother of Liu Hu-lan. Others tell their simple tales of past suffering and show the scars, the rags and the hovels which were their lot. But it remains to be proved that such methods have the desired, and lasting effects on those who experience them. There is sometimes an inverse relation between emotive power and cognitive complexity which borders on the anti-marxist.

Any attempt to evaluate the educational role of the mass media described above, and the other forms through which moral-political teaching is purveyed, must take into consideration the role and effect of censorship. In Russia in 1920 *Agitprop* was established as a department of the CC CPSU (Schapiro, p. 247; Fitzpatrick, pp. 181-5, 195-6, and 244-9 for relations with other educational bodies; Hopkins, p. 77). In 1921 it set up a Press Sub-department which by 1924 had assumed control of the local press and become a full department. It also began turning its attention to creative literature. Press departments of the Party at central, provincial and district level supervised both content and personnel (Hopkins, p. 77).

More important as a censor has been *Glavlit*, the Central Department of Literary Affairs, formerly a Tsarist institution, re-created by a decree of the Council of People's Commissars in June 1922. It was placed under the Commissariat for Education and at the same time worked closely with the internal security police (GPU, then OGPU and now NKVD). Struve comments that 'the exact workings of Soviet censorship are surrounded by mystery, and its history offers many puzzles' (p. 223, n. 3). He goes on to give some references where some 'inadequate' information is to be found. Harper notes the role of the Main Repertory Committee of the Commissariat of Education in the twenties in censoring theatre and film (pp. 314, 328). Hopkins draws attention to the role of various articles of the Criminal Code. Article 70 outlaws

> agitation or propaganda conducted for the purpose of subverting or weakening Soviet power or for the purpose of committing particularly dangerous state crimes: dissemination, for the same purpose, of slanderous fabrications that discredit the Soviet state and social system; as well as the dissemination or preparation or possession for the same purposes of literature with a like content. (Hopkins, p. 129; cf. Reddaway, p. 11)

Article 190-1 reads:

> The systematic dissemination by word of mouth of deliberate fabrications discrediting the Soviet political and social system, or the manufacture or dissemination in written, printed or other form of works of the same content, shall be punished ... (Reddaway, ibid.)

Article 71 prohibits 'war propaganda', article 228 prohibits 'pornographic' works, and there are laws on libel (*kleveta*) and insult (*oskorbleniye*) (Hopkins, pp. 130-1).

Nothing seems to be known about the detailed working of censorship in China. Barnett describes the public security bodies in the ministry, county and commune which he studied, but does not mention responsibility for censorship. He only notes the security classification of documents and the strict secrecy employed (p. 66). The Propaganda Departments of the CCP are probably concerned at one level. Nunn refers to 'organs in charge of publications administration' with which publishing enterprises have to be registered (p. 64).

It is not surprising that censorship operates. The communist governments were established in bitter struggles, and have suffered war and intense hostility since. But the effect may be counter-productive, encouraging apathy, fear and lack of initiative, just those qualities which the censorship is aimed at avoiding. It is clearly antithetical to marxist educational aims of a self-determining and self-conscious human being, for the education of whom access to, and freedom to discuss, the widest range of information is necessary.

3. Politics in the School

Politics can be said to saturate the school, being both explicit and implicit in its organisation. But its form and nature have differed over space and time and we can do no more than point to some of the interesting problem areas here. I shall consider first the curriculum and then the organisation of the school.

Harper quotes from a discussion of pre-school training to show the political aims which Soviet pedagogues of the twenties set for the school 'from the very first stages':

> The future Soviet citizen whom we are training must be a stalwart and healthy proletarian, a class and a revolutionary fighter, a scientifically conscious and organized builder of the new socialist state. He must be a dialectic materialist, armed to the teeth with the necessary knowledge and ability to oppose exploitation and mysticism in all its forms. He must be a collectivist in all economic and social activities, in order steadfastly to oppose private property and individualistic aims, on which the class of exploiters has built up its power... The future citizen must be a revolutionary-activist with habits of self-organization and of organization in common with others. (Harper, p. 268)

Pinkevich, writing for a foreign audience a few years later (1930) expressed it similarly:

> The major aim of general instruction is the development of an outlook upon the world . . . socialistic understanding and marxian evaluation . . . We must educate warriors for socialism. . . (p. 28)

He stressed understanding and evaluation of the 'entire cultural heritage' and allowance for 'the needs of individual development'. Mrs King gives her impressions of what this meant in practice in schools she observed in 1932 and 1934:

> When I visited the USSR in 1932, I found politics colouring all teaching, and it was not coloured a pale shade, but a good deep red. The walls of the nursery-infant schools that I saw were decorated with political posters and slogans, pictures of tractors, and Red Army soldiers. The songs I heard were about completing the Five-Year Plan in four. The information given to the children about foreign countries was more than biased—that is common to all countries—it was in-

correct. All that was post-revolutionary was glorified, all that was pre-revolutionary was regarded as of little value.

The change which occurred within two years was astonishing . . . In 1934, I found the walls of the nursery-infant schools decorated with pleasing, ordinary pictures. The songs the children sang were similar to those sung by children in other countries, except that fairy songs were excluded. I listened to history lessons and geography lessons and the bias was no stronger than in many lessons to which I have listened in English schools. 'Communist education does not mean filling the children's heads with political catchwords such as "bourgeois enemy", "capitalist exploiter", etc.', I was informed by the Director of the institute which trains Marxian psychologists for education, industry, and administration. 'We have no longer any need to fill the history or geography lesson with irrelevant political theorising or generalisations based on no foundation of facts', said the very same Vice-Commissar who two years before had practically insisted that education must be subservient to politics. (King, 1937, p. 30)

No doubt comforting to petty bourgeois and liberal English readers, this account of *volte-face* does not really explain anything. Did it mean, as the Chinese might put it, that the 'academic authorities' had taken over? Were slogans being replaced by real analysis of problems? Only thorough study of contemporary materials might throw light on the matter.

The description of 1932 could with little change apply to China, especially during and since the Cultural Revolution. An extreme example is that of the Yuxiang Kindergarten run by the Air Force of the Peking Military Region, described in the *Guangming Ribao* of 23 December 1967 (*SCMP*, 4106). There children studied Mao's '3 old articles', studied picture exhibitions of the White Haired Girl and the Rent Collector's Courtyard, sang and recited Mao Quotations and fostered the 'proletarian political viewpoint and clear-cut love and hate' by attending mass celebration meetings, such as that to celebrate the current nuclear test. Other examples, also at the pre-school stage, are described by R. Sidel.

The following description by the Alts, visitors to the USSR in 1959 from the USA, show a progression from the description by Mrs King:

In the school, as in the club, on the street, in the park, in the comics and stories that are read to him and that he reads, the Russian child is surrounded by examples of exemplary behaviour and outstanding achievement. The first thing that strikes the visitor on entering the hallway of a school are the photographs and exhibits obviously planned to exert positive influence on the child. Examples of achievement by the children are to be found wherever the children move about. . . The walls of the classrooms as well as the hallways abound not only in photographs of the leaders of the revolution, heroes in battle and the underground during the last war, famous inventors, scientists and athletes, but also in those of classmates who now lead or have led the class, or who excel in sports or otherwise. To emphasize the point, a poster on the wall may depict the best pupil as Sputnik and the worst as a tortoise, each symbol bearing the actual name of the pupil. . .

We sat in on reading lessons in three schools, and without exception the lesson dealt with the lives of scientists, astronomers, geographers, medical workers and inventors as examples of contributors to the common good. The story about the inventor was particularly interest-ing, for, in response to the teacher's question, a pupil pointed out that he was a great and good man because he invented useful machines and was poor and a lover of the people. (H. and E. Alt, pp. 241-2)

The Alts continue with a description of two short films illustrating honesty and the spirit of comradeship (Alt, pp. 242-3). Such stories are typical of pre-Cultural Revolution Chinese primary school books. For example, Book 3 of the selection by Ridley *et al.* (Ridley, p. 255), contains a story about James Watt which begins: 'In England more than two hundred years ago there was the son of a labourer . . . ' (see Price, 1970, pp. 122-3).

The syllabus drawn up for the early years of the United Labour School in the Soviet Union set out the political aspects of the course under the headings 'labour' and 'society'. Studies were practical as well as theoretical. This led pupils and teachers into dangerous conflict sit-uations, not only with parents who were religious or unhygienic, but also with the Party and State officials, something which could not be tolerated in the period of collectivisation and the Five Year Plans. What was required then was loyal enthusiasm to policies handed down from above. The school reforms of the early thirties, restricting political activities and altering the stress to more formal learning must be seen in that context. No doubt many teachers found the change easier and safer. Needless to say, the justifications given for the reforms at the time were couched in quite other terms, of which the following is an example:

Instead of teaching civic history in an animated and entertaining form with an exposition of the most important events and facts in their chronological sequence and with sketches of historical personages, the pupils are given abstract definitions of social and economic form-ations, which thus replace the consecutive exposition of civic history by abstract sociological schemes. (Decree of the Council of People's Commissars of the USSR and CC of the CPSU(B), 'On the teaching of civic history in schools of the USSR', 16 May 1934, quoted in Daniels, 2, p. 39. See also preceding two and following extracts)

Which is not to say that there was no truth in the reasons given. Harper quotes what sounds like an early 'radio Erevan' story, current during his 1926 visit. Asked during a test of *politgramota* what he would do in the event of a revolt against the Soviet government, a student replied that he would take up arms and defend it. A bad answer. The correct one is that such a situation is inconceivable (Harper, p. 268). Harper comments: 'The mere parrot like repetition of formulas in answer to questions has not failed to impress even the most ardent Marxists' (ibid.).

At secondary school level *social science* has been taught as a separate subject for most of the history of the soviet school. In the late twenties it was prescribed for 4 hours a week in grades 5, 6 and 9, and for 5 hours a week in grade 8 (Woody, p. 449). This was reduced when the new syllabus was introduced in 1935 to only one hour a week in each of grades 5, 6 and 7. In the post-World War Two school this subject was replaced by the *Constitution of the USSR*, taught for 2 hours a week in grade 7 (Medynsky, pp. 23 and 26). With the new 8-year school in 1958 this was merged with history, taught through grades 4-8 (Shapovalenko, pp. 92, 95). In 1965 *social science* returned, this time for 2 hours a week. In grades 10 and 11 (Shchukina, p. 190; note the 11th grade was formally abolished the previous year, but still appears in her table).

Some idea of the change of emphasis at the two ends of this develop-ment can be gained from a comparison of the syllabus outlined in King (1937, pp. 164-6) and the textbook, *Obshchestvovedeniye* (1969). Abbreviated outlines are as follows:

1935 syllabus
Class 3: Why the workers love their fatherland (L. 1-12); The country of the soviets needs educated and cultured people (L. 13-24); The country of the soviets needs healthy, courageous and cheerful people (L. 25-38). *Class 4*: Prepare for the defence of your country (L. 1-18); The workers of the soviets—the brothers of the workers of all nations

(L. 19-27); Three generations of fighters for the worker class (L. 28-
38). (This last dealt with the CP, the Komsomol and Pioneers.)

1969 edition of social science
The basis of marxism-leninism: (1) The philosophical notion of the
world and its cognition (matter and movement, materialism and idealism, etc.). (2) Studies of the development of society (the materialist
conception of history; social-economic formations; class and class
war; historical necessity and human activity). (3) Capitalism and its
decline (capitalist production; exploitation; imperialism; to socialism).
Socialism and Communism. (4) The economic system of socialism.
(5) Social-political system of socialism. (6) The foundation of communism (energy, materials, mechanization and automation, organization of production, science). (7) The formation of communist social
relations (town and village; mental and manual work; from the state
to communist social self-government). (8) Education of a new man
(marxist atheism, collectivism and humanism). (9) The Party—our
helmsman. (10) The epoch of the revolutionary change from capitalism to socialism.

While the second work is available in translation (Shakhnazarov) books
and materials used in the first course are difficult or impossible to
obtain now. In any case what is really wanted is the reactions of those
taught and one can only ponder the relations between the kind of material indicated here and the students' other knowledge and experience.

In Chinese schools politics was taught as a separate course for only a
few years before the Cultural Revolution. Monoson gives a teaching
plan for the high schools for 1955/6 in which he shows what he trans-
lates as *politgramota* taught for 2 hours a week in the final year of the
junior high school, and *Constitution of the PRC* for 2 hours a week in
grade 12 (Monoson, p. 115). Klepikov reproduces a teaching plan for
1958/9 in which he shows *socialist education* taught for 2 hours a week
throughout the six years of high school (Klepikov, p. 126). Before this
time and during the sixties these courses were not given and politics
featured within the subject curriculum only as it influenced such subjects
as history, geography and literature (see Price, 1970, pp. 122-7, 132-41;
C.T. Hu, 1968).

Perhaps the fullest account of political education in schools is that
given by Dai Xiao-ai. It conflicts with other evidence in that he asserts
that before the Cultural Revolution the senior high school he attended
in Guangzhou (Canton) gave 'instruction in general politics' four times a

week (Bennett and Montaperto, p. 23). Either this was an exception, or
it was part of the extra-curricula activity which all schools held. It is
worth quoting at some length what Dai says.

> In one sense, politics was at the core of our curriculum. A bad grade
> in general politics could mean expulsion. A bad attitude toward par-
> ticipation in political study at the class and small-group level was
> certain to bring trouble. In general politics we studied different kinds
> of social system—and their historical development. We learned about
> different kinds of exploitation in the capitalist system and how to
> analyze different classes. We also studied international relations and
> learned to interpret the actions of different countries in the light of
> their social systems. . .
>
> General politics was supposed to provide a guideline for other
> kinds of political training. Those exercises were so varied that we
> enjoyed them more than our classroom study.
>
> Each morning every student and every teacher had to spend at
> least one hour in study of the writings of Mao Ze-dong. This was an
> inflexible rule and was never broken whether we were in the school
> or out in the farms and factories. We were supposed to continue the
> practice even when we were home on vacation. We all thought that
> this was important since it was the best way to learn the content of
> these works.
>
> In addition to this, seminars were held at least once each month,
> sometimes at the class level and sometimes for the whole school, in
> which students and teachers who had made a good record in study-
> ing Mao's works would speak. Usually they talked about a specific
> problem that they had faced and then told us how they had applied
> Chairman Mao's Thought to solve it. . . I didn't particularly care for
> these seminars since they were time-consuming and frequently the
> speakers chose problems so personal that they were not of great use
> to the rest of us.
>
> Also, about once a month the whole school would be called upon
> to participate in 'Remember bitterness and think of sweetness' (*yi ku
> si tian*) meetings. A student or a teacher or sometimes even a worker
> from a nearby factory would contrast the hard times he had suffered
> under the Guomindang with present conditions. Sometimes these
> accounts were very moving; I almost always came away with a feel-
> ing that I owed a great deal to the Party and to Chairman Mao for
> making things so much better for me. . .
>
> We also participated in practical programs designed to ensure that

we maintained our political activeness. For example, we spent one month of each term on farms where we lived and worked with poor and lower-middle peasants. (Bennett and Montaperto, pp. 23-4)

Finally, in the tertiary schools of the USSR and China some form of political course has been obligatory since the CPSU established control over the universities. At least two of the Russian textbooks used have been translated into English and are therefore available for study (Lewis, (ed.), *A Textbook of Marxist Philosophy*, n.d., but pre-1944; and Kuusinen *et al.*, *Fundamentals of Marxism-Leninism*, 2nd ed., 1964). Some account of their contents has already been given. In Chinese tertiary institutions political studies have included courses in the history of the CCP (Price, 1970, p. 155).

Anti-religious Education

Anti-religious education has been a feature of education in the USSR and China on a range of levels. At its best it has been an attempt to direct attention and energies to the solving of human problems in the here and now, and the overcoming of beliefs seen to impede this. At its worst it has been a crude practice of repression which must have taught more convincingly than any rhetoric, and some very unmarxist lessons at the same time!

Anti-religious education has drawn its authority from the writings of Marx which we have already examined, and from those of Lenin and Mao respectively. Read dispassionately none of these would seem to justify much that has been done.

Lenin wrote a number of articles on religion. In December 1905, he wrote *Socialism and Religion,* in which he argued the point which he was to repeat whenever he mentioned religion:

Religion teaches those who toil in poverty all their lives to be resigned and patient in this world, and consoles them with the hope of reward in heaven. (Lenin, *On Religion*, p. 11)

Following Engels, he asserted the separation of the State from religion, and the freedom for people to profess any or no religion as they wished. While asserting that for the Party (then the Russian Social Democratic Party) religion was not purely private, since the Party programme was based on 'scientific—to be more precise—upon *materialist* philosophy', he strongly opposed declaring the party atheist, and putting the religious struggle in the foreground. He wrote:

We must not allow the forces waging a genuinely revolutionary economic and political struggle to be broken up for the sake of opinions and dreams that are of third-rate importance. (Lenin, *On Religion*, p. 15)

In *The Attitude of the Workers' Party towards Religion,* published in May 1909, he argued that the Party should not dogmatically ban even priests from membership, but that such cases should be considered on their merits, in the light of the needs of the revolutionary struggle and the activities of the person concerned.

Regarding religious beliefs as a serious barrier to the struggle for a better life on this earth, Lenin advocated various forms of anti-religious education. In *On the Significance of Militant Materialism*, written in 1922, he warned:

A Marxist could not make a worse mistake than to think that the many millions of people (particularly peasants and artisans) who are condemned by modern society to ignorance, illiteracy and prejudices can extricate themselves from this ignorance only by following the straight line of purely Marxist education. It is essential to give these masses the greatest variety of atheist propaganda—to acquaint them with facts from the most diversified fields of life. Every way of approach to them must be tried in order to interest them, to rouse them from their religious slumber, to shake them up by most varied ways and means. (Lenin, *On Religion*, p. 37)

Castigating the 'dull, dry, paraphrasing of Marxism', he advocated publication of some of the great atheistic writings of the eighteenth century. However, long before he had pointed out that religion has social roots in oppression, and the fear of the 'blind forces' of capitalism and of nature:

No amount of reading matter, however enlightening, will eradicate religion from those masses who are crushed by the grinding toil of capitalism and subjected to the blind destructive forces of capitalism, until these masses, themselves, learn to fight against the social facts from which religion arises. . . (Lenin, *On Religion*, p. 20)

In order to accomplish the marxist vision of a free man, liberated from earthly oppression and the dream of a future heaven dependent on present suffering, Party tactics should combine political struggle and intellectual struggle. But the latter should be subordinated to the former so as always to strengthen it.

Mao Ze-dong, perhaps because of the very different nature of religion in China, appears to take a more relaxed attitude to it than Lenin, though at the same time he frequently asserts the dialectical materialist basis of his Party's policies. In his magnificent report on the Hunan peasant movement of 1927 he listed 'the supernatural system (religious authority)' as one of the 'four thick ropes binding the Chinese people' (Mao, *SW* 1, p. 44). While himself doing 'some propaganda against superstitions', he advocated that the Communist Party's policy should be to 'draw the bow without shooting, just indicate the motions'. He added: 'It is the peasants who made the idols, and when the time comes they will cast the idols aside with their own hands' (ibid. p. 46). Thirty years later, in *On the Correct Handling of Contradictions Among the People*, Mao wrote:

> We cannot abolish religion by administrative decree or force people not to believe in it. . . The only way to settle questions of an ideological nature or controversial issues among the people is by the democratic method, the method of discussion, of criticism, of persuasion and education, and not by the method of coercion or repression. (Mao, *Four Essays*, p. 86)

In 1965, talking with Andre Malraux, Mao made the interesting comment:

> When I said, 'Chinese marxism is the religion of the people' . . . I meant that the communists express the Chinese people in a real way if they remain faithful to the work upon which the whole of China has embarked as if on another Long March. (MacInnis, p. 17)

Understanding that 'revolution is a drama of passion' Mao knows that religion for China's masses is more complex than the stifling of revolt by a state-linked church, or the fear and confusion sown by village superstitions. Yet in China, as in Russia, threat of political opposition has led to 'coercion and repression' and many have raised new idols rather than cast down the old.

Religions in Russia and China on the Eve of their Revolutions

Pre-revolutionary Russia was dominated religiously by the Russian Orthodox Church, which as Hecker noted, was 'from its very inception . . . tied to the throne' and 'leaned upon the strong arm of the State'. Not only that, from the eighteenth century on it became 'practically a department of State, something of a police force over the consciences of the people' (Hecker, p. 37). In China there was no state church, and, moreover, the three strands of belief in the supernatural, ethics and ceremony, united in the European Christian Church, in China remained largely separate. True, state ceremonial was linked with the ancestor cult and magical practices connected with the harvests and other matters of popular concern. But ethics was a matter of secular philosophy and the Confucian scholars tended to see beliefs in gods and spirits as matters for the ignorant lower orders. Which is not to make the mistake of saying that religion was unimportant in China. C.K. Yang, pointing to its origin in Legge on the one hand, and Liang Qi-chao on the other, has thoroughly disproved that myth. But it remains true that the situation was significantly different.

(The essentially secular nature of Confucianism was a Chinese interpretation accepted and defended by Matteo Ricci and the Jesuits in China, who at the same time tried to prove a proto-Christian position in the original Confucian *jing* (texts). See the interesting thesis, *K'ung-tzu or Confucius* by Paul Rule.)

Another major religious difference between Russia and China was what Yang describes as 'the highly eclectic nature of Chinese religion' (Yang, p. 25) compared with the distinct and intolerant Christian, Jewish and Moslem religions to be found in the territory of the Russian empire. Yang goes on:

Even priests in some country temples were unable to reveal the identity of the religion to which they belonged. Centuries of mixing gods from different faiths into a common pantheon had produced a functionally oriented religious view that relegated the question of religious identity to a secondary place. (Yang, p. 25)

de Bary *et al.* quote a Chinese saying to the effect that 'the majority of China's millions have "worn a Confucian crown, a Daoist robe, and a pair of Buddhist sandals"' (de Bary, 2, p. 286). Tolerance is indeed an important aspect of Chinese thought, but intolerance is not lacking, especially when ideas were seen as politically threatening. But the mix was different from Russia where the various religions were sharply divided, even when not actually in conflict with one another.

It is always difficult to produce accurate figures for membership in a particular belief, the more so because of the differences in the degree of participation involved. In Russia the Tsarist statistics gave a figure of 69.9 per cent of the 1914 population of 163 millions, a figure which

Kolarz notes is certainly much too high. For the immediate post-World
War Two period a figure of 20m to 30m is more realistic. The numbers of
Old Believers and other 'sectarians' is impossible to estimate. Some
claim a figure of up to 25m at the beginning of the twentieth century
(Kolarz, p. 129). Roman Catholicism was only important among people
of Polish or Lithuanian descent. The Baltic States are said to have con-
tained 81.2 per cent Catholics when they were re-occupied by the
Russians in 1940. Important protestant sects included the Evangelical
Christians and the Baptists who together numbered over 105,000 in
1914. Conquest comments that

> Russian Protestantism was a protest against Tsarist State intervention
> in the affairs of the Russian Orthodox Church; it was also a protest
> against the secularisation of that Church and its support of social
> injustice. (Conquest, p. 98)

The Jews, who suffered all kinds of civil restrictions (debarment from
administrative posts, restricted entry to education and certain professions, and confinement to living within 'the Pale of Settlement', i.e.
certain parts of western Russia) numbered about 3 million after Poland
and the Baltic States had separated from the Soviet Union, but not all
these practised religion. A similar confusion of 'nationality' with
religion occurs for Moslems for which a blanket total is given of over
16m in 1912, 4.6m in European Russia and the others spread through
Central Asia, the Caucasus and Siberia. Buddhism, which entered the
Russian empire from Mongolia in the nineteenth century, was adopted
by the Kalmyks and the Buryats. (Mongol people lived along the Volga
and around Lake Baikal. Conquest notes a figure of some 40 monastery
temples in 1915 while Kolarz gives a figure of 15,000 lamas for the
Buryat region in 1923 when the communists assumed power there.
Neither gives any figures for total believers.)
  For China the quotation of data on the different religions suffers
from the same problems as for Russia, with the additional one that since
religious beliefs and practices are so often overlapping the same person
should be assigned to more than one religion. Or perhaps one should
just say that the overwhelming majority of Chinese have been, and
probably still are, religious in the sense in which Yang describes them.
In the late forties the following figures were given for the main religions:
20m Moslems (with the above-noted confusion between religion and
'nationality'); 600,000 Buddhist monks and nuns, and 3m-4m lay devotees;
several hundred thousand Daoist priests and 'vegetarian women'; 3.3m

Roman Catholics; and about 600,000 Protestants.

In both Russia and China the intelligentsia were led to question religion generally through the social role of the dominant form. In addition to policing the people's consciences, as mentioned above, the Russian Orthodox Church was noted for its lack of interest in any form of education. Hecker notes:

> Up to the eighteenth century illiterate village priests were quite the common rule. Before ordination they had to learn the words of the service by heart and they repeated them ever after with but the least idea of their meaning... the famous High Procurator of the Holy Synod, Pobyedonostzev ... who died in 1907, said: 'Our clergy teaches little and seldom. The Bible does not exist for the illiterate people ... In far off parts of the country the people understand absolutely nothing as to the meaning of the words of the service, not even the Lord's Prayer, which is often repeated with alterations which altogether destroy its meaning' (Hecker, pp. 15-16)

While certain reformers turned to a purified form of religion (Tolstoy, Gorky, Lunacharski—see Kline, ch. 1, 4) others asserted atheism, either in the tradition of the French Enlightenment, or in its later marxist form (Belinsky, Herzen, Chernyshevsky and then Plekhanov). Opposition by the Church to the teaching of science, and even the extension of simple literacy, drove many to question basic beliefs, while probably more simply rejected the Church without really questioning, accepting atheism as part of being progressive.

In China the principles of 'Mr Democracy' and 'Mr Science' were developed during the period 1917-21 known as the May 4th Movement. This movement included an attack on current Confucian values and traditional religion. Chen Du-xiu, in the famous magazine, *New Youth*, in January 1919 explained:

> In order to advocate Mr Democracy, we are obliged to oppose Confucianism, the codes of rituals, chastity of women, traditional ethics, and old-fashioned politics; in order to advocate Mr Science, we have to oppose traditional arts and traditional religion. (Quoted in Chow, p. 59)

(*The Bulletin of Concerned Asian Scholars*, January-March 1976, has devoted a special issue to translations from this period.)

A key problem, filial piety, was rather social than religious in the

usually accepted sense. Lu Xun, writer and critic likened by some to
Voltaire, wrote:

> Even a cow cannot serve both as a sacrificial animal and as a draught
> animal, both for beef and for milking; how can a human being survive
> both for his ancestors and for himself? (in Chow, p. 309)

Some of the psychological aspects of this problem, and the different
attitudes adopted are discussed by R.J. Lifton, who also notes the
connection between liberalism and foreign missionary teaching (Lifton,
pp. 428-9).

It is hard to make a quantitative evaluation, but it is probable that
in both Russia and China the number of the intelligentsia hostile to
religion as they understood it was high at the time of the revolution.
In China such an attitude would be supported both by foreign influence,
and by a return to the classical tradition as interpreted by such people
as Liang Qi-chao. In both countries an important role of education was
seen to be the promotion of a scientific attitude (see the Common
Programme of the People's Consultative Conference, 1949, Price, 1970,
p. 29).

Anti-religious Actions

Any inspection of the social policies of the main religions immediately
reveals the inevitability of clash between them and any communist
group, whether it be a party or the State. Ownership of property is the
first and obvious problem as soon as the question of social ownership
of the means of production is raised. Then there are problems concerning
the role of women in society, especially difficult where the religion is
Moslem, but not easy with other religions. Related to this is the problem
of sex mores and the question of sex education in and out of school.
The teaching of evolution and other concepts in biology have been a
source of conflict with Christian churches outside the communist
countries. Then there are the important ceremonies connected with
birth, marriage and death, and customs and beliefs connected with killing
animals (e.g. Buddhism) and conscientious objection to war. It should,
perhaps, be noted that conflict between different religions on these
matters has been as severe as conflict over doctrinal matters of a more
specifically religious nature. While not offered as an excuse for persecution, it does help to make judgements of some other aspects of Russian
and Chinese state practice more balanced, e.g. the efforts made to win
over sections of the various religions to support of certain communist

social policies.

The young Soviet government almost immediately enacted a law separating Church and State (23 January 1918). Among its 13 articles were:

> 3. Every citizen may profess any religious belief, or profess no belief at all. All restrictions of rights, involved by professing one or another religious belief, or by professing no belief at all, are cancelled and void.

> 9. The School is separated from the Church. Instruction in any religious creed or belief shall be prohibited in all State, public, and also private educational establishments in which general instruction is given. Citizens may give or receive religious instruction in a private way. (Full text, Szczesniak, pp. 34-5)

On 8 April 1929 the comprehensive law, 'Concerning Religious Associations' was passed. Conquest sums up its provisions as follows:

> It laid down that all 'cults' must be registered as 'religious societies or groups of believers', no citizen being allowed to belong to more than one society or group (art. 2). 'Activities' might not begin until after registration with 'the appropriate authority' (art. 4) which could refuse registration (art. 7) or 'remove' individuals from membership of the 'executive organ' of the 'society' or 'group' (art. 14). The decree also introduced new restrictions. Religious organizations were forbidden to establish mutual assistance funds, co-operatives or unions of producers; to extend material aid to their members; 'to organize special prayer or other meetings for children, youths or women, or to organize general bible, literary, handicraft, working, religious study or other meetings, groups, circles or branches, to organize excursions or children's playgrounds, or to open libraries or reading rooms, or to organize sanatoria or medical aid' (art. 17). . . . Article 18 of the decree stated: 'The teaching of any religious faith whatsoever is not allowed in State, social or private educational institutions' . . . The Commissariat of Internal Affairs was, however, empowered to license the opening of special theological courses for people over 17 years of age. (Conquest, p. 22)

Section 3 of a decree of 13 June 1921, prohibited 'the teaching of religious doctrine to persons under 18 years of age' (Brickman, p. 248). The 1935 (Stalin) Constitution of the USSR, art. 124 stated:

> In order to ensure to citizens freedom of conscience, the church in the USSR is separated from the state, and the school from the church. Freedom of religious worship and freedom of anti-religious propaganda is recognized for all citizens. (Brickman, ibid.)

The difference between 'worship' and 'propaganda' was not unintentional!

Legislation in the People's Republic of China followed a similar pattern of separation of the state from religions, and statements of religious freedom. Either because of traditional distrust of written law, or because state and Party control makes it unnecessary there does not seem to be any law specifically prohibiting religious teaching in schools or to the young. The two major policy statements have been the Common Programme of 1949 and the Constitutions of 1954 and 1975. The former stated:

> Article 3: Rural land belonging to ancestral shrines, temples, monasteries, churches, schools, and organizations, and land owned by public bodies, shall be requisitioned.

> Article 5: The people of the People's Republic of China shall have freedom of thought, speech, publication, assembly, association, correspondence, person, domicile, change of domicile, religious belief, and the freedom of holding processions and demonstrations. (MacInnis, p. 21)

The 1954 Constitution said simply: 'Article 88: Every citizen of the PRC shall have freedom of religious belief' (MacInnis, ibid.). The corresponding article, 28, of the 1975 Constitution was significantly different: 'Citizens . . . enjoy freedom to believe in religion and freedom not to believe in religion and to propagate atheism.' Curious that in an overwhelmingly Maoist document one finds this Soviet-style formulation! Or is it, like so much else in the Constitution, simply a recognition of reality? In any case, the main lines of policy have since 1949 been those given by Zhou En-lai to the first session of the Third National People's Congress in 1964:

> We shall continue to pursue the policy of freedom of religious belief correctly and to uphold the integrity of state power and the separat-

ion of religion from the state. We must prohibit all illegal activities. We hope that people in religious circles will continue to take a patriotic stand against imperialism, persist in the principle of the independence and self-administration of their churches, abide by government laws and decrees, intensify their own remoulding and actively take part in the socialist construction of our motherland. (MacInnis, p. 34)

In both countries the government set up special organs of state to handle religious questions and encouraged the formation of religious bodies sympathetic to the government. Both stick and carrot were employed to the latter end. In the USSR numerous church leaders were imprisoned and then released when they agreed to co-operate, beginning with Patriarch Tikhon in 1922 (Kolarz, p. 41). Imprisonment in both countries was always on the grounds of illegal political opposition, and while many of the charges are obvious the result of misunderstanding, ignorance and sheer bad faith, there is also no doubt that the various religions did and do form foci of political opposition. Unfortunately few discussants take the trouble to separate the various strands, and supporters of communist social measures too often ignore the injustice and stupidities committed.

Soviet state bodies include the People's Commissariat for Muslim Affairs, set up in 1918 under the Commissariat of Nationalities (Conquest, p. 68), and the Councils for the Affairs of the Russian Orthodox Church and for the Affairs of Religious Cults, both established in 1943 at a time when religious bodies were being used to aid the war effort (Kolarz, pp. 51, 53, 34). In China there is a Religious Affairs Bureau of the State Council. According to a former official of this Bureau now in exile its work includes regular investigations of the activities of religious organisations and their personnel, activities intended to bring religious leaders and the state together to carry out various mass movements, to hold discussion meetings with leaders, both religious and lay, to teach them party and state policies, and to co-operate with the public security officers in controlling counter-revolutionaries working within the religious organisations (Bush, pp. 31-2).

In addition to imprisoning believers the Soviet government has repeatedly attempted to close places of worship on the grounds that they are no longer being used, or that they contravene some regulation. During 1958-64, under Khrushchev, the number of Orthodox churches in use fell from about 20,000 to 10,000 (Reddaway, p. 321). A recent example was described in the underground journal *Chronicle* for October

1969:

> In the town of Kolyvan near Nobosibirsk (in south-central Siberia)
> the Orthodox church has been closed on the pretext of its not con-
> forming with fire safety regulations. When the believers dug a pond
> to conform with the fire regulations, the local authorities filled it in
> again and prohibited church services, despite the fact that permission
> to hold services had been given by Moscow. Moreover the local
> authorities tore down the church's cupolas, killing a 5-year-old child
> in the process. Instead of the church the believers have been given a
> small chapel which does not satisfy fire safety regulations. (Redda-
> way, p. 321)

Examples for earlier periods can be found in Hecker (1929, p. 217) and
Conquest (p. 59).

In China the emphasis has been on thought reform, but a number of
believers have also suffered various forms of detention, especially
immediately after Liberation, and during the anti-rightist movement
of 1957-8. These included some foreign missionaries suspected of
hostile political activities (Lifton, pp. 53-277). The Daoists, traditionally
regarded with hostility by Chinese governments and legislated against
(Yang, pp. 187, 189) have been harassed more than other religions
because their secret societies have been used by the KMT opposition
and by criminal elements. They have also been staunch upholders of
the various practices which the government has attempted to eradicate,
such as geomancy (which often conflicted with production), fortune-
telling and various magic practices (Bush, pp. 382-90). Both in the early
years following Liberation, and recently during the Cultural Revolution,
Buddhist monks and nuns have been encouraged to return to ordinary
life (Bush, p. 299). In other cases monasteries and religious communities
have been persuaded to take up various forms of productive work
(MacInnes, pp. 256-82).

Anti-religious Education

In both the USSR and China the basic anti-religious education occurs
in the school, in the main through the absence of any kind of religious
teaching, and partly through direct attacks on religious beliefs. Beatrice
King, writing in 1936, remarked:

> Anti-religion is not taught as a subject in the schools. But, just as
> religious ideas are inculcated in children in Christian countries, by

the way, whether in a lesson or a story or a picture, so anti-religious
ideas are inculcated in Soviet children. In the school it takes the
form of scientific explanations of natural phenomena, with always a
reference to the absurdity, for modern times, of the religious
explanation. (King, p. 41)

This is not quite accurate, for at least in secondary level grades, marxism
has been taught in one form or another, and in its soviet form (which
in turn is the form in which it arrived in China) it has always stressed
its materialist outlook. The school textbook mentioned earlier (Shakhnazarov) opens with a section on the philosophy of ideas of the world
and its cognition in which seven pages are devoted to 'materialism and
idealism'. There religion is described as:

this fantastic, distorted reflection of the world in the consciousness
of man. In it is found an expression of the helplessness of man in
front of nature, his social pressure. The religious world view is
directly contrary to science. They are antitheses (antipodies). (p.
42)

The science syllabi published for the 8-year school in 1959 included
direct references to the inculcation of a 'materialist, scientific-atheistic
world outlook'. The biology syllabus adds: 'to disclose the reactionary
essence of religious creeds and the harm of superstitions and prejudices'
(Price, 1961, p. 226).

In Chinese schools there is a similar emphasis on science after the
first four grades, and during the period of Soviet influence, when enormous numbers of textbooks and syllabi were translated and used the
treatment must have been the same. Unfortunately no study of such
materials has been published and I have seen few of the books at this
level. The impression one gains is that the emphasis has been on more
directly political aspects, except where a class has contained a believer,
or been involved in some action against superstition locally. During the
1958 '100 flowers' period there were reports of children of believers
being threatened with expulsion from school if they attended Sunday
school (Bush, p. 224). Directly anti-religious education most probably
occurred in political education classes rather than in the basic curriculum,
and in the Youth League. Now and then one catches a glimpse in the
'auntie' columns in the press. Bush describes one such incident in which
a youth whose mother 'worships gods and Buddha' wrote to the *Nanfang
Ribao* describing how he had performed the *koutou* in order to please

his mother. The editor replied:

> As an educated youth you certainly have some scientific knowledge.
> As such, you should get rid of the bondage of feudal and superstitious
> ideas. You should be a promoter in the movement to break down the
> old and establish the new. You should constantly talk to your relatives
> and people around you about atheism and science. As for your
> mother, you must tirelessly work on her, making her see the harm
> done by old ideas and old customs and rid her mind of the con-
> cepts of 'gods and spirits'. (Bush, pp. 416-7, *Nanfang Ribao*, Feb-
> ruary 1965)

In the USSR much of the anti-religious adult education was conducted by the League of the Militant Atheists (or literally, Godless, from the
Russian word *Bezbozhnik*) (Kolarz, pp. 6-15; Conquest, pp. 17-27;
Hecker, pp. 246-65) founded in 1925 at a congress of supporters of
the paper *Bezbozhnik*. Much of the League's efforts were devoted to
publishing. *Bezbozhnik,* first published in 1922, rose to a circulation of
some 473,500 copies and appeared weekly. A more theoretical *Anti-
religioznik* (The Anti-religious) appeared monthly, and other publications
included *Militant Atheism* and *The Village Godless*. In one decade 1,200
titles of books and pamphlets appeared with a total distribution figure
of 40m (i.e. an average of 235,000 per title). Hecker, who examined
some of the untouched volumes on library shelves, warns that distribution and being read is not the same and adds that 'only the manuals
used in group studies are really read' (Hecker, p. 259). Another activity
was the running of anti-religious museums in some 40 cities, often in
the larger and most famous churches and monasteries, such as the
Kazan Cathedral in Leningrad where the visitor can still today sample
this genre (Hecker, p. 260).

The League aimed at a mass membership and was organised in local
cells, of which there were 3,900 by 1928, with a total of 123,007
members. By 1932 there were 5,700,000 members, and by 1937,
2,000,000 (Kolarz, p. 11). But other organisations carried out similar
work, both in co-operation with the League and separately. These
included the Communist Party, the Soviets, the Red Army and the
trade unions. Large numbers of lectures were organised, including a
series on the radio. In 1927 there were 68 anti-religious seminaries and
15 reference centres for the training of anti-religious propagandists
(Conquest, p. 18). Studies were organised at Sverdlov Communist University already in 1921, and in 1928 chairs for the study of religion were

founded in the Communist University and Institute of Red Professors, and in many of the non-party universities. Other activities included the organising of special secular festivals to coincide with the traditional religious ones, the publishing of posters with such messages as 'Guard your children against Religion and Alcohol' (referring to the common association of drunkenness and the festivals of Christmas and Easter), and even the printing of anti-religious verses on sweet wrappers, and cigarette boxes (Hecker, p. 247 for an example).

During World War Two, when religion was called up to support the cause, the League was quietly disbanded. In June 1947 a different, more academic and elitist organisation was founded, the All-Union Society for the Dissemination of Scientific and Political Knowledge (Kolarz, pp. 15-18; Conquest, pp. 41-2). Its 850,000 members in 1959 included professors, teachers, doctors, agronomists and others able to propagate scientific and technical knowledge, still considered the main antidote to religious belief. This is done by means of pamphlets, published in editions of 80,000 to 200,000, and lectures. The Society has been criticised for both the quantity and quality of its work and members admit that their message seldom reaches the target group of believers. The Society President, Academician Mitin, noted that lecture titles like 'Religion, the enemy of the toilers' would deter believers from attending (Kolarz, p. 17).

An example of the content of anti-Christian education still considered suitable in the immediate post-World War Two period is the following outline of themes for lecturers put out by the Publishing House of Cultural-Enlightenment Literature in a pamphlet: *The Origin and Class Essence of Christianity*.

(1) Show that Jesus Christ, accepted by believers as the founder of Christianity, never existed in reality.

(2) Show that Christianity arose as the result of the long process of disintegration of the ancient slave-owning society as a fantastic, distorted reflection of the apparent helplessness of the oppressed and exploited masses of the workers in the struggle against the oppressors and exploiters.

(3) Show that Christianity from the beginning of its existence always played a reactionary role, that the social principles of Christianity justified ancient slavery, acclaimed medieval serfdom, defended and defends today in bourgeois countries the hired slavery of capital; show that the Christian Church always took and takes today, especially in the person of the Vatican, an active part in all measures

of the ruling exploiter classes directed to the oppression and enslave-
ment of the workers.

(4) Show that in our country Christianity with its anti-scientific
world-outlook and reactionary morality does great harm, like all
other religious survivals, to the cause of the Communist education
of the workers. (Conquest, pp. 42-3)

It would be interesting to compare this with more recent material and
to see whether any notice is taken of the worker-priests, the movements
in Latin America, and such people as Paulo Friere. But one cannot be
optimistic. The above is a good example of the half-truths and exagger-
ations purveyed in so much of what passes for a marxist approach in
the USSR. In fact it is thoroughly undialectical.

In China there has been no comparable anti-religious organisation,
nor has anti-religious publishing been on such a scale. In the fifties a
number of translated Russian works circulated (see RMR article, 'A
discussion of translated works on atheism', 30 October 1962, *SCMP*,
19 November 1962, p. 6, and Kiang Meng-kuang's criticism during the
100 flowers period in *Tiang Feng,* 27 May 1957 in *CB* 16, September
1957). Anti-Christian propaganda continued a tradition dating far back
in history, with the addition of current anti-American imperialism elements (MacInnis, pp. 133-7). In 1955 the Shanghai *Liberation Daily*
published readers' letters attacking 'the criminal activities of the anti-
revolutionary group of Cong Bin-mei' (Roman Catholic Bishop of
Shanghai), accusing him of

gathering information, organizing acts of violence, encouraging the
resistance movement, spreading rumours, poisoning the minds of
youth, cruelly killing babies . . . listening to Voice of America broadcasts, etc. (Bush, p. 124)

The reference to killing babies concerns orphanages which took in
infants left to die in the streets in pre-liberation China. Many died
almost immediately and were buried, to be subsequently dug up by
suspicious and often hostile Chinese who accused the foreigners and
their converts of having killed the children. During the Cultural Revolution there was considerable anti-religious activity, though this does
not seem to have been directly encouraged by the Revolutionary Centre
under Chairman Mao. Examples of Red Guard *dazibao* are given in Bush
(e.g. p. 257) and MacInnis (pp. 289-306).

An important part of Chinese anti-religious education has been the attempt to change some of the ceremonies which surround man's marriage and death, ceremonies which have caused misery to many a family through debts incurred. Expensive feasts have been discouraged, together with the traditional heavy wooden coffins and burial mounds which occupied valuable, scarce arable land. Bush refers to an interesting article in the *People's Daily* which not only condemned the old, but proposed new alternatives (*RMRB*, 17 July 1958, in *CB*, 15 June 1958, pp. 24-30, quoted by Bush, pp. 400-2).

An interesting approach to dispelling belief in ghosts and spirits was attempted by the Institute of Literature of the Chinese Academy of Sciences in 1961. They published a collection of traditional ghost stories in which the hero triumphed over the ghost through courage or disbelief. A shorter English edition was published in the same year, from which this short extract is taken:

Once in the privy Ruan De-ru saw a ghost. More than ten feet tall, black with bulging eyes, it was dressed in a dark coat and cap. And this apparition was less than a foot from his side. Quite calm and composed, Ruan told it with a smile: 'People say that ghosts are hideous; they certainly are!' Then, red with shame, the ghost made off. (From *Records of Light and Dark* by Liu Yi-jing of the Southern and Northern Dynasties, in *Stories about Not Being Afraid of Ghosts*, p. 19)

Conforming to the best marxist principle of combining theory and practice, women were organised to build and repair dykes in Guangdong Province in 1952. According to folk belief such a practice would cause disaster, and the strength of this belief was at the time a serious obstacle to the enlistment of women for construction. After the work had been successfully completed propaganda meetings were held to publicise it (Yang, p. 389).

Conclusions

The survival, not to say *re*vival of religion in the USSR is not surprising in view of the 'soulless circumstances' of the years of agony. What decrease in religious belief there has been is probably a tribute to general schooling, with its emphasis on science, and to industrialisation generally, rather than the directly anti-religious education which has been described here. In China monks and Buddhist nuns have been dispersed and places of worship closed, and there are clearly fewer believers in anciently held ideas and practices. But there too it is uncertain to what extent anti-religious education as such has contributed. At the same time it is important to note that the cults of Lenin, Stalin and Mao draw on deep feelings of a religious nature, and much in the Cultural Revolution in China took on religious form.

As was noted at the beginning of this discussion, the social practices associated with different religions inevitably provoke conflict with communism. In attempting as educators to judge the conflict it is necessary to judge separately the social goal aimed at and the methods employed, and also to attempt to understand why the participants acted in the way they did. It is immediately clear that much hurt has been done without achieving the increase in collective consciousness and human freedom which I have defined as the marxist aim. On the contrary, communism has been discredited through identification with such methods.

Turning from the acts of suppression to the propaganda used, this has all too often been of such a crude, even inaccurate nature as to repel believers and reinforce the prejudices of the non-believers without in any way enlightening their minds. But one must remember that this is in part the result of the crude nature of many of the religious beliefs held, not to mention the form of marxism itself. A study of comparable Christian and anti-Christian tracts in, for example, late nineteenth-century England would be interesting.

Seeing that the counterproductive nature of so much anti-religious activity appears so obvious, why has it been persisted in? Partly this has stemmed from the attempt to stamp out political opposition in circumstances when force was seen as the only way and religion has been equated with political opposition. Partly it may also have been that anti-religion has been a field in which certain officials could be seen to be active without incurring serious risk to themselves. That is, it has been an outcome of the bureaucratic nature of the Party and the system.

In view of the breadth of activities described in this chapter it is difficult to make any valid generalisations. The level both of information and theory varies greatly between the higher party school on the one hand and the popular anti-religious meeting on the other. In the USSR, and to a considerable extent in China too, the interpretation of marxism is an authoritarian, technicist one more congruent with traditional patterns of domination-subordination than with the self-determining, free man envisaged by the Marx explicated here. In addition the reality of both the USSR and China remains too similar to the conditions of capitalism to bring about very different life-styles on a mass scale. Only a more profound marxism, combining theory with practice, could perhaps bring about real changes in man's attitudes and habits. To think that political education of the kind I have described, for the majority a ritual rhetoric, could create the 'new, socialist man' is to exhibit a most unmarxist optimism.

7 THE COLLECTIVE AS EDUCATOR

In view of the importance attached to the collective as an educator in both Russia and China it is surprising that few writers have given the subject the special treatment it deserves. In the Soviet *Pedagogicheskaya Entsiklopediya* (1965) the 'children's collective' is given six pages and 'collectivism' another three, while Shchukina's *Course of Lectures in Pedagogy* (1966) contains a whole chapter on 'the collective and the formation of the personality of the pupil'. N. Grant (1964) deals with the educational role of the various Soviet youth organisations without mentioning the concept as such, nor does he mention Krupskaya or Makarenko. B. King (1937) writes at length on the related concept of children's self-government, but also does not discuss the collective. Even Woody (1932) who is aware of the concept and describes his visit to Shatsky's Colony of the Cheerful Life (*Bodraya zhizn*), used his chapter on 'collectivism' to discuss the socio-economic policies and goals of the USSR rather than its educational theories. Bowen (1962), in his discussion of Makarenko and Anweiler (1964) are exceptional in discussing the concept at some length, though almost exclusively in the context of children's colonies.

Shchukina defines the concept collective as follows:

> A collective is a group of children having a single socially valued purpose, for the accomplishment of which the members of the given group organise common activities and enter into definite relations of mutual dependence and mutual responsibilities with the undoubted equality of all members in the rights and duties in the collective. The collective, organised by its organs is tightly connected through the community's aims and organisations with other collectives. (Shchukina, p. 351)

The *Pedagogicheskaya Entsiklopediya* also stresses unity of purpose (aim) and the definite organisation of common work. It gives first place 'in the socialist countries', to the Young Pioneer Organisations, but adds as examples sports clubs, creative groups in culture palaces and pioneer houses. Scott Nearing, who discussed the concept with Zaloojny, Director of Pedagogical Research in the Kharkov Department of Education in 1925, found they were studying five different types of

269

collective:

1. Brief collectives, organized usually before school age, and for the purpose of play. Of very short duration.
2. Self-organized collectives, more or less permanent. Usually organized to carry out a project of common interest to the group—to build a house, make a raft.
3. Temporary collectives, but, for the period of their duration, developing a system of social machinery—the club, or meeting—with its officers and rules of procedure.
4. A permanently organized simple collective, having in view some specific purpose. A literary society.
5. A permanent complex organization for general social purposes. A student social club or fraternity. (Nearing, p. 116)

The research group was using a questionnaire to discover:

1. The social background of the children; homes from which they come; school life; general social experience.
2. Situation under which the organization arose.
3. Stimulus that brought it into being.
   (a) Stimulus from inside the group of children.
   (b) Stimulus from outside the group.
4. Reactions (results) of the operations of the collective. Duration; reactions on the group life; development of other collectives. (Nearing, ibid.)

Zaloojny pointed out that they were trying to find out if there was a particular form of organisation suited to particular groups of children. Interestingly, he expected on the basis of current practice that in the towns the children would organise themselves, but that in the villages, especially the small ones, the lead would have to come from the teachers. Speaking of the shift of emphasis in research from the individual child to the group, Zaloojny said:

Under our system of pedagogical research, a normal child is one who is successful in group life. Any child who functions well in a group we classify as normal. All other children we classify and treat as abnormal. (Nearing, p. 115)

In the decades which have followed that statement the chances for spontaneous organisation have been minimal, which may account for the complaint of the Alts in their study of *The New Soviet Man*:

With all the emphasis in the Soviet Union on the principle of collective education and on utilization of the group in the education of the individual, it is paradoxically true that Western educational theory has concerned itself more with examination and analysis of the influence of the group on the individual than has Soviet theory. (p. 152)

It is paradoxical that the Russians, who place so much reliance on the group as a medium of character formation, have done so little to study the processes of social interaction within a group. The emphasis has been on the mechanics which sustain the group activities rather than on their content and quality. (p. 293)

Bowen concurs with this last when he says that during the period from October 1923, to March 1926, Makarenko was concerned with

the nature of the imperative behind the collective, the location of authority in the collective, the relation of the individual to the collective, the nature of the 'adhesive' that binds a collective together . . . (Bowen, p. 92)

Anton Semyonovich Makarenko (1888-1939), son of an Ukrainian railway workshop painter, is probably the best-known Soviet educator. His books describing his leadership of colonies of *besprizornii* (waifs, street-children) have been circulated in large editions in many languages, and there now exists a big literature of comment on his methods (bibliographies in Anweiler, *ASM*; Bowen; and Hillig). The publicity he has received and the fact that the second colony he ran was supported by the OGPU (security police) is probably not coincidental, but, as Anweiler warns, he cannot be dismissed simply as a stalinist (Anweiler, *ASM*, p. 24). He saw himself as a Soviet educator, training the 'new man' in the 'era of the dictatorship of the proletariat' (Makarenko, *RTL*, 1, p. xvi), and he was conscious to the end of how little he understood the complex processes he sought to master (Makarenko, *LTL*, p. 644: 'It was only during my work in the Dzerkhinsky Colony that I realized—and I felt it very keenly—how little I mastered the complex process of educating the new man'). He violently rejected the characterisation of his charges as 'moral defectives' and asserted:

The children who came to me were unhappy, life had been difficult
for them in the circumstances in which they had been living. . . Just
give them normal living conditions, demand certain obligations from
them, provide them the opportunities to fulfil those obligations and
they will become ordinary people, living in full accordance with
human standards. (Makarenko, *LTL*, p. 646)

Makarenko believed that in the collective the interests of the individual
and the group could and should become one. Only when this was so
could not only outward behaviour and habits be formed, but also the
necessary moral *feelings*. Where the individual failed to fit in Makarenko
blamed his own lack of understanding of group processes. Asserting that
'the interests of the collective are higher than those of the individual'
(quoted in Hillig, p. 282), Makarenko could at times express an emotional, even religious attitude. Describing the impending move to Kuryazh
he wrote:

The colonists did not so much know, as feel in the air the necessity
of subordinating everything to the requirements of the collective,
and that without any sense of sacrifice.
    It was a joy, perhaps the deepest joy the world has to give—this
feeling of interdependence, of the strength and flexibility of human
relations, of the calm vast power of the collective, vibrating in an
atmosphere permeated with its own force. (Makarenko, *RTL*, 2, p.
340)

Makarenko gradually worked out a number of principles by which
he ran his colonies. The main ones were a strong external form; the
importance of a nucleus; and 'no standstill'. The 'external form' began
almost by accident in 1923 when they first organised into 'brigades' for
work. Some of these were permanent, while others were 'mixed', or
temporary, organised only for particular jobs, such as weeding potatoes
in a particular field, carting a particular consignment of manure, or some
other similar task (Makarenko, *RTL*, 1, ch. 25). Each brigade was headed
by a commander, those of the permanent brigades belonging to the
Commanders' Council which ruled the colony. Efforts were made to
ensure that all took their turn at commanding at least a mixed detachment (ibid. p. 356). Commanders were originally appointed by Makarenko, but later by democratic decision of the Council, which could
increase its membership by co-option. Significantly Makarenko remarks:

It was long before commanders were appointed by general election and made accountable to the electors, and I myself never considered, and still do not consider, such free election as an achievement. (ibid. p. 352)

More to a marxist taste is:

One very important rule, preserved up to the present day, was the absolute prohibition of any privileges whatsoever for commanders, who never got anything in the way of extras and were never exempted from work. (ibid.)

This statement, however, forgets that the one privilege which commanders everywhere prize above all else is to command. The test of real progress towards communism will be when there is regular and frequent interchange of the leaders and the led. In addition to this structure of sub-groups within the collective a uniform was introduced for formal occasions, flags and 'colours' were instituted, and life was regulated by bugle calls. Bowen draws attention to the displeasure this caused the local education authorities at the time (Bowen, p. 123; Makarenko, *RTL*, 3, p. 234).

The need for a nucleus, a group whose leadership the rest will follow, Makarenko recognised early and he put the idea to good use when they took over the broken down, demoralised colony of Kuryazh. Splitting up the 80 Gorky Colonists amongst the 320 Kuryazhites and relying on their superior appearance, morale and working discipline, Makarenko achieved the impossible.

The principle of 'no standstill' was arrived at in response to the tragic failure with Chobot (Bowen, p. 102; Makarenko, *RTL*, 2, p. 277). As with the individual, so with the collective, there must always be new demands to stretch and inspire it. But the incident commented on by Bowen (p. 193) is interesting. Factory workers were building levees to stem a flood. When one of their number refused to leave at the end of his shift, far from praising him for his heroic attitude (as in similar Chinese stories) his mates blamed him:

'And you've no discipline', Minayaev goes on to say, 'We don't need your heroism at the moment. There are plenty of heroes like you here. But you seem to want to show off, as if you were better than anyone else.' (Bowen, p. 193; Makarenko, *BFP*, p. 397)

Here demand must be tempered with discipline and the collective enforces the latter.

Makarenko was not the only educator to theorise about his experiences in running children's homes. The *besprizornii* numbered 540,000 in 1921-2 (*Ped. Enc.* 1, p. 193), and before them there had been others. Combining schooling with the labour of self-maintenance was more than pedagogical theory, and provided the binding force of the collective in a way which is difficult to transfer to other situations, such as the prdinary school classroom. Shatsky describes how in 1916 at *Bodraya Zhizn* they experimented for a short while with a system of individual responsibility for the agricultural plots. Within a week or two this had repercussions on the whole collective, setting up conflicts between the socially organised and 'private' work. Pupils urged freedom to organise according to the dictates of conscience. The first day all went well, with the older children working in the kitchen and looking after the animals. But the next day deterioration set in, and first and major casualties were the artistic and musical activities. Children hung around or went for walks. At the end of a week the colonists met again and resolved that (1) all work was to be compulsory; (2) nobody was to be excused work; (3) singing, drawing and artistic activities were also to be compulsory; (4) those who didn't want to work would have to leave the colony; (5) first, the colony's work, then one's own (Shatsky, 2, pp. 126-33). Summing up this experience, Shatsky puts his finger on the problem: how to organise the social life of the collective so that it does not paralyse the individual, depriving him of his interests and stifling his creativity (ibid. p. 133).

Shatsky's colony was run by a General Assembly of all pupils which met every ten days. Each class had a leader, or *dezhurnia*, and committees for sanitation, instruction, the economy, and other functions. These were elected and served for a month (Woody, p. 54). There were none of the military trappings which Makarenko used. More important, Shatsky's ideas ranged much wider, to the villages around, to all levels of schooling from kindergarten to adult, and he had more interest (talent?) for the arts than Makarenko. While Makarenko's colonies appear to have had minimal contact with the surrounding villages whose inhabitants Makarenko often seems to have regarded as 'negative examples' if not downright *kulaks*, Shatsky's Colony appears to have turned out towards the village more, seeing its role as a stimulus to the general enlightenment. Shatsky, and his wife, were concerned not only with the school, but with organising libraries, concerts, lectures, including special meetings for women's liberation, for the adults of the surrounding villages

(Woody, pp. 50-60). But this is to go beyond the topic of the collective.

Mention must be made of Krupskaya's ideas on the collective. Herself a Ministry functionary without experience of running any colony, she took an intense, personal interest in many of those being run, and spent much of her life among children, observing their behaviour and talking with them. She wrote extensively on the work of the Young Pioneers and Komsomol (See vol. 5 of her *Pedagogical Works*). She recognised children have a natural collective sense which she felt formed a natural basis for communism, given the right development (Krupskaya, *PW* 5, p. 133). She repeatedly contrasted Soviet with bourgeois methods of education, accusing the latter of developing the individual *against* the collective (ibid. pp. 205, 508). She wanted the collective to be organised in such a way that it would stimulate the individual to independent, creative activity, while at the same time subordinating his will to that of the group. She repeatedly stressed the need for creative tasks and socially useful work for the collective in order to encourage the right attitudes. At the same time such work must *interest* the children concerned and be suitable for their age (ibid. pp. 241, 275). While she saw the teacher as essential the role must not be that of dictator, but rather showing what can and should be done, how, and then leaving the collective free to choose what action to take (ibid. p. 279). At one point she comments that study circles do not always have to have a teacher present. Without one sometimes, they will learn independence (vol. 5, p. 178). Here one wonders whether Bowen is right when he says:

> it was a symptom of the colonists that in moments of decision they proved themselves incapable of acting alone, and not infrequently did they go to Makarenko for an answer. (Bowen, p. 100)

Is this really a failure of the collective to develop independence, or were the incidents which Makarenko describes the kind which we would all want to talk over with another person? In any case, there is no doubt of the difference of emphasis between Krupskaya and Makarenko. For her the individual was the centre of interest and the collective was to be shaped for his needs, with no thought of mystic, transcendent group values over-riding those of the members of the group. She was also well aware that the group can be cruel and tyrannical. She pleads for the building of collectives where the members feel themselves comrades (ibid. 5, pp. 295-6), and she is against the collective having the power of punishment (*Ped. Enc.*, p. 431). As the *Entsiklopediya* comments:

how then can one combine freedom and discipline? 'This is an unresolved question.' One is reminded of just how unresolved it is when reading articles in the Soviet press like that of L. Ochakovskaya in the *Literaturnaya Gazeta*, 12 June 1966. She describes a home for difficult children in Nizhny Tagil, and mentions a 'famous school' where under the guise of pupil self-government severe punishments were being meted out on offenders. In the school the studies director explained: 'Our YCL committee passed a resolution to shave the head of anyone caught smoking in the restrooms' (*CDSP*, 20, no. 27). In the children's home a girl had her head partly shaved for running away and a boy was badly beaten up for the same offence. During the past year some 20 children had ended up in the city hospital from democratic punishment of this kind. When the writer spoke to the children she was told:

> We're sick and tired of bothering with that kind. They run away and then none of us are permitted to go to the movies. And standing up in formation in the hall for a couple of hours is no fun either. . . We all have to stand so that anybody who's thinking of running away will remember when he does that the others are being punished for him. (ibid.)

The writers comment is interesting, and the attitude of the teachers, as reported, leaves little grounds for hope of early change. Ochakovskaya writes:

> Vasya was beaten cruelly, and I am sorry for him. But, to tell the truth, I am far more sorry for those who did the beating. I think they were done even greater harm in this fray than he who was beaten. Just think how the human principle must have been broken and twisted and what dark instincts must have been aroused and encouraged to make a gang of children avidly hurl themselves on a single person and beat him up . . . (ibid.)

Tsang, writing about 'the most formative institutions' in China 'fostering the social and cultural values', describes the various associations (*hui*) which still remain important in such places as the Chinese community in New York, or in Hong Kong. These are the associations of people with the same surname, from the same district (native associations), from the same school (England being not alone in favouring the 'old school tie'), or working in the same office. These all came under attack in the early fifties in what was called the 'Down with the

Five-identity Relationship Campaign' (Tsang, pp. 90-93). Other important groups were those known as secret societies (Chesneaux). All of
these different organisations were infused with traditional authoritarian
values and relations were between leader and led rather than between
peers in the group. As Solomon writes: 'the need (is) to have an author-
itative individual or friends who can be relied upon to give help or take
responsibility in solving life's problems' (Barnett, 1969, p. 301). Group
life is traditional, perhaps more so than in the capitalist societies of
Western Europe and North America. A Chinese scholar wrote: 'The life
of a single individual is an incomplete life' (Yang, *CCS*, p. 166; also
Barnett, 1969, p. 279), and Yang adds: 'Western individualism as a social
ideal. . . did not have much attraction for the traditional Chinese mind'
(Yang, *CCS*, p. 172). In his study of Nanching, a village near Canton,
Yang comments:

> . . . the clans so dominated the collective life of the village that an
> individual without clan membership was socially isolated and looked
> down upon. . . he and his family would be only on-lookers at the
> grand ceremonial events that . . . imparted joy and a sense of belong-
> ingness to the participants. (Yang, *CCS*, p. 101)

The attitudes which these various forms of collective inculcated, suggests
Solomon (Barnett, 1969, p. 324) were those attacked by Mao Ze-dong
in his article, *Combat Liberalism*:

> To let things slide for the sake of peace and friendship when a per-
> son has clearly gone wrong, and refrain from principled argument
> because he is an old acquaintance, a fellow townsman, a schoolmate,
> a close friend, a loved one, an old colleague or old subordinate. Or
> to touch on the matter lightly instead of going into it thoroughly, so
> as to keep on good terms. The result is that both the organization
> and the individual are harmed. (Mao, *SW* 2, p. 31)

Since the relations within the group have been seen in terms of
authority to the leader, and the avoidance of expression or action
which might lead to difference (Barnett, 1969, pp. 301-4) it is not surprising to find that Mao Ze-dong writes about the need for criticism
and self-criticism and 'full and frank expression of views and great
debates' (*The Polemic on the General Line*, p. 472). In this context
must be seen his call for discussion of all matters of substance at Party
committee meetings and the injunction that

the committee members present should express their views fully and reach definite decisions which should then be carried out by the members concerned. (Mao, *SW* 4, p. 267; see also his *Methods of Work of Party Committees*, ibid. pp. 377-81)

While holding firmly to the need for leadership, Mao argues consistently, and from his earliest writings, for active participation by the led, both in policy determination and in its carrying out. The responsibility for developing this rests with both of them. For example an early Mao, speaking about physical education, writes:

. . . the installation of a school and the instruction given by its teachers are only the external and objective aspect. We also have the internal, the subjective aspect. . . we should begin with the individual initiative. (Quoted in Schram, 1969, p. 155)

The collectives which in China are today attempting to foster new social-political attitudes are first of all the Chinese Communist Party and the youth organisations under its guidance, and the People's Liberation Army (PLA). Other important organisations include the trade unions and the women's organisations. But for the mass of the people it is the unit (*danwei*) where they work which is the key collective. Here they are, to a greater or lesser degree, exposed to the methods of 'group therapy' worked out during the civil and anti-Japanese wars in the Party and Red Army-PLA.

Various accounts of the process are available, but all too many of them are from those who have left the PRC and for this and reasons of social position are probably not the best witnesses. However, the form is clear and also the reactions of at least some of those who participated. In the main there are three types of group activity relevant to our purpose: investigation and study (*xuexi*); criticism and self-criticism (*piping* and *jiantao*); and struggle meetings (*douzheng hui*). The first of these require little explanation. Party documents, *People's Daily* articles, or marxist writings, especially those of Chairman Mao, are studied and immediate problems are discussed in the light of principles derived from these readings. Examples of such meetings are described, for the Red Army by Snow (pp. 296-302), and for a village during land reform by Hinton (Fanshen, pp. 400-16). In the criticism and self-criticism sessions members of the group are encouraged to do just that, both verbally and in writing. In some cases the questions are less serious and the atmosphere relaxed (Jenner, p. 77). In others the atmosphere is tense and individuals are under pressure to confess to various misdemeanours of both personal and political significance. Here we have to rely on what can only be described as hostile witnesses (M. Yen, p. 157; Lifton, ch. 14). The struggle meetings are the final step in attempting to 'cure the illness to save the patient' (Mao, *SW* 3, p. 50). The group is there organised to attack (mentally rather than physically, though the latter has happened) the one selected as a struggle object (*duixiang*), in order to bring about the required change of *sixiang* (thought). Schurmann describes the process as follows:

> Essentially, the technique consists in the usually temporary alienation of a single member from the group through the application of collective criticism. One member is singled out for criticism, either because of faulty ideological understanding, poor work performance, or some other deviance. He is not only subjected to a barrage of criticism from the members, but also joins in and begins to criticise himself. The avowed purpose of the procedure is to 'correct' (*gaizao*) the individual. Under normal circumstances, the individual is 'reintegrated' into the group after the 'temporary alienation'. The experience of temporary alienation by the one criticized and collective criticism by the group members is, in theory, supposed to have the general effect of maintaining the group's cohesion and effectiveness. Great fear exists on the part of those potentially criticizable that they may become victims of a more permanent alienation. Fear of such a permanent alienation serves to strengthen the bonds within the group. (Quoted by Solomon in Barnett, 1969, p. 326)

An exceptionally interesting account of these processes and the participants reactions to them is given in A.L. George's study of Chinese prisoners-of-war, captured in Korea. The smallest collectives were the groups of three men into which the squads were divided. These met frequently to indulge in criticism and self-criticism, and each was expected to keep a check on himself and the other two. Criticism sessions were held regularly at squad, platoon and company level, and criticism of non-commissioned and commissioned officers was encouraged. The soldiers reported that there was strong dislike of public criticism and that men tried to behave in such a way as to avoid it (George, pp. 77-81). The graphic terms *beetroots* and *radishes* were applied to those who were 'red all through' or only managed a surface conversion (George, p. 89). The latter was said at times to be the result of 'overcriticism' (George, p. 80).

From these introductory paragraphs it will be seen that while in the USSR attention has been directed at organised collectives, in China more attempt has been made to create collectives within work situations where the collective organisation had been less overt or directed to different ends. Certainly collective pressure on the individual appears to be more intense and all-embracing in China at least recently than in the USSR where in the past two decades there has been a development towards the privatisation of life typical of suburban capitalism.

This raises the question of marxist attitudes to such phenomena. Wittig has said flatly that 'the concept of the collective is foreign to Marx's thought' (Hillig, p. 282). Much of the 'village tyranny' that occurs in both countries under the guise of collectivism or democracy certainly is. But as Krupskaya noted, Marx 'always spoke about the masses, of unity, of collectivism, and not of the single hero, spoke of the genuine individual who can only unfold in the collective' (*PS* 5, p. 218). Like the *Pedagogicheskaya Entsiklopediya* (2, p. 439) she is thinking of passages like the following from the *German Ideology* where Marx wrote:

> Only in community (with others has each) individual the means of cultivating his gifts in all directions; only in the community, therefore, is personal freedom possible. (*GI*, p. 93)

That the collectives described here are still far from such 'communities' is obvious, but it is less obvious that some of them may be a necessary transitional stage.

I shall now turn to a consideration of three particularly important collectives, the family, the youth organisations, and the army.

The Family

The importance of the family as an educating, socialising agent has been recognised both by its defenders and opponents. I shall concentrate here on two aspects which have received most attention: the inculcation and maintenance of sex roles; and the instilling of patterns of authority, especially between parents and children, but also, of course, between husband and wife.

In the *German Ideology* (1846) Marx and Engels describe the family historically as 'to begin with . . . the only social relationship' (p. 40) which 'becomes later . . . a subordinate one'. The family's connection with production and property they describe as follows:

With the division of labour . . . which in its turn is based on the
natural division of labour in the family and the separation of society
into individual families opposed to one another, is given simultaneously the *distribution* and indeed the *unequal* distribution, both quantitative and qualitative, of labour and its products, hence property:
the nucleus, the first form, of which lies in the family, where wife
and children are the slaves of the husband. (*GI*, p. 44)

Later in the book they speak of the bourgeois family 'in which boredom and money are the binding link', adding: 'Its dirty existence has
its counterpart in the holy concept of it in official phraseology and
universal hypocrisy' (*GI*, p. 195). Marx and Engels continued their
castigations of the bourgeois family in the Communist Manifesto (1848),
and in *The Origin of the Family* (1884) Engels looked forward to a
time when 'private housekeeping is transformed into a social industry'
and the position of *'all* women also undergoes significant change' (p.
139). (This controversial work is best approached through the introduction by A.B. Leacock.) The family as we know it will disappear.

The nub of the vision of the future is man's relation to man, the
touchstone for which Marx saw as the relation of man to woman. This
he expressed in this famous passage from the 1844 *Manuscripts*:

The direct, natural, and necessary relation of person to person is
the *relation of man to woman*. In this *natural* relationship of the
sexes man's relation to nature is immediately his relation to man,
just as his relation to man is immediately his relation to nature—his
own *natural* function. In this relationship, therefore, is *sensuously
manifested*, reduced to an observable *fact*, the extent to which the
human essence has become nature to man, or to which nature has to
him become the human essence of man. From this relationship one
can therefore judge man's whole level of development. It follows
from the character of this relationship how much *man* as a *species
being*, as *man*, has come to be himself and to comprehend himself;
the relation of man to woman is *the most natural* relation of human
being to human being. It therefore reveals the extent to which the
human essence in him has become a *natural* essence—the extent to
which his *human nature* has come to be *nature to him*. In this relationship is revealed, too, the extent to which man's *need* has become a
human need; the extent to which, therefore, the *other* person is a
person has become for him a need—the extent to which he in his
individual existence is at the same time a social being. (Marx,

EPM, p. 101)

Set in the context of his critique of 'crude' communism where 'the poor and undemanding man' has 'not only failed to go beyond private property, but has not yet even attained it', this passage embodies on the one hand an evolutionary conception of the development of man from a procreating beast, and on the other a measure for the road still to be travelled. Woman is no longer to be reified as sex object, household ornament or drudge, bearer of the heir to property, or breadwinner, but is to be treated *as a person*. Here too is the often forgotten point, that while woman is the oppressed, and for too long has borne the larger part of human suffering, the solution is not simply to transfer the burden, but to effect a double liberation. Man in the above passage is the neutral form, the human being of either sex, whose relations can only be judged human when members of both sexes treat the other *as a person,* and not as a thing to be exploited, manipulated, or perhaps ignored. The point is made, if often implicitly, in the writings of contemporary feminists. (Germaine Greer, e.g., p. 331, Kate Millett, e.g., p. 363 and Shulamith Firestone. For other pictures of the bourgeois family see Ibsen, *The Doll's House,* and Dickens, *Dombey and Son*.)

Engels, looking back to earlier forms of society qualified his and Marx's earlier comment on wives and children being the slaves of the husband. Where 'the economy did not involve the dependence of the wife and children on the husband' 'decisions were made by those who were carrying them out'. Women then had 'decision-making powers commensurate with their contribution' (Leacock in Engels, 1972, pp. 33, 34). Mao makes a similar point:

> As to the authority of the husband, this has always been weaker among the poor peasants because, out of economic necessity, their womenfolk have to do more manual labour than the women of the richer classes and therefore have more say and greater power of decision in family matters. (Mao, *SW* 1, p. 45)

Engels and Mao both looked to changes in the wider society to liberate women in the family. Mao wrote in 1955:

> In order to build a great socialist society, it is of the utmost importance to arouse the broad masses of women to join in productive activity. Men and women must receive equal pay for equal work in production. Genuine equality between the sexes can only be realised

in the process of the socialist transformation of society as a whole. (Mao, *Quotations*, p. 297)

Lenin took up the same theme of liberation through labour. Like Marx and Engels he spoke in terms of liberation from the 'drudgery of the kitchen and the nursery' and of the need for women to play an increasing part in social administration (Lenin, 1972, pp. 81, 78).

Mao Ze-dong expressed his profound sympathy with women on various occasions. In 1919 he wrote a piece on the suicide of a Miss Chao, attributing her death to the 'three iron nets' in which she was enclosed, 'society, her own family, (and) the family of her future husband' (Schram, 1969, p. 335) and calling for a 'family revolution', a 'great wave of the freedom of marriage and of the freedom to love' to 'sweep over China' (ibid. p. 336). In the Jiangxi Soviet Republic, in 1931, Mao, as Chairman of the Central Executive Committee, signed a marriage decree which declared that 'the oppression and suffering borne by women is far greater than that of man' and advocated placing 'the greater part of the obligations and responsibilities entailed by divorce upon men' (ibid. p. 337). Mao's best-known statement occurs in his 1927 report on the Peasant Movement in Hunan, where he speaks of the 'four thick ropes binding the Chinese people'.

As for women, in addition to being dominated by these three systems of authority (political authority, clan authority and religious authority), they are also dominated by the men (the authority of the husband). (Mao, *SW* 1, pp. 44-6; *Quotations*, pp. 294-5)

In 1958 he commented:

After maybe a few thousand years, or at the very least several hundred years, the family will disappear. Many of our comrades do not dare to think about these things. They are very narrow-minded. But problems such as the disappearance of classes and parties have already been discussed in the classics (of marxism). (Schram, 1974, p. 116)

One might speculate whether Mao himself would have been broad-minded enough to follow Shulamith Firestone's attempt to 'take the class analysis one step further' and add the dimension of sex to historical materialism.

Turning to the relation of parents and children, Marx and Engels wrote in the *Communist Manifesto*:

Do you charge us with wanting to stop the exploitation of children by their parents? To this crime we plead guilty... The bourgeois claptrap about the family and education, about the hallowed correlation of parent and child, becomes all the more disgusting, the more, by the action of modern industry, all family ties among the proletarians are torn asunder, and their children transformed into simple articles of commerce and instruments of labour. (Marx and Engels, *SW* 1, pp. 223-4)

Today, in late capitalism, where the demand for labour has declined these remarks require qualification. Exploitation has become psychological rather than economic, and is less obvious.

The attack on the bourgeois family and the demand for the liberation of women and children was taken up by the communists in both Russia and China. *The ABC of Communism* contrasts 'bourgeois society' where 'the child is regarded as the property of its parents' with the 'socialist outlook' whereby 'the individual human being does not belong to himself, but to society, to the human race'. Therefore 'to society, likewise, belongs the primary and basic right of educating children'. The authors strongly reject the parents' right to 'impress upon the children's psychology their own limitations', the more so that the 'faculty of educating children is far more rarely encountered than the faculty of begetting them'. 'Of one hundred mothers, we shall perhaps find one or two who are competent educators.' They add:

Social education will make it possible for socialist society to train the coming generation most successfully, at lowest cost, and with the least expenditure of energy. (Carr, pp. 284-5)

A.V. Lunacharski, first Commissar of Education, wrote as late as the early thirties:

Our problem now is to do away with the household and to free women from the care of children. It would be idiotic to separate children from their parents by force. But when, in our communal houses, we have well-organized quarters for children, connected by a heated gallery with the adults' quarters, to suit the requirements of the climate, there is no doubt the parents will, of their own free will, send their children to these quarters, where they will be supervised by trained pedagogical and medical personnel. There is no doubt that the terms 'my parents', 'our children', will gradually fall out of usage, being replaced by such conceptions as 'old people', 'adults', 'children', and 'infants'. (Geiger, pp. 47-8)

L.M. Sabsovich went even further, wanting to separate children altogether from their parents in special 'children's towns'. Such ideas brought a sharp rejoinder from N. Krupskaya, who commented that children belonged neither to their parents nor the 'society', but to themselves. Looking ahead to the withering away of the state she envisaged that 'the parental sense will not be suppressed, but will flow in another channel; it will afford much more joy to children and to parents' ('O bytovykh voprosakh', p. 22, in Geiger, p. 49). At the same time she was a strong supporter of pre-school institutions, youth organisations and other forms of social support both as a means of freeing the mother from traditional fetters, and as a means of educating the young. In this she came near to A.M. Kollontai, the famous exponent of women's liberation, who wrote in *Communism and the Family* in 1920:

The care of children by the parents consisted of three distinct parts: (1) the care necessarily devoted to very young babies; (2) the bringing up of the child; (3) the instruction of the child. As for the instruction of children . . . it has become the duty of the State, even in capitalist society. The other occupations of the working class, its conditions of life, imperatively dictated even to capitalist society the creation, for the benefit of the young, of playgrounds, infants' schools, homes, etc. . . But bourgeois society was afraid of going too far . . . The capitalists themselves are not unaware of the fact that the family of old, with the wife a slave and the man responsible for the support and well-being of the family, that the family of this type is the best weapon to stifle the proletarian effort towards liberty, to weaken the revolutionary spirit of the working man and working woman. . . Contrary to the practice of capitalist society . . . communist society will consider the social education of the rising generation as the very basis of its laws and customs. . . Not the family of the past, petty and narrow, with its quarrels between the parents, with its exclusive interest in its own offspring, will mould for us the man of the society of tomorrow. Our new man, in our new society, is to be moulded by socialist organizations, such as playgrounds, gardens, homes, and many other such institutions, in which the child will pass the greater part of the day and where intelligent educators will make of him a communist who is conscious of the greatness of this sacred motto: solidarity, comradeship, mutual aid, devotion to the collective life.

(Schlesinger, p. 65)

The attitude to the family and the upbringing of children changed by the early thirties, though the same support for pre-school facilities and youth organisations continued to appear in propaganda. Writing in 1936, Trotsky referred to Marx's earlier remark about 'generalised want' and the impossibility of providing the material alternatives to family care, and neglect, of the young. He added:

> The most compelling motive of the present cult of the family is undoubtedly the need of the bureaucracy for a stable hierarchy of relations, and for the disciplining of youth by means of 40 million points of support for authority and power. (Trotsky, p. 153)

In the sixties in the USSR, with World War Two now well in the past and a new stage of relative well-being reached, fresh debate began on questions of child rearing. One of the early shots was fired by academician and economic planner, Stanislav Strumilin in the journal *Novii Mir* (1960, no. 7, pp. 206-9). Noting the increased facilities for communal feeding, and of nurseries, kindergartens and boarding schools, and 'recognizing that communal forms of upbringing have an unquestionable superiority over all others', he went on to advocate total institutionalised upbringing, with visits by parents 'as it is permitted by the established schedule' (Bronfenbrenner, in Brown, pp. 112-3). He conceived the family, 'reduced to the married couple' somehow would 'dissolve within the context of the future social commune'. Quite contrary views were expressed in the ensuing discussion. Psychologist, Professor Viktor N. Kolbanovsky, summarising readers' letters to *Novii Mir*, commented

> that communal upbringing has its proper and important place in the Soviet way of life, 'but this in no sense implies that the family is to be alienated from the process of rearing children. . . The Party has never considered it possible to supplant the family by society. (Bronfenbrenner, ibid. p. 114)

(See Kharchev, 1960, 1963; Solov'ev, 1962; Levshin, 1964 and refs. in Bronfenbrenner, ibid.)

Current Soviet attitudes are expressed in similar terms by Shchukina in her course of lectures on *Pedagogy* (1966) and Rimashevskaya in the pamphlet *The Soviet Family* (1975). The former claims the 'correct stand' is to rely on parents for upbringing (*vospitanie*) and society, the school, for learning (*uchenie*). Her whole chapter (23 of 648 pages) is written in the characteristic 'imperative-indicative' of soviet prose and is replete with lists of good and bad qualities to be instilled or prevented. Rimashevskaya begins by distorting Marx's attitude to the family (p. 3) and goes on to claim:

> Under socialism, the basis on which the family is formed . . . shifts . . . to the sphere of moral, psychological and intellectual interests stemming above all from the obligations of raising the children . . . which can only take place within the framework of the family structure. (p. 3)

Her pamphlet ends with the 'narrow-minded' view of the future: 'the development of the family and home life under socialism have to be further consolidated and developed' (p. 16)

In China today when interest focuses on the family it is on such questions as family planning and equitable distribution of household duties. Attempts were made during the Cultural Revolution to make the family one centre of political study. Since then families have been drawn into the after-school education of children, but the focus has been the residents' committee or wider group.

1. Traditional Family Patterns

Post-revolutionary ideas and practice have to be seen against the pre-revolutionary family patterns. The modern Soviet family has emerged from a peasant past with its patrilocal and extended family. Authority passed from the head of the household through his wife to their son. As a symbol of his authority he, in turn, would hang the knout presented by his respectful, but traditionally unloving wife, above their bridal bed (Vakar, p. 36). Drinking, smoking, fighting, swearing and infidelity are regarded as male traits, if not to be admired, at least to be tolerated. But once consummated a marriage was expected to be permanent. As one peasant father put it: 'Marry once, even if she's an onion and your tears flow' (quoted in Geiger, p. 219). But one would suspect that it was the women whose tears were the more frequent. Wife-beating was common, and is even occasionally practised today. In all relations, from the sexual to the social, the wife was expected to be submissive. Geiger describes the relation:

> A peasant woman described the proper position of husband and wife in marriage as follows: 'In the majority of good families the wife sub-

ordinates herself to the husband. Now, with us, when my son comes home my daughter-in-law takes off his boots, cleans them for him, and you see how it is. She is obedient and devoted to her husband. There is no other way.' Subordination, obedience, and a slavish devotion comprise the duties of the wife; the husband is the ruler. Anyone who has visited in a traditional Russian peasant household knows the deferential quality of the wife's demeanor. She guards her silence when her husband speaks, serves the food for husband and guest, and remains standing while they eat. If differences arise between the couple, it is the wife who is expected to give in. A young collective farm wife says: 'If my husband shouted at me because of the children I just remained silent, so there would be no quarrels.' (Geiger, p. 217, quotations from interviews conducted under the Harvard Project on the Soviet Social System)

In such a family the double standard is transferred to the children. Wildness is tolerated in the boys, if not encouraged, while his young sisters are from an early age taught to serve. The horizon is limited and for both sexes the dominant theme is obedience to custom and authority.

In China, while the cultural veneer was different, the patrilocal extended family was the same. In Confucian philosophy, the official standard for two thousand years, the family is the basis of the wider society, and filial piety the central principle of the family. While in poor families only the paternal grand-parents might share the family roof, the ideal was the walled compound in which four generations would be gathered under the authority of the family head. (See the novel *Family* written in the 1930s by Ba Jin.) The ideal behaviour put before the young included the following:

Young men should be filial when at home and respectful to their elders when away from home. They should be earnest and faithful. They should love all extensively and be intimate with men of humanity. When they have any energy to spare after the performance of moral duties, they should use it to study literature and the arts. (Analects, 1.6)

In serving his parents, a son may gently remonstrate with them. When he sees that they are not inclined to listen to him, he should resume an attitude of reverence and not abandon his effort to serve them. He may feel worried, but he does not complain. (Analects, 4.18)

Studying the *Classic of Filial Piety*, students read:

> Filial piety at the outset consists in service to one's parents, in the middle of one's path in service to one's sovereign, in the end in establishing one's self. (Xiao jing, in Hughes, 1942, p. 113)

As contact with the outside world strengthened in the first decades of this century young Chinese rebelled against this system. Hu Shih wrote:

> All the much-idealized virtues of filial piety simply could not exist, and in those rare cases where they were consciously cultivated, the price paid for them was nothing short of intense suppression, resulting in mental and physical agony. (Lifton, 1961, p. 418)

But, especially in the villages, old ways die hard and old family patterns persisted into the period following the revolutionary Marriage Law of May 1950. Something of the harshness of the traditional family, the real face behind the Confucian smooth words can be gauged from accounts such as are given in Yang (p. 66) in the many biographies and novels which treat family life (A.-L.S. Chin, 'Family relations in modern Chinese fiction' is an interesting study). One particularly striking example illustrates the traditional opposition to the remarrying of widows:

> A woman whose family name was Chen was married to a man named Xu. The husband died 8 years after the marriage, and both the woman's and the husband's families did not permit her to remarry. In 1949 the widow took the matter into her own hands and married the head of a neighbouring village. Two months after this, the woman's uncle, a local bully, and her own brother, ordered her to hang herself. She begged for mercy from her own brother, saying, 'Brother, I have worked for you for years, won't you have mercy on me as my brother?' and she turned to her uncle saying, 'Uncle, won't you do some talking for me?' Both turned a deaf ear to her pleas. She then requested to see her children and to put on her good clothes before dying, but this was also denied. She adamantly refused to hang herself; so her own brother strangled her to death, then hung her body up below the roof. (Yang, p. 48)

Any consideration of the difficult transition which the traditional family is undergoing in Russia and China needs to realise the additional burden which has been placed on women, perhaps especially urban women, at a period when the poverty of the country has been unable to compensate. Geiger describes the situation soon after the Revolution in Russia:

> Without replacing childrearing, food purchase and preparation, and the like by the family, the Revolution simply brought an additional burden to women. They remained tied to the family and home and often, in addition, had to work in a factory or office. Studies made in these years showed that women were on a day-to-day basis generally busier than men. Since they could spend less time in public or political work, study, and even sleep, they were less able to develop themselves and become the equals of their husbands. Trotsky wrote in 1937: 'One of the very dramatic chapters of the great book of the Soviets, will be the tale of the disintegration and breaking up of these Soviet families where the husband as a party member, trade unionist, military commander or administrator, grew and developed and acquired new tastes in life, and the wife, crushed by the family, remained on the old level.' (Geiger, p. 60)

In China in 1951 there is the same picture of women's burdens,

> State Cotton Mill of Shanghai no. 1 employs a large number of women. Almost 80 per cent of these women workers are married and 70 per cent of the married women workers have children. These mothers, even those returning home from night shift, have to cook, care for the children, wash clothes, and can sleep only three or four hours a day. This is the average picture of the female textile worker in other places. Some of them even have to wait on their husbands and parents-in-law when they go home from work and suffer from beating and malnutrition. (Xin Zhongguo Fu-nu, no. 25-6, December 1951, pp. 12-13, quoted in Yang, p. 149)

What these conditions mean in terms of the education/socialisation of the various members of the family can easily be imagined, but are less easily available for scientific treatment.

To end this section I would like to quote two aspects of traditional patterns persisting into China's present. Jack Chen, an artist working for the Peking Foreign Language Press had been sent to a Henan village for education after the Cultural Revolution. He describes the New Democratic 'free-choice' marriages there:

the tentative choice of a partner for son or daughter and the initial arrangements for betrothal and marriage are made by the parents. Then the two prospective partners meet each other. If they agree, the betrothal takes place to be followed almost certainly by the wedding. There have been local cases of the prospective bride breaking the engagement. There was even one notorious case, not in our hamlet, where a girl had broken two engagements. But no one could recall an instance where a young man had backed out of his commitment. (Chen, 1973, p. 73)

He also comments that:

The idea of romantic love followed by personal courtship and marriage never crossed their minds except as something that happened in operas. (Chen, 1973, p. 72)

Chen describes the second traditional aspect of behaviour in the following passage which shows how social relations are dominated by old family mores:

We gathered that if a young man found that he could approach and make friends with a girl rather easily he would be very chary of marrying her himself or advising any of his friends to do so. She would be considered too 'easy' or even 'loose' in her relations with men. Of course, young men and women work together in the small work teams and groups, but propriety demands that an adult be in charge of the team or group. Anyway, the girls chaperone themselves. In rest periods they will sit slightly apart, and the boys would not be so forward as to intrude on them. The sons or daughters of families that are close neighbors will, of course, mingle together in the family groups, eating together with the rest and chatting together of an evening, but this is always in the family group, never tete-a-tete. (Chen, 1973, p. 77)

In the USSR, particularly in Soviet Central Asia, many similarly traditional patterns persist, often reinforced by religious beliefs. One example must suffice.

In the Karasu District of Tashkent the Komsomol Secretary in 1950 was one, Khamid Erkakhodzhaev. His wife, an ex-Komsomol, did not eat with guests, nor was she taken to the cinema or for walks with her husband. The Secretary excused himself, saying: 'Do you want me to quarrel with my relatives?' On the rare occasions when they did go out together he was careful to walk two paces in front of his wife (Meek, p. 227).

2. Laws and Practice

This section can do no more than draw attention to one or two relevant areas worthy of further study.

In both the USSR and China parent-child relations are covered by major legislation. In the former, according to the Code of Laws of 17 October 1918, parents could exercise paternal rights over a male child to the age of 18 years, and over a female child to the age of 16; decide the religion of their children under the age of 14; were entitled to decide the manner of upbringing and instruction, but could not contract for their employment between the age of 16-18 without the children's consent; and should keep their children with them, and maintain them. Conversely, children were obliged to maintain needy parents (Schlesinger, pp. 39-40). The legislation warned that 'Parental rights are exercised exclusively for the benefit of the children' (art. 153, ibid.), and added

> Parents are bound to take care of the development of their children under age, of their education and their training for a useful activity. (art. 154, ibid.)

Chapter 4 of the 1950 Marriage Law of the PRC makes similar provisions. Article 13 states:

> Parents have a duty to rear and to educate their children; the children have a duty to support and to assist their parents. Neither the parents nor the children shall maltreat or desert one another.
>   The foregoing provision also applies to foster-parents and foster-children. Infanticide by drowning and similar criminal acts are strictly prohibited.

Article 8 in the previous chapter is also relevant:

> Husband and wife are in duty bound to love, respect, assist and look after each other, to live in harmony, to engage in productive work, to care for their children and to strive jointly for the welfare of the family and for the building up of the new society.

This elaborates the basis for marriage set out in the first three articles of the Law:

1. The New Democratic marriage system, which is based on free choice of partners, on monogamy, on equal rights for both sexes, and on protection of the lawful interests of women and children, shall be put into effect.

3. Marriage shall be based upon the complete willingness of the two parties. Neither party shall use compulsion and no third party shall be allowed to interfere.

4. A marriage can be contracted only after the man has reached twenty years of age and the woman has reached eighteen years of age.

Of course, in reality, in the cities at least, family planning dictates that men marry at the age of 26-9 and women at 24-6.

Revolutionary situations and civil wars bring about painful crises of conscience and exacerbate conflicts between parents and children. The Communist Parties of both the USSR and China have attempted to use children as change agents and have on occasion publicly dramatised children's condemnation of their parents' anti-socialist behaviour. A notorious Soviet example occurred during the terrible period of the collectivisation of agriculture. The *Great Soviet Encyclopedia* describes it in these terms:

Morozov, Pavlik (Pavel Trofimovich, 1918-1932) a courageous pioneer who, after selflessly struggling against the kulaks of his community during the period of collectivization, was savagely killed by a kulak gang. The pioneers were carrying on an active struggle against the kulaks. M. exposed his own father, who had been at that time (1930) chairman of the village Soviet, but had fallen under the influence of kulak relatives. After telling his representative of the district committee of the party about how his father was secretly selling false documents to exiled kulaks, M. then testified in court in his father's case, and labelled him a traitor. The kulaks decided to settle matters with M. He was killed, together with his younger brother, on September 3, 1932, in a forest, by kulak bandits. The name of Morozov was given to the kolkhoz which was organized in Gerasimovka after his death, and also many other kolkhozes, pioneer palaces, and libraries. (quoted in Geiger, p. 54)

Yang describes a similar incident in China which received publicity in
the Hong Kong *Da Gong Bao*. (Yang, pp. 176-8) During the tense years
of 1950-2 a number of children publicly denounced famous fathers—
the son of Hu Shi and the daughter of Lu Zhi-wei, President of Yanjing
University (Fraser, 1965, pp. 25, 136-40). Chinese examples need to be
judged against the enormous repressive power of filial piety which probably needs drastic measures if it is to be overcome. Conditions in old
Russia lack that excuse, but they share the more general problem of
the relative value of principles of common humanity as opposed to
particular family interests. Judgement here is only clouded by the
Morozov case, out of which no one emerges well.

The Youth Organisations

The youth organisations in both the USSR and the PRC have always
been considered as basic collectives with a fundamental educational
role to play. They have been structured to cater for three age ranges in
both countries, and for the majority of the time since the respective
revolutions have been the only such organisations tolerated. In China
briefly during the Cultural Revolution independent Red Guard organisations, large and small, were formed with varying degrees of independence. Since then some of these have been formalised and now operate
alongside the reconstituted Youth League, the latter aiming at a smaller
membership devoted to leadership training.

In order to evaluate the youth organisations a number of questions
need answering. What proportion of the potential membership are enrolled? What kind of people belong—by geographical area, social class,
and sex? What do the youth organisations aim to teach, and how congruent with their aims is their practice? In the following pages I shall
supply some evidence on which judgement will be based.

The Youth League

The Komsomol came into being at a meeting of various worker and
peasant youth organisations in Moscow between 29 October and 4 November 1918. From the beginning CP members were in control, and
throughout its history the Komsomol's subordination to the Party has
been made clear in theory and practice. This meeting, later regarded as
the 1st Congress of the Komsomol, laid down that an annual All-Russian
(later USSR) Congress was to be the supreme authority, while in
between sittings an elected Central Committee would handle affairs.
However, in August 1919 a joint resolution of the CCs of the Party
and the Komsomol redefined power more clearly in favour of the Party.

It laid down that:

> The CC of the Komsomol is directly subordinated to the CC of the RCP (Party) . . . The local organizations of the Komsomol work under the control of the local committees of the RCP. (Fisher, pp. 12-13)

Foreshadowing the difficulties which such a position would inevitably lead to, and as if wishing them away, the resolution went on:

> The spontaneity of the RCLY is a foundation of its work and an indispensable condition of its existence. Therefore the Party's control over the League must not bear a character of guardianship, or of trifling interference in the organizational, agitational, cultural-educational, and other work of the League, and must be conducted only within the framework of the Regulations of the League and the instructions of the CC of the RCLY. . . All misunderstandings between local organizations of the Party and the League are submitted for settlement to higher echelons of the Party and the League. (Fisher, p. 13)

Over the years the position of subordination has been maintained. The preamble to the rules issued in 1961 includes this passage:

> The Komsomol is the active assistant and reserve of the CP of the Soviet Union. The Komsomol helps the Party to bring up youth in the spirit of communism, to draw it into the practical construction of the new society, to prepare a generation of well-rounded people who will live, work, and direct societal affairs under communism.
>
> The Komsomol works under the direction of the CP of the Soviet Union. The strength of the Komsomol lies in the CPSU's direction, in the ideological conviction and devotion to the cause of the Party. The Komsomol learns under the Party to live, to work, to struggle, and to win, in a Leninist way. The Komsomol sees the entire sense of its activity in the realization of the great program of the construction of the communist society that was adopted at the 21st Congress of the CPSU. (*Komsomolskaia pravda*, 21 April 1962, quoted in Kassof, p. 51)

The Chinese Communist Youth League (*Zhongguo Gongchanzhuyi Qingnian Tuan*) was set up on the initiative of the CC CCP in 1949. At the first congress, from 11 to 18 April 1949 it was established as the China New Democratic Youth League (*Zhongguo Xin Minzhuzhuyi Qingnian Tuan*), the name Communist Youth League only being adopted at the third congress in May 1957. The Constitution adopted at the second congress in June 1953 described the organisation as:

a mass organization of progressive youth, led by the CCP, and it is also the lieutenant and reserve force of the Party.

The League shall assist the Party to educate youth in the spirit of communism, so that they may become a young generation with a deep love for their motherland, being loyal to the people, educated, disciplined, brave, industrious, lively, and ready to face any hardship. They will follow the direction pointed out by our great leader, Chairman Mao Ze-dong, for the gradual realization of national industrialization and the gradual transition to socialism.

The entire members of the League shall be required faithfully to carry out the decisions of the Party and the Government . . . (Fraser (1) pp. 198-9)

It further lays down that:

The entire work of the League shall be conducted under the direct leadership of the CCP, and the local organs of the League shall accept the leadership and supervision of the Party organs at the same level. (ibid.)

The 'relation between the Party and the Communist Youth League' is also dealt with in a special chapter of the Constitution of the Party itself, adopted in 1956. Article 55 echoes the early Russian pattern:

The CC of the League accepts the leadership of the Party's CC. The League's local organizations are simultaneously under the leadership of the Party organizations at corresponding levels and of higher League organizations.

Article 56 deals with the League's role as the 'Party's assistant'. Article 58 both facilitates the Party's control over the League, while at the same time suggesting the League's role as a preparation for Party membership.

Members of the YCL shall withdraw from the League when they

have been admitted to the Party and have become full Party members, provided they do not hold leading posts or engage in specific work in the League organizations.

The description 'mass organization' has been applied to both the Chinese and the Russian youth league (cf. Fisher, p. 18, in 1919, and p. 182, in *Program of the League*, 1936) on many occasions, but an examination of the selection of members and the proportion of the age-group enrolled show that this is by no means correct. From the beginning in Russia pre-requisites other than age have been laid down and there has been a system of candidate membership preceding full membership. While worker and peasant youth have had few barriers to joining, students and offspring of 'alien classes' have had to find Party members or League members of (by 1936) one year's standing to vouch for them (Fisher, pp. 31, 72, 190). The aim has been to enrol 'the foremost tested youths loyal to the Soviet government', the 'foremost politically literate, toiling youth of town and countryside' (Fisher, p. 190). In the post-World War Two years barriers appear to have disappeared, and membership to be open to all comers. (See Kassof, p. 121: 'In its early days the Komsomol, it will be recalled, was a stepping stone to the party. Although the Komsomol was not necessarily popular, belonging to it was at least a distinction. But with the advent of a mass-membership policy, inaugurated before world war two, the esprit de corps of a few came increasingly to be replaced by the apathy of the many.') In China membership has in theory been open to

all youths, irrespective of sex, above the age of 14 and under the age of 25, who recognize the constitution of the League, participate and work in one of its organizations, implement its decisions, and pay membership dues. (Fraser (1) p. 199)

But in practice local branches have demanded such qualities as (1) a clear personal history; (2) good class status; and (3) being 'progressive in thinking and active in labour' (Report of the work committee of the Young Peasants' Department of the YCL CC, *China Youth Journal*, 21 March 1961). Dai Xiao-ai, former Red Guard in Canton describes how students from the 'backward classes' had difficulty in joining the League (Bennett and Montaperto, p. 4), while the 'Later Ten Points', an important document of the Socialist Education Movement condemns the practice of expelling members simply because they were from landlord and rich peasant families (Baum and Teiwes, p. 93).

Membership figures for the Komsomol show that until 1949 it remained a fraction of the relevant age-group (not to mention that many of its members were in fact over-age!). Table 7.1, taken from Fisher, gives some idea of its growth and composition.

Table 7.1

Membership as percentage of the age-group:	
1926	5.5%
1930s	c. 10%
1949	c. 20%
1954	35%
Membership over 23 years:	
1925	4%
1928	16-17%
1936	30%
Rural youth:	
c. 1924	36%
1926	51%
1954	tiny minority
Female members:	
1924	15%
1926	19%
1928	23%
1936	34%
1949	42%

The minute percentage of rural youth members in 1954 and subsequently must be seen against the whole picture of industrialisation and the neglect of the Russian villages.

Membership figures for the Chinese Youth League are incomplete, especially in recent years, but they show a similar pattern.

Table 7.2

Total membership:		Breakdown of 1957 total:	
1951	5,180,000	in villages	16.4m
1953	9,900,000	in schools	3.6m
1959	c. 25,000,000	in industry	2.28m
		in the army	1.8m

Breakdown of 1957 total:	
in government offices	970,000
in commerce	680,000
national minorities	600,000

With a population aged between 15 and 24 of about 130m, this would give a membership of 18 per cent of the age-group. According to an editorial of the *China Youth Journal* of 2 September 1964:

> Rural League members of the nation account for only 13% of the total number of rural youths. About 10% of production teams do not have League members, and about 30% have only one or two League members. Obviously such a state of affairs is incompatible with the needs of the vigorous development of farm production. (Quoted in Kirby, p. 128)

Activities of the League

The activities of the Komsomol have included military affairs, economic construction and conscription, mass campaigns, protection of young workers, and responsibility for political leadership among school students. At different periods the stress has been on different activities. Protection of young workers was early discouraged and disappeared with the ascendance to power of Stalin, and especially with the declaration of the arrival of socialism (Fisher, p. 182). Military duties naturally prevailed during the Civil War and World War Two, but in the form of various defence activities persisted at other times. Economic construction was particularly important during the first Five-Year Plan, and again in the post-World War Two period. In the late thirties, as during the twenties' struggles with the Trotskyist 'opposition', the Komsomol played its part in hunting out heretics, and more recently it has again been prominent in the defence of public morality among the young.

The Komsomol played a dual role in military affairs. It encouraged preparatory training of various kinds, for many years through the Society for the Promotion of Defence and of Aviation and Chemical Industries (Osaviakhim), encouraged those drafted for service, and promoted exemplary performance while serving. In addition the Komsomol supported the services through a system of patronage (*shefstvo*). This started at the 5th Congress on 16 October 1922, when it was voted to assume patronage of the Red Navy. Following the Kronstadt uprising

of 1921 over 2,000 Komsomols had entered the navy. Now they were
to give 'help and support' and establish close 'moral and material ties'.
Komsomols and other 'toiling youth' were urged to 'daily help the
Red Navy and its sailors: to correspond with sailors, to help their
families, to take up collections and arrange allotments, and to propagate
the idea of creating a mighty Red war fleet' (Fisher, pp. 99-100). In
January 1931 the Komsomol became patron of the Soviet Air Forces.
It was announced at the time that Party and Komsomol members
together formed 70 per cent of the Air Forces in 1930 (Fisher, pp.
174-5).

In the field of economic development the Komsomol has played a
not insignificant role. Most spectacular has been their contribution to
such projects as Dneprostroi, the Turksib railway, the building of the
city of Komsomol'sk-on-the-Amur, the re-building of Stalingrad after
World War Two, and the cultivation of the 'virgin lands' under Khrushchev in the late fifties. But they have also played a part in encouraging
technical skills through worker education, and in short- and long-term
recruitment to key industries or crash programmes such as gathering
the harvest. Numbers recruited have been impressive. Between 1920
and 1931 350,000 Komsomols went sent into various sectors of
industry, while in 1954 100,000 farm machine operators were sent to
the 'new lands'. The extent to which initial enthusiasm was maintained
is another matter. Speakers at the 1931 9th Congress reported a desertion rate of some 45-47 per cent among 15,000 Komsomols sent to the
factories and mines of the Donets Basin (Fisher, pp. 162, 257).

The Komsomol has always put propaganda for a new socialist morality high on its list of priorities. Among the means employed have been
accounts of the lives and exploits of actual or fictionalised Komsomols.
Perhaps the most famous of these is Pavel Korchagin, hero of the novel
How the Steel was Tempered by Nikolai Ostrovsky. Dictated by the
author during 1930-33 when he was paralysed, the book is partly auto-
biographic (he suffered ankylotic polyarthritis, possibly brought on
through prolonged over-exertion in various military and economic construction exploits). Translated into many languages, the book has
inspired many young people. Wu Yun-to, Chinese explosives-expert,
writes in his autobiography, *Song of the Working Class*:

I remembered how back in the spring of 1943 the Party had called
on us to model ourselves on Pavel Korchagin and so give ourselves a
deeper political understanding. I'd borrowed the book from a friend
who had the only copy in Huainan. It had already passed through

many hands and its pages were worn and dog-eared. For several nights Pavel Korchagin and I kept vigil together over a tiny lamp! (Wu Yunto, p. 199)

He quotes the famous passage, poignant when one remembers that its author was lying paralysed and in pain:

Man's dearest possession is life, and it is given to him to live but once. He must live so as to feel no torturing regrets for years without purpose, never know the burning shame of a mean and petty past; so live that, dying, he can say: all my life, all my strength were given to the finest cause in all the world—the fight for the liberation of mankind. (Wu, p. 198; Ostrovsky, 2, p. 105)

In the same tradition were Zoya Kosmodemyanskaya, tortured and killed by the Germans for partisan activity at the age of 19, and her brother Alexander, killed at the front, also a Hero of the Soviet Union, at 17! Their story is told by their mother: *The Story of Zoya and Shura*, by Lyubov Kosmodemyanskaya. These and many like them, perhaps not quite as perfect as the legend which surrounds them, must be balanced against the bureaucrat and the cynic, the prig and the preacher, with whose exploits the pages of *Komsomolskaya Pravda* have become so often spattered. (For other heroes see Fisher, p. 218, where he mentions Fadeev's novel, *The Young Guard*, serialised in *Kom. Pr.* 8 April 1945–1 March 1946).

Where the issues have been less clearcut than economic construction, the collectivisation, or war, Komsomol activities have been earnest, but hardly heroic or attractive to a wide section of youth. Inspection teams, sometimes referred to as 'light cavalry' have been used from the early years to hunt down petty crime and bureaucracy. Bukharin suggested their use at the 8th Congress in 1928 (Fisher, p. 158). In the fifties and sixties numerous reports attest to their use, and also to how far the USSR is from producing the much-talked of 'new man'. In one example

... the Komsomol patrols ... apprehended ... a certain Ignaty Shcherbak... He was living luxuriously, had his own private car, slept during the day, and stole collective-farm goods at night. When Shcherbak was apprehended, 300 kg. of stolen corn ears were found in his car...

The application of the new law on intensifying the struggle against swindlers, loafers, and antisocial and parasitic elements must be com-

bined with an increase in vigilance and with a strengthening of the
protection of public wealth. The Komsomol committees of state
and collective farms can and must play a great role here. The Komsomol committees of collective and state farms and enterprises must
make wide use of such tested forms of Komsomol and youth participation in the protection of public wealth as Komsomol posts,
Komsomol patrol groups for the protection of the fields, and Komsomol 'light cavalry' raids. (Kassof, pp. 114-5, quoted from *Kom.
Pr.*, 12 May 1961)

The following account from *Izvestiya*, 31 March 1961, shows the same
means extended to different ends.

A few days ago . . . the Moscow City Komsomol Committee carried
out a 'raid check on the appearance of young people'. At five o'clock
in the afternoon of that day my daughter Yelena, a Komsomol
member and a student in the 10th grade, and a girl friend of hers
were detained at the State Department Store by young people who
said they were authorized to do so as members of an operational city
Komsomol detachment.

It was later explained to me that my daughter had done nothing
reprehensible and had been detained only because her kerchief had
been tied around her head in a certain way. This served as the basis
for taking Lena to the 117th Militia precinct station where a large
group of drunken hooligans and female speculators was in custody.
This group greeted the girls with a stream of unbridled bad language.

The young people whose duty it was to maintain order held an
insolent three-hour interview with my daughter and myself. Especially
prominent in this was an unshaven young man who threatened physical force.

This was how the opening of the holidays was 'celebrated'. Two
girls were insulted and their families' peace of mind was destroyed.

All this happened under the very eyes of the militia captain on
duty . . . V. Sokolov, instructor in charge of the Moscow Komsomol
Committee, is in charge of the raids. (Kassof, pp. 135-5, quoted from
Izvestiya, 31 March 1961)

Among students the Komsomol has a tendency to pry into intimate
details of their family and sex life (Kassof, pp. 104-6). Disregarding for
the moment the arbitrary and narrow moral views held by the organisation, the results, in their own terms, suggest that their methods are

unsuccessful.

In recent years, as news has become somewhat franker, more details have emerged of the Komsomol's failures (there has always been *ritual* self-criticism). D. Meek quotes the problem of neglected children during the fifties and the comment that while the Komsomol passed resolutions on the subject 'they put so little heart into this work' in practice that nothing effective was done. As for the way in which officials were able to further the interests of their members, one hopes that the following incident is not typical.

> A Komsomol official came to a North Caucasian manager with a request to set aside a room in the plant for young workers' boxing. The manager yelled at him: 'Turn left. What do you see? The door? That's right. . . ' The official obediently marched out. (Parry, p. 167, ex. *Kom. Pr.,* 13 May 1965)

In China the Youth League's activities have been to organise and make propaganda. From published references to the League it would seem that there has been less glamour attached to the organisation than in the USSR, and perhaps less attempt to give it credit for spectacular ventures. Nevertheless it would appear to have been powerful in such institutions as schools and tertiary institutes and universities, and it reaches a wide audience through *China Youth*, the *China Youth Journal*, and publications of the China Youth Press (*Zhongguo Qingnian Chuban She*).

Dai Xiao-ai, ex-Red Guard, gives an interesting account of the League in a Canton school, where just less than half the students appear to have been members in 1966. The League secretary and assistant secretary were both teachers in their twenties, the former a Party member and the latter probably an applicant for membership. The importance of the League is shown by the fact that all the officers of the Student Association and almost all the class officers and small-group leaders were YCL members. Dai comments:

> We League members were the most active students who played a leading role in all activities. Everyone expected us to set an example in deportment, study, and political activism; all of us were proud of our membership. We had hopes of entering the Party as soon as possible and knew that this would depend upon the record we made while in the YCL.
>
> Once a week we participated in League Life (*tuan shenghuo*)

meetings, where we discussed the texts chosen by the propaganda members of the YCL committee. These were part of a regular curriculum for all YCL members. Usually we met in our YCL small groups with branch meetings coming second. The general branch met only for such matters as approving new members, hearing directives, and discussions of the League constitution. Since almost every school · cadre was also a League member, our League Life meetings proved a good way of keeping up with events in the school.

Sometimes we would have special general branch sessions where events of unusual importance would be announced. I first heard about the Cultural Revolution in this way when the Principal told us about a report on Luo Rui-qing. We had many privileges of this sort but our responsibilities were also greater. We received criticisms not only from our ordinary classmates but also from our fellow League members. This made our jobs twice as difficult, but most of us felt it to be worth the price. (Bennett and Montaperto, pp. 18-19)

From the early fifties the YCL has been expected to lead youth in work and recreation. Hu Yao-bang, speaking to the 2nd national congress in 1953 about the work of YCL branches in schools said:

. . . organizations in schools should, first of all, teach the New Democratic Youth League [as it was then called] members to observe the school discipline, to fulfil pedagogical plans, to study their lessons, and use concrete actions to influence and help their fellow students in study. . . Further, under the centralized plans of the schools, provided normal study is not handicapped, the NDYL organizations should unite the students to take part voluntarily in the necessary social activities and public welfare work in the schools, thereby to cultivate students' disposition to labour for the public cause and contact with the masses. The NDYL organizations in schools should also show constant attention to the health conditions of the students and assist the schools in developing physical culture and cultural activities, thereby to enable every student to have proper rest and the required physical training. (Fraser, 1, p. 187)

Speaking to the 4th (renumbered the 9th) congress in 1964 Hu stressed the importance of 'other young people' who had often been neglected by the League. He said:

A fundamental question for the YCL is to keep close contact with
the mass of young people. We should unite and organize them to
the fullest possible extent. All League cadres and members must
show concern for other young people, approach them, find out their
views and needs, and become their bosom friends. . . The YCL
should give full consideration to the two aspects of the life of young
people—their work and study, and their recreation, physical culture
and rest; it should take all-round care of their growth. We should
do our work in a more lively and dynamic way. (Hu Yao-bang, pp.
37-8)

Reporting a year later on how this call to action had been followed up,
Miaodi Production Brigade YCL in Shanxi admitted that they had had
no meetings 'for a long time'. Of the 201 youth spread through 6 natural villages, only 37 were YCL members. They organised in 7 propaganda teams and set out to be the 'most positive and most active shock
force for agricultural production'. At their first Mao Ze-dong Thought
study group meeting only 5 non-members turned up, but later more
joined in. When they invited Wu Yu-zhi, hero of the Volunteer Force
in Korea, to come and speak an audience of 120 came and 'all received
a profound education'. They organised a campaign to emulate Lei
Feng and accomplished 'over 300 pieces of good work' in less than a
month. They used 110 yuan earned for voluntary labour to establish a
cultural room with a small library. There they performed plays, sang
songs and told revolutionary stories. At the same time they made a
special point of trying to win over 'backward' youth, including eight
offspring of former landlord and rich peasant families whom they had
formerly avoided.

In all their activities the initiative appears to have come from the
Party, and the prestige earned was for it, or perhaps more for the
Thought of Mao Ze-dong which guided it. This is apparent in the
accounts of the various heroes proclaimed over the past 23 years. Their
membership in the YCL has been recorded in a majority of cases, and
they have even been proclaimed Model Youth League Members. (See
Qingnian de gushi—Stories of Youth Heroes, e.g. p. 116, bk. 544.) But
more often they have passed quickly through the League of the Party,
or been posthumously awarded Party membership.

The Young Pioneers

The Young Pioneers, 'pioneers of the new society', were set up on the
recommendation of the 5th Congress of the Komsomol in 1922. Formed

for children aged 10-14, the groups were to inculcate class consciousness, a collective sense, respect for labour and learning, and willingness
to subordinate personal interests to those of society (Fisher, p. 96). By
October the new organisation registered some 4,000 members, and
while it grew substantially, by March 1926 it only constituted some
8 per cent of the potential membership. Only in the post-world war
two years did it embrace the great majority of its age-group.

In China the Young Pioneers were first set up as the Children's Corps
of China by the CC YCL in October 1949, and assumed the more familiar name in June 1953 (*Zhongguo Xiaonian Xianfengdui*). Organised for
children aged 9-15, membership rose to 7 million in 1953 and 50
million by 1962. The latter figure is perhaps in the region of 70 per
cent of the age group—assuming an even spread of population across the
range 5-14. But membership has probably been greatest in the towns.
Tsang's comment, 'the Chinese Communist Young Pioneers' Brigade is
found in every school' needs the rider that not every child goes to school
and in remoter villages where there is only a part-work school, or even
no school, a Pioneer Brigade is still probably rare (Tsang, pp. 168-9).

In both countries the Youth League has been expected to look after
the Young Pioneers, staffing it with youth leaders and giving it other
support. But in China direct Party supervision may perhaps be stronger.
(Hu Yao-bang, in 1953, refers to the Party 'entrusting' the YCL to organise the YPC, and further, 'the Party has decided to rename the Young
Pioneers as Young Vanguard'—Fraser, 1, p. 188. Ji Zhong-zhou, leader
of the Pioneers at Liu Lin village is a Party member and does not mention the YCL—Myrdal, pp. 384-9.) Sufficient support has not always
been forthcoming. The 1924 Komsomol Congress received a report
that in that year about a quarter of the Pioneer leaders were former
Scout leaders and other non-Komsomols (Fisher, p. 134). 39 per cent
of the leaders were girls. In 1954 the report on the Pioneers again
reported poor leadership. Half the professional senior Pioneer leaders
remained less than a year with one troop. Of the 51,000 professional
leaders, more than 9,000 had not had secondary education and only 56
per cent had received teacher-training. Again the complaint was made
of a shortage of male leaders! (Fraser, p. 267). In China, where the *China
Youth Journal* of 30 January 1964 reported a total of about 1,200,000
Young Pioneer leaders, the importance of training for the job is recognised, and the Journal called for intensified efforts in 'raising their class
consciousness, political ideology and professional levels' (*SCMP*, 3167
and Kirby, p. 127).

The familiar red scarf, representing a corner of the red flag,

symbol of workers' power, and impressive ceremony are common features to Russia and China. The new member is welcomed in a ceremony
in which he takes a solemn pledge. In the USSR the pledge goes:

> I, a Young Pioneer of the Soviet Union, solemnly promise in the
> presence of my comrades.
>> — to warmly love my Soviet motherland
>> — to live, to study, and to struggle as Lenin willed and as the
>> Communist Party teaches. (*Kom. pr.*, 26 December 1957, p. 1,
>> quoted by Kassof, p. 79)

As a Pioneer the young person must promise to obey the following
Rules for Pioneers:

> The Pioneer loves his motherland and the CP of the Soviet Union.
> He prepares himself for membership in the Komsomol.
> The Pioneer reveres the memory of those who have given their
> lives in the struggle for the freedom and the well-being of the Soviet
> motherland.
> The Pioneer is friendly with the children of all the countries of
> the world.
> The Pioneer studies diligently and is disciplined and courteous.
> The Pioneer loves to work and to conserve the national wealth.
> The Pioneer is a good comrade, who is solicitous of younger child-
> ren and who helps older people.
> The Pioneer grows up to be bold and does not fear difficulties.
> The Pioneer tells the truth and guards the honor of his detachment.
> The Pioneer strengthens himself and does physical exercises every
> day.
> The Pioneer loves nature; he is a defender of planted areas, of
> useful birds and animals.
> The Pioneer is an example for all children.
> (Kassof, p. 79)

A little booklet published by the Youth Press in Peking in 1966, entitled *Why you should wear the red scarf* describes an initiation ceremony
there. The troop lines up. Red flags flutter around the ground and in
front is a picture of Chairman Mao. Saluting the flag they sing the Pioneer
song, after which the 'little Chairman' leads new members in the oath:

> I am a member of the Chinese Young Pioneers. Under the troop flag

I pledge: I will resolutely follow the teachings of the Communist Party, to study well, work well, labour well, preparing to devote all my strength to the communist cause.

At the end of the ceremony a representative of the Youth League Branch fastens on their red scarves and says to them:

Comrades, as a representative of the League Branch I bring you warm congratulations. From today on you are all glorious Young Pioneers. I want you after entering the Pioneers firmly to remember Chairman Mao's words: study well, go forward every day, be a good child of Chairman Mao, be an excellent Young Pioneer.

After that, in accordance with the Regulations of the Pioneers, the new members went off to perform a good deed (*Weishenme yao dai hong lingjin*, pp. 20-3).

Activities of the Pioneers

A problem at the Pioneer stage has always been to find the right kind of activities. Krupskaya, a keen supporter of the Pioneers, wanted Pioneer detachments to be warm, supportive groups which would in many ways act like a family. In the early years in Russia activities swung first towards athletics and outdoor activities of the Boy Scout type, and then towards purely political discussions and social duties (Fisher, p. 134). In the early thirties the older children worked in factories as shock workers, and wrote wall newspapers exposing the shortcomings of 'backward' workers. In the villages Pioneers took part in the anti-kulak campaign, and helped with the collective farming. Pioneer groups were centred on the work place at this time (Fisher, pp. 168-9), but in mid-1931 were transferred to the school and participation in political and economic activities outside the school were severely limited. The 1936 Program and Regulations of the Komsomol separated the first 7 school grades, Pioneer grades, from the 8-10th grades of the new ten-year schools which were to be reserved for Komsomol activities (Fisher, p. 201). Basing the Pioneers on the schools facilitated grouping members by age and thus more easily organising suitable activities. At the same time it removed meetings from private homes where Pioneers were exposed to bourgeois influences and indulged in 'bourgeois games' and 'very dubious tea' (Fisher, p. 202). The shift was towards study in school circles, and for the lucky ones, in the various Pioneer Palaces which were set up. By 1956 the following institutions were reported, not all of them confined to use by Pioneers:

Palaces and houses of pioneers	2,382
Young technicians stations	258
Young naturalists' stations	214
Excursion-tourist stations	135
Children's parks	135
Children's libraries and divisions of libraries	5,923
Puppet theatres	101
Children's railways	229
Sports schools	806
Stadiums	33

(Bereday and Pennar, p. 206)

In the big cities the Pioneer Palaces are large buildings with halls, games rooms, rooms for music, model-making, and all kinds of arts and sciences. They are often lavishly equipped by local standards, but they can only handle a fraction of the demand (see Bereday and Pennar for further description).

Study circles tend to concentrate on the sciences: chemistry, physics, biology, mathematics, and radio, automobile and tractor repair. The principles involved were described in a 1950 manual as:

Technical activity helps the Pioneers to deepen and to strengthen their knowledge of the basis of such sciences as mathematics, physics, chemistry, and allows them to carry these into practice. The young technologist learns that without elementary mathematical calculations, for example, it is impossible to build even the simplest model. . .

Children's technology . . . plays an important part in preparing the children in constructive and technological habits. It helps the school to fulfill the task of preparing the students for future practical activity. (*Pionerskaia organisatsiia*, 1950 edn, pp. 102-3, quoted by Kassof, p. 98)

The Protestant ethic flavour of the attitude to study is brought out in the following quotation from a 1955 book for youth leaders in schools:

Knowledge is strength.
Knowledge is as important as a rifle in battle.
Study is your job.
Learn how to study.

If you lose an hour, you will not make up the time in a whole year.
The price of a minute.
Save each minute.

(Klassnye rukovoditeli o svoei rabotv s komsomoltsami i pionerami,
class directors on their work with Komsomol members & Pioneers;
Moscow, 1955, p. 11, quoted by Kassof, p. 95)

In the late fifties there was renewed emphasis on participation in factory and farm labour. While excursions to work places had persisted
from the thirties, together with socially useful labour, such as helping
with the harvest, there was now a new attempt to link studies with work.
Under the 1958 Komsomol instruction to establish permanent relationships with a particular enterprise plans were worked out aiming at
experiences such as described in *Komsomolskaya Pravda* in these
words:

> Although (these particular) Pioneers have often passed through the
> (factory) gate, each time they feel a festive excitement . . . These 10-
> 12 year-old children are going to the factory where their fathers,
> brothers, and mothers work. The children also have serious business
> here.
>   Enriching the knowledge that they have received during school
> lessons, they are becoming acquainted with the production process,
> and sometimes even stand at a machine getting practice. . .
>   Now the Pioneer detachment has come, not for an excursion (as
> in the past) but for the purpose of participating side by side with the
> workers in socially useful tasks. In the Red Corners of the shops,
> Pioneer flags, horns, drums, children's libraries, diaries, and albums
> have appeared. And many of the factory's Komsomol members have
> begun to wear red Pioneer neckties. They are Pioneer leaders. . .
>   The Pioneers will see at closer range the life of the workers' collect-
> ive, will understand the meaning of such words as socialist competition,
> work enthusiasm, plan fulfilment; they will discover by whose energies
> our country is being enriched. *(Kom. Pr.,* 9 February 1958, p. 3,
> quoted by Kassof, pp. 96-7)

Much of the activity of both Russian and Chinese Pioneers consists
of moral-political studies of one kind and another. At the younger age
these are more local and concerned with doing good. At the older age
more attention is paid to reading newspapers and studying what the
Chinese refer to as 'past bitterness and present sweetness'. In both

countries Pioneers collect stories of the bitter past from old people, heroic stories of war veterans, and recently in China have prepared and eaten meals of the kind endured during extreme poverty and near-famine conditions. The result has inevitably been the depiction of black-and-white images hopefully capable of instilling the desired emotional effect. In the USSR the sudden changes of policy, most recently the abrupt ending of the adulation of Stalin, must have created considerable crises of confidence, seriously weakening the Pioneers' influence as educators (see Kassof, pp. 89-90).

Little Octobrists

Between 1924 and 1926 children in the age range 8-11 were organised in the Little Octobrists. In the latter year they were said to have 200,000 members, and by 1931 may have numbered 700,000 (Fisher, pp. 134, 170). Regarded as a preparatory organisation for the Pioneers, formalities have been few and membership open to almost any child who wanted to join. In the thirties Octobrists were organised in groups of 25, ideally with a Komsomol as leader, though responsibility rested directly with the Young Pioneers. Activities included singing and dancing, outdoor activities of all kinds, including sports, and especially at the older age range, induction into the rules, duties and traditions of the Young Pioneers which they will hopefully join (cf. King, pp. 249-50; *Ped. Ents.* (3), p. 195; and Grant, p. 64).

In China there has been no similar organisation. At first the lower age limit for the Pioneers was nine, but it was later reduced. Children of 7-12 years were organised in Children's Teams (*Ertong Dui*) and those of 12-15 in Early Adolescent Teams (*Xiaonian Dui*) of the Pioneers (Tsang, p. 169).

The Red Guards of the Chinese Cultural Revolution

The Cultural Revolution was probably unique in China's history for the freedom it gave to youth. They organised into large and small groups with various revolutionary names. Generically these were referred to as *Hongweibing*, the Red Guards. Some youth went on trips right across the country, often stopping to work in places they passed through. Some became deeply involved in political activities while others withdrew into a private world of fishing and reading novels. Organisations and individuals were manipulated by political leaders seeking various ends. Many young people suffered and inflicted serious violence. While the experience only lasted some two years it must have left profound impressions. Studies so far have been concerned with the political level.

The educational balance sheet has yet to be drawn (studies include Bennett and Montaperto; Hinton; Domes; Hunter).

Evaluating the Youth Programme

Concluding his discussion of the Soviet youth programme Kassof remarks:

> there is a very strong concern with knowledge, a respect for science, education, competence, and technical proficiency, faith in the power of reason, in the constructive possibilities of social action, and in man's capacity for purposeful self-improvement through planning and effort. That these themes have often been sacrificed to political expediency, or have been neglected by professional bureaucrats, has by no means eliminated them or precluded the possibility that they will receive greater emphasis at some future time. (Kassof, p. 181)

It is the very strength and success of this programme which produces one problem, both for the pro-industrialisation bureaucrats, and those more concerned with social change of a marxist nature. This has been expressed in similar terms in the two countries. In the USSR *Komsomol-skaya Pravda* for 20 March 1954 carried a report by Komsomol leader, Shelepin. He complained of youth who avoided physical work:

> The schools and the Komsomol are not doing enough to imbue the pupils with work habits and to draw them into work appropriate to their strength. Rural schools are doing a poor job of arousing in their pupils an interest in farm work. It is wrong when some Pioneer lead-ers and Komsomol officials, and also teachers, tell the school children only: 'Study hard and you're sure to be a scientist, engineer, or writer'—and fail to interest him in becoming a skilled workman, mechanic, tractor driver, or combine operator. (Quoted by Fisher, p. 262)

Yao Wen-yuan, attacking Tao Zhu in 1968 wrote:

> Tao Zhu says that it is a 'lofty ideal' always to keep in mind that 'one will become a navigator, aviator, scientist, writer, engineer, teacher. . . ' He lists one expert profession after another, but makes no mention at all of any worker, peasant or soldier. (Yao, p. 8)

Considering the youth organisations from the point of view of developing self-fulfilling and self-determining individuals in the marxist sense, it must be obvious from the above description that such an aim is neither set nor achieved. True, they do widen horizons, develop skills and promote self-confidence. But that is within a system which limits information, and trains members in obedience to dictation from above. Apart from the constitutional support for Party initiative and control, there has been the persistent record, especially in the Komsomol-Youth League, of over-age members. Their occupation of key posts stifled initiative and encouraged apathy—the typical situation of systems of misrepresentative democracy elsewhere. It has also encouraged the growth of a bureaucracy with interests of its own, often very different from those of the ordinary membership. One example, quoted in *Izvestiya* in 1962, illustrates the problem. An organisation affiliated to the Komsomol, in Dnepropetrovsk province, had a salaried staff of 25 full-time workers.

> In all, these people received approximately 500,000 rubles in wages in 1961. Yet membership dues collected in the province came to no more than 156,400 rubles.
> What are the society's salaried workers being paid for? Frankly I could find no answer to this question. . . All the committee chairmen do is give out receipts for the payment of membership dues and read and answer directives.

Readers familiar with the operation of bureaucracies will not be surprised that the response to criticism in this case resulted in raising staff salaries (*Izvestiya*, 29 August 1962, p. 3, quoted by Kassof, pp. 126-7).

Throughout the history of the USSR, and certainly too in China, there have been those who wished to give the youth more chance to experiment in governing themselves. Krupskaya was one of these (Fisher, p. 6). Many others over the years must have echoed Trotsky's burning comment, made abroad:

> Having no experience of class struggle and revolution, the new generations could have ripened for independent participation in the social life of the country only in conditions of soviet democracy, only by consciously working over the experience of the past and the lessons of the present. *Independent character like independent thought cannot develop without criticism.* The Soviet youth, however, are simply denied the elementary opportunity to exchange thoughts, make mistakes and try out and correct mistakes, their own as well as others'. All questions, including their very own, are decided for them. (Trotsky,

p. 162, emphasis added)

But where such criticism is voiced aloud it dares not touch on the really vital question: politics. Here is one example:

> Often, we regard political-educational work as cumbersome, boring meetings and discussions similar to classroom lessons; throwing together any kind of montage, putting out a wall newspaper with long leaders from the newspapers. But surely children can feasibly take part in surrounding life and can assist adults. It is essential to put serious, large assignments to Pioneer members, to explain the importance of these tasks to children. . . (*Kom. Pr.,* 24 March 1961, quoted by Kassof, p. 132)

In China the situation has not been more encouraging for the marxist position set out here. Though there have been plenty of quotations from Mao Ze-dong advocating independence and self-reliance the same pattern of paternalism has been followed, while the actions of Red Guards during the Cultural Revolution when they had relative freedom was far from encouraging. It remains to be seen whether the future will be different.

The Army as Educator

Military Tradition and Marxist Ethic

A neglected agent of education of various kinds is the army—strictly, the armed forces—which takes in the young and healthy at what is a formative period of their lives. To different degrees the army influences not only those who join it, but also the wider society. A little thought about traditions in Britain, Germany, and many another country reveals the importance of the armed forces, directly and indirectly, in shaping the dominant ethos. While many youth, especially males, have served both in peace and war, others have been influenced by school cadet corps or derivative organisations, such as the Boy Scouts (Wilkinson, 1969). In all countries, and especially in those which are commonly regarded as 'under-developed', a large number of youth learn basic skills during their service in the armed forces. 'Join the army and learn a trade' is a slogan which does not apply only to Britain where the army has used it in recruiting advertisements. In addition to skills, and more important in the long run, moral-political attitudes and habits are acquired which often persist long after the soldier (sailor or airman) has returned to civilian life. Nor do these attitudes only affect the service personnel, but diffuse through his relatives to the wider society. The military ethic is also transmitted directly to the civilian sphere by other channels of propaganda, many of them more subtle than the campaign to 'learn from the PLA' launched in China in 1964. The attitudes of people in the imperialist nations towards the colonial peoples among whom their soldiers have served have certainly been influenced by this experience. As with other spheres of human experience discussed in this book, the process is a mixture of socialisation and direct education. Britons who served in World War Two will recall the activities of the Army Bureau of Current Affairs. More recent education, for 'counter-insurgency', is described in an important book by Brigadier Frank Kitson (1971). The following pages will outline some aspects of the problematic in the USSR and China, limiting discussion to the activities of the services themselves. Again one must bear in mind the dialectic of present attitudes and present experience from which the future springs. No simple model of stimulus-response conditioning is suggested here. On the contrary: the results are clearly diverse.

Beginning with the qualities associated with the military tradition, it is interesting to speculate on the distinction between masculine and feminine qualities traditionally associated with these roles, and possible links with agricultural and pastoral ways of life. Needham writes:

> The Confucian and Legalist social-ethical thought-complex was masculine, managing, hard, dominating, aggressive, rational and donative—the Daoists broke with it radically and completely by emphasizing all that was feminine, tolerant, yielding, permissive, withdrawing, mystical and receptive. (Needham, p. 59)

In a later section he contrasts the command-psychology required for the management of animals or the safety of a ship, with the Daoist principle of *wu-wei*, or non-interference, which is more conducive to the growth of plants (Needham, pp. 576-7). While talk of national characteristics is dangerous, there is much suggestive evidence for a difference in the degree to which Russia and China can traditionally be regarded as militaristic in this masculine, aggressive sense. As recent years have proved, this is not to say that Chinese cannot make good soldiers. But it may have contributed to the special qualities of the PLA.

In discussing the relations between the military and the Party in the USSR Kolkowicz contrasts a number of traits 'natural' to the military with those desired by the Party. While I would want to question some of the latter in the light of Soviet practice there is little doubt that they describe the Party's theoretical stand reasonably accurately, and bring out the tendency to conflict between these two groups.

'Natural' military traits:	*Traits desired by the Party:*
Elitism	Egalitarianism
Professional autonomy	Subordination to ideology
Nationalism	Proletarian internationalism
Detachment from society	Involvement with society
Heroic symbolism	Anonymity
(Kolkowicz, p. 21)	

Another view of the military virtues was given by Major General Makeev, editor-in-chief of *Krasnaia zvezda*:

> The concept of military honour has existed since time immemorial; it is as old as armies . . . Even in the old Russian army there were good traditions—bravery, selfless dedication, and military skill were revered. (Kolkowicz, p. 317)

In 1955, at the All-Union Conference of the Union of Soviet Writers, Rudni instructed Soviet writers:

> It is necessary to show in what way he (the officer) differs essentially from the people around him, who obey him without contradiction, not only because they are formally subordinated to him, but from deep inner respect. The high moral qualities of this man must be shown, his courage and bravery. . . as a commander, that is, in relation with his equals and the high command. (Kolkowicz, p. 120)

The early Bolshevik dream of a militia which would 'inculcate conscious discipline without the elevation above the army of a professional officers' corps' (Trotsky, *Revolution Betrayed*, p. 216) perished in the flames of civil war. By 1924 Bukharin was forced to admit:

> Our army is in a high degree similar to the quite ordinary bourgeois army. Once upon a time we thought the structure of our army would look quite different: no forced discipline, only conscious discipline. But experience showed that the forms of conscious discipline in this literal sense are inapplicable, though naturally this consciousness plays a larger role with us than in other armies. Therefore we

have various measures of compulsion in the army, and that is absolutely necessary: we even shoot deserters. . . The formal structure is like that of a bourgeois army. But that is not the decisive thing. The decisive thing is its different class character. (in Carr, 1970, 2, p. 430)

Frunze, then Deputy People's Commissar for War (to replace Trotsky as Commissar in 1925) took up the same point in a speech to army officers in November 1924:

This 'democratic spirit' (shown by some officers) is the crudest perversion of any and every rule of discipline in our Red Army. A command is a command. To persuade and exhort men to carry out orders is in itself a crude breach of discipline. (ibid.)

As the *ABC of Communism* already explained in 1920,

. . . Red soldiers . . . in the last resort . . . are commanded by the whole working class, through the instrumentality of the workers' State and its military staff. Thus the discipline of the Red Army is the submission of the minority (the soldiers) to the interests of the majority of the workers. (Carr, *ABC*, p. 261)

Over the years reliance on the trappings of rank and other methods of enforcing discipline characteristic of 'bourgeois' armies were strengthened. In September 1935 ranks were reintroduced ranging from lieutenant to marshal (Kolkowicz, p. 54), and following the disastrous purge of 1937 further privileges were granted. In 1942 strict separation was made between privates, sergeants, officers (a former taboo word, now reintroduced), and generals (ibid. p. 67). 'Military epaulettes were added to uniforms, pointing up differences in ranks' (ibid. p. 68). Commenting in 1936, Trotsky wrote:

The resurrection of hierarchical caste is not in the least demanded by the interests of military affairs. It is the commanding position, and not the rank, of the commander that is important. Engineers and physicians have no rank, but society finds the means of putting each in his needful place. The right to a commanding position is guaranteed by study, endowment, character, experience, which need continual and moreover individual appraisal. The rank of major adds nothing to the commander of a battalion. The elevation of the five senior commanders of the Red Army to the title of marshall, gives them neither new talents nor supplementary powers. It is not the army that really thus receives a 'stable basis', but the officers' corps, and that at the price of aloofness from the army. (Trotsky, *Revolution Betrayed*, p. 223)

While many observers would see the Party exhibiting the same kind of elitist commandism over the non-Party masses in the Soviet Union as the officers increasingly did over the lower ranks, some writeɪ ̮ ̣ave seen the system of political commissars within the army as a check. Writing about the relations between the army and Party after the death of Stalin in 1953, Kolkowicz listed the following Party aims:

(a) to minimize the conditions that breed elitism by forcing egalitarian, collectivist procedures and values on the military community, (b) to 'open up' the military community to the impartial, and not necessarily sympathetic, scrutiny of civilian Party organs, (c) to deprive the officers of their automatic authority as commanders and force them to reclaim it in each instance from the collective authority of the Party organizations in their units, and (d) to undermine the officers' security by exposing them to the ritual of criticism/ self-criticism, including the ignominy of criticism from the professionally and militarily lower-ranking Komsomols. (Kolkowicz, p. 347)

It is ironic to read Marshall Zhukov, in his *Memoirs*, paying special tribute to the officers and admitting the possibility of 'making a difference' between officer and man:

Brilliant examples were set by officers of all ranks—from junior lieutenants to marshals—ardent patriots of their country, experienced and fearless organizers of the multi-million strong armed forces in military actions. Those who make a difference between the Soviet soldier and officer make a bad mistake, for equal in origin, way of thinking and acting, they are equally loyal to, and are the true sons of their Motherland. (Zhukov, p. 691)

He forgets the inequalities, yet these are important when it comes to evaluating the lessons learnt: obedience, a sense of powerlessness, and an acceptance (or rebellion against?) hierarchy.

The style of the PLA was built up during the long years of civil war, beginning with the establishment of the base on the Jinggang Mountains by Mao Ze-dong in September 1927. A mixed bag of peasants, lumpen proletariat (*éléments déclassés* in Schram) and former KMT soldiers were turned into a force whose behaviour has won it the admiration of all who have witnessed it. Mao, in a report submitted to the CC CCP in November 1928, made a point which has remained essentially true ever since:

> Apart from the role played by the Party, the reason the Red Army can sustain itself without being exhausted, in spite of such miserable material conditions and such incessant engagements, is the thoroughness of its democratic practice. The officers do not beat the soldiers; officers and soldiers have the same food and clothing and receive equal treatment; soldiers enjoy freedom of assembly and speech; cumbersome formalities and ceremonies are abolished; the financial administration is absolutely open to (the inspection) of all; and the soldiers' representatives inspect the final accounts . . . (Schram, 1969, pp. 270-71; cf. Mao, *SW* 1, p. 83, where the wording has been slightly altered)

A note in the 1960 edition adds:

> Of course, democracy in the army must not transcend the limits of military discipline, which it must serve to strengthen and not weaken. Therefore, while a necessary measure of democracy should be promoted, the demand for ultra-democracy, which amounts to indiscipline, must be combated. (Mao, ibid. p. 103)

On this problem Mao wrote *On Correcting Mistaken Ideas in the Party* in December 1929. During the period of Soviet influence in the mid-fifties new regulations gave greater stress to formal discipline (Gittings, pp. 147-8), and ranks and medals for officers were awarded in February 1955 (Gittings, pp. 152-5). The revolutionary tradition reasserted itself, however, in May 1965, when the State Council abolished officers titles, and ruled that as previously functional forms would be used (Gittings, p. 251). Already in 1956 there was a reaction against too great reliance on the Soviet model, and increasing attempts were made to bring officers and men closer together (Gittings, pp. 166-7, 193-5).

The Forces: Composition and Military Role

Any evaluation of the influence of the armed forces must take into consideration the number of people who serve in them, in what capacity, and for what length of time. Exact figures are difficult to impossible to obtain, and have varied widely over time.

In Tsarist Russia about one and a half million men were normally kept under arms during the pre-revolutionary decades. In 1921, just after the Civil War, there were 4,400,000 in the forces. This figure was reduced to 560,000 in 1923 (Carr, 1970, 2, p. 417). At that time this figure could be maintained by calling up only one third of the potential conscripts (280,000 out of 800-900,000). In addition to these regular forces another 250,000 served in the Territorials, spending about 2 months a year training for 5 years. By 1934-5 the regular forces had risen to 1,300,000, and in 1960 it was reported to be 3.6 million. The numbers involved during World War Two can be guaged from the losses, put at 7 million (Blackett, p. 199; cf. 10.2 million civilian dead).

Duration of service for conscripts has varied. In 1925 it was 2 years for the regular forces, 8-12 months in short periods over 5 years, and 6 months without enrolment for certain trainees (Carr, 1970, 2, p. 425). All between the ages of 21-40 were liable for call-up. In 1939 conscription for the army was for 2 years; for the Coastal Defence, 4 years; for the Navy, 5 years, later reduced to 4 (1955); for the Ministry of the Interior troops, 2 years; and the Frontier Police, 3 years (Saunders, p. 129). Saunders puts the size of the Soviet Navy (c. 1958) at 750,000.

In addition to the armed forces one should also count the members of the Society for Promotion of Aviation and Chemical Defence (OSOAVIAKHIM) which played an important role in training people in military sports. Founded in 1927 by amalgamation of 4 previously existing organisations, it had 2,950,000 members. By 1932 it was said to enrol 20 million. After World War Two it was replaced by 3 new organisations which were then re-united in the Voluntary Society for Assistance to the Army, Air Force, and Navy (DOSAAF). No figures for membership of this organisation are currently available (Kolkowicz, p. 52, cf. 55).

Figures for service in the PLA, which includes an air and naval arm, are given by Griffith as 2.3 million in 1967 (Griffith, p. 219). Detailed tables for the anti-Japanese War period (1937-45), the third civil war, (1946-50), and the early post-Liberation period (1950-58) are given by Gittings (Gittings, pp. 303-5). These show a possible total of more than 5 million involved either as regulars or guerrillas during the 1946-50 period, and a regular strength of 2.5 million in 1958. The figure for total recruitment during 1950-58 was in the order of 4.5 million, while about 6.8 million were demobilised in the same period.

Conscription was introduced in China in 1955 and may account for three fifths of the PLA since 1958 (Gittings, p. 149). The potential conscripts greatly outnumber those required so the process is highly select-ive. Those not called for service are placed in the reserve and are liable either within 5 years of registration, or during a national emergency. Terms of service in years are shown in Table 7.3.

Table 7.3

		1955	1965
Army:	Infantry	3	4
	Special Arms	3	5
	Public Security Forces	3	5
Air Force:		4	5
Navy:	Shore Arms	5	5
	Fleet	5	6

Source: Gittings, p. 150.

Any consideration of the skills learnt while serving requires a know-ledge of the arming, training, and the way in which personnel are dis-tributed among the different branches of the services. Here it must suf-fice to note that both the Soviet and Chinese armed forces have grad-uated from relatively simply armed infantry forces to a modern force armed with rockets and nuclear weapons. The PLA is relatively less well equipped in the field of naval and air equipment, and it is probable that a smaller proportion of its forces receive a high degree of technical train-ing than is the case in the USSR.

Another important consideration in attempting to judge what a person learns during army service, whether in the socialisation sense or the intentional, educational sense, is whether such service is active, or takes place during conditions of peace. Both the Soviet Red Army and the PLA in China were born in the flames of war, in both cases, though significantly differently, in war against foreign powers which subsequently turned into civil war. The Soviet army then went through 19 years of peace, which was broken in Finland in the west and Khalkhin-Gol in the east in 1939. The bitter years of World War Two followed the German invasion of 21 June 1941, ending with their surrender on 9 May 1945, seven days after the Soviet army won the battle for Berlin.

The PLA had hardly time to recover from the unexpectedly quick end to the civil war when they were drawn into the conflict in Korea. Going officially as the Chinese People's Volunteers, some 180,000 men crossed the Yalu in October 1950, to be followed by reinforcements which brought the total up to about 700,000 in the summer of 1951 (Gittings, pp. 75-9). This war may have cost 300,000 Chinese lives before it ended in 1953. The only other military excursion outside the borders of what all Chinese, KMT or communist, consider to be China, was the brief campaign against India in October 1962 (see Neville Maxwell, *India's China War*). In neither case were Chinese troops faced with the conflict of material cultures which Russian troops experienced in their long march to Berlin (see e.g. Kolkowicz, pp. 69-70). But the superior weapons the Volunteers met in Korea, and a morale different both from previous experience, and probably from that predicted by political propaganda, must have created problems (Griffith, p. 165).

The Party Commands the Gun

This principle, put in these words by Mao Ze-dong in 1938 (Mao, *Quotations*, p. 102) was observed from the first days of the Russian revolution. The Russian leaders, looking over their shoulders at the great French Revolution, were very conscious of the threat of Bonapartism, and also knew that many of the militarily competent they were forced to employ were no communists. They therefore developed a method already begun under the Kerensky government of attaching political commissars to the army, a measure which from the first led to controversy about dual authority. Kolkowicz points out that the Russian system of Party control is a complex of socio-economic privilege for the officers, 'indoctrination and supervision', and 'intimidation and coercion' (Kolkowicz, pp. 28-30). The first and last are in conflict with the content of the second, which is one factor making for the widespread opposition to political classes during the more recent decades. In both the USSR and China there have been problems over the relative duties of political and military leaders within the army, with attempts to combine the two. (See Zhukov, p. 92; in the winter of 1926 he combined the duties of commissar and military commander of the 7th Cavalry Division.) There have also been conflicts over the time devoted to political rather than military training, and the practice has varied from time to time (see e.g. Gittings, pp. 145-8).

The similar organisational structure of the Party within the military establishment is brought out by the two diagrams below (Kolkowicz, p. 376 and Gittings, p. 306). Kolkowicz sums up the duties of the regimental *zampolit* (political deputy) as follows:

> participation in all military planning and training as well as in political education; organization and direction of all political work in the unit;

personal conduct of educational activities of personnel; responsibility for the work of the Party organization, which he organizes together with the Party *biuro*; control of all activity coming under the heading of 'socialist competition'. (Summarised from Kolkowicz, p. 377)

He is subordinate to the regimental commander, and in matters of Party-political work to the political section of the higher unit (*soedinenie*), but he is directly above personnel. Peltier notes that Political Assistants—here in the navy—are capable of exerting considerable influence in a ship because men have direct access to them, by-passing the usual hierarchy (Saunders, p. 127). The duties of the political officer in the PLA at the time of the Korean War, as elucidated by interrogation of prisoners of war, are given by Griffiths as:

1. Investigation of the loyalty, efficiency, and thought of all individuals in the unit; 2. propaganda; 3. political education; 4. Supervision of administration (personnel; logistics); 5. Organization of Party members; 6. Supervision of all Party activities; 7. Approval of promotion, transfer, and demotion of all enlisted men. (Griffiths, p. 261)

An interesting, idealised, account of the work of a political instructor is given in the recent novel, *The Song of Ouyang Hai* (especially ch. 12).

In both the Soviet forces and the PLA a broad range of educational activities are carried on. In the early years of the Soviet Union, and still in China, classes in literacy were provided. Col. Evans Carlson, a US military observer, described how the Chinese Red Army learnt on the march:

When units are on the march lesson papers are pinned to the back of the cap of the man ahead so that the soldier may study as he walks. (Griffith, p. 65)

Zhukov recalls:

Everyone in the army had an overwhelming desire to study and master his subject well. . . . This was a result of the extensive work done by the Party to raise the general cultural level of the Red Army men as well as a result of the far-flung educational system . . . By 1937 illiteracy in the Red Army was wiped out completely. (Zhukov, p. 141)

Figure 7.1 Party Controls in the Soviet Military Establishment

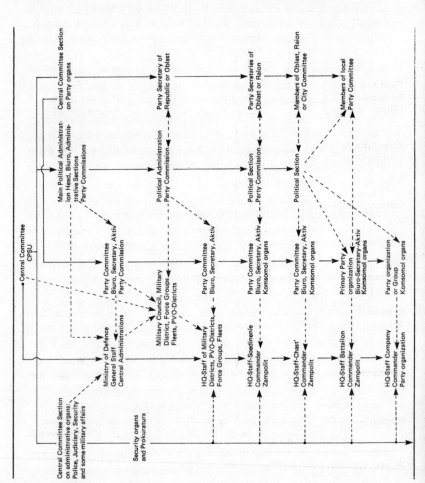

Source: Kolkowicz, 1967, p. 376.

Figure 7.2. Political Control Structure of the PLA

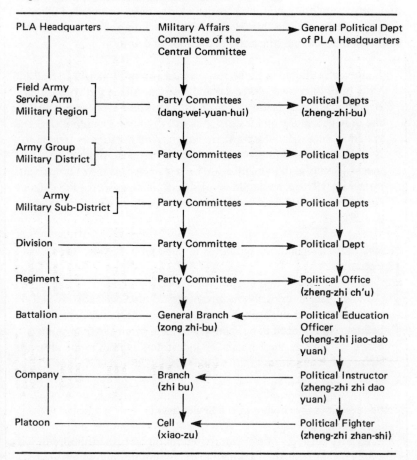

Source: Gittings, 1967, p. 306.

He goes on to describe the system of Red Army clubs, radio relay centres, film projection units, and the libraries whose collection totalled 25 million volumes in the late thirties. The Webbs, writing about the same period, title their section 'the army as a school' and write:

> If any men still join as illiterates, they are promptly taught to read and write both their own vernacular and Russian. All are put through an educational course lasting throughout their whole service, in which not only geography and history, but also economics and 'political grammar' (naturally Marxism) are imparted by instructors trained to be both simple and interesting in their expositions. All men are taught to sing, and, as many as desire it, to play one or other musical instrument. There are a number of special newspapers for the defence forces with an aggregate circulation of a quarter of a million. (Webb, p. 126)

A Soviet official handbook published in 1960 set as the aim of political education:

> ... to explain thoroughly the advantages of the Soviet society and state system over the capitalistic system; to indicate the successes in building communism in our country ... and to inculcate in soldiers a love for their motherland and an indestructible faith in the ultimate victory of communism in the whole world. (Quoted in Kolkowicz, p. 93)

Peltier describes the process in the Soviet navy:

> ... chatty get-togethers or lectures either on matters of theory or upon current affairs ... are held in the 'Lenin Rooms' which are to be found both aboard ship and in stations ashore. In this way the Political Assistants work round to expositions of Marx-Leninist principles, which vary in complexity according to the audience; perhaps they explain to the men the reason for some disciplinary action meted out during an exercise; or clarify to them, still in the light of Marx-Leninism, the official motives behind the adoption by the Soviet Union of such and such a position in the world, or its attitude in the face of international problems. (Saunders, p. 126)

A programme for senior officers of the PLA put out by the General Political Department in January 1956 included the study of the history of the Chinese Communist Party, the history of the Soviet Communist Party, political economy, dialectical materialism, and the party constitution (Gittings, p. 168).

A feature of both Soviet and Chinese forces has been sessions for *criticism and self-criticism.* These have varied in scope and importance over time, and for the USSR there is evidence that many officers resented them (Kolkowicz, pp. 132-3, 146-7, 158-60). In the PLA meetings were held before and after battles in the civil wars and in Korea (Griffith, pp. 261-2).

In addition to all this activity the forces of both countries operate a number of schools which concentrate on purely military training. Zhukov describes the situation in 1937. There were 75 military schools enrolling youth with at least 7 years of schooling. There were 13 military academies, one military college, and 5 military departments at schools of higher learning (Zhukov, p. 142). De Witt gives 22 tertiary military academies for the late fifties, comprising 8 for Command Staff and Political Officers, 10 engineering establishments, and 4 medical and veterinary colleges (Science Policy in the USSR, para. 717). In China the military schools are headed by the PLA General Staff and War College in Nanjing, and include aviation, artillery, armoured and naval schools.

The Army for Labour

In 1943 Mao Ze-dong wrote:

> We have an army for fighting as well as an army for labour. For fighting we have the 8th Route and New 4th Armies; but even they do a dual job, warfare and production. (Mao, *Quotat ons*, p. 101)

It is common enough for all armies to include some forms of production among their activities. Army engineers construct roads and bridges, signals troops construct often elaborate communications systems, and other soldiers service equipment. In the special conditions of pre-Liberation China poverty and the political need to prove they were different from the ravaging warlord armies which had scourged the peasant drove the Red Armies to produce—food, clothing, and arms. This tradition has been maintained to an extent in the post-Liberation period. In Xinjiang a majority of the state farms were started by the PLA, which pioneered modern farming methods there (Gittings, p. 177). While the majority of labour went on helping agriculture, both for its own consumption (a British delegation reporting in the *Observer* supplement for 7 November 1971 gave a figure of four-fifths of its own food) and

328   *The Collective as Educator*

for the civilian market, the PLA also built factories, laid railways, roads, collected scrap metal, and built ships (Gittings, pp. 176-85; *China Pictorial*, 1971, 5, pp. 36-45; 1971, 9, p. 44; 1972, 8, pp. 1-11).

The Soviet armed forces, with their different origin, have probably devoted less activity to production, though this is difficult to assess. In 1920, during the period of 'war communism', 'units of the Red Army, released from the front, were turned on to the economic front instead of being demobilised, to deal with the fuel and transport crisis . . .' (Dobb, p. 119). In the same year Zhukov recalls:

. . . the poorer Cossack and Red Army men's families were aided in every way possible. This was very important for the Red Army's prestige, since before it took over, the White troops had oppressed the poor, often robbing them of their last loaf of bread and humiliating them in every way (cf. China).

I remember the regimental commissar coming to our squadron one evening and suggesting we should work for a few days repairing houses, barns and farm implements for the families of Red Army men and poor families in general. We were all enthusiastic.

Our commissar undertook the hardest job—cleaning the public well which the White troops had filled with garbage. (Zhukov, p. 63).

The only other non-military activity which Zhukov recalls is the giving of political lectures in factories and offices by members of the Party cell in 1930 when Zhukov was Assistant Cavalry Inspector in Moscow. (Zhukov, p. 106).

Kolkowicz, in a memorandum prepared for the Rand Corporation in 1962, gives an account of productive work performed by the Soviet army in the late fifties. The work included agriculture, assistance in repairing equipment and training peasants to use it, and 'miscellaneous work' such as the collection of scrap metal. Kolkowicz attributes the renewed emphasis on such work to a shortage of labour, and to the desire of the Party to strengthen its hold over the military, and he describes the shift in stress back to military duties and 'concern about the soldiers, their food, rest and cultural services' (Kommunist Vooruzhennykh Sil, no. 14, 1962, Kolkowicz, p. 37) which occurred about 1962. Gittings describes similar differences of opinion in the PLA over productive, political and military activities.

The Role of the Demobilised

In the early years of the USSR and still in China today the demobilised soldier is often the bearer of skills learnt in the army to some branch of civilian production where they are in short supply. At one level it is a 'PLA spirit' of alertness, confidence and integrity—in strong contrast to the general morale of the just-collapsed KMT bureaucracy which the PLA were sent to strengthen. A Soviet journal of 1928 wrote:

> Absorbing into itself the mass of raw young peasants, the Red Army every year gives them back to the countryside politically and culturally transformed . . . Demobilized Red Army men are often the most active element in rural social life. (Carr, 1971, pp. 333-4)

In the last decade in the USSR, with a well-developed school system providing the required industrial cadre, the demobilised soldiers, particularly the officers, have not found their prospects attractive. Kolkowicz probably does not exaggerate when he writes:

> As civilians, they now faced a bleak future, in which it would be difficult for them to earn a livelihood and support their families in an environment that had no need for their craft and did not encourage their way of life. Demobilization thus meant *demotion from a privileged social group to the lowest class of workers.* (Kolkowicz, pp. 153-4, emphasis added)

Conclusion

In evaluating the educational-socialising role of the military one must distinguish its effect on the service personnel themselves, their relatives, and the wider public. It is also necessary to distinguish between what is consciously taught and what has come to be called 'the hidden curriculum'. The real difficulties begin with any attempt to assess to what extent military values are internalised in these groups, and to what extent they are passively ignored or even rebelled against. As has been noted in other connections, education must be regarded as a highly personal, peculiar and particular process, and no two individuals can experience the same event, i.e. in exactly the same way.

The preceding description of Soviet and Chinese armies is an attempt to provide a framework within which these questions can be considered, and to point in directions the investigation should take. One difficulty is that writers on the military have other interests and do not always provide the help they might. They are concerned with such problems as possible conflict of Party and military, with power struggles between different arms, or with military efficiency. Matter relevant to education usually only occurs in such frameworks. Where information of direct interest is given the context may be insufficient for evaluation (Parry, p. 131).

The question for the marxism explicated here is, of course, to what extent the armed forces in the USSR and China assist or hinder the development of self-conscious, self-determining, free men. Or do they rather reinforce an authoritarian, hierarchical and alienated society? Looking at the Soviet army with its rigid formal discipline and its privileged officer caste one has few hesitations in giving the latter answer. With the Chinese PLA the answer is more difficult to determine. In its Maoist model there seems hope that a more human army is being created. But as long as armies are necessary real freedom is impossible and it is doubtful whether military discipline can ever be truly free.

The criterion of treating other people 'as persons' in the sense in which Marx used this phrase, presents difficulties bordering on the impossible for any armed forces. Granted, armies have traditionally valued comradeship, but they have limited its application drastically within ranks, and they have of necessity cultivated hostility, not to say misunderstanding, of the enemy. One might even argue that modern war, with long-range weapons and policies of saturation bombing of civilian populations by forces distanced from possible retaliation is more dehumanising than hand-to-hand combat. But in the end all war, however necessary a marxist might recognise it to be, is to a degree dehumanising.

In an under-developed country the possibilities for the army to play a positive educational role are much higher than in an industrial country with a highly developed school system. Engaging in all kinds of labour, with or separate from the civilian population, it trains itself in wanted skills and shows the civilians that the army is their friend. As the economy develops, the required tasks become more specialised and only certain sections of the army are sufficiently trained to carry them out. Nor is there the same need to use cheap and disciplined labour which can be directed at will. More importantly, the skills necessary for society are being taught in other institutions, and the wealth of society allows young people to travel freely without having to 'join the army/navy to see the world'. The educational role of the army in an industrialised society shrinks more and more to the narrowly military-political sphere, and the possible conflict of interest between the military and civilian spheres becomes more important (see recent Soviet military leaders' complaints that Soviet youth is becoming too pacifist—Kolkowicz, p.

318).

Turning back to the wider question of the collective and the marxist vision of dealienated man, one can only restate the point made by Marx in the 1844 Manuscripts: 'what is to be avoided above all is the re-establishment of "society" as an abstraction *vis-à-vis* the individual' (Marx, 1959, p. 104). Dealienated man would understand the groups which he chose to belong to and would ensure that they served to support and encourage the full and varied flowering of the human spirit. Collectives like some of those discussed in this chapter would be rejected for the manner in which they crush and constrain the individual within narrow, uniform limits. They would be rejected because it would be understood that appearance differed from essence: that the ostensible aims and purposes were contradicted by the 'hidden curriculum' of the group. A utopian dream? Perhaps, but one which serves as a challenge and a measure for the critical consciousness.

8 EDUCATION AND THE SOCIAL-POLITICAL REALITY

This chapter is a reiteration and an extension of a theme which has been running through this book, that reality speaks louder than rhetotic, and that explicit teaching must be congruent with implicit learning if education is to be successful. Educators are apt to forget this and concern themselves with aims or the content of what is taught rather than the more difficult problem of what is learnt. It would be simplistic to attribute this to their vested interest in the extension of schooling. Nor should one forget that with the spectacular failure of mass secondary schooling in the rich urban areas of the metropolitan countries many educators have been forced to ask fundamental questions (among them Reimer, Illich, Holt, Goodman, and perhaps the closest to the marxism explicated here, Friere). The marxist criterion of educational success being the self-conscious, self-determining man, the question is to what extent experience of the social-political reality encourages the development of such a man and to what extent it frustrates it. To what extent does reality produce open, questioning minds interested in a wide variety of subjects, and to what extent does it foster closed, incurious minds shut into the confines of parochial conservatism? To what extent does it reinforce the ruling ideology and to what extent does it suggest contrary ideas? Does it foster co-operation or competition? Some aspects of this problematic have been studied by non-marxist scholars under the rubric of *political culture*, or *political socialisation,* though so far rather little has been done on either the USSR or China. (J.W. Lewis has a chapter on China in J.S. Coleman, *Education and Political Development*; Myrdal, 1963; Lifton, 1967; Barnett, 1967; Solomon, 1971; and the Harvard Project, reported variously by Inkeles and Bauer, are all relevant.)

Political culture has been variously defined. For Roy Macridis it is 'the commonly shared goals and commonly accepted rules'; for Samuel Beer it is 'values, beliefs, and emotional attitudes about *how* government ought to be conducted and about *what* it should do'; while for Dennis Kavanagh it is 'the emotional and attitudinal environment within which the political system operates' (Kavanagh, p. 10). Sidney Verba gives a definition which is even more pertinent to our present purpose:

As we use the term 'political culture' it refers to the system of beliefs about patterns of political interaction and political institutions. It refers not to what is happening in the world of politics, but what people believe about these happenings. And these beliefs can be of several kinds: they can be empirical beliefs about what the actual state of political life is; they can be beliefs as to the goals or values that ought to be pursued in political life; and these beliefs may have an important expressive or emotional dimension. (Pye and Verba, p. 516)

Some aspects of this question have already been discussed in relation to the family, schools, youth organisations, the army, and work in the economy. This chapter will consider briefly other important agents of political education whose implicit teaching requires elucidation. The Communist Party has so far only been considered as an explicit educator. Also important are the State legislative organs, the Soviets in the USSR and People's (Revolutionary) Congresses in China; the State bureaucracies of ministries, local departments and other agencies; agents of the law and Public Security; and the trade unions and other mass organisations. All that will be attempted is to point to some aspects of these various agents which appear to be influential, and to the kinds of evidence which is available on which judgement might be based. Student self-government will be briefly discussed as an early experience of political realities and evidence touching on the question of class differences cited in order to show the kinds of evidence and the problems it presents.

Self-consciousness and self-determination in the sense used in this book requires that people become issue-oriented rather than allegiance-oriented. They must act in accordance with understanding of their situation and interests, rather than from loyalty to kin or charismatic leader. It would seem that at present the lesson which group-membership teaches, whether the family, the army, or the Communist Party, is the value of allegiances. Loyalty to persons would seem to be more important for many if not most, and to override loyalty to principle. Or rather, loyalty to persons is the major principle recognised. This certainly seems to be the case in traditional China. (Robert Thaxton is a useful start to reading on this question.) What educators need to know is the relation between issues and allegiances in particular societies and instances, and what are the factors making for changes in behaviour from allegiance-orientation to issue-orientation.

Turning to possible lessons taught by the realities of the Communist Party, the State and mass political institutions, it is necessary to consider separately their effect on those who experience them from the outside. Concerning the first group, important questions are who and how many persons participate, for how long and what interchange there is between them and what might be called 'the general public'. To what extent does the experience of being a Party member or a deputy to the Supreme Soviet or People's Congress set one apart and inculcate ideas of a 'new class'? The answer to the last question must depend on precisely what members of these institutions *do*, just what is their working *style*. Studies to date, with quite a different perspective supply some of the evidence, but are usually far too general for more than provisional hypotheses to be made. There are also insufficient comparative studies of the USSR and China.

Membership in the ruling Communist Party, while it has risen substantially in both countries since the acquisition of power, remains a small percentage of the population consistent with its elite theory. The Bolsheviks were only some 24,000 in March 1917, 'a small and relatively insignificant conspiratorial party' as Merle Fainsod describes them (Treadgold, p. 69). By the end of that year they reached some 115,000, or perhaps about 0.8 per cent of the whole population (*c.* 150m). By the middle of the seventies the number of Party members stood at 14m, a figure representing 5.7 per cent of the whole population or some 7.5 of the adult one (Lane, p. 133). In China, as Fainsod notes, the Party of 4.5m in 1949 was of a different quality since the Chinese Communist Party had by then already governed a substantial population and territory in the course of the long civil war. Rising to a figure of more than 20m members by the seventies, the percentage of the total population changed from about 0.8 per cent to something in the order of 3.0 per cent. However, these global figures tell little and the difference by level within the Party hierarchies, by occupation and various other categories need to be studied. (For the USSR see Lane, pp. 132-42 who quotes Rigby; for China see Schurmann, pp. 128-39). Lindbeck notes that in China 'a very sharp distinction exists between the party mandarinate and ordinary members' (Treadgold, p. 96) and puts the distinction between members at and above county (*xian*) level and those below. He refers to the speech of Deng Xiao-ping at the Eighth National Congress of the CCP in 1956 who said:

> if we make strict demands on every rank-and-file Party member, we
> need to make still more strict demands on the Party cadres. Since the
> key functionaries in the Party organisations at all levels enjoy greater
> confidence from the Party and the people, then obviously they have

a greater responsibility to the Party and the people than the rank-and-file members. (Teng Hsiao-p'ing, *Eighth National Congress–Documents*, 1, p. 220)

Deng gave a figure of 300,000 such key members which Lindbeck extrapolates to 500,000 for 1962. Significantly, Deng spoke of training such cadres 'to master production technique and various branches of professional knowledge' (ibid. p. 221). Coupled with the greater responsibility there is the greater exposure, the greater danger of being held responsible for failures. In the USSR, especially in the thirties through to the fifties, this danger was strikingly severe and thousands of Party officials suffered the labour camps, torture and death. In China Mao's policy of 'curing the sickness to save the patient' (Mao, 1966, p. 262) has reduced the suffering, though struggle meetings and self-criticism, and the threat of reform through labour (*laodong gaizao*) are there. Leaving out 'greater social and political security', Lindbeck was right in saying that

> both the party member and his non-party associates are aware . . . that party membership confers real advantages–inside knowledge through party sources and meetings, influence with local or higher decision-makers, better opportunities for superior positions and rewards, greater ability and opportunity to injure or assist others . . . (Treadgold, pp. 103-4)

Applicable to both Communist Parties, the question for educators is how these advantages are used and what effect this has on both members and non-members.

Membership in the state legislative organs, the various Soviets and People's Congresses, is large but to an extent overlaps with Communist Party membership, particularly at the higher levels. Townsend gives the number of basic-level deputies in China in 1958 as 4.5m (p. 106). In the USSR the comparable figure for 1965 was just over 2.0m (Lane, p. 154). While the following summary states the limitations it is the positive actions and life-style of the deputies which shapes the consciousness of actor and audience.

> Basic-level congresses are not intended to function as decision-making bodies. They have the right to discuss certain subjects and pass resolutions, but all of their actions are, in effect, subject to review by higher-level authorities. . . Topics to be considered are normally det-

ermined in advance and meetings are filled with ritualistic speeches
and reports. Although deputies may, on rare occasions, raise questions on their own initiative, they cannot offer any comments or proposals that conflict with central policies. (Townsend, p. 114)

Deputies, or more correctly, representatives, function to solicit opinions
from their constituents (Townsend, p. 112), and 'to carry out political
communication between government and Soviet citizen' (Lane, p. 157).
At the same time, particularly members of the higher bodies take up
grievances or further particular interests of their constituent members
and organisations (Lane, p. 157).

One aspect of our problematic about which there is information is
the manner in which cadres are selected and also what (for China)
Oksenberg calls their 'exit pattern' from office. Numerous writers have
commented on the importance of Party control over appointments
through the state bureaucracy, the economy and the major cultural
organisations. (For the USSR see Lane's description of the system of
nomenklatura, pp. 219-24. Barnett describes personnel management in
China, 1967, pp. 48-63. There, Schurmann comments: 'The Chinese
communists have always been opposed to the idea that anyone except
the Party should have control over personnel questions', p. 344. Useful
detail is to be found in articles by Oksenberg and Kau in Barnett, 1969.)
The lack of an exit path other than death or disgrace and dismissal for
those on the higher rungs of the ladder has guaranteed rule by the aged
which, for other reasons, has not been unknown elsewhere. But this rule
of 'once a cadre, always a cadre' hardly makes for participatory democracy and the learning of government by the ordinary workers who in
communist party mythology are supposed to form the ruling class. (Mao,
at a work conference attended by 7,000 cadres in January 1962, said:
'Why should a person only go up and never down?' He should have gone
further and advocated periods as ordinary workers, rather than simply
recommending that 'cadres at all levels must participate in collective
labour' while remaining cadres, as the 1975 State Constitution does—
article 11. cf. Schram, 1974, pp. 160-61.)

While the educational effect on and of these cadres and bureaucrats
is partly determined by their small number and length of service which
serves to cut them off from the majority of working people it depends
perhaps even more on their working style. Described in party materials
as either democratic centralism or the mass line, it is the reality of this
rather than the theory which is important here. Hough has shown in his
study of the role of local Party organs in industrial decision-making how

in the USSR this has come to be a modified form of what Barrington Moore called a rational-technical society. What is significant for marxist education is not the absence of strict conformity with rules and laws (Hough, p. 282), or the persistence of political over technical considerations (Hough, pp. 283-4), but rather the central assumptions of technological rationality to which Mandel refers (1975, pp. 500-22) and which I described earlier. The USSR has evolved, and many in China would also ascribe to this model in which government is performed by professionals, the 'brains', while the majority of the people perform the work of, albeit willing, 'hands'. (Professional is used here in the sense defined by Brugger: 'as not only someone who knows his job and is committed to its values but a person who also evaluates the *rest of society* according to the values of his job. The professional defines a layman in pejorative terms as one who lacks those values to which he the professional is committed.' Brugger, 1973, p. 27.) Such a society seems doomed to produce apathy if not outright hostility and disruption on the part of the 'hands', though an alternative reaction is a retreat into 'familial intimacy and consumerism' as discussed by John Alt. (Expression of a variety of responses can be seen in the official press—cf. Parry, or Meek—in the underground publications, *samizdat*, e.g. Reddaway, 1972, and in comments by expatriate Russians, cf. Inkeles and Bauer, pp. 324-32. Chinese materials are similarly full of examples of attitudes which the party is trying to overcome.)

Student Self-government

The system known as pupil or student self-government (*samoupravleniye*) in the USSR is for many children their first experience of 'political' organisation. The term used suggests the microcosmic nature of the system and the literature stresses the shaping influence on behaviour of importance in later life. (The topic is discussed at length in Soviet materials. See *Pedagogicheskaya Entsiklopediya*, vol. 3, pp. 788-91; Kairov, ch. 13, especially pp. 318-20; and Shchukina, ch. 14, especially p. 360. I know of no comparable Chinese discussions of the concept, which is translated *ertong zizhi*.)

Krupskaya commented repeatedly on the topic. She returned again and again to a few simple principles: self-government should relate to the child's life and interests (vol. 3, pp. 32-3, 40); the form should arise out of the tasks (ibid. p. 40); teachers should lead, but not dominate (ibid. pp. 59-60); the aim should be the learning of organisational habits (ibid. p. 56) in order to live and work wisely (ibid. p. 332). Referring frequently to the role of the youth organisations in self-government,

Krupskaya saw them as necessary aids in its development, but objected
to their dictating (ibid. p. 175). She also contrasted the soviet way to
that of 'the bourgeois', commenting in one place that with the latter
the head directs while the masses only serve (ibid. p. 465). For her the
emphasis was on learning to live co-operatively and for this she believed
that all should practise the roles of both leader and led.

Woody, writing in 1932, quotes two Soviet authors who put the
aims of student self-government in a critique of 'bourgeois' forms which
has a strangely contemporary ring:

> The aim which the bourgeoisie put before their schools, is to make
> an obedient citizen who has no wish to make basic changes in the
> existing structure. This aim defines the content of the work and the
> internal structure of the school. Self-government serves the same end.
> [Bourgeois] self-government . . . has the aim of eliminating the
> struggle between the teacher and the class, to raise the authority of
> the teacher . . . the teacher is the unlimited ruler . . . in countries
> where the bourgeois-democratic republic has become deeply rooted
> . . . another type of self-government is introduced . . . with all its
> attributes: elections, courts, even prisons . . . and then pupils . . .
> are allowed a certain amount of freedom within the framework of
> this constitution. Such a type of self-government has the aim of rear-
> ing 'citizens' of a bourgeois republic, serving it most conscientiously.
> (Lvov and Sirotkin, *Self-organization of School Children*, pp. 21-2, in
> Woody, p. 170)

The influential textbook, *Pedagogy*, edited by I.A. Kairov and others
in 1956 devotes a long chapter to 'The student collective in the school'.
Leadership, organisation, discipline and communist organisation are the
organising concepts and self-government appears only in the description
of the work of the Students' Committee (*Uchenicheskii komitet*), the
Pioneers and the Komsomol. Throughout the aim of inculcating habits
of organisation is stressed. Major attention is given to the work of the
Pioneers and Komsomol and it is clear that the Students' Committee is
subordinate to these. Organs of the 'student collective' mentioned
include the editorial committee of the wall newspaper, the sanitary
(hygiene) committee, and the school radio committee (for internal
broadcasting). Shchukina, following much the same argument, does
employ the term children's self-government in the course of her exposition.

While what we are considering here is student self-government it is relevant to note that only rarely have student representatives been included on the School Councils which administer the schools (see Nearing, p. 112; Shapovalenko, p. 397; Kessen, p. 10). The Regulations on Children's Self-government laid down by Narkompros in 1932 made the position quite plain:

> The School Director or Head is responsible to the Education Authority for the condition of work. He should direct the Children's Self-Government so that it participates in school work, helps in the development of children's initiative and activities. Teachers must be attached to all self-government organizations for practical help. They are responsible to the administration for the conditions of the work, but they must not destroy the children's initiative by their authority. (King, 1937, p. 99)

The 1959 Statutes on the Eight-year and Secondary Schools had similar directions (Shapovalenko, pp. 399, 410).

Woody gives one of the fullest descriptions of the way in which student self-government has worked in Soviet schools. He found usually four 'commissions' working under the students' council: economic; sanitary; reports; and cultural. The first of these dealt with problems of furnishing, feeding, production where it occurred, and was specially important in boarding schools where it was responsible for student welfare (Woody, pp. 193-6). The sanitary commission was responsible for hygiene, then often at the level where children were inspected daily to see whether hands, necks and ears were dirty (cf. picture in Kesson, p. 114). Often the commission moved out of the school to tackle problems at the village level (ibid. pp. 184-5). The cultural commission was probably the most spectacular, organising study circles, dramatics, choirs, the teaching of illiterates (done by children in the 12-14 age group) and the school wall-newspaper (ibid. pp. 185-93). The reports commission was responsible for keeping a record of the activities of the school and its personnel (ibid. pp. 196-9).

For China Myrdal, reporting on the school at Liu Lin, makes no mention of a students' council, but describes class leaders whose job it was to 'help the teacher maintain order . . . help organise the pupils when on excursions and that sort of thing' (p. 379). Classes also elected officers to organise study, and to help organise the domestic economy of the school (cleaning, gardening, etc.). Kessen's description for primary schools is similar (pp. 131-2). For secondary schools Kessen's outline (p. 167) is amplified by that of former Red Guard, Dai Xiao-ai. His description shows how many of those taking part were conscious of training for future leadership in state or party bureaucracies. Dai describes how all students at the school automatically belonged to the student association (*xuesheng hui*) and during the first few days of the school year elected, by secret ballot, the committee for the year. Nominees were proposed by the outgoing committee and approved by the Party Committee. The committee included a chairman, two vice-chairmen and five members. The last shared responsibility for study, labour, physical education, culture and recreation, and student life. Dai was himself the study member. He had three main jobs:

> First, I had to find out what students thought about their curriculum and their teachers. Second, I had to keep tabs on students who were in academic difficulty. Finally, I was in charge of the school's wall newspaper. (Bennett and Montaperto, p. 11)

Student committee members kept in close touch with the officers elected by the school classes. Attempting to evaluate the system, Dai comments:

> I suppose one could say that the class officers were agents of information and that we Student Association officers received that information, evaluated it, and took such action as we deemed necessary. If a matter was serious, we reported it to the administrative department concerned and worked out a plan of remedial action which drew in the department head, ourselves, the class, and the small-group leaders. Less serious things were simply referred back to the class for action with the appropriate executive officer taking responsibility to see that the problem in question was solved. (ibid. p. 14)

Dai complained of two weaknesses. The leaders of the small groups were too close to their members and therefore 'could not evaluate problems objectively', and this resulted in strained relations. The other complaint was the familiar one of 'excessive demands upon our time'. Dai's summing up is significant:

> On balance, it must be said that the student organisations had no real power. But we could and did exert influence by virtue of our administrative responsibilities. The Party committee would always back us up because, in effect, *we were simply administering their decisions*. They had to support us. As a result, our position was really something special. The absence of real power didn't bother us that much anyway.

We were young and all of us recognised that we needed training in
the techniques and principles of collective leadership. We thought of
the student organisations as a training ground. Personally, I was glad
to have the chance to develop my skills.(ibid. p. 15, emphasis added)

It would seem to be clear from all this that *'self*-government' is a mis-
nomer and that this institution probably plays a negative role so far as
the marxist aim of self-determination is concerned. However, a more
detailed examination of it might reveal the contradiction between being
a 'transmission belt' for adult initiatives and an organiser and inspirer of
initiatives in the young which is typical of most youth organisations
throughout the world.

The Problem of Evidence

Because of the complexity of the situation, including the fact that
human beings react differently to the same situation, it is difficult to
get beyond speculation, but that is an advance on the position of many
educators who ignore the process of socialisation altogether. Evidence
available includes reportage in newspapers and journals; fiction and
biography; accounts by former citizens now living abroad; accounts by
official visitors and tourists; and for the USSR the findings of sociological studies made during the past two decades. Since, except for
some of the last, the information supplied by these sources has been
reported for quite other purposes it is often insufficient and quite
difficult to relate to our problem. There are also considerable difficulties
with quantification. Examples of the attitudes which are pertinent are
often quoted by official sources as examples of attitudes which are
those of a minority, or which have been eradicated. They are seldom if
ever expressed directly by the persons holding the attitude. Examples of
this kind are frequent in the Chinese press, e.g. in the education debate
unspecified numbers of people are said to favour 'going to the countryside to become gold-plated', or to send their children to school 'in order
to become an official'. Here the traditional stylised, symbolic mode of
expression presents another barrier. I shall take two classes of evidence
to show some of the possibilities and problems. They relate to a question which has recurred through the book: the persistence of social classes
in the USSR.

The first evidence concerns attitudes to different kinds of occupation.
Table 8.1 from Inkeles and Bauer is based on the Harvard Project which
questioned some 3,000 Soviet refugees in 1950-51 (p. 77).

Table 8.1

	In the Soviet Union		In the United States	
Occupation	Rating	Occupation		Rating
Doctor	75	Physician		91
Scientific worker	73	Scientist		86
Engineer	73	Civil engineer		80
Factory manager	65	Member of corporation board		82
[Foreman]	[65] [a]	_____		
Accountant	62	Accountant for a large business		77
Armed forces officer	58	Captain in regular army		76
Teacher	58	Teacher		73
Rank-and-file worker	48	Machine operator in factory		51
[Brigade leader (farm)]	[46]	_____		
[Party secretary]	[41]	_____		
[Collective farm chairman]	[38]	[Farm owner and operator]		[71]
Collective farmer	18	Farm hand		38
Median number of respondents	1989			2900

a. Occupations in brackets are ones for which there are either no comparable data or no comparable occupations in both countries.

It is interesting to compare these findings with surveys conducted within the USSR a decade later. In one of these Leningrad youth were asked to rank forty occupations according to their estimates of creativity. The rankings by the sons and daughters of industrial workers were as shown below.

Numerous studies testify to the low esteem in which village life and work continues to be held. I.T. Levikin describes the investigations of sociologists of the Orlov Pedagogical Institute in an article entitled: 'The life plans of village youth' (Yadova, pp. 116-32). Between 22-40 per cent of respondents, depending on age, sex and whether working in a kolkhoz or sovkhoz, declared they did not like working in the countryside. When asked: 'Where do you reckon it is better for your children to live?', the answers are shown in Table 8.2.

Table 8.2. Occupation Rankings

Boys	Girls
1. Research physicist	1. Research physicist
2. Radiotechnics engineer	2. Worker in literature and the arts

Boys	Girls
3. Worker in literature and the arts	3. Doctor (medical)
4. Radio engineer	4. Medical research worker
5. Ship builder	5. VUZ teacher
6. Doctor (medical)	6. Youth leader
7. Machine construction engineer	7. Chemical engineer
8. Construction engineer	8. Construction engineer
9. Research mathematician	9. Radio engineer
10. Medical research worker	10. Research geologist
11. Pilot	11. Research mathematician
12. VUZ teacher	12. Radiotechnics engineer
13. Chemical engineer	13. Secondary school teacher
14. Automatic machine repairer	14. Pilot
15. Research geologist	15. Machine construction engineer
16. Turner	16. Metallurgical engineer
17. Tailor, seamstress	17. Philosopher
18. Metallurgical engineer	18. Tailor, seamstress
19. Mechanic, operator	19. Philologist
20. Secondary school teacher	20. Agronomist
21. Fitter, mechanic	21. Cultural-education worker
22. (Automobile) driver	22. Ship builder
23. Culture-education worker	23. Cook, waiter
24. Steelworker	24. Turner
25. Automatic machine operator	25. Chemical worker
26. Philosopher	26. Animal husbandry worker
27. Agronomist	27. (Automobile) driver
28. Youth leader	28. Steelworker
29. Philologist	29. Mechanic, operator
30. Building assembly worker	30. Fitter, mechanic
31. Chemical worker	31. Agricultural worker
32. Cook, waiter	32. Painter (house/sign)
33. Combine-tractor driver	33. Automatic machine repairer
34. Railway worker	34. Combine-tractor driver
35. Painter (house/sign)	35. Building assembly worker
36. Agricultural worker	36. Automatic machine operator
37. Animal husbandry worker	37. Shop assistant
38. Shop assistant	38. Railway worker
39. Secretary, clerk	39. Worker in public utilities
40. Worker in public utilities	40. Secretary, clerk

Source: Yadova, pp. 93-5.

Table 8.3

Answers	Men		Women	
	Kolkhoz	Sovkhoz	Kolkhoz	Sovkhoz
In the town	41.5	41.4	51.3	56.3
In the country	32.0	39.1	30.2	31.5
No reply	26.5	19.5	18.5	12.3

Source: Yadova, p. 129.

Some flesh and blood is given to figures like these in such accounts culled from the newspapers as those collected by A. Parry in his *The New Class Divided*. Some concern 'separate living in the quiet behind the high fences' (p. 160) and the yearnings 'to live the way the doctors of sciences do' (p. 234). Others concern the privileges which foreign travel or better schooling can lead to (p. 260). Apathy to political studies and various forms of social work is frequently expressed (pp. 131, 145, 288). None of this adds up to a marxist analysis of the present class structure and its relation to the social realities of contemporary Soviet society, but it does suggest that attitudes and behaviour patterns persist which belie claims that class differences are disappearing.

Conclusions

Marxism in the USSR has in the main degenerated into official apologetics, or a technicism of economic growth and bureaucratic planning. The goal of free, classless man has been embraced only to empty it of real content. In China the marxist vision reappears in Mao who both understands the distant future of its possible realisation and the need to struggle for it now. Hence the slogans of the Cultural Revolution: 'never forget class struggle' and 'to rebel is justified'. But Mao appears as almost a lone voice opposing powerful interests: the old conservative, even Confucian traditions, and the new 'modern revisionist' ones in the Party and State bureaucracies.

The reality—economic and social-political—whose major importance for education I have stressed, has in both countries been one of spectacular economic growth and advance, and at the same time of poverty and relentless toil. In the USSR arbitrary rule and terror has gradually given way to bureaucratic forms, neither phase really conducive to genuine participation in other than subordinate roles. China, which succeeded in collectivising agriculture without the worst horrors and destruction suffered in the USSR is still today relatively poorer than her neighbour, with a significant difference in standards between urban and rural areas. Party dictatorship and bureaucracy have been supplemented by mass campaigns and a system of small-group democracy whose effects are still uncertain.

In education there has been an enormous growth of schooling and impressive democratic reform, but little of this should be judged marxist in the sense explicated here. Rather, it is pre-marxist, necessary but not sufficient. While enlightenment has been broadly spread and, especially in the USSR, and in the realms of science and technology and the performing arts a high standard of excellence has been achieved this has done little to break down class barriers. In some ways the very success of specialised education has worsened the prospect of a classless society. But the real barrier to that is the monopoly of power and information by the Communist Parties and state bureaucracies. These are closely connected with the schools. Recruitment of students to particular schools; success within the schools; and the advance of graduates into powerful posts in the Party and State form a familiar pattern and create new vested interests making increasingly difficult a genuine marxist educational policy. Only Mao Ze-dong in China has attacked this situation and suggested ways in which changes leading in a different direction might be brought about. Among these have been a period of work between school and college and a different method of selection for tertiary schooling; worker-teachers; and a conception of linking education with productive labour which would break down the present gulf between school and the world outside. Here Mao is trying to reverse the world trend to prolong childhood dependence and deprive youth of a meaningful place in 'the great work of social production' without robbing them of support or the joy of freedom to experiment.

Mao's concept of education is a praxis, theory and practice in a dialectic which is to result in man's ever more conscious control of his own destiny. It is not that easy liberal belief in sweet reason and the power of talking through problems so that the lion and lamb lie down together, but education in a web of conflicts, some 'antagonistic' and some 'non-antagonistic', which can only be resolved through practical struggles over a more or less protracted period. His position is a reassertion of the Marx who wrote that 'circumstances are changed by men' and that 'the educator himself must be educated' (Marx, *SW* 1, p. 472). It is wrong to call this voluntarism, for Mao is challenging man in a process of self-education to assert his freedom to re-make himself within the limits determined by a natural world of which he is an active part. In all this Mao asserts the whole Marx against the part, against the mechanical determinist interpretations of today's Soviet leaders for whom the school has become a reification which will, given time, certify us all as classless.

Finally, marxism assumes a dialectic of man and his environment in which the individual personality is shaped by the ongoing interplay of what he is with what he experiences. Now one and now the other side of this contradiction produces a qualitative change in the other. If mankind is to progress towards a communism like that envisaged by Marx the individual human being must increasingly come to understand and dominate this interplay.

ABBREVIATIONS

Organisations, Events, etc.

CC	Central committee
CCP	Chinese Communist Party
CP	Communist Party
CPSU	Communist Party of the Soviet Union
GPCR	Great Proletarian Cultural Revolution (China, 1966-9)
KMT	Guomindang, or Nationalist Party of China
Komsomol	Union of Communist Youth
PRC	People's Republic of China
RSFSR	Russian Soviet Federative Socialist Republic

Publications

The titles of many of the works quoted are abbreviated, especially those of Marx and Engels:

AD	*Anti-Duhring*, Engels
CM	*Communist Manifesto*, Marx and Engels
CGP	*Critique of the Gotha Programme*, Marx
CPE	*Critique of Political Economy*, Marx
CPR	*Critique of Hegel's Philosophy of Right*, Marx
DN	*Dialectics of Nature*, Engels
EPM	*Economic and Philosophic Manuscripts*, Marx
GI	*German Ideology*, Marx and Engels
HF	*Holy Family*, Marx and Engels
PP	*Poverty of Philosophy*, Marx

Collections of works by Marx and Engels:

ET	*Early Texts*
EW	*Early Writings*
FIA	*First International and After*
GC	*General Council of the First International*, 1864-1866
OR	*On Religion*
R.1848	*Revolutions of 1848*
SW	*Selected Works*

The following English-language translations are prepared by the United States Consultative General in Hong Kong:

CB	Current Background

ECMM	Extracts from China Mainland Magazines
SCMP	Survey of China Mainland Press

EPMC	*An Economic Profile of Mainland China* (see bibliography)
JFRS	Translations by the Joint Publications Research Service, Washington, DC
SWB	*Survey of World Broadcasts*, published by the BBC, Reading, England
CDSP	Current Digest of the Soviet Press, published by the Institute of Soviet Studies, Glasgow University
Kom. Pr.	*Komsomolskaya Pravda*
RMRB	*Renmin Ribao* or People's Daily
GMRB	*Guangming Ribao* or The Illuminating Daily

Glossary

Glossaries of varying content and sufficiency exist in Grant, Price (1970), Schurmann (1966/8). The fullest is:

Hu, C.T., and Beach, B. (ed., trans.), *A Russian Chinese English Glossary of Education*, New York, Teachers College Press, 1970.

Chronologies

Useful chronologies are to be found in Price (1970); Hawkins (1974), and Brickman (1972).

The Chinese Transcription used

The system used is that adopted in the People's Republic of China, known as *hanyu pinyin*. This is described in various Chinese language books and in Price, 1970, pp. 296-8.

BIBLIOGRAPHY

This bibliography is a partial one, consisting only of those works quoted, or which have especially contributed to the writing of this book. More complete bibliographies will be found in:

Wittig, H.E., *Karl Marx, Bilung and Erziehung,* Paderborn, F. Schoningh, 1968.

McLellan, D., *Karl Marx, his Life and Thought,* London, Macmillan, 1973.

Brickman, W.W., A Bibliographical Introduction to Soviet Education, *School and Society,* April 1972, pp. 259-70.

Fraser, S., *Chinese Communist Education: Records of the First Decade,* New York, Wiley, 1963.

Fraser, S. and Hsu Kuang-liang, *Chinese Education and Society: A Bibliographical Guide to the Cultural Revolution and its Aftermath,* White Plains, International Arts and Sciences Press Inc., 1972.

*Academic Freedom under the Soviet Regime—*a symposium of refugee scholars—Conference at the Carnegie Endowment for International Peace Building, United Nations Plaza, New York, 3-4 April 1954, Institute for the Study of History and Culture of the USSR, Munich 1954.

Adler, N., and Harrington, C., *The Learning of Political Behaviour,* Glenview, Scott, Foresman & Co., 1970.

Afanasyev, V.G., *The Scientific and Technological Revolution—Its Impact on Management and Education,* Moscow, Progress Publishers, 1975.

Alt, H. and E., *The New Soviet Man—His Upbringing and Character Development,* New York, Bookman Associates, 1964.

Alt, J., 'Beyond Class: the Decline of Industrial Labour and Leisure', *Telos,* 28, 1976, pp. 55-80.

Althusser, L., *For Marx,* Harmondsworth, Penguin Books, 1965/69.

——*Lenin and Philosophy and Other Essays,* London, NLB, 1971.

——*Politics and History,* London, NLB, 1972.

—— and Balibar, E., *Reading Capital,* London, NLB, 1970.

Amalrik, A., 'Will the U.S.S.R. survive until 1984?', *Survey,* August 1969, pp. 47-49.

Amin, S., *Accumulation on a World Scale: A Critique of the Theory of*

Underdevelopment, New York, Monthly Review Press, 1974.

Ammende, E., *Human Life in Russia,* London, Allen & Unwin, 1936.

Anweiler, O., *Geschichte der Schule und Padogogik in Russland vom Ende des Zarenreiches bis zum Beginn der Stalin-Ara,* Berlin, Quelle & Meyer Verlag, 1964.

——*Bildungforschung und Bildungspolitik in Osteuropa und der DDR,* Hanover, Schroedel, 1975.

——and Meyer, K., *Die Sowjetische Bilungspolitik seit 1917,* Heidelberg, Quelle & Meyer, 1961.

——and Ruffmann, K.H., *Kulturpolitik der Sowjetunion,* Stuttgart, A. Kroner Verlag, 1973.

Aron, R., *et al., The Soviet Economy: a Discussion,* London, Secker & Warburg, 1956.

Asia Yearbook, 1973, Far Eastern Economic Review, Hong Kong, 1973.

Avineri, S., *The Social and Political Thought of Karl Marx,* Cambridge, The University Press, 1970.

Barendsen, R.D., *Half-work, Half-study Schools in Communist China,* Washington, US Departmert of Health, Education and Welfare, 1964.

Barnes, L., *Soviet Light on the Colonies,* Harmondsworth, Penguin Books, 1944.

Barnett, A.D., *Cadres, Bureaucracy, and Political Power in Communist China,* New York, Columbia University Press, 1967.

——(ed.), *Chinese Communist Politics in Action,* Seattle, University of Washington, 1969.

Baum, R. and Teiwes, F.C., *Ssu-ch'ing: the Socialist Education Movement of 1962-66,* Berkeley, University of California, China Research Monographs, 1968.

Bennett, G.A. and Montaperto, R.F., *Red Guard: the Political Biography of Dai Hsiao-ai,* London, Allen & Unwin, 1971.

Bennigsen, A. and Quequejay, C., *The Revolution of the Muslim Nationalities of the U.S.S.R. and their Linguistic Problems,* Oxford, St Antony's College Press, 1961.

Bereday, G.Z.F., and Pennar, J. (ed.), *The Politics of Soviet Education,* New York, Praeger, 1960.

Blackett, P.M.S., *Military and Political Consequences of Atomic Energy,* London, Turnstile Press, 1948.

Blaug, M., *Economics of Education* (2 vols), Harmondsworth, Penguin Books, 1968.

Bowen, J., *Soviet Education: Anton Makarenko and the Years of*

Experiment, Madison, University of Wisconsin Press, 1962.

Braverman, H., *Labour and Monopoly Capital: the Degradation of Work in the Twentieth Century,* New York, Monthly Review Press, 1974.

Brickman, W.W., 'Atheism, religion, and education in the Soviet Union', *School and Society,* April 1972, pp. 246-253.

Brown, D.R., *The Role and Status of Women in the Soviet Union,* New York, Teachers' College.

Brugger, W., 'China: the educational environment', *Aspects of Education in China*—papers presented at a conference held at La Trobe University, 13-14 July 1973, Melbourne, Centre for Comparative and International Studies in Education, 1973.

——*Democracy and Organisation in the Chinese Industrial Enterprises, 1948-53,* London, Cambridge University Press, 1976.

Bunge, Mario. *Causality: the Place of the Causal Principle in Modern Science,* New York, Meridian Books, 1962.

Bush, R.C. Jr., *Religion in Communist China,* New York, Abingdon Press, 1970.

Carlo, A., 'Lenin on the party', *Telos,* 17, 1973, pp. 2-40.

Carnoy, M., *Education as Cultural Imperialism,* New York, David McKay, 1974.

Carr, E.H., *The Bolshevic Revolution 1917-1923,* 3 vols, Harmondsworth, Penguin Books, 1966.

——*The Interregnum, 1923-1924,* Harmondsworth, Penguin Books, 1969.

——(ed.) *Bukharin and Preobrazhensky, The ABC of Communism,* Harmondsworth, Penguin Books, 1969.

——*Socialism in One Country,* 3 vols, Harmondsworth, Penguin Books, 1970.

——*Foundations of a Planned Economy, 1926-1929,* vol. 2, London, Macmillan, 1971.

——and Davies, R.W., *Foundations of a Planned Economy, 1926-1929,* vol. 1, London, Macmillan, 1969.

Chan, Wing-Tsit, *Religious Trends in Modern China,* New York, Octagon Books, 1969.

Chao, Yuen-ren, *Language and Symbolic Systems,* Cambridge, The University Press, 1968.

Chauncey, H. (ed.), *Soviet Preschool Education,* 2 vols, New York, Holt, Rinehart & Winston, Inc., 1969.

Chen, C.S. (ed.), and Ridley, C.P. (trans.), *Rural People's Communes in Lien-chiang,* Stanford, Hoover Institution Press, 1969.

Chen, J., *A Year in Upper Felicity: Life in a Chinese Village during the Cultural Revolution*, London, Harrap, 1973.

Chen, Qing-zhi, *Zhongguo jiaoyu shi* (A History of Chinese Education), Taiwan Shangwu Yinshuguan, 1963.

Cheng, Chu-yuan, *Scientific and Engineering Manpower in Communist China, 1949-1963*, Washington, DC, National Science Foundation, 1965.

Chesneaux, J., *The Chinese Labour Movement, 1919-1927*, Stanford, Stanford University Press, 1968.

―― *Secret Societies in China in the 19th. and 20th. Centuries*, London, Heinemann, 1971.

Chin, A-l.S., 'Family Relations in Modern Chinese Fiction', in Freedman, M., *Family and Kinship*.

Chin, C-M., *The Song of Ouyang Hai*, Peking, Foreign Languages Press, 1966.

Chow, Tse-tsung, *The May Fourth Movement*, Stanford, Stanford University Press, 1960.

Churchward, L.G., *The Soviet Intelligentsia*, London, Routledge & Kegan Paul, 1973.

Clarke, R.A., *Soviet Economic Facts, 1917-1970*, London, Macmillan, 1972.

Clopton, R.W., and Ou, T-C., (eds. and trans.), *John Dewey, Lectures in China 1919-20*, Honolulu, University Press of Hawaii, 1973.

Cohen, S.F., *Bukharin and the Bolshevik Revolution, a Political Biography, 1888-1938*, London, Wildwood House, 1974.

Colletti, L., *Marxism and Hegel*, London, New Left Books, 1973.

―― 'Contradiction and contrariety', *New Left Review* 93, 1975, pp. 3-30.

――Introduction to Marx, *Early Writings*, Harmondsworth, Penguin Books, 1975.

Conquest, R., *Power and Policy in the U.S.S.R.*, London, Macmillan, 1962.

―― *Religion in the U.S.S.R.*, London, The Bodley Head, 1968.

Cornforth, M., *In Defence of Philosophy Against Positivism and Pragmatism*, London, Lawrence and Wishart, 1950.

Cosin, B.R., (ed.), *Education: Structure and Society*, Harmondsworth, Penguin Books, 1972.

Croll, E., *The Women's Movement in China: a Selection of Readings, 1949-73*, London, Anglo-Chinese Educational Institute, 1974.

Crook, I. and D., *The First Years of Yangyi Commune*, London, Routledge & Kegan Paul, 1966.

Daniels, R.V., *A Documentary History of Communism,* New York, Vintage Books, 1960.

Davidow, M., *The Most Human World: the Soviet Union through the Eyes of an American,* Moscow, Novosti Press, 1974.

Davies, R.W., *The Development of the Soviet Budgetary System,* Cambridge, The University Press, 1958.

Dawson, R., *The Legacy of China,* Oxford, The Clarendon Press, 1964.

Day, R.B., *Leon Trotsky and the Politics of Economic Isolation,* Cambridge, The University Press, 1973.

Deineko, M., *Public Education in the U.S.S.R.,* Moscow, Progress Publishers, n.d.

de Bary, *et al., Sources of the Chinese Tradition,* New York, Columbia University Press, 1960/65.

D'Encausse, H.C. and Schram, S.R., *Marxism and Asia,* Allen Lane, London, Penguin Press, 1969.

Denzin, N.K., *Sociological Methods,* London, Butterworths, 1970.

Deutscher, I., *The Prophet Armed (Trotsky 1879-1921),* London, Oxford University Press, 1954.

—— *The Prophet Unarmed (Trotsky 1921-1929),* London, Oxford University Press, 1959.

—— *The Prophet Outcast (Trotsky, 1929-1940),* London, Oxford University Press, 1963.

—— *Stalin, a Political Biography,* Harmondsworth, Penguin Books, 1966.

De Witt, N., *Soviet Professional Manpower: Its Education, Training, and Supply,* Washington, DC, National Science Foundation, 1955.

—— *Engineering and Professional Employment in the USSR,* Washington, USA National Science Foundation, 1961.

Dobb, M., *Soviet Economic Development since 1917,* London, Routledge & Kegan Paul, 1948/53.

Dodge, N.T., *Women in the Soviet Economy,* Baltimore, Johns Hopkins Press, 1966.

Domes, J., 'Generals and Red Guards', *Asia Quarterly,* 1971, vol. 1, pp. 3-31, and 1971, vol. 2, pp. 123-159.

Donnithorne, A., *China's Economic System,* London, Allen & Unwin, 1967.

Draper, H., *K. Marx and F. Engels: Writings on the Paris Commune,* New York, Monthly Review Press, 1971.

East Europe Unit of Comparative Research Branch, *Social Science in Soviet Secondary Schools,* Washington, US Department of Health,

Education and Welfare, Office of Information, 1966.

Eckstein, A. (ed.), *Economic Trends in Communist China*, Chicago, Aldine Publishing Co., 1968.

Education in China, Modern China series No. 5, London, Anglo-Chinese Educational Institute, 1974.

Eighth National Congress of the Communist Party of China (documents), vol. 1. Peking, Foreign Languages Press, 1956.

Emerson, J.P., 'Employment in mainland China: problems and prospects', *An Economic Profile of Mainland China,* studies prepared for the Joint Economic Committee of Congress of the United States, Washington, US Government Printing Office, 1967, pp. 403-470.

Engels, F., *Dialectics of Nature*, London, Lawrence & Wishart, 1940-46.

—— *Anti-Duhring: Herr Eugen Duhring's Revolution in Science*, Moscow, Foreign Languages Press, 1962.

—— *The Origin of the Family, Private Property and the State* (ed. and Introduction by E.B. Leacock), London, Lawrence & Wishart, 1972.

Evans, S.G., *A Short History of Bulgaria*, London, Lawrence & Wishart, 1960.

Fediaevsky, V., and Hill, P.S., *Nursery School and Parent Education in Soviet Russia*, London, Kegan Paul, Trench, Trubner & Co., 1936.

Feuerwerker, A. (ed.), *History in Communist China*, Cambridge, Mass., MIT Press, 1968.

Firestone, S., *The Dialectic of Sex*, London, Paladin, 1972.

Fisher, R.T. Jnr., *Pattern for Soviet Youth: A Study of the Congresses of the Komsomol, 1918-1954*, New York, Columbia University Press, 1959.

Fishman, J.A., *Language and Nationalism*, Rowley, Mass., Newbury House, 1972.

Fitzpatrick, S., *The Commissariat of Enlightenment*, Cambridge, The University Press, 1970.

Fokkema, D.W., *Literature Doctrine in China and Soviet Influences, 1956-1960*, The Hague, Mouton, 1965.

Francis, S. (ed.), *Libraries in the U.S.S.R.*, London, Clive Bingley, 1971.

Fraser, S., *Chinese Communist Education: Records of the First Decade*, New York, Wiley, 1965.

Freedman, M., *Family and Kinship in Chinese Society*, Stanford, Stanford University Press, 1970.

Freire, P., *Pedagogy of the Oppressed*, Tenbury Wells, Fowler Wright, 1968/70.

—— *Cultural Action for Freedom*, Harmondsworth, Penguin Books, 1970/72.

Front Line Heroines, Stories of Ten Soviet Women, London, Soviet War News, 1945.

Fundamentals of Marxism-Leninism, 2nd edn., Moscow, Progress Publishers, 1964.

Galt, H.S., *A History of Chinese Educational Institutions*, London, Arthur Probsthain, 1951.

Gamble, S.D., *Ting Hsien: a North China Rural Community*, Stanford, Stanford University Press, 1954.

Geiger, H.K., *The Family in Soviet Russia*, Cambridge, Mass., Harvard University Press, 1968.

Gittings, J., *The Role of the Chinese Army*, London, Oxford University Press, 1967.

Goodman, P., *Compulsory Miseducation*, Harmondsworth, Penguin Books, 1962/71.

Gorky, M., *Literature and Life*, London, Hutchinson, 1946.

Gorokhoff, B.I., *Publishing in the U.S.S.R.*, Indianapolis Indiana University Publications, Slavic & East European Series, vol. 19, 1959.

Gorz, A., 'Technical Intelligence and the Capitalist Division of Labour', *Telos*, Summer 1972, No. 12, pp. 27-41.

Grahl, B., and Piccone, P., *Towards a New Marxism: Proceedings of the First International Telos Conference, October 8-11 1970*, St Louis, Mo., Telos Press, 1973.

Grant, N., *Soviet Education*, Harmondsworth, Penguin Books, 1964-1972.

—— 'Teacher training in the U.S.S.R. and East Europe', *Trends in Teacher Training*, London, Comparative Education Society of Europe, British Section, 1969.

Gray, J. (ed.), *Modern China's Search for a Political Form*, Oxford, The University Press, 1969.

—— and Cavendish, P., *Chinese Communism in Crisis*, London, Pall Mall Press, 1968.

Greer, G., *The Female Eunuch*, London, Paladin, 1970/72.

Griffith, S.B., II, *The Chinese People's Liberation Army*, London, Weidenfeld & Nicholson, 1968.

A Guide to New China, Peking, Foreign Languages Press, 1952.

Gurley, J.G., 'Capitalism and Maoist economic development', *Monthly*

Review, vol. 22, No. 9, February, 1971, pp. 15-35.

Hans, N., *The Russian Tradition in Education,* London, Routledge & Kegan Paul, 1963.

Harper, S.N., *Civic Training in Soviet Russia,* Chicago, University of Chicago Press, 1929.

Harrison, J.P., *The Communists and Chinese Peasant Rebellions: A Study of the Rewriting of Chinese History,* New York, Atheneum, 1971.

Hawkins, J.N., *Mao Tse-tung and Education: His Thoughts and Teachings,* Hamden, The Shoe String Press, 1974.

Hecker, J.F., *Religion and Communism—A Study of Religion and Atheism in Soviet Russia,* London, Chapman & Hall, 1933.

Hillig, G. (ed.), *Makarenko in Deutschland, 1927-1967, Texte und Berichte,* Braunschweig, G. Westermann Verlag, 1967.

Hinton, W., *Hundred Day War,* New York, Monthly Review Press, 1973.

――― *The Historical Experience of the Dictatorship of the Proletariat,* Peking Foreign Languages Press, 1960.

Hoffman, J., *Marxism and the Theory of Praxis,* London, Lawrence & Wishart, 1975.

Holmes, B. (ed.), *Comparative Education Tour to the Soviet Union,* University of London, Institute of Education, 1970 (mimeographed).

Holt, J., *How Children Fail,* Harmondsworth, Penguin Press, 1964/70.

――― *The Underachieving School,* London, Pitman, 1970.

Holubnychy, V., 'Mao Tse-tung's Materialistic Dialectics', *The China Quarterly,* Jul-Sept 1964, No. 19, pp. 3-37.

Hopkins, M.W., *Mass Media in the Soviet Union,* New York, Pegasus, 1970.

Horecky, P.L., *Libraries and Bibliographic Centers in the Soviet Union,* Washington, Council on Library Resources Inc., 1959.

Hough, J.F., *The Soviet Prefects,* Cambridge, Mass., Harvard University Press, 1969.

Hu, C.T., 'The Teaching of History in Communist China', *Education in Communist China,* Bruxelles, Centre d'etude du Sud-est Asiatique et de l'Extreme Orient, 1969, pp. 162-183.

――― 'The Chinese People's University: Bastion of Marxism-Leninism', *Universities Facing the Future,* The World Year Book of Education, London, Evans Bros., 1973.

Hughes, T.J., and Luard, D.E.T., *The Economic Development of Communist China, 1949-1960,* London, Oxford University Press, 1961.

Hunter, N., *Shanghai Journal,* New York, Praeger, 1969.

Huxley, J., *Soviet Genetics and World Science—Lysenko and the Meaning of Heredity,* London, Chatto & Windus, 1949.

Illich, I.D., *Deschooling Society,* London, Calder & Boyars, 1970/71.
—— *Celebration of Awareness,* London, Calder & Boyars, 1969/71.
Inkeles, A., 'Industrial Man, the Relation of Status to Experience, Perception and Value', *American Journal of Sociology,* LXVI, No. 1, July 1960.
—— and Bauer, A., *The Soviet Citizen—Daily Life in a Totalitarian Society,* Cambridge, Mass, Harvard University Press, 1959.
Israel, J., *Alienation, From Marx to Modern Sociology,* Boston, Allyn & Bacon, 1971.

Jackson, B., and Marsden, D., *Education and the Working Class,* 1962.
Jenkinson, A.J., *What do Boys and Girls Read?* London, Methuen, 1940.
Jenner, D., *Letters from Peking,* Oxford, Oxford University Press, 1967.
Jiang Qing (Chiang China), *On the Revolution of Peking Opera,* Peking, Foreign Languages Press, 1968.
Johnson, W.H.E., *Russia's Educational Heritage,* New York, Octagon Books, 1969.
Juviller, P., 'Mass Education and Justice in Soviet Courts: the Visiting Sessions', *Soviet Studies,* vol. 18, No. 4, April 1967.

Kairov, I.A., *et al.* (eds.), *Pedagogika,* Moscow, Gosudarstvennoye Uchebno-pedagogicheskoye Izdatel'stvo, 1956.
Kalinin, M.I., *On Communist Education,* Moscow, Foreign Languages Press, 1950.
Kamenka, E., *The Ethical Foundations of Marxism,* London, Routledge & Kegan Paul, 1962.
Kanet, R.E., *The Behavioral Revolution and Communist Studies,* New York, The Free Press, 1971.
Kassof, A., *The Soviet Youth Program: Regimentation and Rebellion,* Cambridge, Mass., Harvard University Press, 1965.
—— *Prospects for Soviet Society,* London, Pall Mall Press, 1968.
Kavanagh, D., *Political Culture,* London, Macmillan, 1972.
Keat, R. and Urry, J., *Social Theory as Science,* London, Routledge and Kegan Paul, 1975.
Kessen, W. (ed.), *Childhood in China,* Newhaven, Yale University Press, 1975.
King, B., *Changing Man,* London, Gollancz, 1937.
—— *Russia Goes to School,* London, New Education Book Club, 1948.
Kintner, W.R. and Scott, H.F. (ed. and trans.), *The Nuclear Revolution*

in Soviet Military Affairs, Norman, Oklahoma, University of Oklahoma Press, 1968.

Kirby, E.S. (ed.), *Youth in China,* Hong Kong, Dragonfly Books, 1965.

Kitson, F., *Low Intensity Operations,* London, Faber & Faber, 1971.

Klepikov, V., 'Narodnoe obrazovanii v kitajskoj narodnoj respublike za 10 let', *Sovetskaja Pedagogika* (Moscow), II, 1959, pp. 119-31.

Kline, G.L., *Religious and Anti-religious Thought in Russia,* Chicago, University of Chicago Press, 1968.

Kolakowski, L.,*Positivist Philosophy*,Harmondsworth,Penguin Books,1972.

Kolarx, W., *Religion in the Soviet Union,* London, Macmillan, 1962.

Kolkowicz, R., *The Use of Soviet Military Labor in the Civilian Economy: A Study of Military 'shefstvo',* Santa Monica, The Rand Corp., Memorandum RM-3360-PR, November 1962.

—— *The Soviet Military and the C.P.,* Princeton, NJ, The University Press, 1967.

Korol, A.G., *Soviet Education for Science and Technology,* Cambridge, Mass., MIT Press, 1957.

Krupskaya, N.K., *Pedagogicheskie Sochineniya v Desyati Tomax,* Moscow, Akademii Pedagogicheskix Hauk, 1957.

Labour Laws and Regulations of the People's Republic of China, Peking, Foreign Languages Press, 1956.

Laird, R.D. and B.A., *Soviet Communism and Agrarian Revolution,* Harmondsworth, Penguin Books, 1970.

Lane, D., *Politics and Society in the U.S.S.R.,* London, Weidenfeld & Nicolson, 1970-72.

Langrish, J., Gibbons, M., Evans, W.G., and Jevons, F.R., *Wealth from Knowledge,* London, Macmillan, 1972.

Lawton, D., *Social Class, Language and Education,* London, Routledge & Kegan Paul, 1968.

Lenin, V.I., *Socialism and War,* London, Lawrence & Wishart, 1942.

—— *War and the Workers,* London, Lawrence & Wishart, 1942.

—— *The Essentials of Lenin in Two Volumes,* London, Lawrence & Wishart, 1947.

—— *Where to Begin/Party Organization and Party Literature/The Working Class and its Press,* Moscow, Foreign Languages Press, n.d.

—— *Lenin o Narodnum Obrazovanii,* Moscow, Akademii Pedagogicheskix nauk RSFSR, 1957.

—— *Materialism and Empirio-criticism,* Moscow, Foreign Languages Press, n.d.

—— *Lenin on Culture and Cultural Revolution,* Moscow, Progress

Publishers, 1970.

Lenin, V.I., *The Emancipation of Women*, New York, International Publishers, 1972.

—— *On Religion*, London, Lawrence & Wishart, 1940.

Leonhard, W., *Die Revolution Entlässt Ihre Kinder*, Frankfurt/M, Ullstein GMBH, 1962.

Levitas, M., *Marxist Perspectives in the Sociology of Education*, London, Routledge & Kegan Paul, 1974.

Lewis, J.W. (ed.), *A Textbook of Marxist Philosophy*, Lakshmi Narain Agarwal, Agra, 1944.

—— *Party Leadership and Revolutionary Power in China*, Cambridge, The University Press, 1970.

—— (ed.), *The City in Communist China*, Stanford, Stanford University Press, 1971.

Lifton, R.J., *Thought Reform and the Psychology of Totalism*, Harmondsworth, Penguin Books, 1967.

Lindbeck, J.M.H., *China: Management of a Revolutionary Society*, London, Allen & Unwin, 1972.

Liu Shao-qi, *On the Party*, Peking, Foreign Languages Press, 1950.

—— *How to be a Good Communist*, Peking, Foreign Languages Press, 1965.

Lu Ting-yi, *Education Must be Combined with Productive Labour*, Peking, Foreign Languages Press, 1964.

Lukacs, G., *History and Class Consciousness*, London, Merlin Press, 1968.

Lun jiaoyu yu shengchan laodong xiangjiehe, Peking, Zhongguo Qingnian chubanshe, 1958.

Macfarquhar, R., 'A Visit to the Chinese Press', *The China Quarterly*, vol. 53, Jan-Mar 1973, pp. 144-152.

Macinnis, D.E., *Religious Policy and Practice in Communist China*, Hodder & Stoughton, London, 1972.

Mackerras, C., *Amateur Theatre in China, 1949-66*, Canberra, Australia National University Press, 1973.

Makarenko, A.S., *The Road to Life*, Moscow, Foreign Languages Press, 1951.

—— *Learning to Live: Flags on the Battlements*, Moscow, Foreign Languages Press, 1953.

—— *A Book for Parents*, Moscow, Foreign Languages Press, 1954.

Manacorda, M.A., *Marx e la Pedagogia Moderna*, Rome, Editori Riuniti, 1966.

—— *il marxismo e l'edicazione, testi e documenti*, Rome, Editore

Armando Armando, 1971.

Mandel, E., *The Formation of the Economic Thought of Karl Marx*, New York, Monthly Review, 1971.

—— *Late Capitalism*, London, New Left Books, 1975.

—— *Marxist Economic Theory*, London, Merlin, 1968.

Manhattan, A., *The Catholic Church Against the Twentieth Century*, London, Watts, 1949.

Mao Ze-dong (ed.), *Socialist Upsurge in China's Countryside*, Peking, Foreign Languages Press, 1956.

—— *Selected Works of Mao Tse-tung*, vols. 1-4, Peking, Foreign Languages Press, 1965.

—— *Quotations from Chairman Mao Tse-tung*, Peking, Foreign Languages Press, 1966.

—— *Four Essays on Philosophy*, Peking, Foreign Languages Press, 1966.

—— *Miscellany of Mao-Tse-tung thought (1949-1968)*, Parts 1 and 2, Arlington, Virginia, Joint Publications Research Service, JPRS-61269-1 and 2, 20 Feb 1974.

—— *Selected Readings from the Works of Mao Tse-tung*, 1971.

Marcuse, H., *Reason and Revolution*, London, Routledge & Kegan Paul, 1955.

—— *Soviet Marxism: A Critical Analysis*, London, Routledge & Kegan Paul, 1958.

—— *One Dimensional Man*, London, Sphere Books, 1968.

—— *An Essay on Liberation*, London, Allen Lane, 1969.

The Marriage Law of the People's Republic of China, Peking, Foreign Languages Press, 1965.

Marx, K., *The General Council of the First International, 1864-1866*, Moscow, Foreign Languages Publishing House, n.d.

—— *Capital*, vol. 1, New York, The Modern Library, Reprint of Kerr edition of 1906, n.d.

—— *A Contribution to the Critique of Political Economy*, Calcutta, Bharati Library, reprint of 1904 edition, n.d.

—— *Early Writings*, Harmondsworth, Penguin Books, 1975.

—— *The General Council of the First International, 1868-70*, Moscow, Progress Publishers, 1964.

—— *The Poverty of Philosophy*, London, Martin Lawrence, n.d.

—— *Critique of the Gotha Programme*, London, Lawrence & Wishart, n.d.

—— *Selected Works*, 2 vols., London, Lawrence & Wishart, 1942.

—— *Theories of Surplus Value*, London, Lawrence & Wishart, 1951.

—— *Economic and Philosophic Manuscripts of 1844*, Moscow, Foreign

Languages Press, 1959.

Marx, K., *Critique of Hegel's 'Philosophy of Right'*, Cambridge, The University Press, 1970.

―― *Grundrisse, Foundations of the Critique of Political Economy, (Rough draft)*, Harmondsworth, Penguin Books, 1973.

―― and Engels, F., *Collected Works*, vol. 1, London, Lawrence & Wishart, 1975.

―――― *On Religion*, Moscow, Foreign Languages Press, n.d.

―――― *Selected Correspondence*, London, Lawrence & Wishart, 1934/ 43.

―――― *The German Ideology*, London, Lawrence & Wishart, 1965.

Matthews, M., *Class and Society in Soviet Russia*, London, Allen Lane, The Penguin Press, 1972.

Maxwell, N., *India's China War*, Harmondsworth, Penguin Books, 1970/ 72.

Mayers, W.F., *The Chinese Readers Manual*, London, Probsthain, 1874/ 1939.

McAuley, M., *Labour Disputes in Soviet Russia, 1957-65*, Oxford, Clarendon Press, 1969.

McLellan, D., *The Young Hegelians and Karl Marx*, London, Macmillan, 1969.

―― *Marx Before Marxism*, London, Macmillan, 1970.

―― *Marx's Grundrisse*, London, Macmillan, 1971.

―― *Karl Marx, Early Texts*, Oxford, Basil Blackwell, 1971.

―― *Karl Marx, His Life and Thought*, London, Macmillan, 1973.

McNeal, R.H., *Bride of the Revolution: Krupskaya and Lenin*, London, Victor Gollancz, 1973.

Medynsky, Y., *Education in the U.S.S.R.*, London, Soviet News, 1950.

Meek, D.L., *Soviet Youth: Some Achievements and Problems*, London, Routledge & Kegan Paul, 1957.

Meszaros, I., *Marx's Theory of Alienation*, London, Merlin Press, 1970.

Mickiewicz, E.P., *Soviet Political Schools*, New Haven and London, Yale University Press, 1967.

Miller, J., *Life in Russia Today*, London, B.T. Batsford, 1969.

Millett, K., *Sexual Politics*, London, Sphere Books, 1969/72.

Mitchell, G.D., *A Dictionary of Sociology*, London, Routledge and Kegan Paul, 1968.

Model Regulations for Advanced Agricultural Producers' Co-operatives, Peking, Foreign Languages Press, 1956.

Monoszon, E.I., 'Narodnoe obrazovanie v kitajskoj narodnoj respublike', *Sovetskaya Pedagogika*, Moscow, 2, 1957, pp. 106-16.

Montagu, I., *The Red Army: 50 Questions Answered,* London, Russia Today Society, n.d. (*c.* 1941).

Morton, A.G., *Soviet Genetics,* London, Lawrence & Wishart, 1951.

Morton, M., *The Arts and the Soviet Child: the Esthetic Education of Children in the U.S.S.R.,* New York, The Free Press, 1972.

Munro, D.J., 'The Chinese view of "alienation"', *The China Quarterly,* vol. 59, July-Sept 1974, pp. 580-582.

Myrdal, J., *Report from a Chinese Village,* Harmondsworth, Penguin Books, 1963.

——— and Kessle, G., *China: the Revolution Continued,* Harmondsworth, Penguin Books, 1973.

Nearing, S., *Education in Soviet Russia,* London, The Plebs League, 1926.

Needham, J., *Science and Civilization in China,* vols. 1-4, Cambridge, University Press, 1954-1971.

New Steps in Soviet Education, Moscow, Novosti Press Agency Publishing House, 1973.

Noah, H.J., *Financing Soviet Schools,* New York, Teachers College Press, 1966.

Nove, A., *The Soviet Economy,* London, Allen & Unwin, 1961/68.

——— *Economic History of the U.S.S.R.,* London, Allen Lane, Penguin Press, 1969/70.

Nunn, G.R., *Publishing in Mainland China: MIT Report no. 4,* Cambridge, Mass., MIT Press, 1966.

Obshchestvovedeniye, Izdatel'stvo Politicheskoi Literaturui, Moscow, 1968.

Oksenberg, M., 'The Exit Pattern from Chinese Politics and Its Implications', *China Quarterly,* 67, Sept 1976, pp. 501-18.

Ollman, B., *Alienation, Marx's Conception of Man in Capitalist Society,* Cambridge, the University Press, 1971.

Orleans, L.A., *Professional Manpower and Education in Communist China,* Washington, National Science Foundation, 1961.

——— *Every Fifth Child: the Population of China,* London, Eyre Methuen, 1972.

Osipov, G.V. (ed.), *Industry and Labour in the U.S.S.R.,* London, Tavistock Publications, 1966.

——— *Town, Country and People,* London, Tavistock Publications, 1969.

Parry, A., *The New Class Divided: Science and Technology Versus*

Communism, London, Macmillan, 1966.

Pedagogicheskaya Entsiklopediya, Moscow, Sovetskaya entsiklopediya, 1964.

Pemberton, A.R. (ed.), *Trends in Teacher Education,* Report of a conference held at the University of Reading, 12-15 Sept 1969, London, Comparative Education Society of Europe, British Section, 1970.

Petrovsky, I.G., *Higher Education in the U.S.S.R.,* London, Soviet News, 1953.

Pinkevitch, A.P., *The New Education in the Soviet Republic,* New York, Day, 1929.

―― *Science and Education in the U.S.S.R.,* New York, Putnam, 1935.

Planification Debats et problemes du socialisme, *Recherches internationales a la lumiere du marxisme,* Mai-Juin 1965, numero 47.

Ploss, S., *Conflict and Decision-making in Soviet Russia,* Princeton, N.J., Princeton University Press, 1965.

―― (ed.), *The Soviet Political Process,* Waltham, Mass., Ginn & Co., 1971.

The Polemic on the General Line of the International Communist Movement, Peking, Foreign Languages Press, 1965.

Postman, N. and Weingartner, C., *Teaching as a Subversive Activity,* Harmondsworth, Penguin Books, 1969/71.

Poulantzas, N., *Political Power and Social Classes,* London, NLB & Sheed & Ward, 1973.

―― *Classes in Contemporary Capitalism,* London, New Left Books, 1975.

Prenant, M., *Biology and Marxism,* London, Lawrence & Wishart, 1938.

Preobrazhensky, E., *The New Economics,* Trans. B. Pearce, with Introd. by A. Nove, Oxford, Clarendon Press, 1965.

Price, R.F., 'The Content of the Soviet School Science Course', *The School Science Review,* no. 148 & 149, Oct. & Nov. 1951.

―― *Education in Communist China,* London, Routledge & Kegan Paul, 1970.

―― 'Mao Ze-dong Thought and education', *Aspects of Education in China,* Melbourne, Centre for Comparative & International Studies in Education, 1973, pp. 34-57.

―― 'The Part-work Principle in Chinese Education', *Current Scene,* Sept 1973, vol. XI, no. 9, pp. 1-11.

―― 'Labour and Education in Russia and China', *Comparative Education,* vol. 10, no. 1, March 1974, pp. 13-23.

―― *What Chinese Children Read About,* Melbourne, Centre for Comparative & International Studies in Education, 1, 1972, 2, 1975.

Prybyla, J.A., *The Political Economy of Communist China,* Scranton, Penn., International Textbook Co., 1970.

Pye, L. and Verba, S., *Political Culture and Political Development,* Princeton, Princeton University Press, 1965.

Qingnian Yingxiongde Gushi, 2 vols, Peking, Zhongguo Qingnian Chubanshe, 1965.

Reddaway, P. (ed./intr./trans.), *Uncensored Russia–the Human Rights Movement in the Soviet Union,* London, Jonathan Cape, 1972.

Redl, H.B. (ed. & trans.), *Soviet Educators on Soviet Education,* New York, The Free Press, 1964.

Richman, B.M., *Industrial Society in Communist China,* New York, Random House, 1969.

Ridley, C.P., Godwin, P.H.B., and Doolin, D.J., *The Making of a Model Citizen in Communist China,* Stanford, Hoover Institution Press, 1971.

Rigby, T.H., *Communist Party Membership in the USSR, 1919-1967,* Princeton, New Jersey, 1968.

Rimashevskaya, N., *The Soviet Family,* Moscow, Novosti Press, 1975.

Reimer, E., *School is Dead,* Harmondsworth, Penguin Books, 1971.

Robinson, J., *The Cultural Revolution in China,* Harmondsworth, Penguin Books, 1969.

—— *Economic Management, China 1972,* London, Anglo-Chinese Educational Institute, Modern China Series No. 4, 1973.

Rosen, H., *Language and Class, a Critical look at the Theories of Basil Bernstein,* Bristol, Falling Wall Press, 1974.

Rule, P.A., *K'ung-tzu or Confucius? The Jesuit interpretation of Confucianism,* Ph.D. thesis, the ANU, 1972.

Rutkevich, M.N., *Dialekticheskii Materializm,* Sotsialno-ekonomicheskoi Literatoori, Moscow, 1960.

—— *The Career Plans of Youth* (M. Yanowitch, ed. & trans.), New York, International Arts & Sciences Press, 1969.

Saunders, M.G., *The Soviet Navy,* New York, Praeger, 1957.

Schacht, R., *Alienation,* London, Allen and Unwin, 1970.

Schapiro, L., *The Communist Party of the Soviet Union,* London, Methuen, 1960/63.

Schiff, B., *Die Reform der Grundschule in der Sowjetunion,* Berlin, Quelle & Meyer, 1972.

Schlesinger, R., *The Family in the U.S.S.R.,* London, Routledge &

Kegan Paul, 1949.

Schmidt, A., *The Concept of Nature in Marx*, London, New Left Books, 1971.

Schram, S.R., *The Political Thought of Mao Tse-tung*, Harmondsworth, Penguin Books, 1969.

—— 'From the "great union of the popular masses" to the "great alliance"', *The China Quarterly*, vol. 49, Jan-Mar 1972, pp. 88-105.

—— *Authority, Participation and Cultural Change in China*, Cambridge, The University Press, 1973.

—— *Mao Tse-tung Unrehearsed: Talks and Letters, 1956-71*, Harmondsworth, Penguin Books, 1974.

Schulman, E., *A History of Jewish Education in the Soviet Union*, New York, Ktav Publishing House, 1971.

Schurmann, F., *Ideology, and Organization in Communist China*, Berkeley, University of California Press, 1966/68.

Schwartz, H.G., 'The Ts'an K'ao hsiao-hsi: How Well Informed are Chinese Officials About the Outside World?', *The China Quarterly*, 27, July/Sept 1966, pp. 54-83.

Selden, M., *The Yenan Way in Revolutionary China*, Cambridge, Mass., Harvard University Press, 1971.

Seybolt, P.J., *Revolutionary Education in China*, documents and commentary, White Plains, New York, International Arts & Sciences Press Inc.

Shakhnazarov, G., *et al.*, *Man, Science and Society*, Moscow, Foreign Languages Press, 1965.

Shatskii, S.T., *Pedagogicheskie Sochineniya*, Moscow, Akademii Pedagogicheskix Nauk RSFSR, 1963.

Shchukina, G.I. (ed.), *Kurs Lektsii pedagogika*, Moscow, 'Prosveshcheniye', 1966.

Sheridan, M., 'The emulation of heroes', *The China Quarterly*, vol. 33, Jan-Mar 1968, pp. 42-72.

Sheringham, M., 'Peking university—the debate goes on', *China Now*, vol. 37, Dec 1973, pp. 5-6, 11.

—— 'Which door to Peking university?', *China Now*, vol. 38, Jan 1974, pp. 7-8.

Shimoniak, W., *Communist Education: Its History, Philosophy and Politics*, Chicago, Rand McNally & Co., 1970.

Shirk, S., 'The 1963 temporary work regulations for full-time middle and primary schools: commentary and translations', *The China Quarterly*, vol. 55, July/Sept 1973, pp. 511-46.

Sidel, R., *Women and Child Care in China*, New York, Hill & Wang, 1972.

Simon, B., *Intelligence, Psychology and Education: A Marxist Critique*, London, Lawrence & Wishart, 1971.

Simsova, S. (ed.), *Lenin, Krupskaia and Libraries* (G. Peacock and L. Prescott, trans.), London, Clive Bingley, 1968.

Sloan, P., *How the Soviet State is Run*, London, Lawrence & Wishart, 1941.

Snow, E., *Red Star Over China*, London, Gollancz, 1937.

Sohn Rethel, A., *Geistige und Körperliche Arbeit*, Frankfurt am Main, Suhrkamp Verlag, 1970.

Solomon, R.H., *Mao's Revolution and the Chinese Political Culture*, Berkeley, University of California Press, 1971.

Some Basic Facts about China: 10 Questions and Answers, Peking, China Reconstructs, 1974.

Sorlin, P., *The Soviet People and their Country*, London, Pall Mall Press, 1969.

Sosnovy, T., *The Housing Problem in the U.S.S.R.*, Ann Arbor, Edwards Brothers, Inc., 1954.

Stalin, J.S., *Problems of Leninism*, Moscow, Foreign Languages Press, 1945.

―― *Works*, vols. 1-13, Moscow, Foreign Languages Press, 1952-1955.

Stories about Not Being Afraid of Ghosts, Compiled by the Institute of the Chinese Academy of Sciences, Peking, Foreign Languages Press, 1961.

Strive to build a Socialist University of Science and Engineering, Peking, Foreign Languages Press, 1972.

Struve, G., *Russian Literature under Lenin and Stalin, 1917-1953*, London, Routledge & Kegan Paul, 1972.

Sun, Bang-zheng, *Liushi nian laide zhongguo jiaoyu* (60 years of Chinese education), Zheng Zhong Shu Ju, 1971.

Surveys and Research Corporation, *Directory of Selected Scientific Institutions in Mainland China*, Stanford, Hoover Institution Press, 1970.

Svalastoga Kaare, 'Social differentiation', in Faris, R.E. (ed.), *Handbook of Modern Sociology*, Chicago, Rand McNally & Co., 1964.

Szeczesniak, B., *The Russian Revolution and Religion*, Indiana, University of Notre Dame Press, 1959.

Tandler, F.M., *The Workers Faculty (Rabfak) System in the U.S.S.R.*, Ph.D. thesis, Columbia University, 1955.

Thaxton, R., 'Tenants in revolution: the tenacity of traditional morality', *Modern China*, vol. 1, no. 3, July 1975, pp. 323-358.

The Tenth National Congress of the Chinese Communist Party (documents), Peking, Foreign Languages Press, 1973.

The U.S.S.R. in Figures for 1973, Moscow, Statistika Publishers, 1974.

Thompson, E.P., *The Making of the English Working Class,* Harmondsworth, Penguin Books, 1963.

Townsend, J.R., *Political Participation in Communist China,* Berkeley, University of California Press, 1968.

Trace, A.S., Jnr., *What Ivan knows that Johnny doesn't,* New York, Random House, 1961.

Treadgold, D.W. (ed.), *Soviet and Chinese Communism: Similarities and Differences,* Seattle, University of Washington Press, 1967.

Troitsky, D.N., *Training Technicians in the Soviet Union,* London, Soviet News Booklet, 1957.

Trotsky, L., *The Revolution Betrayed,* New York, Pioneer Publishers, 1945.

—— *Literature and Revolution,* Ann Arbor, University of Michigan Press, 1960.

Tsang, Chiu-Sam, *Society, Schools and Progress in China,* Oxford, Pergamon Press, 1968.

U.S.S.R., a Reference Book of Facts and Figures, London, Soviet News, 1956.

U.S.S.R., 73, Novosti Press Agency Year Book, Moscow, Novosti Press Agency Publishing House, 1973.

Vakar, N., *The Taproot of Soviet Society,* New York, Harper Brothers, 1962/63.

Vazquez, A.S., *Art, and Society: Essays in Marxist Aesthetics,* New York, Monthly Review Press, 1973.

Vigdorova, F., *Diary of a School Teacher,* Moscow, Foreign Languages Press, 1954.

Vogel, E., *Canton under Communism: Programs and Politics in a Provincial Capital, 1949-1968,* New York, Harper & Row, 1969/71.

Walton, P. and Gamble, A., *From Alienation to Surplus Value,* London, Sheed & Ward, 1972.

Watson, A., 'Sian revisited', *China Now,* vol. 16, Oct-Nov 1971, pp. 5-6.

Webb, S. and B., *Soviet Communism: A New Civilization,* London, Gollancz, 1937.

Weishenme yao dai hong lingjin, Peking, Zhongguo Quingnian Chuban She, 1966.

Wheelwright, E.L., and McFarlane, B., *The Chinese Road to Socialism,* New York, Monthly Review Press, 1970.

Whyte, M.K., 'Educational reform: China in the 1970s and Russia in the 1920s', *Comparative Education Review,* February 1974, pp. 112-128.

Wilkinson, P., 'English youth movements, 1908-30', *Journal of Contemporary History,* vol. 4, no. 2, April 1969, pp. 3-23.

Winner, T., 'Problems of alphabetic reforms among the Turkic peoples of Soviet Central Asia', *The Slavonic & East European Review,* XXXI, vol. 76, 1952, pp. 133-147.

Winter, E., *Red Virtue: Human Relationships in the New Russia,* London, Gollancz Ltd., 1933.

Wittig, H.E., *Die Marxsche Bildungskonzeption und die Sowjetpadagogik,* Bad Harzburg, Verlag Fur Wissenschaft, Wirtschaft und Technik, 1964.

―― *Karl Marx: Bildung und Erziehung, Studientexte zur Marxschen Bildungskonzeption,* Paderborn, F. Schoningh, 1968.

Wolfe, T.W., *Soviet Strategy at the Crossroads,* Cambridge, Harvard University Press, 1964.

Woody, T., *New Minds: New Men? The Emergence of the Soviet Citizen,* New York, MacMillan, 1932.

Wright, F.O., 'Class Boundaries in Advanced Capitalist Countries', *New Left Review* 98, Jul/Aug 1976, pp. 3-4.

Wright, M.C., *The Last Stand of Chinese Conservatism,* Stanford, Stanford University Press, 1957.

Wu, E., 'Recent developments in Chinese publishing', *China Quarterly,* Jan-Mar 1973, No. 53, pp. 134-8.

Wu, Y-l. and Sheeks, R.B., *The Organisation and Support of Scientific Research and Development in the Mainland of China,* New York, Praeger, 1970.

Xrestomatiya po istorii pedagogiki―V.Z. Smirnov (ed.), Moscow, Gosudarstbennoe uchebno-pedagogicheskoye izdatel'stvo, 1961.

Yadova, V.A. and Dobrinina (eds.), *Youth and Work* (in Russian), Moscow, Young Guard, 1970.

Yang, C.K., *Chinese Communist Society: the Family and the Village,* Cambridge, Mass., MIT Press, 1959.

―― *Religion in Chinese Society,* Berkeley, University of California Press, 1970.

Yang, I-fan, *The Case of Hu Feng,* Hong Kong, Union Research Institute, 1956.

Yao Wen-Yuan, *Comments on Tao Chu's Two Books,* Peking, Foreign Languages Press, 1968.

Yelyutin, V., *Higher Education in the U.S.S.R.,* London, Soviet Booklet, No. 51, 1959.

Yu, F.T.C., *Mass Persuasion in Communist China,* New York, Praeger, 1964.

Zaleski, E., *et al., Science Policy in the U.S.S.R.,* Paris, Organisation for Economic Co-operation & Development, 1969.

Zepper, J.T., 'A study of N.K. Krupskaya's educational philosophy', Ph.D. thesis, unpublished, Missouri, 1960.

—— 'Recent and contemporary Soviet educational thought', *School & Society,* January 1972, pp. 31-43.

Zhamin, V., *Education in the U.S.S.R.: its Economy and Structure,* Moscow, Novosti Press Agency Publishing House, 1973.

Zhdanov, A.A., *On Literature, Music and Philosophy,* London, Lawrence & Wishart, 1950.

Zhukov, C.K., *The Memoirs of Marshal Zhukov,* London, Jonathan Cape, 1971.

INDEX

achievement, testing of 103
administration 103-5, 106
agriculture, collective 174, 183, 214,
    293, 327, 344; exploitation of
    172, 173; textbooks dealing with
    192; training in 198
aid, Soviet (to China) 169; withdrawal
    of 170
alienation 16-19, 20
allegiance, value of 333
alphabet, simplicity of Russian as
    compared to Chinese 146
apathy, in political studies 344
aptitude, testing of 103
argument, importance of 228
arithmetic, teaching of 209
artist, the, importance of 231, 232-3
arts, the 345; relation of, to class
    230; function of 233
atheism 45, 46, 252, 256, 259, 262,
    263

behaviour, control of 120
belief, freedom of 258-9
biology 257
brigade system 272-3; abolition of
    153
Buddhists, the, pre-revolutionary
    numbers of 255

capital, dominating class (qv); effect
    of 32; foreign 168; valorisation of
    73n
capitalism 59, 69; as inferior to state
    system 326; decline of 249; effect
    of 252; exploitation in 250; in
    USSR suburbia 280; monopoly
    44-5; rejection of 72; similar con-
    ditions to in China and USSR 267;
    state, outline of 163-4
categorisation, social 30
Catholic, Roman 256; pre-revolutionary
    numbers of 255
censorship 213, 233, 238, 240, 243-
    4
centralism 66, 172-3; democratic 35
certification 180, 182
character, change of 68

chemistry 212, 214, 309
child care 109-10
children, as informers of their par-
    ents' behaviour 293-4; dependence
    of 345; exploitation and separ-
    ation of by and from parents
    284-5; moral qualities of 117
Christianity, social principles of
    47
class, abolition of 72; desertion of
    227-8; determination of 174-5,
    179 passim; persistence of 29,
    195, 322, 333, 341, 345
cognition (of marxism-leninism) 161,
    249, 262
collective, the, student 338 passim
collectivisation 116, 168, 221, 236,
    247, 301, 302, 331
college, the, Chinese, types of 90-1;
    factory 93; village 210
Common Programme, the 222-3
communications (in China) 171
communism, as instrument of trans-
    ition to socialism 34-8; 'crude'
    282; Marx's vision of 19-25; in
    regard to education 68; scientific,
    laws of 227; time required for
    transition to after Bolshevic
    Revolution 22
Communist Party, Chinese, develop-
    ment of 36
Communist Party, Russian, develop-
    ment of 36; elitist nature of
    membership of 334-7; membership
    of Komsomol stepping-stone to
    297; 'world outlook' of 61
competition 310, 323
comprehensive system, the, establish-
    ment of 77
Confucianism 122, 222, 238, 254,
    256, 288, 315
conscience, freedom of 259
consciousness, socialist 51, 62, 71,
    72, 93, 126, 189, 193, 223, 235,
    243, 262, 306; change of 68;
    collective, failure to achieve 267;
    critical 184, 331; group, in pre-
    schooling (qv) 116; mystical 26

conscription 320-1
consumption, communal 15-16
contradiction 56-7, 62, 64-7, 74n, 75n,
  193, 231, 253, 346
councils, academic, Soviet, duties of
  106
creativity, fostering of 188, 189;
  importance of 117
creche, the 110, 112, 116, 121-2
crime, petty, role of Komsomol in
  controlling 301-2
criticism 57, 68, 314, 327; importance of 313; in wall newspapers
  (qv) 237-8; military 318; need
  for 277, 278; see also self-
  criticism
culture 93; in collectives 269; political 332-3; proletarian 232
curricula, boredom in 215-16; relating
  to politics 245-51; relating to
  religion 262; students' opinion of
  340

Daoism 255, 315
Daoists, persecution of 261
day, working, shortening of 21
de-alienation 331
degrees, types of 91
dialects, difficulty of assimilating
  into educational pattern 143-4
diamat 63
diplomas, types of 91
director, institutional, responsibilities
  of 106
discipline 276, 326; as socialist ethic
  221, 222; breaches of 180; lax
  military 319; military 316-17, 319,
  330
discrimination, abolition of 99
distribution 23-4

economics 229, 326
economy, the, base of 40-1; bourgeois
  58; development of, as allied with
  educational development 163;
  political 63-4, 327; relation of,
  to education 181-3; socialist,
  construction of 23
electives 161
empiricism 58
equilibrium, theory of 62
examinations, entrance, abolition
  of 100, 101; return to, by Soviets
  102

experience, lived 43; see also praxis
experimentation, with period of
  secondary courses (in China)
  85

factory, the, as educational base 87
factory system, the 70
finance 107-8; combination of local
  and state 217

general knowledge, teaching of 209
geography 212, 249, 326
Gotha Programme, the 47, 73n, 74n
grades 77, 84; changes in 160-1; separation of 308

Harvard Project on the Soviet Social
  System, the 99-100
Higher Party School, the 225
history 212, 229, 249, 251, 326;
  merged with Constitution of the
  USSR 248; metaphysical nature
  of 27-9; replaced by economic
  and social formations 248; taught
  in polytechnics 202
home visiting 125
humanities, problem of 151; provision for 194-5

ideas, production of 39-40
illiteracy 235; in Red Army 323,
  324
illiterate, the, teaching of 339
imprisonment, of religious 260, 261
individual, the, 17-18, 22, 55, 72, 75n;
  constraints upon 331; cult of 36;
  disparities in classes of 70; freedom of 259; importance of in
  Krupskaya's (qv) view of the
  collective 275; interests of 66;
  pressure upon 280; relation of,
  to the collective 271; solitary
  experience of 329; temporary
  alienation of 279
individualism, Western, as a social
  ideal 277
indoctrination 326, 328; political
  322-3
Industrial Labour College, the, enrolment at 213-14
Industrial Training School (USSR)
  87
industrialisation, confusion of interpretations of 236

industry, investment for 173; Soviet management of 172
insult, laws on 244
intelligentsia, encouraged to reject religious precepts 256; hostility of, towards communism (*qv*) 232; position of, regarding religion 257
intensification 24
interaction, social (within collectives) 271
internationalism, socialist 227

Jewry, restrictions imposed upon 255

knowledge, acquisition of 51-2; evaluative criteria referring to 60
Kollontay, A.M. 285
Krupskaya, N.K. 187-91, 196, 269, 275, 280, 285, 313; comments of on student self-government (*qv*) 337-8; supporter of Young Pioneers 308
Kruschev, N.S. 23; agrarian reforms of 233, 300; educational reforms of 84, 96, 154, 182, 200, 218, 219, 235; reduction of numbers in Orthodox Churches under 260-1

labour 11-13; productive 71, 73*n*, 129, 151, 184, 187, 191, 196, 199, 216; distinctions between types of 184-5; division of 21, 281; education in 120-1; effects of delivery of 14; link with education 147, 182, 345; of the individual (*qv*) 17; participation in 310; reform through 335; supplement to theory 251; teaching children value of 117; teaching of in nursery schools (*qv*) 115; theme of in integrated course syllabus 147, 151, 153; training in 196-8
Labour Reserve School, the 88
land, partial requisition of 259
language 143-5, 214; legislation on (USSR) 145; reform of 146; teaching of 209
'Later Ten Points', the 297
leadership, collective 341; poor, in Young Pioneers 306
learning, as against what is taught 332

'learning by doing' *see* praxis
Legalism 315
legislation, in parent-child relations 292
leisure 24
'levelling down' 62
libel, laws on 244
liberalism, as related to foreign missionary teaching 257; combating of 277
literacy 145-6; classes in 323
literature 233, 249
Little Octobrists, the 311

machine, the 18
man, Marx's conception of 14-1|5
man-power, high-talent 101
management, collective 106
manager, the, factory, opposition of to part-work 219
mass-line theory, the 36, 37, 135, 173, 336; with regard to administration (*qv*) 104
materialism 52-7, 60, 74*n*, 75*n*; as ethic of religious classes 262; dialectical 61-7, 245, 327; historical 59, 283; mechanical 65; principles of 63
mathematics 212, 213, 214, 309; in nursery schools (*qv*) 114; in polytechnics (*qv*) 203
matter 53
May 4th Movement, the 256
media, the 229, 243
memorisation 114
metaphysics 55
method, the 58-9
militarism, role of Komsomol in 299-300
military ethic, the 315-16; service, deferrence from 88
morality 193, 272; new Soviet 222; private, Komsomol's incursion into 302-3; problems of 228; public, defence of by Komsomol 299, 300-1
Moslem, the, pre-revolutionary numbers of 255
museum, the 242-3; anti-religious 263

nationality, as confused with religion 255
naturalism 52

nature 61, 117; appreciation of 189; determination of life of 56; dialectics of 75*n*; man's relationship to 281; non-human 57, 71; theme of course syllabus of 147, 153
New Economic Policy 168
newspaper, wall 237-9, 308, 314, 338, 339, 340

orphanages, Christian 265

parent committee, the 105
parents, the, co-operation of with educational collective 94, 119; duty of 292; influence of 196
Paris Commune, the 32
peasantry, decline of 174
pedagogy 270, 274, 284, 304
peoples tribunals (in China) 169
personnel, trained, proportion of as related to economic needs 182
physics 212, 214, 309
piety, filial 289, 294
planning, military 322
play, role of toys and equipment in 121-2
polytechnic, the 75*n*, 186-91, 196-203; distinction of between and technical training 188, 216; mistaken notion of in China 219
positivism, relationship of with marxism 60; anti- 75*n*
'positivist marxism' 57
practice 48-9, 51-2, 65, 195, 310; effect of 206; *see also* praxis
pragmatism, as distinguished from practice (*qv*) 48-9
praxis 75*n*, 126, 211, 266, 268, 345; *see also* practice; theory
pre-schooling 84, 115, 116, 245-6, 285, 286
press, the 233-9, 341, 344; freedom of 230
priest, worker, the 265
production 28, 65; as determinant of all activities 51; based on exchange value 22; capitalist mode of 29-30, 31; changes and development in 50; commodity 29; common ownership of means of 20; economic 21; efficiency of 70; military 28; mode of 28; profit from 218; separation of students from 192; social 70

profit, economic 185
proletariat, the, campaign on the dictatorship of 163; capitalist (*qv*) concept of family stifles 285; dictatorship of 32-3, 38-9, 72, 74*n*, 271; exploitation of 242; historic role of 30-1, 49; ideology of 198; necessary advance of 229; politics of 192; role of, in making revolution 42; statesmen of 223-4
propaganda 52, 244; anti-religious 267; atheist 252, 253; by Chinese Youth League 303-4, 305; by Komsomol 300; thought teams 107
property, personal possession of 14, 20, 24, 26, 28, 257, 280, 281
Protestant ethic, the 256, 309
Protestantism, pre-revolutionary 255
punishment 275-6
pupil-teacher ratios 85, 129-30

radio 239-40
rank, academic (USSR) 91; Chinese 92; military 317-18, 330; teachers' 122-3
rationality, technological, assumption of 337
realism 53, 54; emphasis on in nursery schools (*qv*) 118; socialist 232
reality 58-9; as educational aim 147-8; as understood by proletariat (*qv*) 142; historicity of 56
reductionism 63
reflection theory of ideas, passive 41
reform 77, 84, 87, 127-8, 142, 247, *see also* Kruschev, N.B., educational reforms of
relation, imaginary 43
religion 45-6, 48; as focus of political opposition 260, 267; class bias of 47; conflict with state over 257; criticism of 253; separation of, from the state 251-3; survival of 266
Republic Higher Party School, the 226
revisionism 219; criticism of 227
revolutionary committee, the 107
revolution, continuous 39
routine, importance of, in nursery schools (*qv*) 116

Russian Democratic Labour Party
34
Russian Orthodox Church, pre-revolutionary status of 253-4, 255,
256, 260

school, the 86, 87, 88, 95, 101, 107,
108, 182, 188-9, 191, 193, 197,
205, 206, 212, 227, 228, 229,
258, 259, 322, 326, 327, 332;
half-day 205; high 77, 211-12;
high, agricultural, work schedules
in 211; nursery 110-13, 118, 286;
part-work 192, 194, 204, 206-18,
219, 229, 306; primary 84, 209-10;
rural 154, 192, 204; secondary
76, 84; technical 212-13; urban
154
science, advances in (USSR) 345;
social 248, 249
'scientific Socialism' 26
'scissors crisis' 168
selection 100-3
self-consciousness 330, 332, 333
self-creation 12-13
self-criticism 224, 277, 278, 303, 318,
327, 335
self-determination 330, 332, 333,
341
self-government, student 333
self-improvement 312
sense, bases of 41
sinification (in China) 145
socialism 50, 68, 183, 249, 341
Socialist Education Movement 297
society, as theme of integrated
course syllabus 147, 153
specialisation 92, 213
speech, freedom of 230, 231
spontaneism 44
sport, military 320
staff, appointment of 106-7
standards 101-2
starvation, pre-revolution 167
structuralism 58
struggle meetings 278, 279, 335
student, the, social composition of
98-100
study circle, the 228, 275, 278-9,
309, 339
style, teaching of 118
suppression, anti-religious 267
Supreme Attestation Commission
91

teacher, the 122-33, 137-42, 148,
340, 337, 339; dissenting 134-5;
non- 128-9; worker- 129-52,
345
teaching 261-3; abandonment of
authoritarian 142; anti-religious
263-5; progressive 152; subject
system of 153-4
technology 23, 75*n*, 309, 345
television 239-40
theory, importance of 190; combination of, with practice 192, 193-
4, 195, 203; specialist 213
theory and practice *see* praxis
trade unions 37, 74*n*, 88, 108, 243,
263, 278, 333
training, extension correspondence
institutes 92-3; lack of 160; military, schools in 322, 327; monotechnical 216; physical 304, 305;
polytechnical 216; vocational
188, 191, 199-200, 201
truth 55; criterion of 51; William
James' concept of 48-9

unity, law of 62
university, the, communist, closure
of 225; necessity for 89-90
upbringing, communal 286-7

vacation, the, duration of 131
value, surplus 29-30, 74*n*, 184
vanguard party, the 49-50

wages, differentials in, Stalin's recommendation of 222; industrial, as
compared with teachers' salaries
132-3
War Communism 168, 328
women, liberation of 109-10, 274,
278, 281, 282-3, 285, 290; role
of, as effected by religion (*qv*) 257
work, physical, avoidance of by youth
312
worker, the, opposition of to partwork 219; separation of students
from 192; training of 224-5; young,
Komsomol's protection of 299
worker control 32, 74*n*, 103, 219
Workers' Faculty, the 88

Ze-dong, Mao 22-3, 25, 29, 33 *passim*,
51, 63 *passim*, 89 *passim*, 107,
110, 114, 122, 124, 126-7, 134,

151, 163, 171, 172, 173, 174,
181, 186, 187, 191-5, 209, 212,
223, 227-8, 229 *passim*, 250, 253,
265, 267, 278, 282-3, 296, 305, 307,
307, 308, 314, 318, 319, 322,
327, 330, 335, 336, 344, 345-6